The Complete Climber's Handbook

SECOND EDITION

Jerry Cinnamon

**RAGGED MOUNTAIN PRESS /
MCGRAW-HILL**

Camden, Maine • New York • San Francisco •
Washington, D.C. • Auckland • Bogota •
Caracas • Lisbon • London • Madrid • Mexico
City • Milan • Montreal • New Delhi • San
Juan • Singapore • Sydney • Tokyo • Toronto

*This book is dedicated to the friends and fellow climbers
who helped shape my vision of what is possible.*

Ragged Mountain Press
A Division of The **McGraw·Hill** Companies

10 9 8 7 6 5 4 3 2 1

Copyright © 1994, 2000 Charles Gerald Cinnamon
All rights reserved. The publisher takes no responsi-
bility for the use of any of the materials or methods
described in this book, nor for the products thereof.
The name "Ragged Mountain Press" and the Ragged
Mountain Press logo are trademarks of The
McGraw-Hill Companies. Printed in the United
States of America.

Library of Congress Cataloging-in-Publication Data
Cinnamon, Jerry.
    The complete climber's handbook / Jerry Cinnamon.
        p.   cm.
    Rev. ed. of: Climbing rock and ice. c1994
    Includes bibliographical references and index.
    ISBN 0-07-135755-6 (alk. paper)
    1. Rock climbing. 2. Snow and ice climbing. I.
Cinnamon, Jerry. Climbing rock and ice. II. Title.
GV200.2 .C55 2000
796.52'23—dc21   00-024812

Questions regarding the content of this book should
be addressed to
Ragged Mountain Press
P.O. Box 220
Camden, ME 04843
http://www.raggedmountainpress.com

All photos by the author except for the following:
Bob Giolito, page 23; Kevin Kubota, pages 32 (bottom) and 33; Bob Lockhart, page 39, Stewart M.
Green, pages 2, 68, 148, 160, 258; Greg Epperson,
pages 52, 59, 90; Cliff Leight, pages 31, 126, 274,
235; Petzl America, page 53; Eldorado Wall, page 32
(top).

Questions regarding the ordering of this book should
be addressed to
The McGraw-Hill Companies
Customer Service Department
P.O. Box 547
Blacklick, OH 43004
Retail customers: 1-800-262-4729
Bookstores: 1-800-722-4726

This book is printed on 70# Citation

Printed by R.R. Donnelley, Crawfordsville, IN
Design by Joyce C. Weston
Production management by Janet Robbins
Page layout by Eugenie S. Delaney
Edited by Dorcas Susan Miller, Nancy N. Green,
    Pamela Benner, and Terry Belanger
The author has made all effort to reproduce trade-
    marked terms accurately.

WARNING: This is an instructional book for
potentially dangerous activities. Rock climbing, ice
climbing, and mountaineering may subject you to
climbing falls; rock and ice fall; avalanches; injuries
from exposure, such as frostbite and hypothermia;
drowning; and many other hazards that can lead to
serious injury and death.

Brand-name items of equipment mentioned or
shown in this book are for purposes of illustration or
discussion only and do not constitute a recommendation for their use.

This book is not intended to replace instruction by
a qualified instructor nor to substitute for your personal judgment.

In using this book, the reader releases the author,
publisher, and distributor from liability for any
injury, including death, that might result.

Contents

Preface

This book grew out of many years of teaching climbing to individuals, many of whom have become masters of the sport. My premise has been that novices begin to learn under the tutelage of an experienced friend, instructor, or guide and eventually reach a point of mastery where they can climb safely with peers and perhaps teach others.

This book should remain valuable to you throughout your climbing career for review, as a guide to skill presentation, as a source of additional references, and to introduce you to new areas to master, such as working with groups.

You can enjoy and practice climbing throughout your life at whatever level of athletic ability or conditioning you possess as long as you are aware of your own limits. More than athletic ability, climbing demands thought and decision-making. This book tries to show currently accepted techniques and procedures of climbing, but it can never replace your own judgment as to how to apply them in the fluid situations that climbing offers.

The book is divided into three parts. Part 1 focuses on locations and tools for climbing rock because the central focus of climbing is movement in the vertical world, supported by companions, gear, and techniques. Chapter 1 teaches individual movement techniques and sequences and when to use them. Chapter 2 explores the climbing gym, where climbers are introduced to the sport and where many climbers train and practice movement skills. This chapter explores wall design, route setting, competition climbing,

and the important differences between climbing in the gym and in the outdoors. Chapters 3 through 11 focus on the tools to climb rock: basic knots, harnesses and helmets, rope, protection, and anchor systems, as well as the techniques of belaying and rappelling. A chapter on leading rock (chapter 9) and a discussion of fall forces (chapter 11) round out this section.

Part 2 covers the special skills needed for movement on ice and snow, the kinds and use of protection in this environment, the nature of ice, and the techniques of climbing on steep ice. Throughout this part, I assume that the reader is already familiar with the information in Part 1, especially the sections concerning ropes, belaying, and anchors as used in rock climbing. Part 2 also deals with avalanches, an environmental hazard that occurs in terrain where snow and ice climbing take place.

Part 3 is written for experienced climbers who wish to help manage a climbing site when working with organized groups, and who recognize that the dangers of climbing also require management for safety.

Appendices on first-aid programs, fitness, lightning, and pulleys conclude the book.

The climbing community has come to recognize that great climbs can be accomplished by both women and men. Results depend largely on the amount of time and effort that individuals wish to spend learning, training, and putting skills to use. Throughout the book I have attempted to use gender-inclusive terminology, except when referring to a specific, illustrated climber.

Acknowledgments

I wish to take this opportunity to thank the following individuals who have contributed to my personal growth or have directly contributed to the success of this book by sharing adventures, modeling for photographs, critiquing illustrations and text, or providing support: Jeff Alexander, Rich Baker, Tom Davis, Jim Ewing, Gene Francis, Dave Getchell Jr., Dave Getchell Sr., Eric Harms, Geoff Heath, Damon Johnston, Scott Kimball, Dan Koch, Matt Lawler, Jon Leonard, Heather Lindquist, Laurie Little, Mike Lockett, Dan Lowell, Dodi Marvell, Doug McMullin, Dorcas Miller, Chris Misavage, Jim F. Morrisey, Marty O'Keefe, Nick Prvulov, Dot Quimby, Ed Raiola, James Reed, David Smith, Debbie Sugerman, Mark Tenney, Shawn Tierney, Ben Townsend, Steve Tweito, Marjory Ulin, Kathy Dixon-Wallace, Peter Wallace, and Mary Ward, as well as others whom I might have inadvertently omitted. Thanks to the Unity College Board of Trustees, who granted a semester of free time to initiate this book, and to other members of the college community for their support.

I wish to thank the following individuals and their organizations for reviewing the text, transmitting information, and making it possible for me to further my education on subjects related to specific chapters: Roger Damon and the Eastern Division of the National Ski Patrol; and John (Jed) E. Williamson and the American Alpine Club.

Thanks also go to the following individuals and organizations for permission to use copyrighted works: Michael L. Benge, managing editor of *Climbing* magazine, to quote from an article by Paul Piana in volume 110 on the Salathé Wall; Yvon Chouinard to quote from his book, *Climbing Ice*, concerning the origin of the radically drooped ice-axe pick; Bruce Temper, editor of the *Avalanche Review*, to quote from the 1991 article "White Death: A Review of Fatal Accidents in Colorado, 1950–91" by Dale Atkins; John (Jed) E. Williamson and the American Alpine Club to quote individual case studies from *Accidents in North American Mountaineering*.

Finally, I wish to thank the generations of climbers before me who have contributed to the literature, technique, and knowledge of climbing.

Introduction

Climbing is about having fun. It is about pumping adrenaline, enjoying the outdoors, ascending impossibly vertical or smooth walls, viewing space beneath our feet, sitting quietly on a ledge reflecting on nature, and sharing tall tales and adventures with friends. At its heart, climbing is about moving our bodies from one spot to another, at our best, with the accomplished, graceful steps of a dancer.

Dancers are not born as masters with the gift of springing into the air and landing softly again on their toes to hold an audience in rapture. Like dancers, climbers start as apprentices; we rehearse our steps time and again to move fluidly and to develop grace. We practice by climbing, whenever we can, at the cliffs, on rock walls, or in the gym. One type of climbing, bouldering, was originally practiced on small glacial boulders but can be practiced on any climbing surface low enough from which to safely jump. Bouldering frees us from encumbering ropes, rope partners, and tools. We use our hands, climbing shoes, and bodies to move for long periods of time and to try movement problems at our current limits. This promotes muscular endurance and power, increases fluidity of motion, and allows us to spend time doing what we enjoy most. Practice gives us the opportunity to incorporate thinking about climbing technique, or mind knowledge, into actual climbing, or body knowledge.

Climbing was once the pastime of a few privileged Victorians with the money and leisure to climb mountains. Its popularity gradually spread during the 1900s to a wider public looking for physical challenges. During the 1960s, with the introduction of advances in ice tools, ice climbing became a separate sport from mountain climbing. A rapid revolution of tools, protection, boots, and clothing followed to make this cold-weather sport more enjoyable and safer than ever before. During the 1980s, "sport" cliffs, indoor climbing walls, "sticky" shoes, and technologically advanced gear made rock climbing accessible to tens of thousands of climbers.

Currently, novices—men and women alike—can begin the sport close to home under the supervision of accomplished friends, climbing gym personnel, school climbing clubs, or guide services. Anyone of average physical ability can profitably spend the first climbing season under the tutelage of a seasoned climber to gain familiarity with the sport. If you want to do advanced intermediate climbs, you will need to develop a general fitness program that involves endurance and strength training. This program can become highly specialized as you train to climb at an advanced level.

Climbing includes a number of disciplines, including bouldering, rock climbing on small and large cliffs, sport climbing, water-ice climbing, and mountaineering. These disciplines present opportunities to develop new skills and knowledge; to encounter diverse internal responses to the effort demanded, ranging from exhaustion to heightened states of awareness; and to gain new summits. The view from the top of any climb is both beautiful and far. On the way to the top, you will see new places, meet new people, make new friends, and experience successes as well as failures. All of these experiences will seep into you and, upon reflection, enrich your daily life.

As you read and as you practice climbing, think positive thoughts and enjoy yourself!

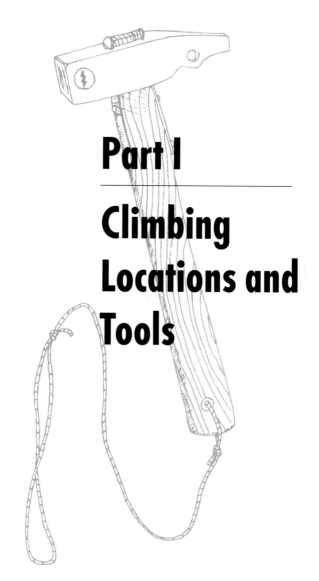

Part I

Climbing Locations and Tools

1

Movement

FACE CLIMBING

Cliffs range from low-angle to very steep indeed. Climbers began exploring cliffs by using cracks that split otherwise featureless faces: the cracks provided handholds, or *jams*, and places to insert artificial *protection*—anchors used to shorten a fall—to safeguard the climber. (This is known as *crack climbing*, and we will come to it later in this chapter.) Climbers did venture out onto the rock face, but often were limited by the scarcity of protection. Today you have a multitude of specialized protection pieces that, in combination with sticky climbing shoes, safeguard you in what was once an alien place. As a result, you can find many of today's *test pieces*—climbs on the cutting edge of the sport—as well as fun climbs on faces, where you need precise footwork, concentration, and excellent balance.

Basic Moves

When you climb, you use your feet in combination with your hands to keep yourself on the rock. Since good balance requires that you posi-tion your feet below your hands and not off to the side, you must often make a choice between using the largest footholds available or using the largest handholds. When resting, you will probably choose the largest footholds to stand on. When attempting to pull up with your arms on a steep wall, you will often use the largest handholds and whatever small footholds are directly underneath your hands. On less steep walls with positive, or jutting, footholds, you may find that you can balance from foothold to foothold without much use of your hands to support your body weight. As handholds get smaller and the wall gets steeper, take shorter steps a few inches apart to help maintain balance. As a general rule, the higher you step, the larger the handhold you will need to maintain balance. The two common techniques used on these small holds are *edging* and *smearing*.

When small positive edges or the tops of semidetached rock flakes are available, you edge on these, as shown in figure 1-1. This means that you use the inside edge of your shoe, adjacent to the big toe; on bigger holds, you use the inside ball of your foot. When you take this stance with both feet turned outward, you can bring your body closer to the rock while remaining upright. Alternatively, you can stand on the outside edge of your foot, which puts much of your weight directly over the bone structure of your foot but usually feels less secure than inside edging because your foot and ankle tend to roll. You can counteract this by tensing involved muscles. Most climbers use an outside edge as a transitory move on small holds while trying to get to better holds where they can pause.

When the rock on steep faces and slabs offers you holds that are rounded so you cannot edge, you place your entire foot on the hold, at right angles to the fall line—the most direct line up and down the cliff—to create the maximum contact area between the bottom of your foot and the rock. You use the maximum surface area of the bottom of your foot. This is called *smearing*. You can use any small surface that is

of a lower angle than the overall cliff (fig. 1-2).

On low-angle rock slabs, extend both the smearing concept and shoe-to-rock surface contact by pointing the toe of your shoe up the fall line (fig. 1-3). This is the *friction foothold*. Do not attempt to edge on rounded holds, as edging reduces the area of the shoe making contact with the rock.

For any single friction move there are usually places to step on that are less steep than the general overall angle of the rock. Place your foot on one of these spots and then shift your body weight over your foot. You want a smooth shift from one foot to the other, as if you were ice skating. Climb by linking these moves until you get to a resting place where you can place protection and start over. Moving directly up the slope is easier than moving sideways, where a pronounced weight shift is necessary to transfer from one foot to the other. If the route requires you to move sideways, it is almost always easier to plan ahead and ascend in a diagonal line rather than a horizontal one.

Handholds and Finger Holds

You can grip handholds and finger holds in many ways, as shown in figure 1-4. Possible grips include the open, cling, vertical, pinch, finger grip, and finger wrap.

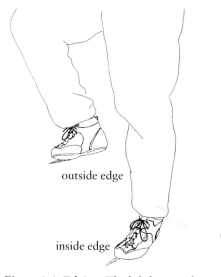

outside edge

inside edge

Figure 1-1. Edging: The left foot, at the lower right corner of the figure, is edging on the inside. This places body weight directly over the inside of the big toe. The right foot, at the upper left corner of the figure, is edging on the outside of the foot. Body weight is over the outside of the ball of the foot.

Figure 1-2. Smearing on Rounded Holds

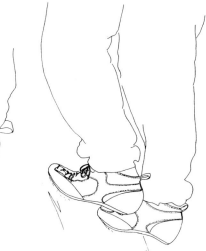

Figure 1-3. Frictioning

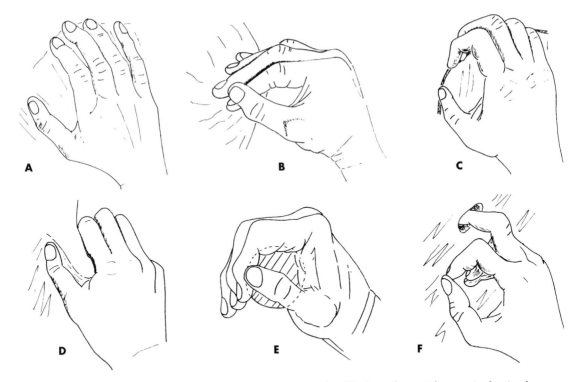

Figure 1-4. Handholds and Finger Holds:
A—Open grip; B—Cling grip with thumb as stabi-
lizer; C—Vertical grip; D—Pinch grip;
E—Finger wrap; F—Finger grip.

In the open grip (A) you use a maximum amount of surface area of your fingers and hand to grip a hold; this works well on large and rounded holds. You can use the friction of your palm, called *palming*, to increase the security of the hold. Use a cling grip (B) when the pads of your fingers fit on the hold. You can stabilize the grip by placing your thumb over the adjacent finger to provide support and additional strength.

On narrow positive holds, use the vertical grip (C). Bend your fingers at the second joint and fold the first two joints into the third, forming your hand into a hold-grabbing hook. This grip transfers your weight to the rock through your fingertips. The hold does place stress on the bone structure and tendons of your fingers, so using this grip extensively can damage finger tendons. The ends of your fingers

are also likely to hurt. The vertical grip does allow you to *crank*—pull your hardest—on the smallest of positive holds and to feel relatively secure while you do. On very small holds you can make the vertical grip more secure by hooking your fingernails over the rock crystals to provide a powerful but potentially painful hold.

Use the pinch, or squeeze, grip (D) on holds with two surfaces that you can pinch together. On large holds this grip can engage the whole hand; on holds the size of a pebble you use a couple of fingers. On small holds pinch the hold between your thumb and the side of your index finger for the greatest holding power.

You can often more securely hold protruding rounded knobs and even large protruding crystals that you might otherwise pinch-grip by using a finger wrap (E). Wrap your small finger, and as many other fingers as you can, around the knob to create maximum surface contact between your fingers and the rock. Maximize contact between the side of your small finger and the rock, and hook the bend in the second joint of this finger over an upper sharp bend in the knob. Pressing your thumb against either your fingers or the knob may help to stabilize the wrap.

You can use a finger grip (F) in thin cracks, piton scars, and small pockets. Insert a finger into the hole and *cam*, or twist, your finger. Combine this with a pull to the side to enhance the cam. Fitting two or more fingers side by side in the hole increases the strength of the grip. Stack fingers on top of each other in holes that are taller than they are wide. Experiment with different ways of inserting your fingers to determine what works best. Remember that handholds should help you maintain balance, while footwork actually moves you up the cliff. Pulling up mostly on finger strength can be very strenuous and may lead to injury.

Balance and Progression in Face Climbing

Once you know individual foot and hand techniques, you need to put them together. Do you use a vertical grip while edging with the inside of your left foot, or do you use an open grip while smearing with both feet? Is it better to go fast or slow? How do you transfer body weight from one hold to another? To use the dance analogy, these problems are like knowing the individual steps to a dance, and then learning how to link them together into a graceful choreographed pattern that flows over the dance floor.

Face climbing, like dance, emphasizes balance over the feet and smooth body shifts. By standing upright over your feet, you use gravity to stay on the rock, as shown in figure 1-5. If you stand upright on a slab, the downward force of gravity pulls you into the rock. If you lean into the rock, on the other hand, gravity pulls your feet away from the rock, resulting in a slide down the rock face.

Small steps, often measured in inches, help you maintain balance. They also bring the power of large leg muscles into play and substitute leg strength for that of weaker forearm and upper-arm muscles, so you will not need to hang off small finger holds as much.

The Hand Traverse on a Slab

In a hand traverse, you have positive holds for your hands while your feet smear, friction, or occasionally edge. A classic rising hand traverse leading diagonally across a slab illustrates how you put together different foot and hand techniques. The climber in the photos on page 6 maintains his center of gravity by squatting over his feet and leaning back on his arms. This stance keeps his body weight over his feet so that they do not slide out from under him. He frictions with his feet, but will smear on rounded holds and stand on his inside shoe edge if appropriate holds appear at points on cross-

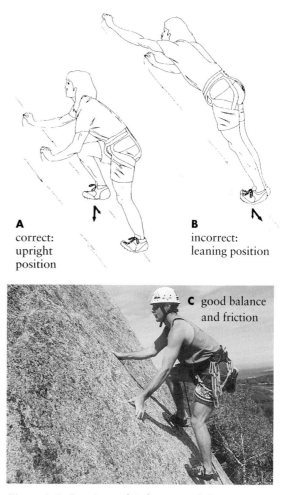

A
correct:
upright
position

B
incorrect:
leaning position

C good balance
and friction

Figure 1-5. Gravity and Balance on Slabs

A Classic Hand Traverse across a Slab:
A—Leaning back and frictioning; B—Working up the crack; C—Crossing hands; D—Finishing the crossover.

ing the slab. As you hand-traverse up a crack with your feet frictioning on the slab, you may cross hands, as the climber does in B and C in the photos above, to reach from one good hold to another as you move your feet to keep them beneath your body.

Mantleshelves

A mantleshelf is a rock shelf with a wall behind it. (The shelf found above a fireplace is a mantelshelf.) When you approach this shelf from below, it first provides handholds. Climbing past the shelf presents problems of balance that become greater if the shelf slopes outward, if it has a rounded edge, and if the wall behind gets steeper and more featureless.

Mantling, the act of surmounting the shelf, is a skill that can be broken up into a number of steps. For a wide shelf (see A in the photos at right), mantle facing the rock. From below, feel around on the shelf for the best finger holds so you can start pulling yourself upward; leave room for your foot on the shelf so you do not step on your hand. If the shelf is not too high, you may be able to place your palm on the shelf to bear weight as you move up in the next step.

In the second step, hoist your upper body as high as possible to enable you to cock your arm next to the wall. You can use small footholds or friction with your feet to assist upward movement. You need to get high enough to lean your upper body over your cocked arm and the palm of your hand. This places your body's center of gravity over your hands and allows you to straighten your arm. This position also uses your triceps efficiently to push your body weight upward. If you do not get high enough to get your body weight over your cocked arm, the mantle move will fail and you will have to reverse the movement in order not to fall. To succeed in mantling you must commit to an active, forceful, or dynamic move (as opposed to a slow-motion, near-static move) and a vulnerable position of balance to get your body weight well over your palm. This challenge makes hard mantles interesting.

As you move your body upward, you can rotate your hand on the shelf to bear your body weight over your palm if you could not do so in the initial setup. It takes coordination to hoist yourself and turn your hand at the same time. Getting as much friction as possible on the palm of your hand is important when the shelf slopes outward and is slippery.

You can mantle onto small shelves by turning your body sideways (see B in photos at right), a position that allows you room to lean forward. If the shelf is very small, you can place one hand on top of the other to leave room for your foot. Otherwise you may find that you have to place your foot on top of your hand, making it difficult to stand. (Some experienced climbers have actually fallen and broken bones after standing

Two Sequences of Mantling onto a Shelf: A—Directly; B—On one side.

on their own hands.) Once you are positioned sideways, hoist yourself upward and lean forward to get your body weight over your cocked arm. Stabilize your balance in this position before attempting to bring a foot up onto the shelf. Then press your body upward to complete the mantle sequence. Finish by bringing a foot up onto the mantleshelf and standing up.

Small handholds or finger holds above the shelf that enable you to pull downward or to the side will greatly enhance this final move onto the shelf. In the absence of positive holds, you can try smearing the palm of your hand on the steep wall behind the shelf to create a tenu-

ous friction hold. While you are using one hand on the wall behind the shelf, you can use the other hand to push up off the shelf or even off your foot (which is on the shelf) to help you stand. The act of standing is easier if your foot is underneath your body, rather than out to the side. This movement means you need to use your leg muscles to help walk your foot sideways, in a series of small movements, until you can load it fully.

On some steep face routes, climbers run into a situation where there is a large positive foothold slightly off to the side, but almost no handholds to help you stand up. You can over-

come this problem by placing your instep and heel, rather than the ball of your foot, over the hold before standing up, using leg power to lift you over the hold. This maneuver works because it places your center of gravity over your foot as you attempt to stand. Combine it with mantle technique and side pulls to aid in standing.

Counterforces: Underclings, Liebacks, and Stemming

Counterforce is a general technique applied to many types of climbing. You generate forces that act in opposite, or counter, directions to create friction and provide balance. You can create these forces by opposing your hands, as if you were attempting to spread open a crack, or your feet (*stemming*), or you can produce a counterweight to help balance your body over your feet, or by leaning off holds as in underclinging, liebacking, and stemming.

Underclings and liebacks differ in the orientation of the holds used for opposition. Underclings involve using your hands palm up in an upward pull that you oppose by pushing downward with your feet (see photos at left). A pure undercling allows you to make a long reach from beneath a horizontal overhang or flake. With your feet smearing, edging, or frictioning, you push down with your feet and walk them higher, while pulling up with your arms. This produces forces in opposition that glue you onto the rock while you make that long reach to a high hold. Many undercling sequences last only one or two moves, although you can undercling rock flakes for long stretches.

Liebacks often follow vertical cracks for long distances between stances that allow you to rest. You can use lieback technique one move at a

The Undercling to a Long Reach: The climber initiates the undercling by pushing insecurely against the roof of the horizontal crack while his feet push downward onto thin edges. He stands to gain a higher handhold in a dynamic movement that converts the push of his hands into a powerful upward pull directed in opposition to the push of his feet. Small downward-pointing flakes also can be used to create opposition.

time, but you can also use continuous lieback technique to climb cracks in 90-degree corners or flakes on a wall. You climb lieback corners using your feet against one wall while your hands pull in the opposite direction to produce the counterforce, as shown in the photos at right. When the wall is smooth, your toe points directly up it, with the entire sole against the wall to maximize friction. Keep your feet as high as possible to prevent them from slipping off. This position strains fingers, hands, wrists, arms, shoulders, and back muscles and requires commitment to the technique, or you will fall off.

Falls most often occur in liebacking when your feet slip off because you lower them to lessen the stress on your arms and hands. Less frequently, your hands slip off a rounded edge that you are palming. Cracks with sharp edges afford a good grip and make liebacks easier. If there are positive edges or lower-angle spots to friction, then you can stand in a more upright position to relieve stress on your hands and arms. You can occasionally turn your foot at a right angle to insert your toe into a wide spot in the crack to give a foothold.

Because of the strenuous nature of liebacks, climbers usually inspect a lieback for potential rests before starting out. Then they move quickly along to a rest spot, such as a stemming position that has footholds on both sides of the

Liebacking a Corner: A—The climber pulls against the crack with a straight arm and pushes in the opposite direction with his feet against the flat wall. He needs to keep his feet high and close to his hands to generate enough counterforce to adhere to the rock. If he stands upright over his feet, they will slip off the rock and he will fall out of the lieback. Usually, liebacks fail when your feet slip as you attempt to relieve stress on your arms.
B—The climber has moved his right foot upward onto a small edge that allows him to stand up a little straighter without having his feet slip off. This position reduces the counterforce strength that he must generate with his arms. Small positive toeholds allow you to lessen your effort before continuing, but you must still lean back and cannot stay in this position for long before continuing.

Figure 1-6. Stemming on a Steep Face Using Counterforces

The classic stem takes place in a right-angle corner where both walls have positive edges, smear, or friction holds (see photos at right). Stemming in a corner has an advantage over stemming on a face. On a face you can only move your legs so far apart before your hips hurt and you lose balance. In a corner you can increase your stem span by turning and rotating your hip. In doing this you "backfoot" the holds behind you to provide counterforce.

Stemming is a type of face climbing, since upward progress can depend on footwork combined with mantle-type moves, horizontal pull moves, or counterforce moves. In the photos at right the climber frictions with his foot on the left wall, "backfoots" the right wall using a smear foothold, and uses the crack to produce a lieback type of counterforce as he sequentially moves his feet and hands. Occasionally you can find a pull move for your hands to help stand over your feet. Beginners expecting abundant positive downward pull holds may have a very difficult time progressing, while an expert enjoys a relatively easy ascent.

Stemming can be useful even if the corners do not have walls at right angles. You can sometimes stem shallow grooves on steep faces. Rock climbers can ascend overhanging cracks more easily if there is any opportunity to stem on face holds on either side of the crack. Ice climbers can ascend overhanging shallow grooves in a relatively straightforward manner by stemming between walls with crampons. In all cases, stemming effectively brings your body position from leaning backward to vertical and allows you to get weight off your arms onto your feet.

corner. The most difficult part of the lieback in a corner often occurs where the crack becomes less vertical. This difficulty arises because your feet are still on the steep wall, demanding a strong counterforce that you have difficulty providing because your hands no longer have as positive an edge to grip.

Liebacking is often mixed with face climbing, stemming, and jamming.

Stemming

Climbers often stem between flake edges on steep faces. The boulderer in figure 1-6 stands on flake edges using the inside balls of her feet to bring her center of gravity closer to the wall, placing most of her weight over her feet. She establishes and maintains upper-body balance by pinch-gripping rock flakes as she pulls her hands toward each other. The opposition forces created between her two hands counter another set of opposition forces created by her feet, as shown by the arrows.

Weight Shifts

Climbing on a face involves smoothly shifting your center of gravity from one position to another. The climber in figure 1-7 starts a traverse to the left by placing her leading foot onto a distant and slightly higher hold. At the end of this initial movement (A), her center of gravity is slightly left of her right foot, which supports most of her weight. She maintains balance by providing a counterforce off the distance

Stemming in a Corner: The left foot frictions and the right foot "backfoots" and smears, while the arms *provide counterforce to move sequentially both feet and hands.*

foothold while gripping small finger holds. To move her right foot left at this time would place her center of gravity to the right of her feet and upset her balance. The small finger holds would not allow her to apply enough upper body strength to offset the resulting poor balance, and she would fall.

In a correct movement sequence, she moves her hips to the left (B), which shifts her center of gravity in the traverse direction. This allows her to stand in a stemming position with her center of gravity equally spaced between the two

footholds, requiring very little upper body strength. To complete the movement, she moves her left hand and then her right hand in the traverse direction in preparation for the last weight shift. The final weight shift (D) moves her center of gravity first horizontally and then vertically in a smooth flow. She moves her center of gravity horizontally toward her left foot assisted by a pull from her left hand and a springing start from her right foot. She completes the sequence in a flowing manner by pushing upward with her left leg once her center of gravity is over this foot. To continue traversing she may have to change feet in one of the ways described below.

Figure 1-7. Weight Shifts When Traversing a Steep Face from Right to Left

D   C   B   A

Foot Sequences and Changing Feet

On a face, handholds and footholds, body position, and balance depend on each other. Often a sequence requires you to lead onto the next foothold with the left (or right) foot. If you use the other foot, your balance will be upset, your movement on the climb will falter, and you could even fall.

You have two options to put the correct foot forward. You can down-climb back to the last hold big enough to stand on with both feet and start out the second time with the other foot to gain the correct sequence. On a difficult climb you may have to go quite a distance, so a better option is to stay where you are and switch feet.

You can switch feet either statically or dynamically. You can switch statically if there is room on the hold for both feet; when the holds are relatively small, you hop. Figure 1-8 shows a static switch from right foot to left foot. The climber starts with her right toe on the hold (A). She sets her left toe down on the hold and gradually rotates her left foot downward to cover more of the hold (B) as she simultaneously removes her right foot by wiggling it off the hold (C). Notice that the position of her upper body does not alter during the foot exchange; her fingers maintain upper body balance.

The climber in figure 1-9 also begins on her

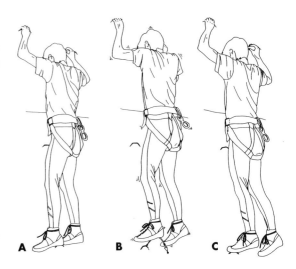

Figure 1-9. Hopping—Dynamic Foot Exchange

right foot and ends on her left. Since she only needs to have one foot on the hold at a time, she covers the hold with the ball of her foot (A). This foot placement requires less effort than that of the static sequence, where only the toe was on the hold. She sets up for the hop by gripping the positive finger holds well and then springing up or hopping off her right foot (B). Her upper body moves upward and downward during the hop; she moves both feet to the right and prepares to land on the inside ball of her left foot (C). The hop is quick and takes very little energy, but requires some coordination, and a couple of small positive finger holds.

Barn Doors and Counterbalancing

When climbing on a steep face, you need to figure out how to keep your center of gravity, located somewhere around your navel, over your feet—or even one foot—as you move from hold to hold. As long as you grip two good handholds with vigor, you can offset poor balance, but you always have to let go of one hold to move on.

The climber in figure 1-10 has a great handhold for his left hand and an adequate finger hold for his right. His right foot is on a small positive hold, and his left foot hangs in space (A). His balance point, somewhere around his

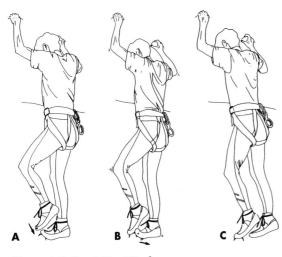

Figure 1-8. Static Foot Exchange

Figure 1-10. The Barn Door—Counterbalancing on a Face

navel, is to the left of his right foot, but he manages to compensate for this by pulling himself to the left using that good handhold. When he lets go of the left handhold, his center of gravity, indeed his entire body, rotates or *barn-doors* around the axis formed by his right foot and right hand (B). He is about to fall off unless he can pull off a most amazing save.

The climber could avoid the barn door by using his body as a counterweight to achieve balance. If the climber is to use the same foothold and finger hold as he did when he barn-doored in figure 1-10, he has a couple of options. To make a high reach overhead (fig. 1-11A), he switches his left foot onto the small foothold and bends his torso to the left; his center of gravity is slightly left of his foot on the hold. He also places his right foot away from his body, using it as a counterweight to shift his center of gravity slightly to the right. He finishes up in balance over the foothold,

Figure 1-11. Using the Body as Counterweight for Long Reaches: A—The long reach overhead; B—The long reach to the side; C—Traversing on a wall with good handholds and few positive footholds; D—Counterbalancing with the left foot while edging on a small positive foothold with the right foot.

assisted by gripping a small finger hold with his right hand.

The second option is to use these same holds to make a long reach to the left (fig. 1-11B). Here the climber begins in the position that previously led to the barn door. This time, however, he repositions his hanging left leg behind the right leg as a counterweight to move his center of gravity to the right. This use of a foot as a counterweight gives him enough balance to cling to the finger hold while making the long reach left to a better hold.

You can also use your leg and foot as a counterweight to maintain balance and to set up subsequent movements during a traverse. The climber (fig. 1-11C) makes long movements to the right on a wall with good handholds but few positive footholds. He moves his left hand next to his right hand (fig. 1-11D), and sets up a long reach and weight shift right by extending his left foot to a smear hold. This allows him to

Figure 1-12. Combined Techniques

support much of his weight on his right foot by edging on one of the few small positive footholds on the wall. From this position, in a subsequent move, he can move right by pivoting on his smeared left foot to a positive edge for his right foot.

Combined Techniques

As you progress up any section of rock, you are likely to combine various climbing techniques. For example, the climber in figure 1-12 edges with the outside of his left foot, smears with his right foot, mantles with his left hand, and starts an undercling with his right hand. He is using these holds to mantle and smear upward so that he can convert a relatively weak finger-grip undercling to a solid hand-grip undercling. After he has this solid hand undercling he will rotate his hip to the right so that he faces the rock. At that point he will move his left hand up to join his right in the undercling and work his left toe onto the mantle hold. Next, he moves his right hand around the right side of the flake so that he can lieback the flake and stand up.

This sequence seems complex, but it is a bit like learning how to ride a bike: you have to program your motor memory. After a few false starts and falls, you will find that very little effort is required. Climbing several grades below what you can just physically manage will allow you to acquire individual techniques and master putting them into sequence.

Rest and Balance on a Steep Face

On steep climbs with sparse large holds, you usually want to move along as quickly as possible, but you occasionally need to rest to conserve energy. Move your midsection (and center of gravity) closer to the rock and over your feet (fig. 1-13). Hold your head back to see the next section of rock and hang your upper body off the bone structure of a straight arm. Placing one foot higher than the other enhances the stability of this position by allowing your midsection to move closer to the rock. The tripod formed between your two feet and straight arm is a restful position.

Figure 1-13. Rest Position: On a face, the climber has one foot higher than the other, with hips swung into the cliff, and grips the higher hold with a straight arm.

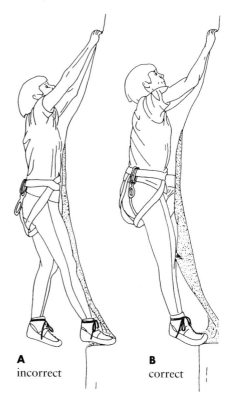

A
incorrect

B
correct

Figure 1-14. Incorrect and Correct Foot Placements under Overhangs

Foot Placement under Overhangs

If you use the large, seductive foot placements often found deep under overhangs, you are likely to destroy your balance during a long reach to good holds above. If, like the climber in figure 1-14A, you incorrectly place your foot deep under the overhang on a large placement and extend your body full-length to reach a positive handhold above, you will lean backward out of balance, your elbows fully extended. You will reduce your ability to power up and you cannot see your next foothold. You will most likely fall if you attempt to move. Instead, return to your starting position and place your toe as far to the outside of the overhang as possible, using a small hold. Your foot will be beneath your center of gravity, enhancing your balance. By standing on your toe you also have a better

reach: your elbows remain flexed and your arms can apply power. You can lean back to view your feet, step higher, and pull over the overhang (fig. 1-14B).

Semirest and Null Moves on Overhangs

Even when you cannot hang off a straight arm, if you rotate your hips into the wall you will place more weight over your feet and less on your fingers, hands, and arms. If you are underneath an overhang, swing your hips into the cliff (fig. 1-15A) in order to exert less effort. In this semiresting position you can get a good look at the holds above before continuing.

You can maintain balance in a static or dynamic manner, but if you move dynamically, passing through a series of small holds to arrive at a large one in a smooth flow, you will use less energy than if you do the moves statically,

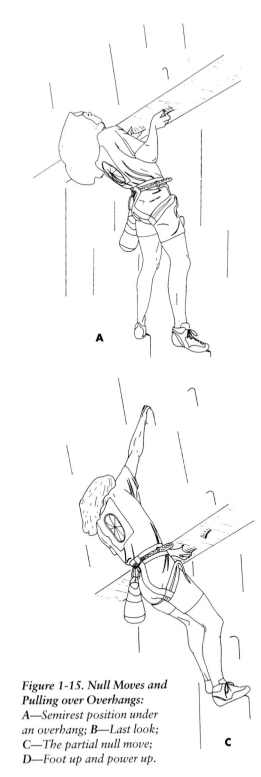

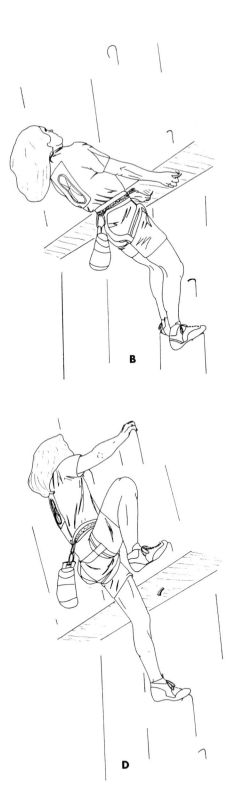

Figure 1-15. Null Moves and Pulling over Overhangs:
A—Semirest position under an overhang; B—Last look;
C—The partial null move;
D—Foot up and power up.

Beyond Barriers in Climbing

Climbers did not invent overnight the techniques described in this book. Rather, they developed them over time by experimenting with new technologies and applications, and refining their tools and techniques. Climbers with disabilities also have used the latest technology in materials and biomechanical concepts to develop special tools and techniques suited to their individual needs as they have passed milestones in climbing. For individual climbers, new technologies have resulted in protective climbing chaps and pull-up ascenders, as well as adaptive feet and legs. A few specific individuals and their adaptations are highlighted below:

- Mark Wellman climbed El Capitan and Halfdome using adaptive equipment. Through his company No Limits, he designs adaptive gear—climbing chaps for paraplegics—and offers videos and books. Look for No Limits at <www.nolimitstahoe.com>.

- Hugh Herr achieved high-standards in rock climbing while ascending with two prosthetic legs and feet.

- Tom Whitaker summited Mt. Everest with the aid of a prosthetic flex-foot.

All athletic individuals who accomplish great ascents, whether disabled or able-bodied, undergo intense, prolonged efforts of training and focus. Mark Wellman's taxing training regime to climb El Capitan would leave most athletes gasping. He did an estimated 7,000 chin-ups on his ascent of El Capitan. Most climbers will never achieve the conditioning and nerve to climb Hugh Herr's Stage Freight in its original unprotected condition. Few of us will display the motivation, perseverance, and physical stamina required to summit Mt. Everest as Tom Whitaker did. What we can learn from the efforts and accomplishments of these individuals is an understanding that first we need to pick a goal, however outrageous, and then train and focus on it until we achieve it.

To read more about climbers with disabilities, consult *Second Ascent: The Story of Hugh Herr* by Alison Osius (Harrisburg, Pennsylvania: Stackpole Books, 1991) and *Climbing Back* by Mark Wellman and John Flinn (Waco, Texas: WRS Publishing, 1992).

---

one at a time. The *null*, or *deadpoint*, move is a dynamic move that requires good timing, courage, and bombproof protection nearby when you are in the learning phase. In its most dynamic form, the null move requires that your hands and feet completely leave the rock in an upward leap for higher holds. At the top of the leap, when you are no longer going upward and not yet started downward, you are momentarily weightless at the deadpoint. Pulling off a null move involves coordination to grip the higher hold in the fraction of a second that you have at the apex. There is the chance that you will miss the hold and fall, so only try this near good protection or with an overhead top-rope belay until you feel comfortable with the technique. Since the null move is so committing and easy to miss, climbers more commonly use a partial null move to progress, as demonstrated by the climber in figure 1-15.

The climber is doing a series of dynamic moves to surmount an overhang. He moves his feet up in opposition to the undercling holds and leans out on straightened arms for one last look before committing to the overhang (B). Between B and C he pivots into the wall over his feet, releases his right hand at the moment that he is no longer rotating forward and before he begins to rotate backward (the *deadpoint*), and reaches quickly but in control to grab the higher hold. During this move the climber's torso first moves into the wall and then upward. After grabbing the higher hold, he hangs from a straight arm to inspect his next move (C).

Leaning backward also leaves room between the rock and the climber's body to bring a foot up for pulling over the overhang. The climber sees another hold to the right of his body that will both give him room to bring his foot up and allow him to lever off a side pull to lift his body over the overhang. He puts a foot up and

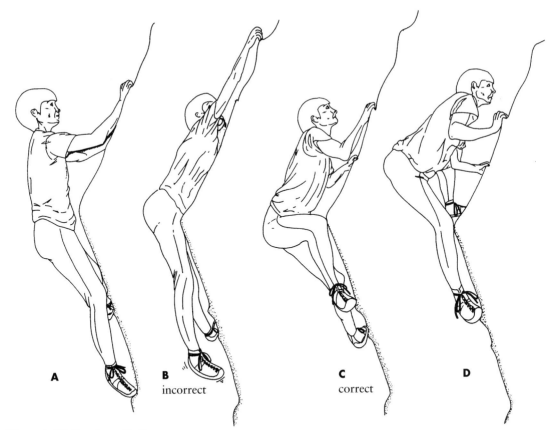

A

B
incorrect

C
correct

D

Figure 1-16. Overhang Exits

moves his hand to the right hold, shifts his center of gravity over the high foothold as he stands (D), and simultaneously brings his left hand up to the higher hold.

Common problems with dynamic technique are lack of commitment to the move, poor timing, and overshooting the hold.

In exiting from an overhang you need to maintain balance between footholds and handholds as handholds become smaller and the overhang hides footholds. Figure 1-16 shows a climber beginning to exit from an overhang. She maintains balance between foot stemming and small finger holds (A). She needs additional holds to complete her exit, and B and C illustrate two options.

In the first option (B), the climber stretches full body length and reaches a high, large hand-

hold with her fingers. Although the finger hold may be secure, the body position is not. Stretched out, the climber cannot see higher foot placements and does not have room to move her feet up. In this position she cannot use the upper body power required for the large handhold. Unbalanced, she is about to fall. This "flop" option is a poor choice.

The second option (C) allows the climber to maintain her balance. Starting from her initial position in A, she leans back on her finger holds. She can see her feet and has room to move them. With her right foot on a small edging hold, she moves her left foot on top of the overhang and then shifts her center of gravity forward to place her weight over this higher foot (D). The next step will take her up the final slab above the overhang to finish.

CRACK CLIMBING

On many cliffs, cracks offer natural lines of weakness that are used to produce climbs of the highest quality. Routes that follow natural crack systems, vertical lines along which a drop of water would fall, are the only flaw in an otherwise smooth face and have long been considered the classic and ideal route up the rock face. Crack climbing ability does not come naturally but requires experience, experimentation, and guidance. It can be strenuous and painful, and you may feel insecure until you have mastered the techniques. Why, then, do some climbers prefer crack climbing to all other forms? It provides good holds, good protection, and challenging routes up otherwise smooth and steep rock.

Crack climbing involves inserting your fingers, hands, feet, or even knees into the crack and camming them so that they lock. This process is *jamming*. Once you have jammed your feet and hands, you are secured to the rock and can remove one hand or foot at a time, move it upward, and jam it again. You repeat the process with the next hand or foot.

Jam cracks are classified by their width, since width determines which part of your body you jam. *Thin cracks* allow for finger jams, *hand cracks* allow for jamming the hand, and *fist cracks* allow for fist jams. Cracks that fall between these sizes require combining techniques. When cracks are larger than fist size, they are called *offwidth* and require specialized techniques.

Much of what has been said about balance and movement in face climbing also applies to crack climbing, with the addition of the specific crack techniques discussed below for handholds and footholds. In crack climbing you often use one foot or one hand on a face hold or on friction to maintain correct body position and upward movement.

Thin Cracks

Thin cracks range from the width of the tip of a small pinkie finger to a size that allows the fingers to be inserted up to the knuckles. As with all cracks, you must choose to insert your fingers thumb up or thumb down. The thumb-down position allows the hand to rotate, or torque, which often makes the jam more secure.

If you can put only the tip of your pinkie into the crack, you usually hold the hand thumb up. (If additional fingers fit into the crack, you *stack* them on top of your pinkie to increase the security of the jam.) A pinkie jam (fig. 1-17) is rather insecure, but you can strengthen it by leaning to one side or the other as in a lieback. If the crack leans to the left, for example, you might have a high pinkie jam with the right hand; your left hand will be low in the crack jamming, liebacking, or using a face hold on the left. Your left foot will usually be active out on the left face, edging any positive hold or smearing rounded holds. The inside edge of your right foot might well be stabilizing you by pushing against any protruding edge of the crack.

When a crack is wide enough to insert your fingers to the knuckle, new possibilities open up for jamming thumb down. You create a *finger lock* by inserting your fingers into the crack and rotating your thumb to create a cam (fig. 1-18A). If one edge of the crack offsets, you can use

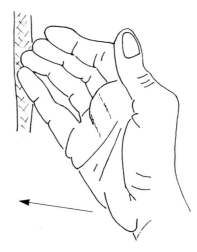

Figure 1-17. The Pinkie Jam for a Thin Crack: Insert your pinkie and neighboring fingers into the crack and rotate your palm to lie against the left wall of the crack to secure the jam before moving on it.

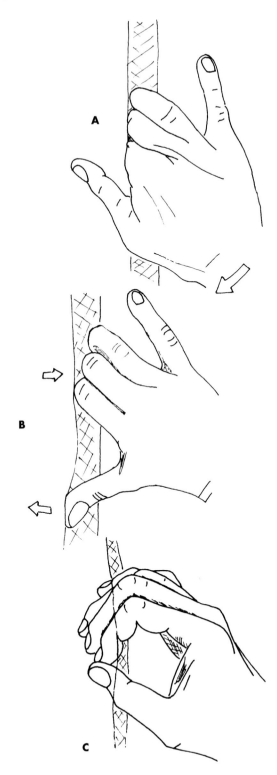

Figure 1-18. Thin Crack Jams with the Thumb Down: A—Finger lock; B—Finger lock with counter-pressure by the thumb; C—Ring jam; D—Combined techniques while jamming.

your thumb on the raised lip to create a counter-force to that created by your fingers (fig. 1-18B). When the crack is wide enough to insert your thumb, you can form a *ring jam* (fig. 1-18C). Your thumb closes upward, with your fingers pointing downward to form a ring. This works especially well if the crack has a narrow spot and flares out above and below. The fingers stack in the taper above the narrows and the thumb pulls upward from below. When the ring closes, you have a kind of pinch grip that firmly welds you to the rock.

The combination of techniques in a movement sequence is illustrated by the climber in photo 1-18D. He is using a fingerlock with his lower right hand, and a finger lock with counter-

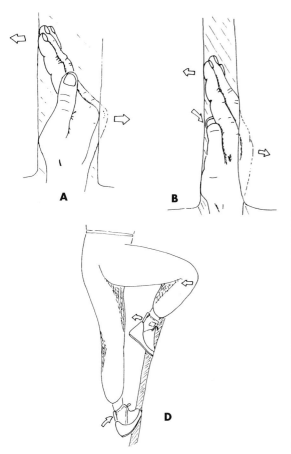

Figure 1-19. Hand and Toe Jams: A—Wide hand crack; B—Narrow hand crack; C—Climber jamming a narrow hand crack; D—Toe jams.

pressure applied by his thumb on his left hand. Both hands were inserted into positions in the crack, which tapers downward to a narrows, so that by pulling downward his hand wedges or slots. He is also using a lieback type of counterforce between his feet and hands. His right foot pushes against the edge of the crack while his left foot frictions on the wall.

Hand Cracks

Many climbers consider a crack that accepts the whole hand to be the perfect crack. You insert your hand with straight fingers, and your thumb is tucked in under your palm or placed on top of your index finger to help stabilize the jam. You create the hand jam by pressing your fingers against one side of the crack while the back of your hand presses against the other side. If

your fingers can grip small knobs, cracks, or irregularities within the larger crack, your hand jam is all the more secure. Hand jams are shown in figure 1-19A and B. The climber in figure 1-19C has tucked his thumb into his palm in a narrow hand crack.

Hand jams are often tight, and you'll have to move your hand to find the most secure position. Some climbers find additional security by leaning to the left or right to lieback the crack off a jam. You can severely abrade the back of your hand or your wrist if you allow your hand to rotate in the crack. To avoid these abrasions, insert your hand straight into the crack, rotating your wrist as you move upward. Most climbers also tape their hands or use commercially available Spider Mitts to prevent abrasions that result from hand rotation.

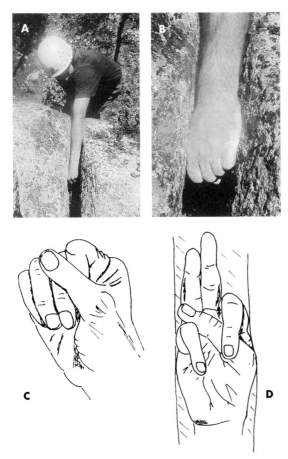

Figure 1-20. Fist Jams: A—Fist jam with palm facing into the crack; B—Closeup; C—View of the fist position with thumb over the fingers; D—Hand position for a narrow fist jam.

In jamming, you often use your upper hand in a thumb-down position while you use your lower hand thumb-up. You do this most often when the crack leans to one side or the other. When the crack is a straight-in vertical crack, you may be able to use both hands thumb up. If you are placing protection, a thumb-down jam overhead allows you to cam your hand for security.

If you use a thumb-down position above a constriction, you can mantle on the jam to make a long reach. Likewise, you can jam your lower hand, thumb up, against a constriction in a crack. As you make the high reach, move your feet up

much as you would do when using an undercling.

A crack that readily accepts a hand jam will be the right size to jam a toe, so that you can move upward by using leg strength as you do in face climbing. Initiate a toe jam by rotating the sole of your shoe to parallel the crack walls, insert it into the crack, and rotate your sole back to a horizontal position to cam it as you stand up (fig. 1-19D). In practice, you can focus on movement of your knee away from and toward the crack, since it controls the position of your foot and shoe sole. Toe jamming, like hand jamming, can be a painful process.

Fist-Size Cracks

In the classic fist jam, your thumb tucks in under your fingers with your palm facing into the crack (fig. 1-20A and B). In wider cracks you can place your thumb over your index finger to form a wider fist (fig. 1-20C), but this position produces a painful jam. In a narrow crack tuck your thumb under your palm, and fold your index finger and pinkie into your palm underneath the two middle fingers (fig. 1-20D).

A fist-size crack is more difficult to jam than a hand crack because you cannot expand your fist as much or with the same amount of force as you can expand your hand. The width of the fist jam is primarily determined by whether you place your thumb under your palm or over your index finger. As a result, fist jams work best just above a constriction and require conscious placement to find the best position.

When a large portion of your foot fits into the crack, you can use a foot jam, which is more secure when placed just above a constriction. Do not insert your foot too far, because the jam produced may be so good that you cannot extract it easily. If you should get stuck, you may have to climb back down a step to reverse the loading sequence.

Offwidth Cracks

When a crack is too large for a fist or a foot, it is an offwidth crack. In narrow offwidths you use your entire arm in an arm bar (fig. 1-21A) to hold yourself in place. Your outside foot moves

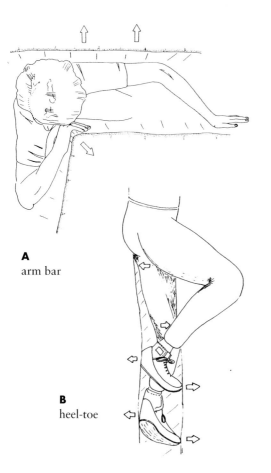

A
arm bar

B
heel-toe

Figure 1-21. Narrow Offwidth Cracks: A—The arm bar in a narrow offwidth. B—The heel-toe sequence.

C—Climbing a narrow offwidth crack.

you up the crack in a heel-toe action, as sketched in figure 1-21B. In a good heel-toe jam you keep your toes below and slightly outside your heel and smear the ball of your big toe. Your inside leg should be in a leg lock that you achieve by rotating your hip, knee, toe, and heel for maximum adhesion. The climber in figure 1-21C has secured his position with a heel-toe jam and a leg lock in the crack while frictioning and stemming against a small rib on the wall. Inside the crack he is gripping a flake and using an arm bar, while his outside hand pushes against the wall to provide counterforce against his arm. This same climber is shown in the photo on page 131 in a slightly lower position in the crack.

The arm bar, inside the crack, opposes the back of your upper arm and elbow against one wall of the crack while your hand pushes against the opposite wall. Arm bars work well if your arm and hand are diagonally down and away from your shoulder, allowing your shoulder to rotate in and over the elbow. The outside hand, on the edge of the crack, can often be low, pushing up on any lower-angle spot.

To make upward progress hold your body in place with the arm bar and inside leg lock while moving the heel-toe jam as high as possible. Then release the inside leg lock and stand up on the new heel-toe jam, with an outward motion of your hips. Finally, release your arms and move

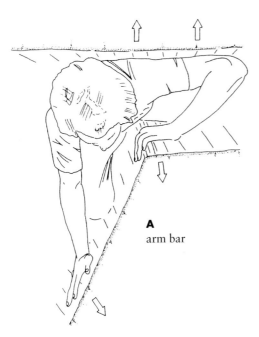

A
arm bar

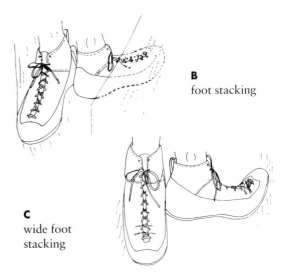

B
foot stacking

C
wide foot
stacking

Figure 1-22. Wide Offwidth Cracks: A—The arm bar in a wide offwidth. B—Foot stacking. C—Wide foot stacking.

your upper body up to reestablish the arm bar. You have now arrived back at the starting body position and are a little higher in the crack.

As the offwidth becomes wider, you can use your arm inside the crack in a wide arm bar. Your outside hand uses whatever hold or friction is available on the edge of the crack (fig. 1-22A). If the crack becomes too wide to heel-toe, stack your feet at angles up to 90 degrees, as shown in figure 1-22B and C.

Not everyone enjoys overhanging offwidth cracks, but a movement sequence created by Randy Leavitt and Tony Yaniro, called *Leavittation*, makes climbing them possible. You hang from a handstack and support your weight on one jammed knee as you move the handstack. For example, in a left-leaning crack that fits your knee, place your left palm against the left-hand crack wall and jam your right fist between your left hand and the right-hand crack wall, palm outward (palm inward for a vertical crack). To move the handstack, support your weight on your knee while palming and liebacking the crack and using your abdominal muscles. After setting the handstack, release the jammed knee, and heel-toe and balance with the

other leg as you move the right foot directly below the handstack. Then, jam your right knee as high as possible and remove your right foot from the crack, and hook your toe against the rock to lock the jam. Blue jeans are a good choice of clothing for this technique because they inhibit knee abrasion, do not stretch, and can be taped at the ankle to prevent bunching around the knees.

Spreading the Crack

When cracks are hand or fist to offwidth in size, you can *spread the crack* by creating opposition force with your hands on the sides of the crack (fig. 1-23). Spreading the crack works particularly well if there are small flakes inside the crack around which you can wrap your fingers, and if the crack is not vertical. Indeed, the technique works well in face climbing if you have opposing flakes as holds. Spreading a crack grows more strenuous as positive holds inside the crack and on its edge become fewer and as the crack becomes overhanging. On overhangs this technique may allow you to set up to move to the next and, you hope, better hold.

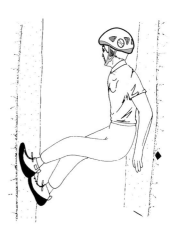

Sit in a higher position and repeat the feetback movement.

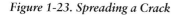

Figure 1-23. Spreading a Crack

Chimneys

Cracks wide enough to accept your entire body are called *narrow*, or *squeeze, chimneys*. These chimneys may also flare—they may be narrower on the inside than on the outside. There is a tendency to move back into a chimney because of the sense of security that comes from being firmly wedged in. However, it is as hard to move up as it is to slip down when you are securely wedged. Climb squeeze chimneys by using off-width techniques involving heel-toe and foot stacking, or bridging if the chimney is just a bit wider. Meanwhile, use an arm in an arm bar. You can often bypass constrictions in a chimney by jamming a hand or fist above the constriction and liebacking around it off the jam.

In wider chimneys your feet, knees, and hands bridge on opposite walls, providing counterforces to hold you in. You are, in effect, camming your entire body. In a wide chimney you unload, move, and then set the body cam—feet against one wall, back against the other. The *chimney feetback sequence* is shown in figure 1-24. This technique can feel precarious, since you unload the cam by using your leg to push upward against gravity. You feel secure only when you are stationary after the cam is reloaded. If you ever have to down-climb a chimney, you will find

Push off with the hand at your waist and stand up.

One hand may be out for stability or on the rear wall to push up.

Begin with your foot back and move your hand(s) to waist height.

Figure 1-24. The Chimney Feetback Sequence

that it is not as insecure as it might seem because gravity helps you move downward into a secure, cammed body position.

TAPING FOR FINGER, HAND, AND FIST JAM CRACKS

When you climb cracks, rotating a jammed finger or hand on protruding crystals can quickly shred the back of your finger, hand, or wrist. Taping can save a lot of pain. You can avoid tearing the skin of a jammed knuckle by simply wrapping a strip of ½-inch breathable athletic tape or medical cloth adhesive tape around each knuckle. You can obtain these tapes from a sporting or medical supply store. Before taping, clean your fingers and hands of dirt and skin oils with soap or alcohol. If your hands are

hairy, you can shave the hair or burn it off, being careful not to cut or burn yourself. (If you do not mind pulling your hair out by its roots when you remove the tape, you may forgo this last step.)

When you tape your hands, the pattern of taping shown in figure 1-25 forms a palmless glove that allows you to feel and grip the rock but protects the back of your hand and has the advantage of being reusable. It works extremely well for hand jams, though it does not protect the side of the hand well; use a wraparound tape pattern or modification of the palmless glove with extended sides for pure fist jamming.

Loop a long strip of 1-inch-wide tape starting from the wrist, up the back of the hand, around a finger, and back down to the wrist (A). Pinch the strip in half where it passes around the fin-

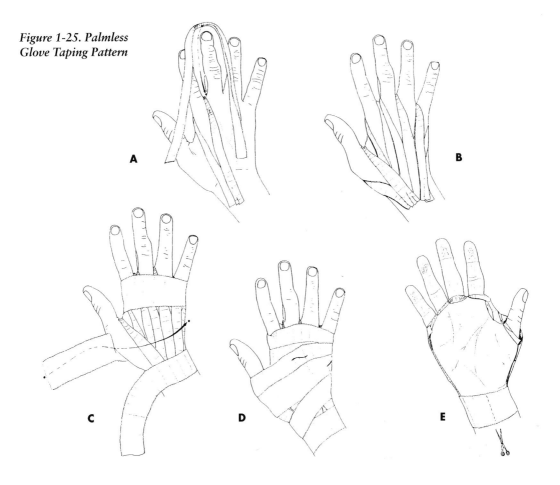

Figure 1-25. Palmless Glove Taping Pattern

ger. Repeat for each finger and the thumb (B). Tie the finger strips together by taping across the knuckles and the back of the hand and around the wrist (C), so that no skin remains exposed (D). (The tape for step C can be any width.) Be sure to flex your hand when taping to allow the hand to bend throughout its full range. Your wrists will swell in the course of a strenuous jamming session: do not wrap them too tightly. Additional strips of tape along the base of the thumb and across the knuckles help tie all of the strips together and close up any holes. Make sure no skin shows through.

At the end of the day, use scissors (rather than a knife) to cut the glove off at the inside of the wrist (E). Peel the tape up over the fingers. Reuse the glove by positioning it over the fingers and thumb and wrapping the wrist with new tape. After about a week of daily use, you may need to make a new glove as the wrist becomes so thickened with tape that its flexibility is limited.

You can tape your knuckles for climbing finger cracks, particularly when you anticipate doing a move involving a jam with one or two knuckles. A simple wrap of the tape around the joint that allows the joint to bend seems to work.

ROCK-CLIMBING SHOES

Many climbers do their first climbs in nothing more than a pair of running shoes, basketball shoes, or boots, and classic first ascents have been done in sneakers. But given a choice, most of us prefer to climb in shoes specially made for climbing. These shoes have evolved a great deal, particularly during the 1980s and 1990s.

Pioneer Victorian climbers led out in smooth-soled boots. To give these boots more friction they began adding soft iron nails to the soles and heels. These nails evolved into special patterns and types arranged around the edge and interior. On modern soles individual rubber lugs mimic the shapes of individual nails worn by the earlier climbers (fig. 1-26A). The pattern of a unique collection of these nails is preserved in the trademarked Vibram lug pattern. (The name

Vibram derives from *Vitale Bram*ani, one of its inventors.) Nailed boots worked to some extent on granite and even helped climbers stand in cut steps on snow and ice. On dolomite rock, a rock similar to limestone, some climbers preferred hemp-soled boots, as frayed strands of rope would catch on sharp edges and protrusions to provide good traction.

During the 1950s shoes with Vibram-type soles predominated, evolving over the course of two decades, and culminating in Royal Robbins climbing shoes. Commonly called RRs, these had distinctive blue suede uppers and a special composition sole. Indeed, if you own a pair, they still work well for climbing Yosemite-type walls, and they work very well for alpine rock climbs. Unfortunately, they are no longer available.

Smooth-soled shoes similar to modern climbing shoes began to make their appearance in the 1960s. The shoes were named after the initials of famous climbers. The RD (René Desmaison), which had brown leather uppers, quickly became popular. Other climbers preferred the high top PA (Pierre Allain) for edging. The soles of both were made of a hard composition rubber. By the end of the 1960s, EBs came to dominate the climbing-shoe market and did so for the next decade. The EB (Edouard Bourdineau) had a softer composition sole that gripped the rock well by standards of the time, but a canvas upper that quickly became brittle from foot perspiration. Because the shoes were made on a narrow European last, some climbers went around with tightly pinched toes. Those who wore small shoes to give them superior edging control suffered great pain and many lost their toenails to a malady called EB Toe or Black Toe.

In 1982, the Fire (pronounced *fee-ray*) climbing shoe, featuring a sticky Spanish rubber, was introduced to the climbing world. This shoe revolutionized both shoe designs and climbing. Wearing sticky rubber, climbers found that they could casually stand on rock slopes where they had slid down previously. A new world of extreme friction and face climbing opened up in the 1980s. Sticky rubber is a softer composition

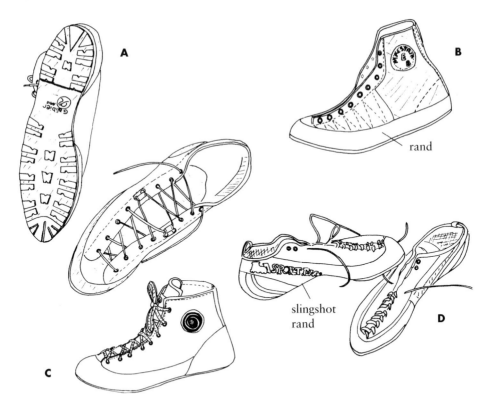

Figure 1-26. Climbing Shoes through Time: A—The Royal Robbins shoe is still considered to be the best big-wall boot. The rubber sole pattern is that used by Galibier, the company that manufactured the shoes. B—The EB dominated climbing in the late 1960s and the 1970s. C—The Fire started the modern shoe revolution in 1982. D—A modern low-cut anatomical shoe for steep edging has a slingshot rand that limits lengthwise stretching.

that deforms well over microcrystals, providing good holding power, but it is less durable than harder rubber when used for edging and therefore wears more quickly.

The 1980s saw an increase in the number of people climbing. Along with the Fires came new protection and greater numbers of fitness-minded individuals who took up climbing, leading in turn to increased interest by shoe manufacturers, who produced shoes that fit better and function better than earlier shoes. You now have your choice of shoes with soft or hard rubber, pointed shoes for steep faces with pockets, and stiff shoes for edging, supple sticky shoes for friction and slabs, high-top shoes with sticky rands (rubber around the edge) and flat toes for cracks, and low-cut shoes for ankle flexibility on overhangs. All of them have a close fit—they average one to one-and-a-half sizes smaller than street shoes—to fill the shoe and eliminate foot roll from small edges. At an extreme, some specialized and painful shoes curl your toes under to allow you to stand on micro-edges. When you choose climbing shoes, remember that they will stretch about one-half size sideways and perhaps lengthwise, depending on material and construction. Most climbing shoes have rubber rands that wrap completely around the bottom edge of the shoe to help grip in corners or cracks. Some newer shoes (fig. 1-26D) prevent lengthwise stretching with a nonstretching slingshot rand that extends from the upper heel to the toe. Remember that you will have to wear tight shoes, living with any pain, until they do stretch.

When buying shoes consider what kind of climbing you will be doing. Shoes for face climbing should be low cut for foot articulation, have an anatomical (close) fit, and allow you to feel the rock through the sole. The rubber should be relatively hard for edging. Shoes for multipitch climbs—climbs that extend for multiple rope lengths—should fit more loosely since you will be wearing them for long periods of time. Most shoe companies produce a relatively comfortable general-purpose shoe that will get you up most hard climbs.

As your skills advance, you can consult catalogs, reviews in climbing magazines, friends, people on the rock, and salespersons to learn the advantages of the latest models.

FOLLOWING THE LEADER

After you practice movement skills and gain initial proficiency, you need to learn how to put on a harness and tie into the rope to accompany an experienced team doing short lead climbs. Ideally, you should join two experienced climbers who will do the leading and belaying while you—climbing between them—learn about the process. Part 1 gives an overview of how the climbing system works so that the instructions that you receive from the experienced team will be more understandable. After becoming skilled in belaying and rope handling, also covered in part 1, you will be ready to support the leader as the second in a party of two. If the leader uses established bolted protection, you can concentrate on movement techniques, since you only have to unclip carabiners from the bolts and hang them from your harness. If the leader places protection, you will need to understand more of how the leader thinks in order to communicate with and work well with her.

The leader initially solves physical movement puzzles and routefinding problems that confront the team in climbing sections of rock, or *pitches*, between belay points. When the leader arrives at the top of a pitch, and has set up a fail-safe belay, it becomes the second's turn to climb.

Many leaders store a map of the pitch in their

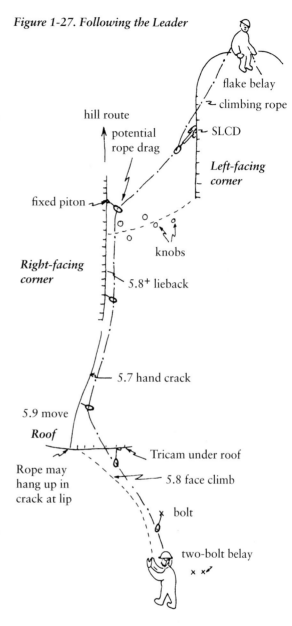

Figure 1-27. Following the Leader

- flake belay
- climbing rope
- SLCD
- hill route
- potential rope drag
- **Left-facing corner**
- fixed piton
- knobs
- **Right-facing corner**
- 5.8⁺ lieback
- 5.7 hand crack
- 5.9 move
- *Roof*
- Tricam under roof
- Rope may hang up in crack at lip
- 5.8 face climb
- bolt
- two-bolt belay

head and use it to communicate with the second. The leader may tell the second how to overcome potential problems with removing protection, managing rope, or climbing difficult sections.

A leader might sketch out a *route topo*, such as the one in figure 1-27. It is important to remember that the symbols of the mental topo remain as an image in the leader's mind even if guidebooks to the area are written in a descriptive essay style. In this particular mental topo, standard guidebook symbols are used for face climbing, corners that face left or right, overhangs, straight-in cracks, liebacks, belay stations, degrees of difficulty, and so on. On the map in the leader's head, a piton or bolt becomes more than just a shaped bit of metal. These objects become landmarks of the climb, along with overhangs and other rock features that mark specific locations.

On the specific climb in figure 1-27, the leader cannot see the second and might ask if the second is at the Tricam under the roof. The leader knows that beyond the Tricam is a particularly difficult section involving thin edging to the jam crack followed by a difficult pullover on a fist jam. If there is too much slack as the second climbs the lower face, the rope may well catch in the crack at the roof lip. The leader might ask the second, who stays in one spot a bit higher for a long time, if he is at the right-facing corner just below the fixed piton, or if he is at the fixed piton at the knob traverse. These are precise locations on the climb that give the leader specific information about the difficulties that the second is about to face. The experienced leader can also anticipate specific problems of rope management or protection removal and communicate these to the second.

Solving physical problems on your own is one of the most appealing aspects of rock climbing. In the initial stages of learning how to climb, you can carefully observe the leader's movement. Did the leader use a lieback at a particular place or stem? Was the left foot or right foot on the large hold, or was that large hold ignored because it might destroy balance? This type of observation requires you to focus carefully on the leader's movement.

REFERENCES FOR FUTURE READING

Graydon, Don, ed. 1992. *Mountaineering: The freedom of the hills.* Fifth edition. Seattle: Mountaineers.

Kopischka, Layne. 1988. Wide-crack technique for intermediates. *Climbing.* 108:112–13.

Leavitt, Randy. 1988. Advanced offwidths: Leavittation makes them manageable. *Climbing.* 109:90–91.

Long, John. 1989. *How to rock climb!* Evergreen, Colorado: Chockstone Press.

Loughman, Michael. 1981. *Learning to rock climb.* San Francisco: Sierra Club Books.

Meyers, George, and Don Reid. 1987. *Yosemite climbs.* Evergreen, Colorado: Chockstone Press.

Peters, Ed, ed. 1982. *Mountaineering: The freedom of the hills.* Fourth edition. Seattle: Mountaineers.

Raleigh, Duane. 1990. Testing the new soft shoes: 1990 climbing shoe review: *Climbing.* 120:86–103.

———. 1990. Shoes, shoes, and more shoes: 1990 climbing shoe review. *Climbing.* 121:80–86.

Climbing Indoors

Climbing indoors is booming with climbing gyms established in big cities to small towns, in vast converted warehouses, in converted racquetball courts, and in private bedrooms. Walls are located in schools, colleges and universities, retail shops, community recreation centers, and private basements and garages. Most indoor walls have in common a relatively short height of 10 to 60 feet, with emphasis on climbing sequences that require intense effort without rest. Indoor climbing walls allow you to climb day or night, in sunny or inclement weather, during summer or winter, without preplanning, and at great distances from the nearest rock.

Experienced climbers are flocking to climbing gyms to maintain or improve their fitness between weekend trips to outdoor crags. First-time climbers enjoy social recreation free of the complex concerns and requirements of outdoor cliffs—indoors, where there is no loose lichen-covered rock or access problem. The ease, safety, and challenge of indoor climbing walls also provide a dynamic medium for teaching problem solving, community building, and self-confidence for groups of novice climbers in challenge and youth-at-risk programs. Both experienced climbers and novice climbers, who focus on climbing as a recreational activity, enhance their fitness and skills in the special techniques required by the steep, overhanging, and continuously difficult routes found indoors.

WALL DESIGN

Climbing walls are versatile in design[1]. Mobile walls mounted on trailers are available for such special occasions as picnics, parties, fairs, and expositions (see photo next page). When these walls arrive on a site, they are set up in minutes to accommodate up to four climbers at a time. Outdoor artificial walls used in competitions can be larger, freestanding, and constructed for the event on scaffolding. Walls designed for neighborhood children's playgrounds are no higher than other playground equipment but often longer and can withstand vandalism,

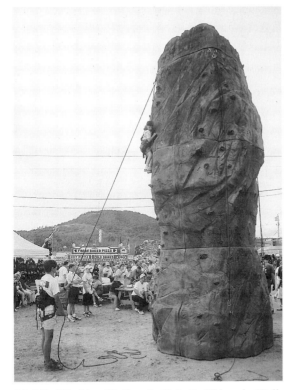

Mobile Climbing Wall at the Fair. By Eldorado Wall.

ing spaces for the climber to explore and admire. Innovative manufacturers have created molds from outdoor rock surfaces to create panel systems (see photo next page) that can be configured to include cracks, overhanging areas, corners, roofs, vertical surfaces or sharp outside corners similar to a ship's prow. The panels are interchangeable and can be reconfigured to create a new look. Many climbing walls are made of plywood or textured plywood and use modular holds. Wall designers can design three-dimensional surfaces with ribs, bulges, pockets, and large handholds or jugs. Climbers can enjoy the result of these innovations and climb on interesting surfaces that can vary in difficulty and be visually stunning.

There are now a number of climbing wall design companies with solid experience in building medium-size to large walls. These and other companies not only engineer, design, and build walls but can also help to direct you toward creating a viable and profitable business to pursue a dream of owning your own climbing gym.

weather, and unsupervised play. Rotating walls are available for gyms, fitness centers, and institutional training. One type of rotating wall operates by counterweights and friction; another type is motorized and programmable[2]. A rotating wall allows climbers to climb several hundred vertical feet, and even to be totally inverted, without ropes, as they maintain a distance of three to six feet from the ground.

Larger climbing walls are located in gyms, ski areas, retail stores, colleges, and buildings where they can form architectural focal points (see photo at right). These walls use plywood with modular holds, sculpted concrete shell structures, or reinforced concrete imprinted panels. They can be built on rigid steel frames, articulating steel frames, or, in the case of most small walls and miniwalls, on wooden frames. Sculpted concrete walls allow three-dimensional climbing and closely resemble natural rock formation when the sculptor creates twisting, flow-

Chelsea Piers Rock Wall. By Entre Prises.

Many climbing wall designers and builders have banded together as the Climbing Wall Industry Group (CWIG) of the Outdoor Recreation Coalition of America (ORCA).[3] CWIG's mission is to promote safety through education, testing, research and establishment of standards for the industry that serves the climbing public. Thus far, it has focused on gathering physical data to determine the loads and forces acting on wall components and to create standards for construction. The good news for climbers or groups wanting to build engineered structures is that CWIG has published *A Guide to Building Your Climbing Wall*, and the British Mountaineering Council offers the *BMC Climbing Wall Manual: Technical Information for Designers, Architects, Leisure Managers, Facility Owners and Climbers*.[4]

CLIMBING IN THE GYM

If you come to indoor climbing after climbing cliffs, you will discover a few differences. When climbing on rock, you warm up and stretch as you hike into a cliff. You usually warm up on a climb that stretches your body while awakening your muscles without more than moderate mental or physical effort. On rock, your first climbs may be on a slab or steeper climb with large enough footholds so that you can support body weight on your feet, and you leave the arm-blowing, finger-ripping, vertical to overhanging climbs until later in the day. In the gym, where climbs are 10 to 60 feet high on vertical to over-hanging walls without rest, even climbs with large holds immediately demand intensive physical effort. You can often start out on slabs indoors, but many climbers tend to move quickly to an overhanging bouldering cave or start a long traverse on a vertical wall where sequences are continually demanding, which leads to a fairly quick muscular pump and an incomplete training session. In the gym, designated routes are designed by route setters to be continuously challenging and without significant rest in the short vertical spaces of the gym, which also leads to a quick muscular pump. This quick

Custom Rock Panels. *By Custom Rock/Entre Prises.*

jump into intense effort and the resulting muscular pump are accentuated as you complete one route and then begin climbing again on the next route just a few feet away.

Without an adequate warm-up and rest between routes, you can suffer a premature pump that limits your overall climbing time or invites serious muscle or tendon injury that can sideline you for weeks or even permanently. Instead, consider stretching well before starting, walking along the base of the wall, as if traversing, and gripping the holds as though you were climbing; once you start, spend 10 or 15 minutes in belaying friends or stretching between demanding climbs. Books and articles by Dale Goddard and Udo Neumann and by Eric Horst, referenced at the end of this chapter, provide useful information on training. Incomplete training suggestions taken from these sources follow. Consult these and other sources to understand training complexities.

You can train for endurance by using holds and wall angles that allow you to move continuously on moderate climbing for 5 to 15 minutes at a time and then rest until you are completely recovered 15 to 20 minutes later. Two to three repetitions of the sequence, or sets, complete the endurance workout. An anaerobic endurance workout stretches both your mental and physical boundaries. Train moving from small to medium-size holds in a sequence of 15 to 40 moves as your strength fails. Each successive hold in the sequence requires great effort to hang on as you attempt "one more move" to muscular failure. Rest 15 to 20 minutes before doing the second of two or three more sets. This type of workout can lead to injury if you attempt it every day and to a performance plateau without incorporating other elements and sequences into your training. If you use this type of workout too extensively, overtraining injuries tend to follow. The opposite of an endurance workout is that of maximum-intensity effort, based on just a few maximum-intensity moves, to increase grip strength, pull strength, and lock-off strength.[5] Do this type of training while minimizing technical difficulty on rounded holds that do not produce pain, with an acute awareness of your limits and susceptibility to injury, and only after you are comfortable with the aerobic and anaerobic endurance aspects of your training.

Climbing indoors is the perfect place to train and learn new movement skills. During this process, you'll go through a number of phases ranging from first thinking about a move or watching others practice the move to your first clumsy and halting attempts at the movement. At this stage, your mind knows about the movement, but your body has not yet learned how to carry it out and you're likely to put forth a jerky and fatiguing effort with only partial success. Your body movements will become smoother and less conscious with practice as your central nervous system "builds in" the movement in co-operation with your brain. With time and continued practice, movements become smooth and flowing. The ultimate state of practice is to achieve a "flow,"[6] in which you perform in harmony with the climb free of conscious thought outside of your immediate relationship to the climb. In this state, you focus on excluding both external and internal distractions to "send flash ascents" as you successfully climb an unknown route smoothly on your first attempt.

Climbers on indoor walls rely on the movement skills discussed in chapter one, but add to those skills to cope with the continuously difficult vertical and overhanging climbs found indoors. When you climb vertical walls gravity pulls you away from the wall and significantly changes the angle at which your hands and feet grip holds. To understand this relationship, first consider how gravity affects you on a slab. By standing upright over your feet on a slab (see fig. 1-5A) gravity pulls you downward into your feet, and you need a small amount of friction to stay on the rock so that you stick in place. If you lean forward, less of your body weight is over your feet and you do not create enough friction on the soles of your shoes as gravity pulls you downward; you slide down the slab. On more vertical walls you employ counterforce techniques. In the undercling (see photos on page 8), you push down with your feet while pulling up with your hand to produce body tension and opposing forces that both stabilize you and allow you to make long reaches.

Stemming on a steep face (see fig. 1-6) also produces counterforces between your feet; counterforces between your hands supply upper body balance as you work to stay over your feet. If you try using the forward facing stemming technique on an overhanging wall, these counterforces won't work. Your upper body sags backward into space without the effort of body tension, and the counterforce provided by your hands is reduced to a weak frictional force against the holds as gravity pulls you backward; the counterforce of your hands pulling toward each other becomes ineffective, and you fall. Your first inclination in this forward-facing stemming position is to grip the holds with an open hand, cling grip, vertical grip, pinch grip, or finger wrap while abandoning counterforce

The Backstep/Drop Knee on an Overhanging Wall

you twist, as you twist the opposite hip into the wall. If you grip the hold with your left hand, as in the photo at left, twist your right hip into the wall to begin setting up a counterforce between your left hand and right foot. To complete the counterforce, step backward with your right foot, now against the wall, onto a hold slightly behind you and drop your right knee, which is also adjacent to the wall. You will finish standing on the outside edge of the foot behind you, here your right; stand on the inside edge of your front foot with your feet in a stemming opposition to each other and with as much body weight as possible over your feet. By dropping your knee, you change the direction of applied force to be more perpendicular to the hold that you are gripping and you will have a better grip. Body tension stabilizes this backstep/drop knee position to allow you to make a long reach to a higher handhold or to take a short rest in this position. Once you grip the upper hold, you will probably twist back to face the rock and you might need to counterbalance with your leg (see fig. 1-11) in order to maintain balance. Quick, precise movements distinguish accomplished climbers on overhanging walls far more than they do on less steep walls.

MOVEMENT GAMES

Your experiences on indoor walls can be enriched by variety and new challenges. If you are fortunate enough to have a number of walls available, occasionally visit each wall. On a home wall, vary your use by focusing on bouldering, top-roping, or leading, if possible. To warm up, you might try floor bouldering. On the floor next to the wall, place strips of duct tape. Use these as footholds, as you use handholds on the wall by placing as much pressure on your fingers and hands as feels comfortable. Start out slowly, warm up your muscles, stretch, and get ready for climbing. A good game with a group, in which everyone can participate, is to add on holds. The first person climbs a three-move sequence. The next person repeats these moves and adds three more moves,

technique. Each of these grips has merit on overhanging walls, but, if used exclusively, they lead to muscular fatigue and to positions where you cannot positively grip each hold.

Your task on an overhanging wall is to find a body position that will allow you to produce counterforces successfully in order to stabilize your body while you reach for the next hold. A technique that does this is to backstep, followed by dropping your knee when required (see photo above). To use this backstep/drop-knee technique to make a long upward reach from a forward facing position, first securely grip a hold between your waist and head that will allow you to twist. The hand with which you grip this hold, whether left or right, will determine which way

and so on. If the first few people use large holds, this can quickly become an endurance game lasting awhile; leave the power moves for the last few climbers.

A variation is the "bleep" game,[7] in which the first climber creates a movement problem about 30 to 40 moves long, then shows it to you once and only once. When you get on the problem and try to do it, any mistake receives one bleep. The route setter shows you the correct sequence, and you have to move back one move before you proceed. After the second time that you fail this sequence, you move back three moves and so on, until you are repeating enough moves that you remember the sequence; your memory and forearms get an endurance workout.

"Pointing" is a game to challenge yourself and a friend or two. One person stays on the ground and points with a stick to the holds that you can use. The pointer becomes a coach-trainer with the objective of getting you to the brink of falling as you pump through difficult sequences, but who gives you a rest before you do falter. Variations of this game allow any handhold to be used while the coach-trainer points at footholds. This allows you to use many different combinations of handholds and body positions to progress while using only the designated footholds. The opposite variation of this game has the pointer picking handholds rather than footholds, with many strenuous hand and finger matches, where you replace the fingers of one hand with those of the other hand on the same hold, that result in long reaches. A complete variation of the game allows the pointer to designate both handholds and footholds to create one boulder problem after another as the game continues. You can play these games while traversing or top-roping. To exhaust yourself totally, change the rules so that you have to get back on the wall and continue climbing and falling until the coach-trainer allows you to stop. Another variation is to set an end to the game by spelling out a word, such as "horse." Take turns with other climbers, and add a letter for each fall.

MODULAR HOLDS AND ROUTE SETTING

The modular holds found on most climbing walls allow route setters to establish easy to difficult routes quickly and to change them often. Many climbing walls, especially plywood-based ones, are drilled with holes in the plywood panels, like Swiss cheese, every eight inches or so. T-nuts are inserted into the back of these holes to fasten to Allen head bolts that are integral parts of the modular holds inserted from the front of the panel. On any given plywood panel, only some of the Swiss cheese holes contain modular holds, and these can be changed or moved to other holes to create different climbs. The modular holds rotate full circle to allow a given part of the hold to be vertical or horizontal on the left or right or in a different orientation; the route setter rotates the hold to create the desired grip in combination with footholds for a route. Strength standards for climbing holds are being investigated by many of the two dozen or so U.S. manufacturers in the Handhold Manufacturers Committee of ORCA.

Holds come in many sizes and shapes ranging from large positive grip holds or jugs designed for ceilings and extreme overhangs to micro-holds designed for extreme crimping on near vertical surfaces. Holds are designed to be used as pulls in counterforce moves, pinch grips, or sloping edges that offer less than positive pull surfaces. Pocket holds simulate the two or three fingerholds found in some limestone areas, and horn holds, although not common in nature, allow for interesting route setting. Small footholds allow for microedging or smearing and can be used as in-between footholds for climbers shorter than the route setter as they move dynamically across small footholds to larger ones. Most manufacturers offer a complete set of holds for home wall builders; you can also purchase holds from a number of manufacturers to gain variety for your wall. Very large holds can be bolted to the wall to simulate elongated rock flakes, columns, or even stalactites to provide variety and challenge to routes.

Holds are available in solid and swirled colors and even can be shaped like numbers or letters of the alphabet. The shapes and textures of climbing holds has changed a bit. First-generation modular holds were designed to simulate holds found on rock, but, like rock, they were often sharp and painful. Modern holds are friendly to the skin and touch and allow climbers to use them for hours.

Route setting is the art of the climbing gym. A good route setter attempts to make routes, marked with a bit of colored tape on useble holds, as diverse, exciting, and realistic as possible. Feasible route moves are sequenced so that they have some similarity to climbing outdoors, but a route setter can also create climbs that emphasize the uniqueness of indoor climbing. Routes should be challenging and rigorous with differing sequences that can be dynamic or static, strenuous for either your arms or fingers, and require good balance and flexibility. Routes should meet the needs of intended users. For recreational climbers, a gym might maintain a bell curve distribution of routes with the average degree of difficulty being around the average climber's ability. Routes for competition should increase gradually in grade so that competitors fall at different points, as they encounter moves that exploit their weaknesses, rather than at a crux where most competitors fall. A good finals competition route will allow one competitor to reach the top while second and third-place competitors fail at proportional distances down the wall. Setting routes is a step-by-step process where the first few holds determine the sequence before and after them.

Sander Culliton, author of the booklet *Route Setting* for CWIG, advises the route setter to imagine a single move or a unique sequence of moves and to build a route around it. Try to incorporate drop knees, flagging, and side pulls pushed or pulled to the side away from the body. Climbers that use these design moves will climb smoothly and under control. Make the most of the limited height of climbing gyms by setting routes that maintain a consistent degree of difficulty. Try to create routes with a steady flow or rhythm, as opposed to a one-move wonder. Keep the grade consistent and the moves challenging. Keep finger size in mind especially when setting routes for juniors. Add additional footholds and small intermediate handholds to enable climbers of all sizes to enjoy your route. Large sloping holds are harder for juniors and people with small hands to hold onto. Rotating handholds off horizontal allows for more creative footwork and creates a need for precise weight distribution, body position, and reading the movement of the route by the climber. Twisting a few handholds this way or that can be the difference between a route graded 5.8 that feels like a ladder and a 5.8 route that excites the climber and offers a challenge. (For more on how routes are graded, see Rating Rock, page 129.)

Route ratings should be consistent throughout the gym in an attempt to create a rough comparison to outdoor ratings. This allows climbers consistently to climb at known grades as they progress systematically in skill and experience. Inconsistent ratings can be frustrating and halt a climber's development. As a result, the route will lose popularity. It might be hard for experienced route setters to rate their own routes because of their familiarity with the holds and the fact that they imagined the hold sequence. The route setter can observe climbers of different abilities and sizes to determine if additional footholds are needed for small climbers or if there is an easy way around an intended crux.

Route setting for playground climbing structures has some different considerations. Most juniors using these routes will not be wearing climbing shoes, so holds should be quite positive. The route setter places holds to the maximum reach of younger climbers, perhaps by using his or her adult-size wrist, forearm, or elbow to establish proper distance. Route setters should consider available footholds, stances, and the finger size of juniors and add additional footholds and small intermediate handholds to enable climbers of small size to enjoy their routes. It is important to make sure that protruding handholds will not be in the way of falling climbers.[8]

COMPETITION CLIMBING

With increased numbers of indoor climbers and the widespread distribution of walls, climbing competitions have become popular events at climbing gyms. Outdoor climbing competitions on natural cliffs and artificial walls are subject to inclement, hot, or wet weather. Also, they are limited in matching a natural set of climbs having desirable characteristics to a confined viewing area. On indoor artificial walls, route setters aim for movement sequencing that is interesting to both participants and spectators and designed to produce a winner at the end of a competition. Climbing competitions most often involve local climbers who are attracted to the sport because they want to be participants rather than just spectators. A limited number of competitions attract elite climbers.

In the United States, the American Sport Climbing Federation (ASCF)[9] sanctions competitive climbing at local, regional, and national levels. The ASCF also selects U.S. Team members and alternates for the World Cup series involving national teams so that everyone, from local weekend climbers to elite climbers with world-class skills and the required dedication to training, can participate in sanctioned competitions. Formats for local competition include bouldering and redpoint or on-sight. There are no set judging or course-setting requirements at the local level or prize-purse requirements for this format. Both the bouldering and redpoint format are similar and differ only by the absence and possible use of ropes, respectively. These formats allow multiple attempts on a problem and the opportunity to watch other competitors climb on the problem prior to an attempt, but climbers return to the end of the line after they fail to complete an attempt. All competitors climb during the same time period but are ranked according to the categories of beginner, intermediate, advanced, and open. Competitors choose from 20 to 50 problems of varying difficulty for a climbing period of two to three hours and earn points on completion of a problem, after potentially up to five attempts.

At the end of the competition, the top five scores recorded by a climber are counted for placement in the field of competitors within his or her own division of beginner, intermediate, advanced or open. Ties are decided in favor of the climber who used fewer tries. The redpoint competition incorporates top-rope climbing or lead climbing with the bouldering competition. Scoring and attempts on routes are similar to those for the bouldering format.

On-sight competitions differ by not allowing the climber to see any other climber in advance or a route prior to attempting it; competitors are kept in isolation while others climb. An on-sight competition might include a combination of bouldering, top-roping, and lead routes all climbed in an on-sight manner. On-sight events can be run with qualifying, semifinal, and final rounds; many gyms use a single round of climbing a minimum of five routes. Gyms might provide an opportunity for a group preview of the routes, in which case the ability to "read" a route from the viewing area is a competitive advantage. On on-sight routes, a climber's score is based on the highest hold reached, each hold having a set point value. Competitors are allowed a single attempt per route with a high point measurement being recorded by the route judge. In on-sight competitions, the route setter attempts to eliminate about half of the field for each round so that only the most accomplished climbers advance to the final round and only one of them will reach the top hold of the route.

Regional competitions sanctioned by the ASCF conclude with on-sight routes. National competitions are conducted only as on-sight competitions with qualifying, semifinal, and final rounds, each having one route per round. Each year, the ASCF reviews its rules that cover details of using inbound or out-of-bound holds, precompetition observation of the wall and holds, time limits to start and how to handle misstarts, clipping protection points, the kinds of equipment such as shoes and harness that climbers can use, how to deal with technical incidents such as holds breaking, and an appeals process to judgments.

Competition climbing thrives at the junior level for climbers under age nineteen through the Junior Competition Climbing Association (JCCA).[10] Climbing at the junior level is designed to be fun with individuals and organizations supporting young climbers who are trying to do their best (see photo at right). These competitions award ribbons and points to give standing within 1 of 15 regions; qualifying climbers can go on to both national and international competition. Junior climbers find that the best part about competition is having fun while making new friends, often from among their age group.

Operating at their best, in a role that supports participants' fun and personal growth, coaches and parents help climbers to determine strategy, and they cheer for all climbers in the competition. The JCCA sponsors local, regional, national, and international competitions, training camps, and knowledgeable coaches who receive advice in motivation, training and periodization, technique drills, and games for working with young climbers. A pilot program encourages junior climbers to compete in teams. The program features the advantages of the supportive effort and companionship found within teams while it minimizes an intense focus on individual achievement.

Junior Competitor Lauren Karcey

Speed climbing competitions are quickly becoming a favorite of spectators. The rules are simple; the first climber to make it to the top of a route wins. The best speed climbing routes have large holds and a bell or object at the end that can be "slapped" at. The visual intensity of the competition is enhanced with two side by side routes for competing climbers in which climbers race each other to the top in heats. If the routes are not identical, each climber climbs both routes, and the winner is the climber with the smallest total elapse time. Speed climbing encourages climbers to take dramatic chances, to skip holds, to climb dynamically and even to leap upward and totally leave the wall in the hope of catching a higher hold at the "dead point" where upward motion stalls just before gravity begins to acceler-

ate a downward plunge. Often, speed climbing competitions are run in rounds with elimination and advancement based on time in each round, but a relatively new format combines difficulty with speed. The lowest time wins, but each climber climbs only once on a lead route with a set upper time limit to finish— usually 90 seconds for women and 60 seconds for men. Climbers are ranked by the highest hold reached on very difficult routes, typically 5.11d for women and 5.12 a/b for men. Speed climbing probably originated in Russia, where this type of competition became popular on outdoor cliffs. Most recently, it has been practiced even on the Big Walls of Yosemite Valley in California, complete with informal records and history.[11]

CLIMBING SMART

Climbers fall frequently; part of the challenge of climbing is to execute a movement at your limit where you might fall. To overcome any harmful consequence resulting from a fall, gyms provide ropes, crash mats, and instruction, and you have to constantly exercise thought and skill to overcome the inherent dangers of falling. Both gym personnel and you as an individual have important roles in creating a safe climbing environment. Many gyms have joined the Climbing Gym Association (CGA) to set common safety standards for climbing gyms and their personnel. On your first visit to a gym, a qualified staff person should discover your climbing experience and knowledge, describe the specific risks of indoor climbing and gym rules, and qualify you as a belayer—to manage climbing ropes—whether you are a new or an experienced climber. Most gyms require climbers to sign informed consent and release waivers that acknowledge the risks in climbing and/or a contract to follow safety policies of the gym.[12] Gym staff might request that you demonstrate the following: the process of putting on a climbing harness; a figure-8 follow-through knot for tying into the harness; a proper belay setup with the harness, including the belay device, carabiner, and rope, with proper belay signals and technique; and the process of double-checking the entire setup before climbing. Techniques and skills learned indoors become foundation skills when applied to the complex outdoor climbing environment, so insist on learning techniques, for example, using a friction plate in belaying, that will serve you well both indoors and out.[13] The concern for creating a safe climbing environment for climbers outdoors, as well as in the gym, has led to the establishment of ORCA's CLIMB SMART! program, which is geared toward educating climbers to the dangers and responsibilities of climbing. This program stresses that climbing is inherently dangerous, instruction is required, climbing equipment is for climbing only, and you are responsible for your own actions.

Climbers, whether in the gym or outdoors, can overtrain and suffer overuse injuries, commonly to the fingers, hands, forearms, or shoulders, involving soft tissue abrasions or finger splitting, muscle strains, ligament injuries, tendon tears, nerve compression, and joint deformity, among others.[14] You can avoid injury, long recovery periods, and even permanent disability by learning about potential climbing injuries and adopting a planned training program. A gym cannot accomplish this for you, but its staff might help you to become aware of proper training and injury prevention. If you do suffer an injury, consult a sports medicine physician for proper treatment.

A limited amount of data indicates that climbing on artificial walls results in a relatively low injury rate, although this does not take into account unreported overuse injuries that occur too frequently among hard-training climbers. A study of injuries on British climbing walls[15] over a two-year period, with an aggregate of more than one million visits, found that upper-body injuries included 6 shoulder dislocations, 2 wrist fractures, 2 adult and 2 juvenile forearm fractures, 1 elbow fracture, 1 elbow dislocation, and 1 wrist ligament injury. Among lower-body injuries were 19 ankle fractures, 14 ankle sprains, 2 heel bone fractures, 1 tibia fracture, and 1 knee ligament injury. The study did not find any of the following conditions related to accident frequency: height of a wall; regulations requiring the use of a rope or helmet; presence, absence, or nature of preliminary instruction; presence of an experienced climber; and method of wall construction or materials. The presence of safety or crash matting did not have an overall effect on the injury rate but did affect the injury pattern. Upper-body injuries tended to occur on thin mats, less than 20 inches thick, which did not seem to absorb adequately the energy released on impact with an outstretched limb. Lower-limb injuries were equally common on these walls, as well as those with movable crash mats; climbers landing with one foot on a mat and the other foot alongside or between mats struck the gym floor. These injuries occurred on different types of walls that variably

Making the Transition to Outdoor Climbing: A sport climb in a setting with limited environmental hazards.

allowed bouldering, top-roping, or leading. The low injury rate suggested to the author of the study that climbers acted to modify their behavior to take into account the nature of the climbing facilities in order to prevent injuries.

CLIMBING OUTDOORS

Outdoor climbing requires new skills and different ways of thinking and behaving than does climbing indoors so as to promote your own personal safety, as well as the safety of others, and to increase everyone's enjoyment in being outside. The remaining chapters in part 1, Climbing Locations and Tools, get you started in understanding concepts and systems as you make the transition from gym to cliff. An accomplished friend with a number of years' expe-

rience in climbing outdoors might be able to provide guidance. Also, many guide services and colleges offer courses providing the hands-on instruction necessary for a safe transfer of your indoor experiences and your understanding of climbing concepts to field practice.

Highlighted here are a few differences between indoor and outdoor climbing (see photo at left). To climb indoors, you park your car, enter the gym, and walk to your staging area in a controlled setting. The outdoor cliff is an uncontrolled environment requiring alertness as you collect and process a stream of information that you need to make decisions. In the gym, you begin at the bottom of the wall, rope up and climb to the top, and lower down after you complete the climb. In the outdoors, you might have to construct an anchor at the cliff top, which can be a rounded surface with loose pebbles or even acrons underfoot that can act as "ball bearings" to send you over the edge if you are unwary. Other climbers could drop gear or rocks on you, or you could encounter loose rock flakes as you climb. They are all potentially dangerous situations that you do not find indoors.

Belaying will be even more complex as you move beyond gym belays and learn to establish belay anchors and "aim" the belay and as you learn how much slack to give a climbing leader beyond that required for safeguarding a climber on a top rope. You will need to learn to place protection while leading with bolts, or more complexly with artificial "nuts," and to learn when climbing protection is questionable, a situation that seldom occurs in the gym but is an ever-present aspect of outdoor climbing. Gym climbing emphasizes face-climbing technique, often to a high standard, but neglects the skills of climbing a low-angle friction slab or a high-angle crack, each of which is a different discipline requiring subtle learned movement and protection skills. You can expect to drop well down in climbing standard as you adapt to new types of climbing and even the peculiarities of a new cliff. You will find that "multipitch" routes require you to operate with far greater efficiency in establishing anchors, climbing and protecting, and route finding than gym climbs or one-pitch road-side climbs.

You might begin one day of outdoor climbing by encountering difficulties in getting to the base of the cliff or finding the climb that you are seeking. Many climbers have joined together in annual workdays to establish set systems of trails to replace the poorly laid out and maintained trails created by wandering lost climbers and to correct erosion problems that result from taking shortcuts across fragile land. These corrective measures help to convince private landowners and public land managers, on whose land the trails and cliffs lie, that climbers are stewards who will use the land wisely. Indeed, climbers have banded together to create and support The Access Fund[16] to bring climbers and landowners/managers together at cliffs of local, regional, and national stature to solve and head off access problems, so that every climber can continue to enjoy outdoor climbing.

Cliffs are home to many wild creatures, such as birds or frogs, which have been protected by the climbing community. On some cliffs, spring peepers, small tree frogs, climb up and down cracks with an ability that a climber can only hope to achieve. The peregrine falcon and other raptors make their homes on cliffs, and soaring birds glide above on thermal currents during midday. Many members of the climbing community help to post and respect closure of numerous climbing sites during the breeding season to allow endangered birds to breed and raise their young.[17] In this way, they help to maintain the wildness of the special cliff environment where they spend enjoyable time and expend hard effort.

The gym is a social place with climbers traversing the length of walls under top-roping climbs and passing knots of climbers, moving from boulder problem to boulder problem, talking to fellow climbers, trading advice on making a dynamic move or a drop-knee move during the next sequence. Outdoors, most climbers readily give social greetings, saying hello and talking for a few minutes, but they might also wish to concentrate on perfecting movement and problem-solving skills that require an extreme focus, which cannot occur in the presence of loud voices or recording systems. Climbers outdoors might also wish to enjoy the special wildness of the cliff environment. Climbing at indoor gyms, as well as up outdoor cliffs, is best enjoyed by being sensitive to the need to create positive interactions between individuals or groups within the context of these different environments.

REFERENCES FOR FUTURE READING

Arran, John, Tony Bird, and Mike Rosser, eds. 1998. *BMC climbing wall manual: Technical information for designers, architects, leisure managers, facility owners and climbers.* 2nd ed. Manchester, England: British Mountaineering Council.

Csikszentmihaly, Mihaly. 1990. *Flow: The psychology of optimal experience.* New York: Harper Perennial.

Goddard, Dale, and Udo Neumann. 1993. *Performance rock climbing.* Mechanicsburg, Pennsylvania: Stackpole Books.

Horst, Eric. 1996. *Flash training.* Evergreen, Colorado: Chockstone Press.

Horst, Eric. 1999. Working your woodie, rock and ice. *The Home Wall Manual.* 95:121–24.

ENDNOTES

1. Many climbing wall and hold manufacturers support World Wide Web sites:
   Comp Wall   <http://www.compwall.com>
   Eldorado Wall   <http://www.eldowalls.com>
   Entre Prises, manufacturer of a range of climbing walls and holds <http://www.ep-usa.com>
   Metolius holds   <http://www.metoliusclimbing.com>
   Nicros   <http://www.nicros.com>
   RadWall   <http://www.radwall.com>
   Realform, Inc.   <http://www.realform.com>
   SolidRock   <http://www.srws.com>
   Sport Rock   <http://www.thegrid.net/sportrock>
   Stoneage   <http://www.stoneage-gear.com>
   Vertical World   <http://www.verticalworld.com>
2. Ascent Products, Inc., produces motorized rotation climbing walls designed for either two

persons (The Rock) or one person (The Rocket). Their Web site is <http://www.ascentrock.com>.

3. The Outdoor Recreation Coalition of America (ORCA), the trade association of the outdoor industry, includes the Climbing Gym Association (CGA), the Climbing Wall Industry Group (CWIG), and the CLIMB SMART! program, <info@orca.org>. This is also the source of the booklet *Route Setting,* by Sander Culliton, mentioned in this chapter.

4. An abbreviated guide is available at <http://www.orca.org/subgroup/CWIG/bldawall. html>. The British Mountaineering Council publishes *BMC Climbing Wall Manual,* referenced above, and coordinates the Climbing Wall Manufacturers Association (CWMA) of Great Britain, <http://www.thebmc.co.uk>. Publications are available from Publications, 177–179 Burton Rd., Manchester, M20 2BB; general mail: office@thekmc.co.uk.

5. Horst, 1999.

6. The concept of flow, introduced by Mihaly Csikszentmihali, has been investigated to explain why participants involve themselves in active sports, including climbing.

7. Many authors report climbing-wall games to keep training fresh and interesting. One of these is Beth Rodden, in "The Training Game: How to Get Hot without Burning Out," *Rock and Ice,* 1999 JCCA series program supplement for the North Face/La Sportiva, Youth Competition Series.

8. The Web site of Beckwith Associates, manufacturers of BOLDR precast playground climbing equipment refers to the need to conform to the *Consumer Products Safety Commission Guidelines for Public Playgrounds*: <http://www.boldr. com>.

9. The ASCF Web site contains information on sanctioning levels, competition formats, rules, and news: <http://www.climbnet.com/ascf>.

10. The JCCA Web site contains rankings, training camps, rules, and application forms: <http:// www.juniorclimbing.org>.

11. Hans Fluorine maintains records of speed climbing ascents in Yosemite at <http://www.speed-climb.com/yosemite/Yosemite/html>.

12. Examples of waiver forms are those of the North Wall Inc. Rock Gym at <http://user.mc.net/ ~ookmuk/waiver.htm>, and of the Granite Arch Climbing Center at <http://www.granitearch. com/waiver.htm>.

13. Safe practices for climbing gyms are under discussion. Examples include Steve Weitzler, "To GRI or Not to GRI—That is the Question," and Jake Kreutzer, "GRI-GRI Use—The Plot Thickens," both in *ORCA: News & Media,* summer 1998, vol. 5, no. 2, pages 5–6 and 6–7 respectively: <http://www.orca.org.news/cs98.html>. An additional reference is Charles Fisher, in "Safety: Safety Programming for Climbing Wall Programs," *The Network Archives,* summer 1998, vol. 1, no. 6.

14. Sports medicine literature contains many references to these injuries, including Peter J. L. Jebson and Curtis M. Steyers, "Hand Injuries in Rock Climbing: Reaching the Right Treatment," *The Physician and Sportsmedicine,* May 1997, vol. 25, no. 5, <http://www.physsportsmed.com/ issues/1997/05may/Jebson.htm>, and Blount Orthopedic Clinic, "Rock Climbing: Reaching New Heights," summer 1997, vol. 9, no. 3, <http://www.blountortho.com/newsindex.html>.

15. Arran, Bird, and Rosser, *BMC Climbing Wall Manual,* 37, cites "Injuries on British Climbing Walls" by David Limb, who studied the 90 most accessible walls in England, Scotland, and Wales and their injury records for a two-year period through June 1993. Sixty-three replies were received, with individual walls having one to two thousand users per week; 94.3 percent of use was at fifty-six walls with access rated "Very Good" to "Excellent." The complete study was presented at an annual meeting of the British Orthopaedic Association.

16. The Access Fund, P.O. Box 17010, Boulder, CO 80308, is an important climber-centered group striving to maintain climbing access: <http:// www.accessfund.org>.

17. The Access Fund maintains a list of raptor closings at <http://www.accessfund.org/info/ rapclo.htm>.

3

Knots

ABOUT KNOTS

Technical climbers use a handful of knots regularly and a few more for special situations. Poor knowledge of knots has contributed to some climbing accidents. It is important to be able to tie knots correctly and without delay. You should practice tying knots in fair weather with an experienced climber to check them, then practice them at home with a short piece of climbing rope or clothesline until they become second nature to you.

Knot Characteristics

Laboratory tests show that tightening knots in a rope lowers the overall strength of the rope 20 to 40 percent. This dramatic reduction in strength does not seem to have any practical effect on rope strength in climbing situations. Ropes under stress fail either because they are cut or because a knot comes untied as a result of improper tying.

A knot is not finished until you dress and set it. *Dressing* means orienting all parts of the knot so that they are parallel to each other and do not overlap, making sharp bends. (When two different knots will serve the same purpose, the stronger knot is the one in which the rope has broader, more symmetrical bends.) Dressing a knot tied in webbing requires special attention because webbing easily folds over onto itself, which prevents the smoothness you want in all parts of the knot. *Setting* a knot means tightening the parts of the knot so that they touch each other, which creates friction that prevents the knot from untying. Some, but not all, knots are not considered complete until they are *backed up* with a second knot that prevents the load-bearing knot from untying. You jam the second knot tightly against the first (see fig. 3-12H, where an overhand knot backs up a bowline on a coil). A well-finished, set, and backed-up knot is a secure knot.

Common Knot-Tying Terms

Knot: A piece of rope tied or folded upon itself; used for fastening two ropes together or fasten-

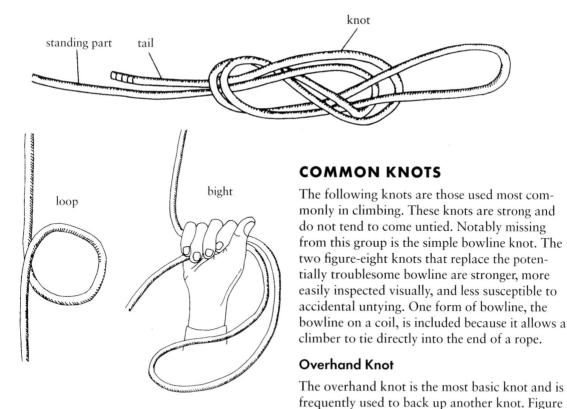

standing part   tail

knot

loop   bight

Figure 3-1. Parts of the Rope in Reference to a Knot

ing a rope to something else. A knot consists of a *standing part* or end, a *bight* or *loop*, and a *running end* or tail (see fig. 3-1).

Bight: A doubled section of rope, formed in the middle of the rope, that does not pass over itself.

Loop: A doubled section of rope that crosses over itself, which leaves an opening between the parts.

Standing Part: The end of the rope that is stationary. Often a knot is formed by passing the rope around the standing part.

Tail or Free End: The short free end of the rope left over when a knot is tied in the end, as opposed to the standing part of the rope. The tail must not slip back through or the knot will untie.

COMMON KNOTS

The following knots are those used most commonly in climbing. These knots are strong and do not tend to come untied. Notably missing from this group is the simple bowline knot. The two figure-eight knots that replace the potentially troublesome bowline are stronger, more easily inspected visually, and less susceptible to accidental untying. One form of bowline, the bowline on a coil, is included because it allows a climber to tie directly into the end of a rope.

Overhand Knot

The overhand knot is the most basic knot and is frequently used to back up another knot. Figure 3-2 shows how the overhand knot is tied.

The water knot is a retraced overhand knot tied in flat webbing. Due to the slippery nature of nylon webbing, the water knot requires a backup to ensure its security.

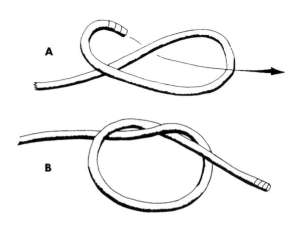

A

B

Figure 3-2. Overhand Knot

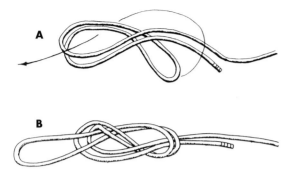

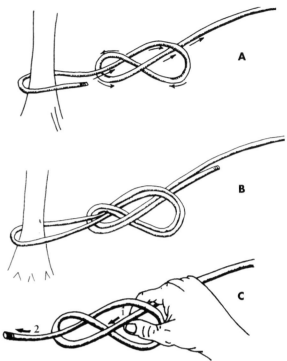

Figure 3-3. Figure-Eight Loop

Figure-Eight Loop

The figure-eight loop is useful when you wish to tie into the middle of a rope. It is very secure and easy to inspect.

To tie this knot, begin with a bight of rope and make a loop of the bight (fig. 3-3A). Then twist this loop around the standing part of the rope and pass it back through the first loop formed (fig. 3-3B). Usually you clip a carabiner into the bight of the knot and attach it either to an anchor or to yourself.

Figure-Eight Retraced or Follow-Through Knot

Figure-eight retraced knots (fig. 3-4) are used to tie around an object. You might use this knot to make an anchor around a tree or to connect the rope to your harness. The knot is tied by a retracing process, a technique used in tying many different knots.

The Clove Hitch

The clove hitch is an adjustable knot that you can tie in the middle of the rope, and it is particularly useful when you set up a cliff-top belay stance near the edge. In laboratory tests, clove hitches slip at approximately 700 pounds, but, in my experience, this low value of slippage appears not to be a problem. (Indeed, on one occasion, I have seen a carabiner broken by force transmitted from the rope to the carabiner by means of a clove hitch tie-in. The knot did not slip.) Given an adequate stance, clove

Figure 3-4. Figure-Eight Retraced: A—Tie a figure-eight knot on a single strand of rope, leaving a long tail. Wrap the tail around the object that you wish to tie around, such as a tree. Then retrace the tail, following the arrows. B—The completed knot. After you set the knot, there should be enough tail— normally 3 or 4 inches—to prevent accidental untying. Some climbers tie an additional backup knot that they jam up against the completed figure-eight. But if the figure-eight retraced is tied properly, with sufficient tail, the backup knot is not essential. C— Adjust the length of the tail by hooking your thumb and finger around the knot to form a closed circle. To increase tail length, pull rope through the knot as indicated by the arrow labeled 1. Then pull the tail in the direction of the arrow at 2. If the tail is more than a few inches long, it will hang down where you might step on it as you are climbing. An overhand knot tied near the end of the tail will prevent this problem.

hitches provide safe, easily adjustable tie-ins to anchor points for belaying. Back them up with a figure-eight knot to be absolutely safe.

You can tie a clove hitch by the method recommended here (fig. 3-5).

Grapevine (Double Fisherman's) Knot

You can use the grapevine knot to tie two different ropes together. It is the knot of choice for tying rappel ropes together and tying cord or webbing slings on climbing protection (nuts). Grapevine knots tied in ropes containing Kevlar,

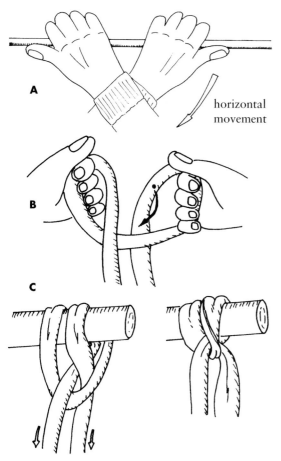

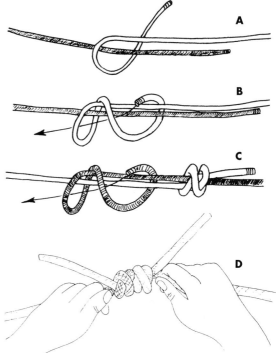

Figure 3-5. The Clove Hitch—Hand Held Horizontally (Viewed from Above)

Step 1. Cross hands with the right hand above the left, palms down and horizontal, thumbs along the rope, as shown in A.

Step 2. Hold the right hand steady and move the left hand beneath the right hand in an arc on the horizontal plane, as indicated by the arrow in A. This should result in two vertical loops (B). Make sure that the two vertical ends of the loop are touching the horizontal connecting strand between the loops.

Step 3. Hold the left hand steady and bend the right loop toward you. Then move it to the left, as shown by the arrow in B, and place it over the fingers of your left hand, on top of the left loop.

Step 4. Transfer these overlapping loops to the anchor point (C).

Step 5. The finished clove hitch in both loose and set forms (C). To set, simultaneously pull the two ends as shown by the arrows.

Figure 3-6. Grapevine (Double Fisherman's) Knot

Step 1. Place the two ends of the rope parallel to each other and loop the distant rope around the near rope and itself (A)

Step 2. Continue looping the rope about itself to form two loops. Pass the tail or free end of the looped rope through the inside of the doubled loop (B) and set the knot.

Step 3. Reorient the ropes so that the remaining untied tail is positioned as shown in C and repeat steps 1 and 2. This sequence helps ensure that the completed double knot is correct.

Step 4. When both knots are completed, visually check that the crossed part of each knot is on the same side and that each knot nestles into the other without a gap, as shown in D. If the crossed parts of the knots are on opposite sides or there is a gap, the knot should be retied.

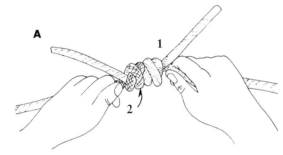

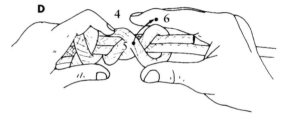

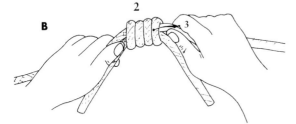

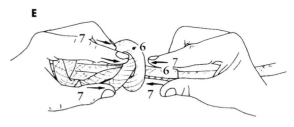

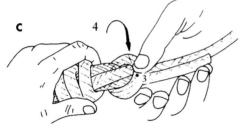

Figure 3-7. Dismantling the Grapevine Knot

Step 1. Examine the crossed "front" side of the knot labeled 1 in A. Then turn the knot over, following the arrow labeled 2.

Step 2. On the knot's "back" side, labeled 2 in B, move spot 3 to the right to new position 3 with your thumb. This takes effort.

Step 3. After moving spot 3, its new position is indicated in C. Now turn the knot to the front side (the arrow labeled 4).

Step 4. The front view, after turning, is labeled 4 in D. Move the spot labeled 5 to the right to new position 6 shown in D and E.

Step 5. Compress the knot from the sides as indicated by arrows labeled 7 in E. This loosens the knot enough to dismantle the right side so that it looks like drawing F.

Step 6. Now pull one end of the knot free as indicated by arrows labeled 8 in F. Dismantle the remaining knot to finish.

a high-strength but slippery synthetic, are more secure with three wraps around the standing part of the rope rather than the two illustrated.

A method for tying the grapevine knot is described in figure 3-6; figure 3-7 shows how to take the knot apart. In this procedure, you undo the right half of the knot first.

Prusik Knot

Named for Dr. Karl Prusik, who invented this knot, the Prusik is useful in everyday climbing and in search-and-rescue operations. Use it as a means of ascending a standing rope, as a tie-off for a rope, as a linkage in a pulley system, and

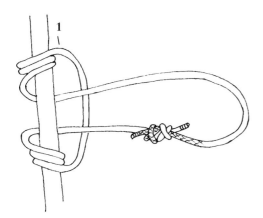

Figure 3-8. Prusik Knot: Hold the small-diameter loop so that the grapevine knot joining the ends of the loop will not interfere with the Prusik knot when it is completed. The grapevine knot also should not be at the end of the loop, where it would interfere with a carabiner clipped into the loop. Wrap the small-diameter loop around the standing rope three or four times. Set the knot and check that it holds in the use intended. If the knot slips, add another wrap of the loop to increase friction. To release tension in the Prusik, loosen the part of the small-diameter loop, labeled 1, that is parallel and against the standing rope. Then loosen the wraps.

as a rappel safety. The knot grips best if you use a small-diameter rope on a larger-diameter rope, but you can use slings of nylon tubular webbing normally carried while climbing. Avoid using Spectra webbing, which is susceptible to friction melting. Tie the knot, as shown in figure 3-8, by wrapping the smaller-diameter sling around the standing rope. The Prusik works by introducing friction that can be alternately set and released as needed. More wraps of the Prusik around the standing rope produce more friction.

Bachmann Knot

The Bachmann knot (fig. 3-9) is a friction knot like the Prusik, but you insert a carabiner into the knot to provide a handle. Place the carabiner through a loop of small-diameter rope or sling material. Position the back of the carabiner against the rope and parallel to it. Now wrap the sling loop around the rope and through the carabiner, working from top to bottom. The free end of the loop at the bottom is the attachment point.

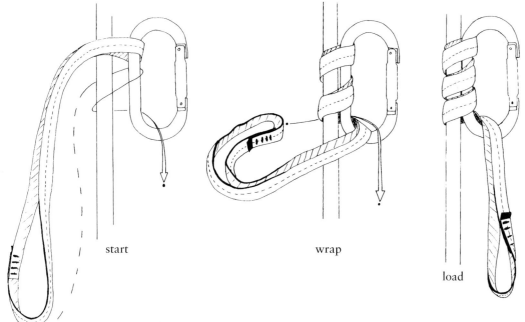

start

wrap

load

Figure 3-9. Bachmann Knot

Figure 3-10. Kleimheist Knot: The arrow shows the direction to apply tension.

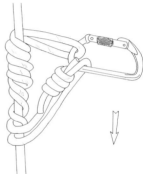

Figure 3-11. AutoBlock: The arrow shows the direction to apply tension.

Kleimheist Knot

The Kleimheist knot (fig. 3-10) is a friction knot that is easier to manage than a Prusik knot using the shoulder-length webbing slings that you normally carry with you when climbing. Wind a sling around the rope in a spiral pattern from top to bottom and pass the bottom of the sling through the top loop. Place tension on the hanging loop to lock the knot to the rope, and release tension to slide the knot with your hand. You can tie a Kleimheist knot around both the rope and a carabiner, in a manner similar to the Bachman knot, to allow the knot to slide easier.

The AutoBlock

The AutoBlock (fig. 3-11) is a friction knot used as a backup knot for rappelling when you use small-diameter rope. This is tied in a manner similar to that of a Kleimheist knot except that the top and bottom loops of the sling are connected by means of a locking carabiner instead of passing them through each other. Five or six wraps should provide the right amount of friction to allow you to slide the knot but yet count on it to lock when needed. Test-load the knot before using it for the proper amount of friction. Retire any ropes or slings obviously worn by extensive use.

Bowline on a Coil

Use the bowline on a coil to tie yourself into the end of the rope. If you are an alpine climber

who mistakenly ventures into an exposed spot without having first put on your harness, you can quickly safeguard yourself by tying into the rope with this knot.

The bowline on a coil also provides the standard tie-in for a backup belay, independent of the rappel anchor and harness, to safeguard novice rappellers who might inadvertently release the controlling brake hand. In this system, one end of the belay rope goes to the rappeller's bowline tie-in, and the other end of the rope attaches to an independent anchor.

The sequence for tying the bowline on a coil is shown in figure 3-12.

Check to ensure that the bowline on a coil is tied correctly. If the loop (fig. 3-12C) is twisted so that the standing part of the rope is away from your body, the bowline is not formed and the coil will slip dangerously when weighted. Visually inspect the loop at step C, and physically test it by attempting to make the knot slip at step G. Push on the bight while pulling on the standing part of the rope with as much force as possible. Remember that your body weight will be applied to this knot if you fall. If the knot slips, it will constrict your diaphragm and keep you from breathing.

Bowlines need to be backed up with a safety knot to prevent accidental untying. Figure 3-12H shows an overhand knot tied for this purpose. Physically test the knot before tying the backup knot.

Figure 3-12. Bowline on a Coil

A—Wrap the rope around your waist with a minimum of three wraps, working upward. The crosshatched area will become a loop and the stippled area will become a bight in the finished knot.

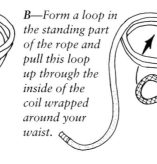

B—Form a loop in the standing part of the rope and pull this loop up through the inside of the coil wrapped around your waist.

C—Make sure that the standing part of the rope is against your body. Turn the loop over the coil around your waist.

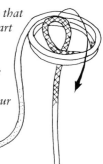

D—Weave the tail through the loop going over the near side, under the standing part, and over the far side of the loop.

E—The tail or free end of the rope now forms a bight (stippled) that weaves through the loop (crosshatched) formed in the standing part of the rope. This loop is passed over the bight in the next step.

F—Tighten the loop once the bight and loop are formed, as shown by the arrow.

G—After tightening, the loop holds a symmetrical bight in the free end. This is the completed bowline. The arrow shows the path of the free end to tie an overhand knot as a safety backup.

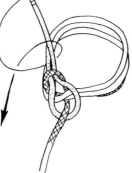

H—The completed bowline with an overhand knot tied tightly against the bowline to keep it from untying.

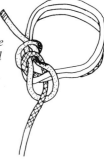

REFERENCES FOR FUTURE READING

Graydon, Don, ed. 1992. *Mountaineering: The freedom of the hills.* Fifth edition. Seattle: Mountaineers.

Padgett, Allen, and Bruce Smith. 1987. *On rope.* Huntsville, Alabama: National Speleological Society.

Peters, Ed, ed. 1982. *Mountaineering: The freedom of the hills.* Fourth edition. Seattle: Mountaineers.

Setnicka, Tim J. 1980. *Wilderness search and rescue.* Boston: Appalachian Mountain Club.

4

Harnesses and Helmets

THE CLIMBING HARNESS

A climbing harness is a system of straps by
which you secure yourself to the climbing rope.
The primary job of a harness is to provide both
comfort and security if you fall, and its secondary job is to serve as a belay seat and a place to
rack gear. In a fall, the harness helps to protect
you from forces of deceleration as your fall is
arrested and provides support as you hang from
the end of a rope. Harness designs vary, and the
one you need depends on the specific type of
climbing that interests you. There are harnesses
for sport or competition climbing, alpine climbing, big-wall or aid climbing, and multipurpose
use. Most climbers rely on commercially sewn
harnesses.[1]

HARNESS DESIGN

A harness consists of a waistband of wide, flat
webbing with leg loops that are either permanently attached or detachable. Harnesses are
precisely stitched together to provide strength

and might have padding, gear loops, haul loops,
belay loops, and brightly colored designs (see the
photos at right). The part of the harness that fastens only around your waist is a *waist belt* or
"swami belt." When you add leg loops meant to
take your weight (during a fall, when rappelling,
or when lowering), you create a *sit harness*.
There are several types of sit harnesses. The sit
harness in A in the photos at right is designed for
rock climbing. It has a comfortable waist belt
equipped with a buckle, leg loops of fixed size,
a belay loop, gear loops, and a haul loop. The
waist belt is padded to be comfortable when you
wear thin clothes and hang in your harness for
very short time periods. If you are a heavier
climber or specialize in multipitch all-day routes,
choose a harness with a wider waist belt and leg
loop webbing and with more padding; thinner
climbers on short gymnastic sport climbs can
choose a harness with a narrower waist belt and
webbing. Alpine climbers need to get in and out
of a harness without removing their boots, and
they need a harness that fits when they wear dif-

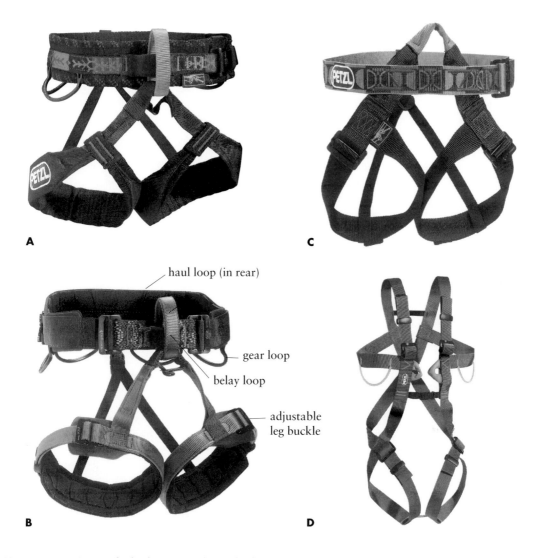

haul loop (in rear)

gear loop

belay loop

adjustable
leg buckle

A

C

B

D

Sit Harnesses: **A**—*Rock climbing;* **B**—*Alpine climbing;* **C**—*Multipurpose climbing;* **D**—*Full body.*

ferent thicknesses of clothes. A harness with adjustable leg loops and a drop seat (see B in the photos above) meets these requirements. Alpine climbers wear medium to thick clothing and require little padding in a harness. A multipurpose harness (see C in the photos above) is equally useful for groups and for rock climbing or alpine climbing; the waist belt and leg loops adjust to many body sizes quickly by means of buckles.

Sewn belay loops connect waist and leg loops and allow you to clip quickly into an anchor. The belay loop is not intended as a tie-in point for your rope as it moves the center of gravity of your tie-in point too high on your body, which potentially could promote injury in a fall. Haul loops, sewn at the back of the waist belt, are useful for attaching trailing ropes or shoes. The number of gear loops on your harness varies by the type and style of climbing that interest you; big-wall climbers might use up to eight loops, whereas sport climbers often use two. Gear loops and haul loops are not intended as a rope tie-in point; they are too weak to hold a fall.

A chest harness, designed to be worn with a sit harness, provides a higher tie-in point to help maintain an upright position in a fall or when ascending a rope. Many alpine climbers like the secure feeling of a full body harness, as well as the stability provided by a higher tie-in point level with their sternums.[2] Full body harnesses (See D in photos previous page) can incorporate the drop seat design of alpine harnesses or be designed to accommodate the body shape of children who are difficult to fit into other harness types' uniform waist, hip, and chest measurements.

FITTING A HARNESS

Harnesses, other than those intended for group use, are designed to taper to fit different body shapes and are designed for height, waist, thigh, torso length, and gender differences. The best way to fit a harness is to choose one indicated by the manufacturer to fit your body shape and adjust it to fit over your normal climbing clothing. If possible, climb or boulder while wearing the harness or stretch to simulate exaggerated climbing movements and hang in suspension from a rope to test its comfort. If you are uncomfortable at the sides, the harness is too big, and, if the harness is too restrictive in the crotch, it is too small. No harness is comfortable for more than a few minutes when hanging from it; after only seven minutes, persons incapable of movement are in extreme danger related to blood circulation restrictions.[3]

To put on the harness, first orient it in front of you, untangling the waist belt and leg loops, in the manner that you will wear it. Now step into the leg loops, and position the harness so

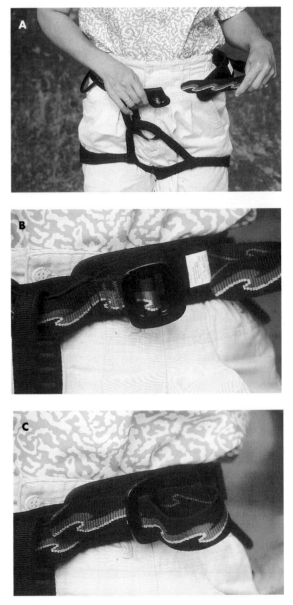

Putting on the Harness: A—*Initial fitting of the leg loops and waist belt.* ***B***—*The buckle.* ***C***—*First pass of the waist belt tail through the buckle.* ***D***—*Doubling back the waist belt tail: This step is critical!* ***E***—*Pulling the waist belt tail snug.*

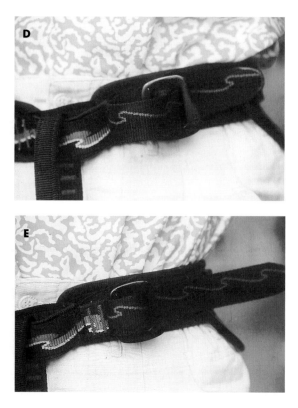

that the waist belt fits on your waist and the leg loops are comfortably fitted at the top of your legs (see A in the photos at left). The waist belt of a commercially sewn harness closes by means of a double pass or double back buckle system similar to that in B in the photos at left. To fasten the buckle, first pass the tail of the waist belt through the buckle (see C in the photos at left), pull the waist belt snug and then double back the waist belt tail through the buckle (see D in the photos above) and pull it snug (see E in the photos above). *Doubling back the waist belt tail is a critical step in putting on the harness; the harness can open in a fall and result in injury or death if this step is skipped.*[4]

Harnesses can have a life of up to five years, without taking wear into account. Cuts, tears, abrasions, and worn or loose stitching indicate general deterioration. Harnesses are typically made of polyamide or polyester fibers that undergo discoloration because of damage from ultraviolet (UV) light. Contact with the air results in a slight decrease of elasticity in time, and acids, such as car batteries and solvents, can degrade the webbing. Repeated rubbing cuts surface fibers and gradually reduces webbing strength. Minute grains of sand can penetrate the webbing and create internal abrasions and cut fibers when a harness is under tension. Keep your harness clean by washing it by hand or machine with a powder according to instructions for delicate fabrics; rinse in clean water; and dry in a ventilated area. Badly fitted harnesses undergo repeated movement that unequally "works" the webbing and sewing. Repeated flexing unevenly shortens the tape and gives it a "knobby" surface appearance. Such repetition stretches the fibers, generates friction of fiber on fiber, and cuts the fibers in the sudden impact force generated by arresting a fall.[5] Replace your harness after a severe fall, when the harness suffers visible wear, or every three to five years because of obvious or hidden deterioration.

HARNESS TIE-IN

Attach the climbing rope directly to the harness by using a figure-eight retraced. (Details of this knot are shown in chapter 3, fig. 3-4). Note that you should not use a carabiner as an intermediate link for this connection in ordinary climbing situations because carabiners can open accidentally, which might result in injury.

To tie into the harness, pass the long tail through the crosspiece of the leg loops and then through the waist belt (see A in photos next page). Tying into the haul loop, gear loops, or belay loop is not acceptable and even can be

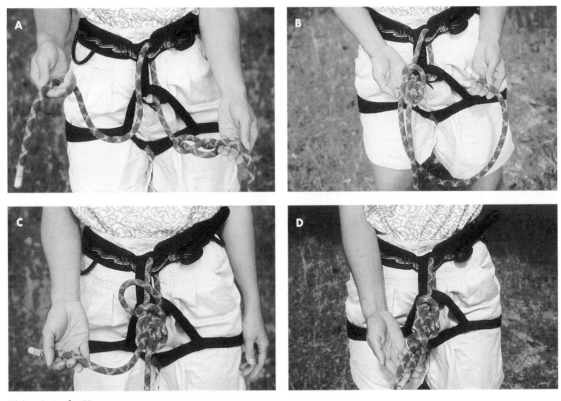

Tying into the Harness

fatal because of lack of strength or incorrect geometry that results. Complete the figure-eight retraced knot (see B and C in the photos above), and tie off the tail with an overhand knot to prevent the loose end from dangling underfoot (see D in the photos above). The overhand knot is not absolutely required as a finishing knot as long as 3 or 4 inches of tail remain outside the knot after you tighten and dress the knot. A lifelong protective habit (for a long life) is to double-check your harness, the double-back buckle, and tie in immediately before you commit to climbing or rappelling.

To create a tie-in point for rappelling, you use a locking carabiner as an intermediate link, as shown in the photo at right. (Rappelling is discussed in detail in chapter 8). This carabiner passes around the harness leg loops and waist

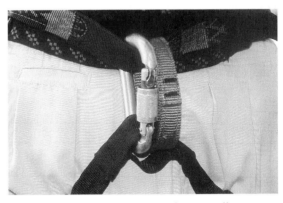

Harness Carabiner Attachment for Rappelling

loop in the same manner as the rope tie-in shown in the photos above. This locking carabiner is the attachment point of a rappel brake (see figs. 8-4 and 8-5 in chapter 8).

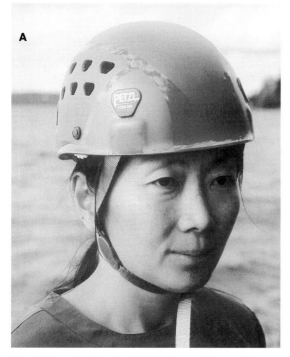

Two Helmet Styles: A—Shell helmet with an adjustable webbing suspension: The Petzl Ecrin Roc.

B—Lightweight sport climbing or cragging helmet: The Petzl Meteor.

HELMETS

Climbers usually wear helmets when they climb waterfall ice or mountains and are increasingly wearing them as they climb rock. Climbers who once could purchase only heavy hand-laid fiberglass helmets now have a choice of helmets made of lighter materials that provide increased comfort, adjustability, ventilation, and style. The lightweight styles, color patterns, and suspension systems of modern helmets are suitable for sport climbers, as well as for multipitch crag climbers. Climbing helmets are designed to meet safety standards set by the Committee for European Normalization (CEN) and the Union Internationale d'Associations d'Alpinisme (UIAA) and bear the CE/UIAA mark. These standards protect against falling rock or a carabiner dropped by overhead climbers and are tested for

this function by the dropping of steel balls and pointed anvils onto their tops. They are also tested to prevent excessive forward or backward motion that would expose vulnerable parts of your skull to falling objects. Helmets are not designed to absorb side, front, or rear impact in a fall, although helmet design can be expected to evolve to handle the needs of gymnastic climbers who fall onto solid protection as a normal practice. Helmets have shells to absorb initial impact and to prevent penetration, and they work with internal energy-absorbing suspension systems. Suspension systems are formed by either a webbing harness (see A in the photo above), with some type of adjustment, or a foam interior (see B in the photo above), with a system to adjust for size.

ENDNOTES

1. Detailed information on harnesses is available from manufacturers. Web addresses for manufacturers are

   Black Diamond   <http://www.bdel/ harnesses1.htm>

   Metolius   <http://www.metoliusclimbing. com/holds.htm>

   Petzl   <http://www.petzl.com>

   General listing   <http://www.rockclimb.org/ manufac.html>

2. If you fall backward, you can turn upside down. Both a chest harness and a full body harness can help to prevent this from happening, but neither type of harness can totally prevent the potential for injury. Helmut Microys, speaking in the context of crevasse falls, reports in *News from the Last Plenary Session of the UIAA Safety Commission*: "It is now known that neither the sit harness nor full body harness are ideal fall protection. The former can lead to inverting and back and head injuries while the latter may produce whiplash injuries during the process of inverting." <http://www. compusmart.ab.ca/resqdyn/articles/UIAA.htm>.

3. A note in *Petzl Technical Manual* indicates "that no matter how comfortable the harness, a person who has lost consciousness or is incapable of movement is in danger of death after only seven minutes of hanging in a harness. The stagnation of the blood actually provokes internal poisoning. That's why it's imperative that a partner has the training to act quickly." <http://www.petzl.com/ english/dir/harnais/fit mercury.html>.

4. For a falling climber caught on the end of a single dynamic climbing rope carrying the CE mark—a safety standard set by the Committee for European Normalization (CEN) and the Union Internationale d'Associations d'Alpinisme (UIAA)—harnesses are designed to survive severe impact forces greater than those expected. The buckle closed with a single pass might release at little more than twice body weight, whereas the buckle closed with a double pass can remain closed at the maximum impact force expected.

5. See "Harnesses: What you should know . . . about harnesses in general," in *Petzl Technical Manual* at <http://www.petzl.com/FRENG/frharness/ harnesses.html>.

5

Rope

CLIMBING ROPE

The classic image of climbing is the climber starting up a slope, pack on back, festooned with hardware, with rope over a shoulder. Historically, climbing has been a "companionship of the rope," the roped leader guiding the way for the team. In the early days of climbing, the most skilled person always climbed first and did not expect—and could not afford—to fall, for fear the rope might break. The rope was used to safeguard the passage of the second climber, who was usually less skilled than the leader. Modern rope construction has changed this way of climbing. So reliable is climbing rope that we now expect leaders on the most difficult climbs to fall repeatedly in order to make progress, to improve their skills, and to have a day of fun. Ropes have come a long way.

Rope Construction

The rope used for rock climbing today is *dynamic kernmantle* (core-jacket). *Dynamic* describes the ability of the rope to stretch as it

absorbs the force of a fall. *Kernmantle* describes the construction of the rope, illustrated in figure 5-1. The kern, a high-strength inner core of twisted nylon threads, twisted first as yarn into cordlets, which are likewise twisted into strands that are "layed" clockwise or counterclockwise, is covered by an outer braided jacket or sheath, the *mantle*. The twisted strands of the core behave like miniature springs, lengthening as they absorb the energy of a fall. They provide most of the rope's strength; the jacket protects the core and determines most of the rope's handling characteristics and abrasion resistance.

Most modern climbing ropes are 45, 50, 55, or even 60 meters long (150, 165, 180, or 200 feet, respectively), and approximately 10 to 11 millimeters in diameter. The 50-meter length was first used extensively in Yosemite Valley where belays were protected by bolts, but this length is becoming essential in other areas where bolt-protected routes have been established. Longer lengths allow climbers to reach the top of many modern sport routes, 27.5 to 30

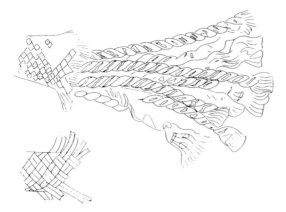

Figure 5-1. Kernmantle Rope Construction

meters (90 to 100 feet) long, and lower off without using a second rope. An 11-millimeter kernmantle rope is a good choice for general climbing, for climbing schools where the rope will experience heavy use, for working with groups, or for guiding. Many climbers prefer a 10.5-millimeter rope because it is slightly lighter; it combines good abrasion resistance with moderate weight. Some experienced climbers use an even lighter 10-millimeter rope. Climbers do not ordinarily use ropes of 9.0 or 8.8 millimeters as single strands. (They do use these ropes in *double-rope* or *twin-rope* techniques to help reduce the friction or rope drag that occurs when ropes turn right angles. Two ropes also allow easier rappelling.)

Rope Retirement

A rope can suffer a harsh existence—being pulled through mud, exposed to the glaring sun, soaked with water, walked on, knotted and fallen on, rappelled on, rubbed across rough rock with sharp edges, and stuffed into the dark bottom of a tiny rucksack. Yet we expect to use it routinely and without much thought as a personal safety device. It is important to know when to retire a climbing rope. The main causes of rope retirement, in order, are probably general misuse leading to premature old age, abrasion to the sheath or cutting, damage to the sheath from falls or aggressive rappelling, core and sheath damage from being

trodden on, invisible wear from abrasive grit particles, normal old age, and chemical attack from acids and other solvents.[1]

The UIAA Safety Commission recommends retiring a rope after about five years of use or 10,000 to 20,000 meters of climbing. To use this method, you need to keep a rope logbook to record the date and distance of each climb. Some rope manufacturers recommend a maximum of four years of use, even if use is occasional. With normal weekend use, two years is a reasonable working life for a rope. But if you are one of the fortunate individuals who climb daily, the life expectancy of your rope can be as little as three months to one year.

To be conservative, retire a rope when it experiences a single severe fall. A fall is severe when the fall distance exceeds the amount of rope between the belayer and the leader, a fall factor of one (the fall factor is very important to take into account in considering the seriousness of a fall on the serviceability of a rope; the subject is examined briefly at the end of this chapter and in detail in chapter 11).

A number of lesser falls can also make the rope unsafe. Rope is not perfectly elastic: each fall takes some of the twist out of the twisted strands, thus reducing the spring of the rope, permanently elongating it a little more, and reducing its shock absorption for the next fall.

Remember that the rope is your lifeline. Replace it more often than you think is necessary: your life is worth more than the cost of a new rope.

After a fall and lowering to the ground or after securing yourself to an anchor, untie and shake out the rope to allow the internal twisted strands to reset and to reset the knot, which also absorbs energy in a fall. Another method of resetting the rope is to tie into the opposite end for the next attempt.

Kernmantle ropes can be damaged internally in a manner that requires close inspection to detect. One standard way to determine rope damage is to inspect the rope sheath with an 8- to 10-power hand lens. Puffs or strands of core sticking out of the sheath and limp or hard spots indicate damage. If you see sheath abrasion (more than 50 percent of the sheath fibers are damaged at any one spot) with a 10-power hand lens, retire the rope. Another way to test the rope is to tension it and check visually and by feel for irregularities.

If damage is confined to the end of the rope, you can cut the damaged part away. Often, enough will be left, particularly with a longer rope, to use for lead climbs or perhaps for top-roping. Cut the rope with a hot knife (the knife will probably lose its temper), so that the blade both cuts and melts through the rope, which fuses the internal fibers of the core to the sheath. A piece of electrical tape around the rope adjacent to the cut completes the process and provides an identifying marker.

COILING ROPE

The two common methods of coiling a rope are the *mountaineer's coil* and the *butterfly coil*. The mountaineer's coil creates a continuous circle that you can carry over your shoulder and neck and allows you to carry a number of ropes at one time.

On the other hand, for a single rope, you can form the butterfly coil faster even if the rope is encrusted with ice, you can make it into a backpack, and it is less likely to tangle during uncoiling.

The Mountaineer's Coil

Many people form the mountaineer's coil by wrapping the rope around their feet and knees when sitting, but this normally creates irregular-length coils. If the rope has been badly twisted, however, this may be the only way you can achieve the mountaineer's coil. Making the mountaineer's coil while standing—though possible only for people who have hands large enough to hold 165 feet of coiled rope in one hand—is faster and gives you greater control over the length of an individual loop once you master the technique. You can never satisfactorily untwist ropes that are badly kinked from a belay plate by this method, and you must either

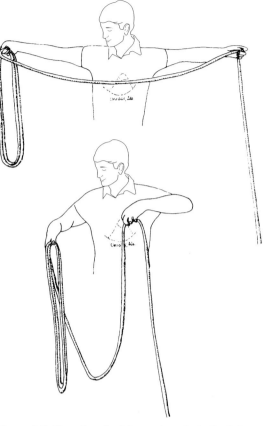

Figure 5-2. Forming the Mountaineer's Coil while Standing, Using the Left Hand to Control Twist

form the mountaineer's coil while sitting or use the butterfly coil.

To form the mountaineer's coil while standing, hold an end of the rope in your *off hand* and with your *control hand* (normally the right hand for right-handed people) stretch out the standing part of the rope two arm lengths across your chest (fig. 5-2). The length of a loop is determined by the distance between your outstretched hands. With the rope stretched out, grasp the rope between the thumb and fingers of your control hand. To remove twist from the coil, give the rope a half-twist and bring the newly formed coil over to your off hand. Use your off hand to grasp and enclose all the loops formed by this process.

Finish the coil by whipping the ends tightly,

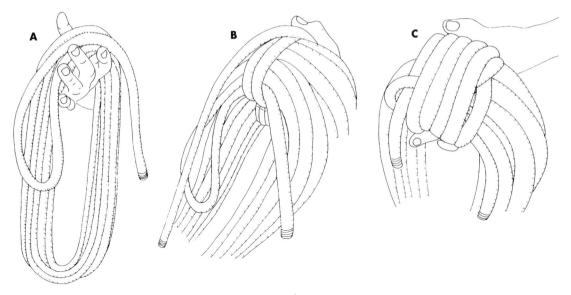

Figure 5-3. Whipping the End of the Mountaineer's Coil

as shown in figure 5-3. You need to tighten each wrap of the whip to gain enough friction to keep the wrap from falling apart. If you do it properly, you will not need to wrap extremely long ends around the coil to secure it. Long ends are unnecessary and even undesirable if you need to use the rope quickly.

The Butterfly Coil

To make the butterfly coil, take both ends in one hand and stretch the doubled rope full length across your chest. Measure out two and a half or three lengths and drop them on the ground: you will use this rope to tie the coil together when you finish (or, if your rope has a middle mark, you can grab the middle mark and skip the step of dropping several lengths on the ground). Now you are ready to form the *butterfly wings*. Take an arm-to-arm length of rope, double it, and drape it over the palm of your hand to form a loop on either the left or right side of the hand. You form the next wing by draping the next doubled length of rope across the same palm with the loop facing the opposite direction, as sketched in figure 5-4A. Do this until all the remaining rope is in the palm of your hand. Now use the lengths of rope you

dropped (or the ends of the rope, if you started with the middle mark) to make three or four wraps around both wings (fig. 5-4B). Form a bight in the standing part of the rope, and pull it part way through the loop at the top of the wrapped coil (fig. 5-4C). Take the remaining end of the rope, and place it over the body of the wrapped coil and through the last formed loop (fig. 5-4D). Tighten to finish the butterfly coil. Form a backpack from the coil by placing it on your back and passing the free ends over your shoulders. Wrap these ends across your chest and waist, and tie them together (fig. 5-4E).

UNCOILING AND STACKING

Organizing an uncoiled rope so that both ends of the rope are available and the rope will run freely without tangling or knotting is called *stacking* or *flaking*. The belayer stacks the rope at the beginning of a climb, before anyone ties into the ends. The leader usually makes last-minute preparations while the belayer stacks. Stacking properly allows the climber to progress smoothly while being belayed safely. This is especially critical for the leader, who should not have to hang on while the second deals with a tangle. To simplify this task and to keep the rope clean, many climbers carry their rope prestacked in a rope bag.

To uncoil and stack a mountaineer's coil, free the lashed ends and hold the coil and one end in one hand. Do not uncoil two ends at the same time or the rope may knot. Put one end on the ground, slightly away from where you are stacking. (If you bury the first end with subsequent loops, you will have to lift the stack, which could tangle it and you would have to untangle and restack it.) With the other hand, undo the coil one loop at a time and drop it on the

ground, out of the dirt (perhaps on a plastic sheet or in a rope bag) adjacent to the belay site. Be careful not to stack the rope where climbers from other teams will walk on the rope or have to step over it. The first end on the ground becomes the bottom end, which the belayer ties into. The leader ties into the top end, which remains in the belayer's hand until the stacking process is completed. If you stack the rope properly, you will be able to feed slack to the leader smoothly as needed.

Once the stack is organized, do not move it by pushing it or lifting it because you can tangle the rope. Any time you move the belay, stack

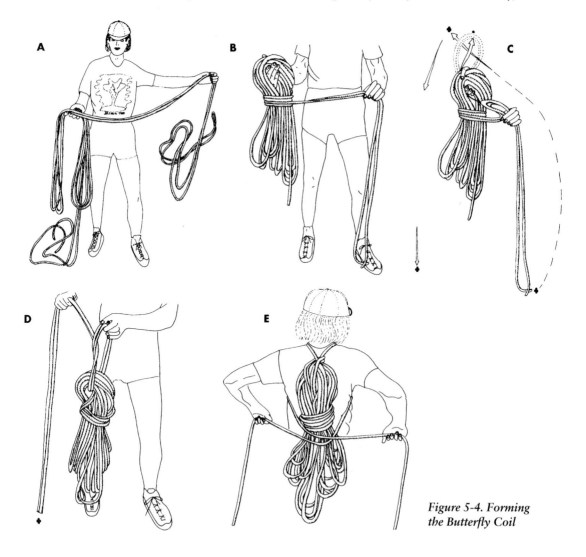

Figure 5-4. Forming the Butterfly Coil

Accidental Cutting

Climbing ropes are basically very reliable. Indeed, climbing ropes without prior damage have not been known to break from the impact of a simple fall. This fact can be misleading, however, because a rope tensioned over a rock edge is very susceptible to cutting. At cliff tops, you should pad the rope with clothing, packs, or custom-made sheaths of canvas or other heavy-duty material. Tie these pads into the anchor so they cannot be lost over the cliff edge. Partway up lead climbs, long runners often allow a rope to stand away from an edge where it might be cut in the event of a fall.

The rope can be cut in a more subtle manner if you step on it. This grinds dirt composed of small, sharp crystals, mostly quartz, into the rope where they cut the fibers of the mantle and core. *Never step on climbing rope!*

the rope at a new site to ensure that the leader does not get stuck in the middle of a pitch because the rope is tangled.

The butterfly coil is not as likely to tangle during uncoiling. To uncoil it, unfasten the finishing hitch, unwrap the coil, and drop the wings on the ground. You will have a doubled rope. To ensure that there will be no tangles, start at one end and stack half the rope; then start at the other end and restack the entire rope, but make sure that both ends are available.

Stacking on Multipitch Climbs

In a stack, the rope to the climber must always come off the top. This happens naturally when two people switch leads on multipitch climbs. The rope end passing to the original leader will automatically finish up on the bottom of the stack as the second climbs. The leader for the subsequent pitch, who was previously the second, now has the end of the rope on top of the stack and is ready to climb. This neat order of stacking changes, however, when one person leads two pitches in a row. The leader's rope will wind up on the bottom of the pile and must be stacked before the same leader can start up the

next pitch. The stacking can be most efficiently done by the belayer, while the leader reorganizes the climbing protection on a gear sling.

On multipitch climbs, you sometimes belay on a stance directly above a crack or flake that could be a trap for a dangling rope. In this case, form butterfly loops with the rope across your feet, a convenient rock horn, or the belay tie-in to prevent the rope from catching on anything below as the leader attempts to make upward progress.

THROWING ROPE

To establish a rappel or top rope, you often need to throw rope directly down a less than vertical cliff or off to the side. A technique that

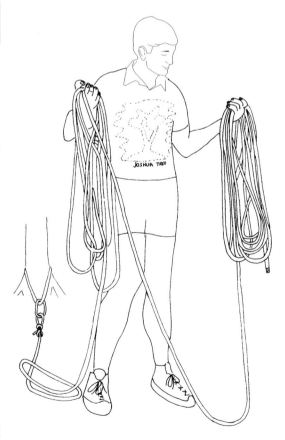

Figure 5-5. Throwing the Rope. Tie in before you do this.

allows you to aim your throw is shown in figure 5-5. Starting from the rope tie-in at the anchor (see chapter 10, Anchor Systems), form seven or eight butterfly or mountaineer's coil loops in the middle of the rope. Leave enough slack to allow the loops to reach over the edge of the cliff. Lay these loops down, out from underfoot, in a handy spot. Starting from the free end of the rope, form seven or eight more loops and leave 10 to 15 feet of slack between the two sets of loops. This second set of loops will be a throwing weight that you can aim. Drop the first set of loops over the cliff edge while you hang onto the second set of loops that includes the free end of the rope. Throw the second set of loops and free end overhand or sidearm hard enough to hit the target. If you misdirect the first throw into a rope-eating tree, reorganize and try again.

PROPERTIES OF CLIMBING ROPES

Perhaps the most significant property of kernmantle rope is that it stretches to absorb the shock of a fall. This property distinguishes the dynamic ropes used for rock climbing from the static ropes used for rope ascending and rappelling in caving. The amount of rope stretch under body weight is a rope's *working elongation*. Dynamic ropes have a maximum working elongation of 8 percent, whereas the working elongation of a static rope of the same diameter rope is usually much less and cannot exceed 5 percent.

The *impact elongation* of a climbing rope is the amount of stretch suffered by the rope during a fall, measured in tests as approximately 20 percent of the rope length between the belayer and the climber. Impact elongation, belay method, rope slippage through the belay, and position and security of rock protection all determine the total distance of a fall. The impact force is the force felt by a falling climber when the rope stops a fall. For the rope to be effective, this force must be within the range that the human body can withstand without injury for short periods of time. Maximum impact force is about

2,000 pounds for the average 11-millimeter rope.

Fall Factor

Dynamic ropes are given a fall rating—they are called 5-fall, 9-fall, or 11-fall ropes—on the basis of a test established by the CEN/UIAA, and ropes that pass this test are given a CE mark. CEN has taken over and adopted UIAA rope standards; in the United States, standards are being developed by the American Society for Testing and Materials [ASTM]). Because CEN/UIAA simply gives a pass-fail to this test, a 9-fall rope is the manufacturer's rating and not CEN/UIAA's. The nature of this test is described in figure 5-6.

A weight of 80 kilograms (176 pounds), approximating body weight, is dropped over a simulated carabiner 10 millimeters in diameter. The weight falls 5 meters onto 2.8 meters of rope attached to a static anchor. This is a severe fall—very near the maximum severity possible. It simulates a locked-off belay that does not allow rope to slip through a belay brake. The ratio between the length of rope (2.8 meters) and the distance fallen (5 meters) is the *fall factor* (here it is 1.78). If the weight were attached directly to the anchor without the carabiner, the fall factor would be 2.8 meters: 5.6 meters, or 2. A fall factor of 2 is the most severe fall possible. This is an important concept, which is examined in detail in chapter 11. Before you launch out on your own as a leader, you must understand the fall factor, since it affects where you should place your first piece of protection, as well as the impact forces that you, the belayer, and the anchor experience in a fall.

To carry the CE mark, a rope must survive at least five severe falls of fall factor 1.78, and the first fall must have a landing or impact force not exceeding 2,640 pounds (15 times body weight). Because climbers do not normally experience real impact forces of this harshness in the field, a 5-fall rope would appear to be safe, indeed, though some ropes are made to withstand up to 11 falls.

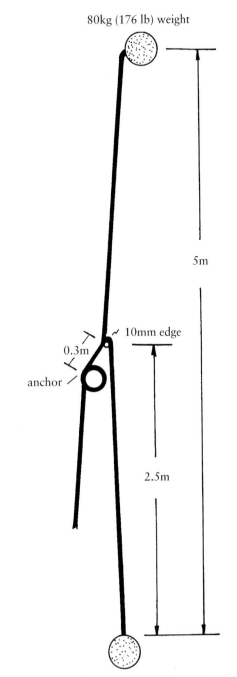

80kg (176 lb) weight

5m

10mm edge

0.3m

anchor

2.5m

Figure 5-6. Schematic of CEN/UIAA Drop Test.
An 80-kilogram (176-pound) weight suspended 2.5
meters above a simulated carabiner (10-millimeter
edge) drops 5 meters onto 2.8 meters of rope for a
fall factor of 1.78. The distance between the anchor
and simulated carabiner is 0.3 meter.

Specific data for individual climbing ropes vary, but statistics for an "average" rope are given in table 5-1.[2] Labels on ropes can underreport rope diameter up to 0.5 millimeter and rope length by 10 percent. This means that climbers are better protected and get more for their money than they pay for.

To obtain information for specific ropes, ask at your local climbing store, look for annual comparisons in climbing magazines, or write to the manufacturer.

Abrasion Resistance, Water Absorption, and Handling Characteristics

Abrasion resistance is another characteristic of interest to the climber. The higher the abrasion resistance, the longer the life of a rope and the less easily the rope can be cut over an edge.

A wet rope is heavier than a dry rope, ices quickly to the point of uselessness in cold conditions, and is weaker than a dry rope. Some ropes are coated to prevent water absorption, either by coating individual threads before weaving them into the rope or by coating the finished rope. In theory, coated dry ropes shed water more easily than uncoated standard ropes, and they might be more abrasion resistant. Tests indicate that ropes with tightly woven sheaths typically absorb less water than loosely woven ones irrespective of their coating.[3] Water absorption can vary between 10 and 50 percent of the rope's dry weight.

Besides damage from abrasion, ropes are susceptible to deterioration caused by ultraviolet waves in sunlight as well as the effects of acids. Climbers are usually concerned about "petroleum products such as gasoline, paint, oil, etc. All of the fiber producers state that no petroleum product will harm nylon, . . . but evidently the information is not being picked up by many climbers."[4] Periodically clean ropes in lukewarm water by using a detergent and gentle action to remove dust and rock fragments, followed by a thorough rinsing.

How a rope feels in your hand—its handling characteristics—and its resistance to kinking are also important for daily climbing.

5-1. "Average" Climbing Rope Statistics

Manufacturer's stated diameter in millimeters	11.0	10.5	10	9
Impact force in pounds	1850–2090	1958–2310	1760–1870	1320–1540
Static elongation % 80 kg loads	5–7.5	4.2–8	1.5–8	5.5–10
CEN/UIAA Falls	7–12	7–9	6–7	7–11*
Weight 165 feet in pounds	≈ 8.5–9	≈ 8	≈ 7	≈ 6

*CEN/UIAA fall number for 9.0 millimeters is for a double rope.

REFERENCES FOR FUTURE READING

Newell, Dick. 1990. Product interview by Larry Coats. *Rock & Ice*. 36: 76–79.

Robbins, Royal. 1979. Climbing rope myths. *Summit*. 25(1): 12–17, 23–25.

Raleigh, Duane. 1991. Hanging by threads. *Climbing*. 126:82–92.

ENDNOTES

1. Reasons cited by Beal Rope at <http://www.bealropes.com/english.dir/care.html>.
2. This is a summary of data collected by Duane Raleigh for a 1991 rope review for *Climbing*.
3. *Ibid.*
4. Newell, 1990, referenced above, and Helmut Microys, 1998, in *News from the Last Plenary Session of the UIAA Safety Commission*. <http://www.compusmart.ab.ca/resqdyn/articles/UIAA.htm>. Tests verify that gasoline, diesel, camper fuel, seawater, Coke, and strong vinegar have no influence on the rope. Do not pee on your rope! The number of falls held in standard CEN/UIAA tests drops off by 30 percent. Wash the rope if it is exposed to seawater or Coke, however, because of possible damage from the crystals that form after these liquids dry. Do not use a Magic Marker to mark your rope (midpoint), as the ink reduces the strength of the rope at the point marked by as much as 50 percent in drop tests.

6

Belaying

BELAYING BASICS

Although the rope provides a classic image of mountaineering, belaying is the reality behind the image. In belaying, two individuals form a team that is much stronger than the simple combination of two individuals' skills. Belaying provides forgiveness in the vertical world and safeguards the team so that a falling climber can be caught and held safely on the rope.

The basics of belaying are the belay chain, the rope-manipulation sequence, and the belay stance. A proper belay comprises many components, including anchors, harness, and tie-ins. Let's start by examining the belay chain, rope-manipulation sequence, and the hand-manipulation sequence that holds the rope against a friction surface. The components of the belay are easiest to illustrate with a waist (body) belay, although belaying with a mechanical plate allows a belayer to safely catch and lower a climber when good protection, as described in chapter 7, is present. (See "Mechanical Plates" on page 80.)

The Belay Chain and Rope Manipulation

Your job as a belayer is to pay out or take in rope as the climber moves, so as to catch the climber with as little slack as possible in case of a fall. To check a fall, you instantly pull the rope against an object (such as your waist or a belay device) to create friction. The principle is the same whether you are using a waist belay or a mechanical belay brake. In order to understand the sequence, look at the *belay chain* shown in the photo at right.

Focus on the climber at the tie-in point, and then follow the rope back to the belayer. The rope passes around the belayer's back, which will become the *braking friction surface* in a waist belay. To hold the rope against the braking friction surface, the back, you use the hand on the side opposite the climber as a brake. This hand is the *braking hand*. The other hand, which grasps the rope before it goes around the back, is the *helping hand*, sometimes called the *feeling hand*. Notice that if you tried to hold the climber with only the helping hand, there would

climber

belayer

helping hand

rope from climber to belayer

braking hand

The Belay Chain: *Starting at the tie-in point of the climber, the rope runs from the climber to the belayer. At the belayer, the rope runs through a carabiner on the belayer's waist belt (to prevent the rope from lifting) and then around a friction surface—the belayer's back—where it is held by the braking hand. The helping hand helps manipulate the rope while the braking hand remains in position to apply the friction at all times.*

be no friction between the climber and you. This means that you would be trying to hold a falling climber with only the strength of one hand, an impossible task.

Novice belayers often mistakenly belay the wrong end of the rope and confuse the braking with the helping hand. These mistakes occur because the novice does not consider the belay chain before concentrating on the hand-manipulation sequence that serves to hold the rope against the braking surface.

To be ready to apply friction instantly, you use your braking hand and your helping hand in a coordinated manner to move the rope past the braking friction surface. As shown in figure 6-1A and B, which illustrate the hand-manipulation sequence without showing belay anchors or other essential components of the belay chain, you begin with the helping hand extended and take in (arrow 1a) rope from the climber. The braking hand starts next to your body and then pulls (arrow 1b) rope across the braking friction surface, your own back. Your helping hand winds up next to your body, and your braking hand extends from your body.

As shown in figure 6-1C, extend your helping hand and grasp both strands of the rope with the helping hand (arrow 3) so that your braking hand remains on the rope between your helping hand and your back. Now slide the braking hand along the rope (arrow 4) to your body. Never let go of the rope with your braking

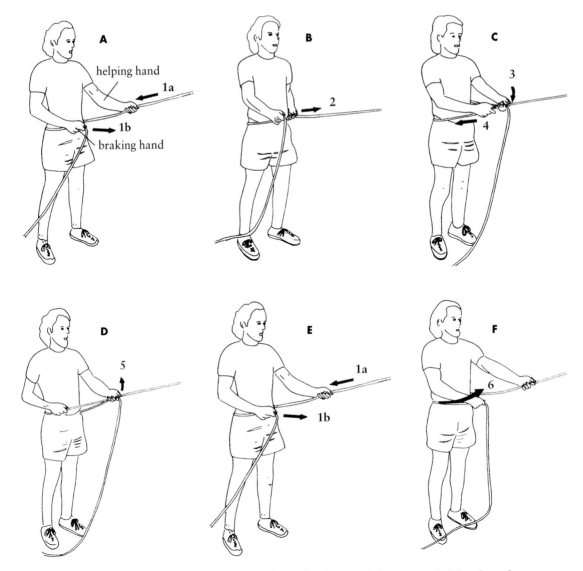

Figure 6-1. Rope Manipulation in Belaying: A—The belayer pulls in the rope from the climber with the helping hand (1a) and pulls it around the friction braking surface with the braking hand (1b).
B—The end of this sequence, in which the helping hand is next to the hip and the braking hand is extended from the body. Holding the rope in the braking hand, the belayer extends the helping hand in the direction of the arrow (2). C and D show the sequence to get back to the starting point.
C—The belayer moves the braking hand and the helping hand together and grasps both ropes with the helping hand (arrow 3). The braking hand remains closed around the rope, and slides along the rope to a position next to the body (arrow 4).
D—The helping hand prepares to drop the rope on the braking hand side (arrow 5). This leads back to the starting position shown in E.
E—The belayer has dropped the braking side of the rope with the helping hand and is ready to repeat the belaying sequence.
F—If a fall should occur at any time during A – E, the belayer gains additional friction by wrapping the rope across the midsection with the braking hand (arrow 6).

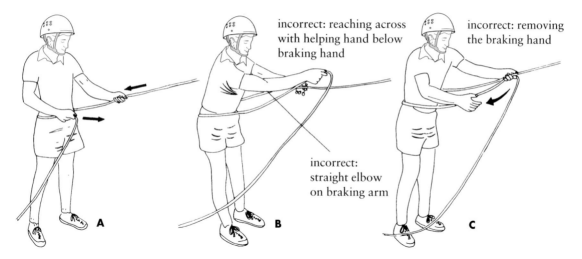

Figure 6-2. A Common Mistake in Rope Manipulation: A—*The sequence begins normally with the braking hand next to the body and the helping hand extended. The braking hand is correctly extended with the elbow remaining bent.*
B—*In an incorrect belaying sequence, the belayer straightens the elbow of the braking hand and bends* over to maximize the amount of rope taken up in one cycle, positioning the helping hand between the braking hand and the body.
C—*The belayer removes the braking hand from the rope. You cannot make an effective belay when you remove your braking hand from the rope.*

hand. If you do, and the climber falls at that instant, you cannot hold the climber with only your helping hand. Release the braking side of the rope (arrow 5) with your helping hand. You are now (fig. 6-1E) in the starting position (fig. 6-1A), ready to repeat the cycle.

A common mistake occurs when you begin normally (fig. 6-2A) but bend at the waist and straighten the elbow on the braking arm in order to take up a maximum amount of rope. In this extended position, it is difficult to reach beyond the braking hand and you can use your helping hand to grasp the two ropes between the braking hand and the body (fig. 6-2B). Because you cannot slide your braking hand to the original position, you must remove it from the rope (fig. 6-2C), and you cannot apply effective, instantaneous braking action. To avoid this problem, leave the elbow of your braking arm bent, do not bend over at the waist, and take in a smaller amount of rope during each cycle.

THE BELAY STANCE

Body position and location of the belay, collectively termed the *stance*, is an important consideration. At stake is your ability to remain in control at all times to prevent injury to yourself and the leader. During the belay, position your body relative to both the force of a falling climber and the anchor. You always need to examine the key points diagrammed in figures 6-3 through 6-6.

1. Make sure that you tie into a belay anchor without slack between you and the anchor. If the climber falls and there is slack (fig. 6-3A), you will be abruptly pulled to the end of the anchor and experience shock forces as the anchor rope suddenly stops your forward motion. You might even be pulled off the ledge or into the cliff face. Besides causing injury, the shock of the sudden stop could cause you to drop the rope and lose control of the falling leader.

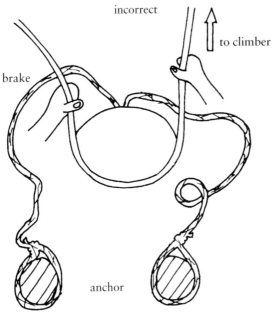

Figure 6-3A. A Slack Anchor Rope

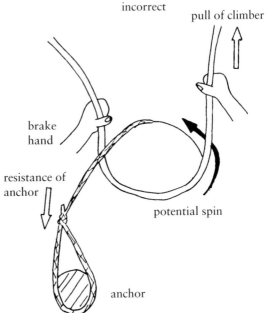

Figure 6-3B. Potential Spin from Shear Forces

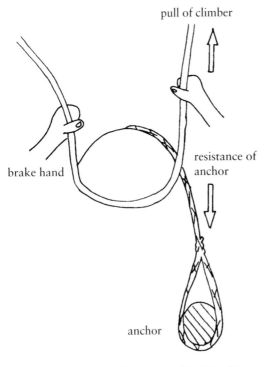

Figure 6-3C. Correct Alignment of the Climbing Rope and Anchor Rope to Prevent Spin

2. Safeguard against forces that might cause you to lose control of the belay. In figure 6-3B, the tie-in point is at the midpoint of the belayer's harness, and the anchor is on the opposite side of the pull applied by a falling climber. This produces unaligned shear forces that will rotate the belayer. To eliminate these forces, pass the anchor rope around the same side as the rope leading to the climber (fig. 6-3C) or interchange braking and helping hands. Using a brake plate reduces rotation because you normally fasten it to the belay loop at the front midpoint of your harness.

3. Couple natural terrain features with body position to brace against a potential fall. For example, you can brace against a low wall with a leg extended on the helping-hand side of the body to counteract the force of a falling leader, or sit in a well-braced position (fig. 6-4). Here you use your left hand as the brake hand and brace your right foot to counteract a pull in the direction of the climber. Even on a flat ledge, you can offset rotational forces

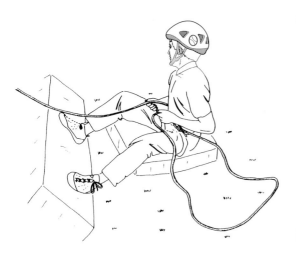

Figure 6-4. A Secure Body Position with Belayer's Right Leg Braced against the Pull of a Falling Climber

by extending your leg on the helping-hand side of the body to counteract the pull of the falling leader. In alpine climbing, there are times when no artificial anchor can be set up and you have to depend on a strongly braced body position alone to hold a fall.

4. *Aim* the belay, so you do not swing during a fall. In figure 6-5, the belayer can rotate and be pulled off the belay ledge. To prevent this situation, use the intermediate protection shown to aim the direction of pull. Sometimes, depending on the location of protection in relation to belay geography, you can aim a belay more effectively by using either your right or left hand as the braking hand. Learn to belay effectively with both hands. You can also reduce the potential rotation shown in figure 6-5 by decreasing the distance to the anchor.

5. In a waist belay, you must guard against the possibility that the belay rope will unwrap from your waist during a fall (fig. 6-6). You can use a carabiner safety, as shown in the enlarged detail of figure 6-6, to hold the rope in place. If the leader falls, this carabiner also keeps the rope from abrading your armpit as the rope is pulled upward. (It is not necessary to take this step when you are using a belay device because the device clips through a carabiner that will hold the rope in position.)

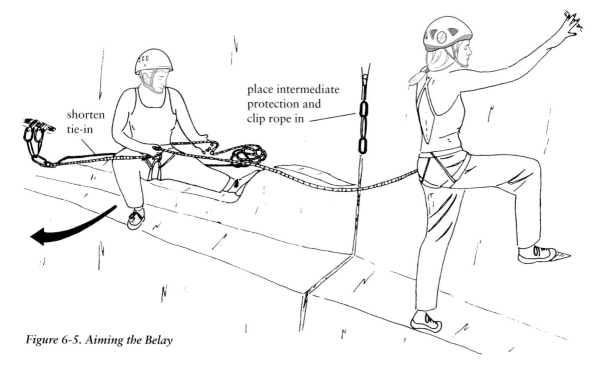

shorten tie-in

place intermediate protection and clip rope in

Figure 6-5. Aiming the Belay

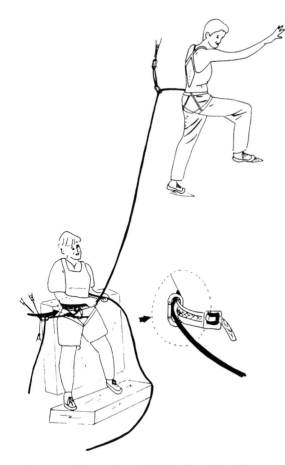

Figure 6-6. Preventing the Belay Rope from Unwrapping: To prevent the rope from unwrapping in the event of a fall, clip the rope through a carabiner on the side opposite from the brake hand.

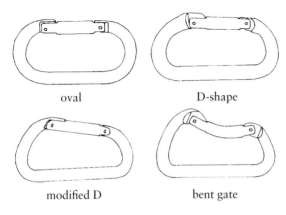

| oval | D-shape |
| modified D | bent gate |

Figure 6-7. Carabiner Shapes

CARABINERS AND ANCHOR BASICS

Carabiners allow the belayer, who remains stationary, to attach quickly to a "bombproof" anchor before the climber moves. This section examines common top-rope belay systems, the amount of slack that you need to provide, and the security of natural tree anchors. Chapter 10 covers belay anchors in greater detail.

Carabiners

You commonly use carabiners to attach ropes to intermediate protection points and belay anchors, to assemble friction brakes for rappelling, and to connect aid climbers to aid points. Usually made of aluminum alloys, carabiners come in three basic shapes (fig. 6-7): the generally useful oval, the stronger D-shape, and the modified D with a large gate opening. The bent-gate carabiner is a modified D designed for quick rope clips in sport climbing. Almost any catalog of climbing equipment will show a wide range of variations of these shapes, some having specialized uses.

In all designs, the load is intended to be applied along the long axis of the carabiner. With the gate closed, carabiners should have a minimum strength of about 2,000 kilograms and a gate-open strength of 600 to 700 kilograms. The D-shape and modified D-shape apply more of the load on the body of the carabiner and hence are stronger, but the gate is the weakest part of the device.

Locking carabiners (fig. 6-8A) are generally stronger than nonlocking because the gate area is reinforced by a threaded screw lock. The threads are covered by the screw lock to prevent accidental fraying of webbing. Locking carabiners offer more security than nonlocking ones and are commonly used for belaying or for setting up top-rope climbs. Currently, twist-lock carabiners that lock automatically are commercially available. When nonlocking carabiners are used for these purposes, two carabiners with the gates *opposed* and *reversed* (fig. 6-8C) should be used.

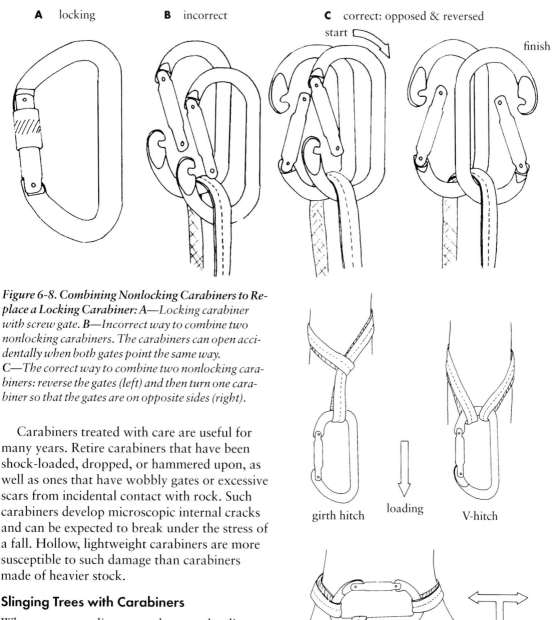

A locking   **B** incorrect   **C** correct: opposed & reversed

start   finish

Figure 6-8. Combining Nonlocking Carabiners to Replace a Locking Carabiner: A—Locking carabiner with screw gate. B—Incorrect way to combine two nonlocking carabiners. The carabiners can open accidentally when both gates point the same way. C—The correct way to combine two nonlocking carabiners: reverse the gates (left) and then turn one carabiner so that the gates are on opposite sides (right).

Carabiners treated with care are useful for many years. Retire carabiners that have been shock-loaded, dropped, or hammered upon, as well as ones that have wobbly gates or excessive scars from incidental contact with rock. Such carabiners develop microscopic internal cracks and can be expected to break under the stress of a fall. Hollow, lightweight carabiners are more susceptible to such damage than carabiners made of heavier stock.

Slinging Trees with Carabiners

When you use a sling around a tree, the sling can form either a girth hitch or, for want of a better name, a V-hitch (fig. 6-9). To form a girth hitch, pass the sling around the tree and through the loop formed by the distant end of the sling. To form a V-hitch, pass the sling around the tree and clip the two ends of the loop with a carabiner. Make sure that the V formed between the

girth hitch   loading   V-hitch

dangerous

triaxial loading

triaxial loading

Figure 6-9. Girth Hitch, V-Hitch, and Dangerous Triaxial Loading

two sides of the hitch is 60 degrees or less to prevent problems (see chapter 11, Fall Forces).

If a sling barely makes it around the tree and you use a carabiner to join the ends (fig. 6-9), you will be loading the carabiner along its axis as well as perpendicular to its axis. This *triaxial loading* is dangerous. If the load perpendicular to the axis pulls on the weak gate, the carabiner will probably break. To avoid this risky situation, lengthen the sling by adding a second sling and fasten the two slings together with a locking carabiner or gate-opposed carabiners.

A BELAY TIE-IN

Whether you arrive at the top of a cliff after a lead or set up the anchor from above, you usually want to stand or sit at the edge to watch or talk to the climber below. Yet available anchor points —large trees or protectable cracks—may be many feet back from the edge. You can solve this problem quickly by tying yourself into a large loop of rope extending from your harness to the anchor and back, as shown in the photo below. If you use this variable-length tie-in, you can still use many different belay brakes and assume many different stances anywhere on the cliff.

The tie-in sequence requires that you establish an anchor, assume a stance, and finally tie yourself to the anchor. First, create an anchor with its attachment carabiner and clip your rope through this carabiner so that it runs freely. A locking

The Belay Tie-In Loop

carabiner or two nonlocking carabiners with gates opposed here give added security. Next, return to the cliff edge, assume a stance that allows you to aim the belay, and finish tying yourself to the anchor. Notice that the rope goes from your harness tie-in point through the anchor carabiner and back over the cliff edge to the climber below. Tie a figure-eight knot into the rope that leads to the climber and clip it to your harness tie-in point with a locking carabiner or two carabiners with opposed and reversed gates. You are now secure at the edge of the cliff, ready to belay and observe the climber below.

WAIST BELAYS FOR TOP-ROPING

When you give a waist belay, as shown in figure 6-10A, your stance determines the amount of friction available to hold the climber. All belayers on the top (or bottom) of a cliff should be tied into and at the end of a taut leash attached to the belay anchor. A standing belayer who is tight against the anchor leash and leaning over the cliff edge can exert almost 250 pounds of friction to control a fall. A short fall—as little as a few feet—can produce this much force if there are no other sources of friction in the system. You cannot exert enough braking friction to stop the rope from slipping around your waist, and the climber will take an "elevator ride" down the climb. On the other hand, by sitting down (fig. 6-10B), you make a 90-degree bend in the rope where it passes over your leg. This bend increases friction by about 40 percent, so that you can hold a maximum of about 350 pounds of force before the rope begins to slip. Thus, a sitting belayer has more control over a short top-rope fall than a standing belayer.

A High-Friction Waist Belay for Top-Roping

In some situations, you might want more friction than a normal waist belay can provide. If you are at the top of a pitch and have only a couple of carabiners available but you want to stand at the cliff's edge to observe the belayer, you prefer to be pulled away from the edge rather than toward the edge in the event that the

A

B

incorrect: standing
waist belay with
minimal friction

correct: sitting
waist belay with
increased friction

Figure 6-10. Friction on Top-Rope Belays

— to climber

A High-Friction Waist Belay for Top Roping

climber falls. If there are good cliff-top anchors available, use the setup shown in the photo above.

At the cliff top, tie in with a clove hitch or figure-eight on a bight and adjust the length of your leash to stand near the edge. To belay, pass the rope through a carabiner on the anchor tree to make a 180-degree turn. This configuration increases the maximum impact force by about 90 percent, to about 450 pounds, before the rope runs dynamically around your waist. You are in control at the edge and have as much belaying friction as a mechanical belay plate provides (an obvious advantage with icy ropes that will not work with the mechanical belay devices). To prevent being pulled toward the anchor and away from the edge during a fall, you would need to place a counter anchor at the cliff edge.

THE SLINGSHOT OR SOCIAL BELAY

Slingshot or social belays allow you to belay at the base of a climb, thus gaining visual contact and casual conversation with the climber, yet use an overhead anchor. The rope runs from the climber at ground level, as shown in the photo at right, through a carabiner attached to an overhead anchor and back to the belayer at ground level. The completed system looks like a stretched slingshot with the V-shaped center of the system at the top of the cliff. A method of setting up a slingshot anchor is described in chapter 10, figure 10-11.

With a slingshot system, the climber usually starts at the base of a cliff and climbs to the top. Then you lower the climber to the ground. Both the waist-belay and the mechanical-belay systems described below give enough friction

The Slingshot or Social Belay (see chapter 10 for setup details)

to control potential falls, but most people prefer that the friction of lowering be absorbed by the mechanical device rather than by their waist.

Belayers often employ a slingshot belay without being tied into a ground-level anchor. This system works as long as you are directly underneath the overhead anchor, have a tight rope on the climber, and weigh more than the climber. The direction of pull on you, in this case, is upward. The force generated in a fall will be offset by your weight coupled with friction of the rope on the upper anchor. If you stand away from the bottom of the climb, however, a fall will jerk you toward the cliff and you could collide with either the cliff or the falling climber. Worse, you could become disoriented, stumble, and drop the climber. Use a tie-in when you belay.

The Proper Amount of Slack

When you belay top-roped climbs, keep the rope tight enough to "feel" the climber. You want neither a tight nor a loose rope, but one that allows you to feel the slightest amount of resistance. Make sure that you belay smoothly, without jerking the climber. Do not let a loop of rope accumulate under the climber's feet or bending knee; allow the climber to focus on climbing without constant concern about rope tension. At the same time, do not exert a distracting pull that destroys the climber's concentration or makes it seem as if you were winching the climber up the route.

Belaying a leader is somewhat different from giving a top-rope belay. You can pull the climber off balance with a rope that is too tight and provide for a fall that is unnecessarily long if the rope is too loose. Your job is to have the proper amount of slack, as shown in the photo on page 69. When the climber is climbing smoothly, there will be 1 to 3 feet of slack forming an arc that you constantly adjust as the leader moves upward.

At the *crux* (the most difficult section of a climb), the leader might experiment with a move two or three times before finally committing. The alert belayer reduces the amount of slack in anticipation of a fall. You can compensate for the leader's up-and-down movement by paying out and taking in slack as the leader works out the moves. (If the climber is leading and has overhead protection at the crux, you take rope in as the leader moves up and pay it out again after the leader passes the protection.)

Limitations of Waist Belays

Use the waist belay in situations where other belay brakes do not work, such as when the rope ices up. The waist belay produces a lower impact force on the protection piece that would hold a fall; marginal protection pieces placed on a dicey lead are more likely to hold. On the other hand, the waist belay allows more rope to slip through the system. The leader will fall farther before stopping, with an increased possibility of hitting a ledge.

A waist belay might not provide enough braking friction to catch a fall for "normal" leads where there is little to moderate friction in the belay chain. A waist belay gives a very dynamic belay that can result in loss of control and friction burns to your waist and hands. Use gloves and heavy clothing to help control the waist belay and protect your body.

HIGH-FRICTION BELAY BRAKES

Both the Munter hitch and mechanical belay plates give you greater holding power than a waist belay and transfer the friction generated in a fall to a carabiner, the rope, or a mechanical plate rather than your waist. Some high-friction belay brakes incorporate tubes to dissipate the heat produced by the friction. As you use belay brakes, carry over your knowledge of the belay chain, friction surface, and helping and braking hands.

The Munter Hitch Belay

The Munter hitch provides a quick, lightweight belay brake that you can use with a minimum of equipment. There are a number of ways to tie the Munter hitch. The method illustrated in figure 6-11 is based on the clove hitch. Begin by forming two loops of rope that touch a crosspiece (A). Take the loop formed behind the crosspiece, here the left-hand one, and bend it forward (B), opening the loop. Now pass the carabiner through the resulting hitch, enclosing the two strands of rope at the top of the loop. You are now ready to belay (C). You reverse the hitch by pulling when you take in rope from the climber (D). Keep your fingers out of the hitch: if a fall occurs, the hitch could trap them.

The Munter hitch works best with a large-diameter carabiner that has a rounded end—the pear-shaped carabiner—fixed in position to your harness or other anchor point. The large, rounded carabiner allows the hitch to "turn over" or reverse without first taking up excess slack better than a smaller carabiner would, so you can change from feeding out to taking in or braking the rope. It can be difficult to reverse the Munter hitch if you do not use proper technique and a pear-shaped carabiner. You can vary the braking friction provided by the Munter hitch by moving your hand and altering the position of the brake, as shown in figure 6-12, from a dynamic, through an intermediate, to a nearly static position. These different braking positions allow the belay to apply between approximately 290 to 590 pounds of stopping force.[1] As a result, you can generate a more static belay with a Munter hitch than with a waist belay or many mechanical-belay brakes. Static belays can stress the protection system more than dynamic belays, as discussed in the following pages.

Mechanical Plates

Mechanical plates magnify the strength of your hand by passing the rope over a metal friction

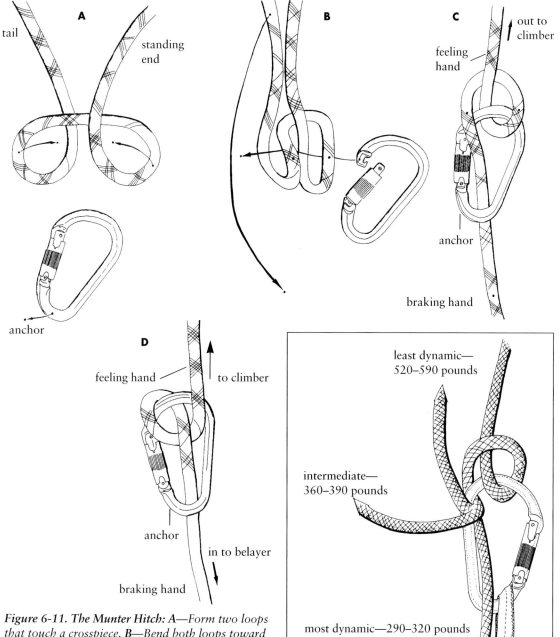

Figure 6-11. The Munter Hitch: A—Form two loops that touch a crosspiece. B—Bend both loops toward you. C—Place a carabiner through the loops and pull the tail of the rope toward your body. This completes the Munter hitch. To feed out the rope to a climber, pull as indicated. D—To take in rope, pull toward you. The action of taking rope in or letting it out reverses the position of the hitch, as shown by comparing C and D.

Figure 6-12. Variable Braking Action of the Munter Hitch. Data based on test by the Ontario Rock Climbing Association reported in Rock Climbing Safety Manual *(1985).*

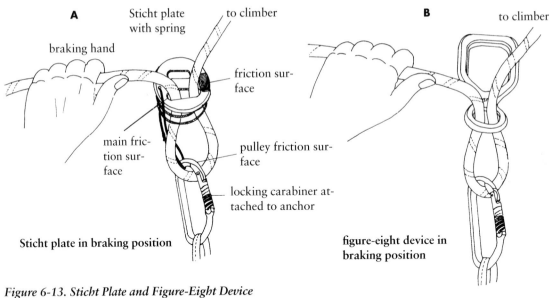

A Sticht plate with spring — to climber

braking hand

friction surface

main friction surface

pulley friction surface

locking carabiner attached to anchor

Sticht plate in braking position

B to climber

figure-eight device in braking position

Figure 6-13. Sticht Plate and Figure-Eight Device Showing Braking Position and Friction Surfaces

surface. Well-known mechanical brake plates include, among many others, the Sticht plate (fig. 6-13A), the Tuber, and the Air Traffic Controller. Figure-eight devices with rectangular holes and rounded corners, similar to a Sticht plate, are also available (fig. 6-13B). A figure-eight descender, normally used for rappelling, can be used in a manner similar to the Sticht plate, although this is recommended only for emergencies. For normal climbing situations, mechanical plates are advantageous and widely used. Attach the plate to the carabiner with a retaining cord to prevent the device from slipping away from you and causing you to lose control of the belay.

Using a Mechanical Plate

To use a Sticht plate, serving here as a prototype of slot-shaped mechanical plates, or a figure-eight device, extend a bight of rope through a hole and then clip a carabiner through the bight, as shown in figure 6-13.

This figure shows how to hook up these devices and which surfaces provide friction. You can transfer the hand sequence that you learned

for a waist belay to belay with these mechanical devices, as illustrated in figure 6-14.

There is another popular hand sequence for mechanical belay plates that differs somewhat from that used for waist belays. This might be a confusing sequence and should be attempted only after you thoroughly understand the belay chain and the functions and locations of the brake hand, helping hand, and friction surface. The major difference from the waist-belay sequence arises from the use of the helping hand as both a helping hand and a second braking hand. The helping hand moves back and forth on the rope to both the climber's side and the braking side of the mechanical plate.

The sequence begins as for a waist belay: pull slack from the climber with your helping hand while your brake hand pulls the rope through the plate. Now the sequence departs from that of a waist belay. With your helping hand, you release the rope leading to the climber and grasp the rope on the brake-hand side. In this position, the helping hand becomes a second braking hand. You can now release the original braking hand and reposition it adjacent to the

Figure 6-14. Hand Sequence for Belaying with a Brake Plate

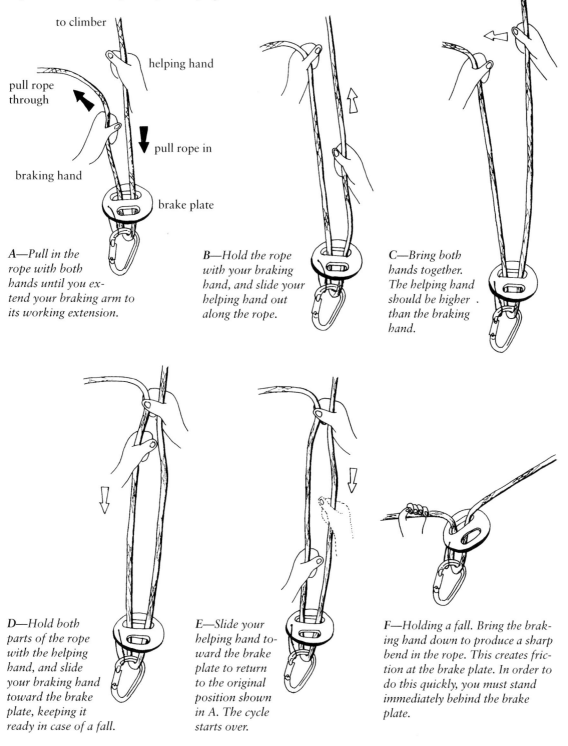

to climber

helping hand

pull rope
through

braking hand

pull rope in

brake plate

A—*Pull in the rope with both hands until you extend your braking arm to its working extension.*

B—*Hold the rope with your braking hand, and slide your helping hand out along the rope.*

C—*Bring both hands together. The helping hand should be higher . than the braking hand.*

D—*Hold both parts of the rope with the helping hand, and slide your braking hand toward the brake plate, keeping it ready in case of a fall.*

E—*Slide your helping hand toward the brake plate to return to the original position shown in A. The cycle starts over.*

F—*Holding a fall. Bring the braking hand down to produce a sharp bend in the rope. This creates friction at the brake plate. In order to do this quickly, you must stand immediately behind the brake plate.*

plate. Then drop the braking side of the rope and return your helping hand to the climber's side of the rope to help pull in slack from the climber. Now you can start the sequence over. What is important is that you always have a functional brake hand on the rope ready to apply braking action. Like a race driver careening around a curve on a cliff edge, you always must be ready to brake instantaneously, so always have a braking hand on the rope and be ready to use it.

In order to brake effectively with a mechanical plate or a Munter hitch, it is important to have the belay plate in front of you so you can pull back on the rope instantly. It is most comfortable about waist height. This occurs naturally when you belay from your harness but might require planning when you belay directly from an anchor.

Because they provide lots of friction and dissipate heat, mechanical plates are useful to lower climbers from the top of a climb. The heat and friction are transferred to the metal plate rather than to your waist, or to the sheath of the rope in a Munter hitch. On a lead climb, the mechanical plate also allows you to hold a fall with less effort because it generates more braking friction—it is more static—and creates less discomfort than a waist belay. For a moderate fall, energy is absorbed mainly by rope stretch, together with deformation of tie-in knots and the climber's and belayer's bodies. The energy of a fall also places stress on the protection piece the leader counts on to catch the fall. As the belay brake provides increasing braking friction, the impact force on the protection piece increases twice as fast as it does on the rest of the system. The static or dynamic nature of different mechanical plates varies in degree.

Choosing a Belay Brake

The art of belaying begins with the choice of belay brake. Belayer and leader together need to consider the needs of each different situation and piece together the right system. You are a team, connected by a rope. Teamwork requires prolonged attention, positive verbal and nonverbal communication, and emphatic commitment to the project at hand, as well as to each other.

Both the design of belay brakes and the strategies for using them appear to be changing as climbing itself changes. At one end of the scale are the braking needs of social-belay novice climbers who work with bombproof protection and overhead anchors; at the other end are the needs of lead climbers who tremble through long run outs to marginal protection. For the first situation, a foolproof belay plate, such as the Grigri, allows novices to lock up the rope safely and prevents the loss of precious height during a fall. The run-out lead climber, however, desires a belay that does not lock up but lets the rope slip through it to keep stress off the marginal protection. The sport leader working with beefy bolts and the adventurous climber placing good protection at reasonable intervals find themselves at the middle of the spectrum. All these different situations place radically different demands upon the belay brake and its effect on protection.

In an "average" lead climb, there is little to moderate friction provided by ropes running over carabiners or around corners. An "average" fall on the lead is also likely to be moderate, onto closely spaced, good protection. For the average top-rope or lead climb, many belay brakes are suitable and recommended[2,3] as long as they do not permit the belayer to apply too little or too much braking force. Too little force will allow the leader to continue falling; too much force may cause the protection to pull and lengthen the fall distance. This subject is examined in greater detail in chapter 11.

Belay techniques that provide too little braking force for lead climbs, and are not recommended even for top-roped sport climbs, include figure-eight descenders used in rappel or sport mode (fig. 6-15). In sport mode, a bight of rope passes through the large hole in the descender directly to a belay carabiner. This generates even less friction—on the order of 200 pounds—than the waist belay, giving rise to the possibility that a belayer might lose control of a falling climber even on a top rope. In the rappel mode, you can

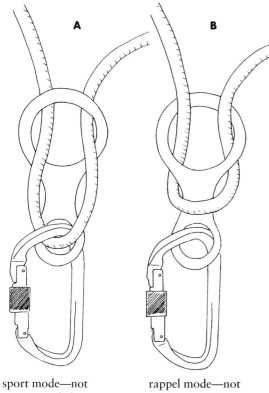

sport mode—not
recommended

rappel mode—not
recommended

Figure 6-15. Incorrect Belay Techniques with a
Figure-Eight Descender: A—The sport mode has too
little friction to control reliably the fall of even a top-
roped climber and can lead to injury. B—The rappel
mode also has too little friction to hold reliably a
top-roped climber; this mode also kinks the rope. Do
not belay a lead climber with the use of either mode.

generate a somewhat higher braking force—
between 240 and 270 pounds—which is roughly
equivalent to the waist belay. This is not enough
braking force to hold the average leader fall
when there is medium to low friction in the system. In addition, the figure-eight descender in
the rappel mode tends to kink the rope, which
may make it impossible for the belayer to pay
out rope to the leader.

The Sticht plate is a useful and recommended
belay device, and it serves as the model for discussion of slot belay devices because it was the
first on the market. The Sticht plate with a

spring provides a more dynamic belay than one
without a spring and may be better suited for
moderate to severe falls on climbs with a
medium amount of friction in the system. Sticht
plates with springs also are suited for easy, low-
fall-factor falls without much friction in the system. Other slot belay devices provide variable
amounts of braking force, listed in pounds of
force in chapter 11.

Many climbers employ the figure-eight descender (see fig. 6-13B) as a springless slot plate,
although this use is not officially recommended.
Springless slot plates can lock up during a severe
fall when there is little friction in the system and
can damage the rope or even cut it. To prevent
lockup, clip an extra carabiner onto the bight of
rope between the plate and your locking carabiner. Tube-shaped plates, used with the large
end against the belay carabiner, appear to prevent lockup, but make sure not to reverse them.

For slingshot belays, climbers may use mechanical belay devices, such as the Petzl Grigri[4],
based on the action of a cam that grips the rope
when it comes under sudden tension and locks
up automatically if the climber falls. For slingshot belays or belaying a second, shock forces
are not expected to be significant, and the
brake can be fixed directly to a good belay anchor point, as is the practice in some climbing
gyms, or to the belayer's harness, which provides give to the system. If this static brake is
fixed directly to an anchor, it is important that
you not allow slack to accumulate in the rope
in order to avoid generating significant shock
forces in a fall. To belay a leader, who might
create a significant shock load in a fall, you
need to introduce elasticity and give into the
system to offset the lockup of the brake. Belay
from your harness, and place your anchor at
waist height or slightly above; during a fall you
will be lifted and your body deformed to absorb energy and make the belay more dynamic.
Of course, you need to be careful that you are
not dragged horizontally, lifted into a ceiling, or
hit by the falling climber, lest you lose control
of the belay or be injured. Static belays, such as
those provided by a cam locking device or a

Static Belays and Marginal Protection

Many belay brakes useful for well-protected sport or lead climbs are not suitable for adventure climbs with long run outs to marginal protection. For example, the Grigri is a device designed to lock off the rope during a fall to provide an absolutely static belay. A Munter hitch in its most static mode, as well as other highly static belay brakes,

also effectively lock off the rope. A locked-off rope transmits elevated stresses to protection pieces. Beefy bolts found on sport climbs and well-protected pieces placed on the lead might withstand these forces. The marginal small to tiny protection pieces, which may be the only protection found on some adventure climbs, probably will not be able to withstand these forces, particularly for a long fall.

If you lead on marginal protec-

tion, you already might have a good idea of what you are getting into. To have the best shot at success, place your belay point farther away from the marginally protected crux rather than closer, use dynamic slings (described in chapter 7), and choose the belay brake that best combines the ability to stop the fall with the likelihood that it will not pull your protection. Stay away from high-friction devices.

Munter hitch in its most static mode, should be avoided for lead climbs on anything less than "bombproof" protection.

BELAYING ON GLACIATED CLIFFS

The soils on cliffs in glaciated areas, covering much of the northern part of North America and northern Europe, are usually very thin glacial till soils that are often a few inches to a few feet thick, as sketched in figure 6-16. These soils formed during the melting of a glacier. They are made up of the rock load pulled off and carried along at the base of glacial ice. Beneath these thin soils, the bedrock of the ledge is polished from the abrasive action of the glacier that occurred before the till was dropped. When exposed at the surface, this polish can produce mirrorlike smoothness and extremely slippery slab climbs. It should be obvious that tree roots do not penetrate this glacial polish, although the rare tree may send taproots into a crack.

Always be suspicious of trees growing in glacial till soils on cliff ledges as belay stations for technical climbing. These trees usually have roots that spread out over the surface of the soil and are not deeply rooted or firmly attached to the ledge. Observe two rules of thumb when belaying from these trees: First, pick a tree that weighs more than the shock force that would be generated on the tree by a falling leader; second, tie off the tree as close to its base as possible to

prevent leverage. Sit, rather than stand, so that your body does not act as a lever and to increase the friction of the belay. Back up the tree with artificial protection pieces, using nuts, if you have any doubt.

Shock forces are discussed in detail in chapter 11. To summarize shock forces briefly: in falling you can generate a force many times your body weight when you stop at the end of the rope. To test this out experimentally, jump up and down on a bathroom scale and read the maximum instantaneous weight, or impact force, recorded on the scale. You jump a few inches, but the scale registers a couple of hundred pounds. Now consider the force if you take a screamer fall and come to an abrupt stop on the end of the rope. This shock force is transferred to the belayer and the belayer's anchor. To absorb a high-value shock force, choose a substantial tree weighing 2,000 to 3,000 pounds, with a girth of several feet. When large well-rooted trees are not available, back up small tree anchors with nuts and use a braced body position.

COMMUNICATIONS

Good communication is required in climbing at all times and becomes more critical when the situation is difficult. When climbers can converse easily, they talk normally and do not need special jargon. As you gain experience, you may

Figure 6-16. Till Soils on Cliffs: A—The belay is incorrect in three ways. First, the tree used for belaying connects poorly to the thin till soil through its spread-out roots. Second, the tie-off point is above the base of the tree and will produce leverage. Third, the belayer increases the effect of leverage by standing, and will rotate outward if a fall occurs.

B—A better belay. The tree used for the tie-off weighs as much as the shock force that will be produced in a fall. The tree is tied off at its base to prevent leverage, and a nut anchor is used to back up the tree anchor. By sitting, the belayer makes a 90-degree turn in the rope across the legs that increases braking force by up to 40 percent. Finally, the belayer will be pulled directly downward into the rock rather than outward if a fall occurs.

find that you will climb under environmental conditions that make it difficult to communicate—in wind storms and other heavy weather, when separated from your companion by overhangs or bulges that muffle sound, or in situations of stress when you must get a request across quickly and unmistakably. Climbers have developed a shorthand communication system that relies on one- and two-word phrases to communicate fundamental requests for rope management. To prevent misunderstanding, these phrases include questioning signals that are always followed by a response acknowledging the original signal. In crowded areas, climbers can use each other's name to differentiate their signals from identical signals being used by other teams. The generally accepted terms used are listed below.

Confusing the Signals

The Pipe Pitch of the Whitney-Gilman Ridge has two cruxes. First comes the Pipe Overhang followed by a platform, then a simple but very exposed mantle out of the void of the Black Dike. The first time I led off this pitch, I almost caused myself to be pulled backward into this void.

Still a bit wobbly after completing the Pipe overhang, I looked around the corner into the void of the Black Dike. There was no protection to minimize a fall during the mantle. I had almost completed the mantle when I said to myself, "I seem to have a lot of drag on this rope." My belayer, two right angles and an overhang below, heard the operational word *rope*. He began taking it in, exerting a slight tug that prevented further progress on my part. I was held in midmantle, firmly committed to completing it or suffering the consequences of going back down. Unthinkingly, I said in a firm but not loud voice, "Take up the rope." My belayer began to pull me backward with an effort that matched the firmness of my voice. Now panicked at what appeared to be an inevitable fall, I screamed at the top of my voice, "Rope!" I started to slide into the void, as my dutiful belayer complied by pulling with all his strength. Just before my foot, or was it a knee, popped off the out-sloping top of the mantle, I realized my error. Reversing my command, I emphatically shouted, "Slack," and my responsive belayer paid out slack. Adrenaline heightened, I clawed and crawled my way onto the ledge and then around the corner when I was able to stand up.

In the more than 20 years since, I have never confused these critical signals again!

Climber: **"On belay?"** Question to belayer.

Belayer: **"Belay on!"** Response to climber.

Belayer: **"Climb"** or **"climb when ready."** Tells the climber it is okay to climb.

Climber: **"Climbing."** Indicates that the climber is starting up; sometimes the belayer is not ready yet and tells the leader so. "Climbing" can also mean that the climber is moving again after stopping for an extended period of time.

Climber: **"Up rope."** There is loose rope in the system and the belayer should take in some of it. There is no spoken response, since it is obvious to the climber that the rope is being taken in. When you are at a top-rope site with several ropes of different colors, it is helpful to mention the rope color in the signal: "Up on blue."

Climber: **"Slack."** The rope is too tight and the climber wants slack. If the belayer pays out rope without the rope becoming slack at the climber (because of friction in the system), the belayer may tell the climber to pull out what is needed. Once the climber starts up again, the signals "Climbing again" and "Up rope" should be given if they are necessary.

Climber: **"Tension."** This signal urges the belayer to make the rope very tight because the climber is in danger of falling or because the climber needs to rest for some reason. A second might have difficulty getting out a piece of protection from a difficult stance, for example, and ask for tension.

Climber: **"Falling."** The climber is falling and the belayer should lock off the belay.

Belayer: **"[Number of]feet."** This tells the leader how much rope is left and gives the leader a chance to set up a belay. Break the number up into its components—such as "two-zero" instead of "twenty"—to make the communication clearer.

Climber or belayer: **"Rock, rock, rock . . . !"** Shouted at the top of your lungs, this tells anyone below to get out of the way of a falling rock, carabiner, nut, etc.

Climber: **"That's me."** This tells the belayer that the rope is not hung up in a crack or bush but has come tight on the climber. This situation often occurs just before the "Belay on" call, as the former leader initiates the belay out of sight of the second.

Climber: **"Watch me."** Not a traditional signal,

this term is used now when climbers are doing a particularly hard move to warn the belayer to be especially attentive.

Belayer: **"I am with you."** This response reassures the leader.

Climber: **"Off belay."** The climber is secure and tells the belayer to break the belay apart.

Belayer. **"Belay off."** Confirms that the belayer has broken the belay apart and tells the climber that the rope can be managed without interference from the belayer.

The question "Belay off?," with the word *off* accented, is not a good way for the belayer to ask the leader if the belay can be taken off because it can be mistaken for a statement. It is usually posed by an impatient belayer whose leader is not setting up the upper belay anchor fast enough for the belayer. The belayer may be cold, hungry, or have other personal needs, and be impatient. If the leader has forgotten to tell the belayer "Off belay," however, the belayer is justified in the question.

Rappeller: **"Off rappel."** The rappeller has not only taken the rappel apart, but has walked away from the area to avoid rock fall that might be caused by the next rappeller.

REFERENCES FOR FUTURE READING

Chisnall, Robert. 1985. *Rock climbing safety manual.* Kingston, Ontario: Ontario Rock Climbing Association.

Gadd, Will. 1992. This ain't no trad weenie roast!: Safety in the sport climbing arena. *Rock & Ice.* 49:94 – 9.

————. 1993. Toys: Belay and descending devices. *Rock & Ice.* 54:106 – 108.

ENDNOTES

1. These figures are supplied by the Ontario Rock Climbing Association in its *Rock climbing safety manual.*
2. Chisnall, 1985, provides a summary of the results of extensive drop tests on different belaying techniques.
3. Gadd, 1993, lists properties and recommendations for belay devices in table form with a brief discussion.
4. Use of the Grigri is discussed in detail by the manufacturer under belaying and technical manual at <http://www.petzl.com >.

7

Protection

THE DEVELOPMENT OF PROTECTION

Being roped to the belayer does not safeguard the leader unless there is a way of attaching the rope to the cliff. On a lead climb, the leader places protection in the rock (see photo at right), uses natural protection, or takes advantage of protection that has been fixed in place by a previous climber. (Modern protection, "pro," includes a wide range of metal devices that can be wedged, pounded, or even drilled into the rock.) The leader clips the rope through a carabiner attached to the pro so that the rope can slide as the leader moves upward. This running protection does not prevent a fall but minimizes potential fall distance.

At the top of the pitch, the leader places several pieces of protection or uses fixed or natural protection and then ties into it. This anchor—the protection at the end of a pitch—ensures that the leader will not be pulled off his or her stance while belaying the second.

Early climbers, with great ingenuity and boldness, used natural chockstones wedged between the walls of chimneys for protection. Arriving at the chockstone, the leader untied from the rope, passed the rope behind the stone, and retied. Of course, not all climbs had natural protection, and those that did might not have had it when it was needed before a difficult section of the climb. Thus, climbers had the incentive to experiment with artificial protection.

Protection developed along two parallel but different paths, which can be divided loosely into protection that was pounded into a crack (wedges and pitons) and protection that was placed in a crack (artificial chocks, including spring-loaded camming devices). Climbers in the United States, for example, drove hardwood wedges into cracks to build a ladder up the side of Devil's Tower in Wyoming and drove a single wedge to protect a traverse across a blank section of the Old Cannon route on Cannon Mountain in New Hampshire.

Europeans also used wood wedges, but, for thinner cracks, they developed soft iron spikes

Placing Protection

called *pitons* or *pins*. Climbers pounded pitons into cracks, where the soft iron molded to the shape of the crack. With pitons, leaders could protect themselves whenever they arrived at a stance with a suitable crack. *Aid climbing*—using the protection to support body weight—became possible and allowed climbers to ascend outrageously overhanging walls for the first time.

Robert Underhill, who apprenticed on European mountains, introduced pitons to the United States in the 1930s. The security of this artificial protection allowed people to climb at a new level and established routes such as Standard on Cathedral Ledge in the White Mountains of New Hampshire and the North Ridge of the Grand Teton in Wyoming.

The next step was rigid steel pitons, first forged from the axle of a Model-T Ford by John Salathé, who used them to pioneer climbs of the southwest face of Half Dome and Lost Arrow Spire in Yosemite Valley, California. Unlike the soft iron pitons, Salathé's pitons could be removed and reused, so only a limited number were needed for a long climb.

In the 1950s, Chuck Wilts introduced rigid and durable pitons of a chrome-molybdenum steel alloy to Yosemite Valley. A decade later, equipment innovator and climber Yvon Chouinard began making and selling rigid pitons as a backyard industry. Eventually, he produced a range of piton sizes and shapes that remain state of the art today. Pitons became the dominant form of artificial protection and raised the standards of climbing. Using pitons, climbers scaled the big walls of Yosemite Valley with increasing frequency and established difficult climbs across the United States. Rigid pitons were the protection of choice until the early 1970s.

Protection for modern *free climbing*—climbing in which the climber does not use protection as a hand or foothold—evolved separately from pitons. In England, climbers collected natural chockstones of various shapes while walking along railroad tracks to the climbing area. They carried the stones in their pockets until they found a likely looking spot to use them on the climb. With the introduction of flat nylon webbing and carabiners after World War II,[1] enterprising climbers began to sling large hexagonal machine nuts with their interior threads filed smooth. Leaders could place these artificial chocks quickly, and seconds could retrieve them for use on the next pitch. In addition, the nuts came in various sizes and could cover a great range of placements. Among the nuts or chocks later developed were cylindrical knurled Pecks, foxhead wedges, and symmetrical hexes.

Yvon Chouinard's introduction of tapered nuts called *stoppers* and passive camming nuts called *Hexcentrics* provided the next landmark. Passive cams allowed climbers to protect parallel-sided cracks for the first time. Greg Lowe experimented extensively with passive cams of all sizes and shapes, but Vitali Abalakov, a climber

---

An Unusual Piece of Protection

A unique example of the evolution of artificial protection that combined the durability of iron with a wedged placement occurred on what is now the Whitney-Gilman ridge of New Hampshire's Cannon Cliff. Bradley Gilman and his cousin Hassler Whitney climbed this prominent ridge, which has an extremely exposed crux without protection. This section was probably the hardest climb in the country in 1929. Even today, the crux, although now considered to be of moderate difficulty at 5.7, prompts hesitation.

In 1931, Robert Underhill and Kenneth Henderson "improved" the route[2] by sliding a long pipe with an iron ring welded to one end into a crack beneath the crux. Subsequently, leaders could come to this spot, untie, pass the rope through the ring, and tie back in. Climbers were undoubtedly grateful to have this protection.

Unfortunately, climbers today cannot enjoy the pleasure of using Underhill's protection: the ring fell off the end of the pipe in the early 1970s, and the pipe itself disappeared after a half-century of use.

---

and engineer in the former Soviet Union, widely introduced these ideas to the West. Ray Jardine developed a spring-loaded camming device, the Friend. Many types of passive and spring-loaded camming devices and tapers are now part of the modern climbing rack. Advances in metallurgy, too, have produced a range of extremely strong nuts sized to fit the smallest of cracks.

By the early 1970s, artificial nuts had almost entirely replaced pitons. Nuts were both quicker and easier to place, and provided the same, or greater, security. In popular climbing areas, such as Yosemite Valley, cracks had been enlarged by the quarrying action of the repeated insertion and removal of pitons. Thoughtful climbers realized that their climbing resource, the rock itself, was being altered rapidly. Doug Robinson's article, "The Whole Natural Art of Protection," in the 1973 *Chouinard Equipment Catalog*[3] and John Stannard writing in *The Eastern Trade*[4] helped popularize this view, and by 1974 the climbing community had turned to pitonless climbing. Today, piton scars provide placements for nuts, fingers, and hands on older free climbs, but most climbers agree that the rock should be preserved in as natural a state as possible and deplore such practices as chipping holds or otherwise altering the rock.

During the 1980s climbers began to use *bolts* designed for industrial anchoring in masonry and concrete, placing them on blank walls that were otherwise without protection. This interest led manufacturers to produce bolts made expressly for rock climbing; whole new areas opened up, and climbing standards rose to a higher level.

NUTS

Aluminum Nuts

A standard wedge-shaped nut made from aluminum is called a *taper*. Most have tapering sides that form faces of unequal width so that they will fit two different size ranges (fig. 7-1). The newest tapers have rounded corners and curve on one side, so that they offer passive camming action. Tapers that curve on both sides provide tremendous holding power—so much that they are often very difficult to remove.

Tapers are designed to slot above a constriction in a crack. To achieve a secure placement, obtain as much contact between the rock and the taper's faces as you can. An incorrect placement (see fig. 7-1) illustrates two mistakes. First, do not place a taper so that one face rests on a protruding nubbin or crystal that may break or allow the nut to slip under the force of a fall. The nubbin may dig into the taper and require a vigorous one-handed effort on lead to remove and replace the nut properly, but it will not hold a fall. Second, be sure to place the nut entirely within the crack so that both faces completely contact rock surfaces.

Tapers usually come with a sling attached, and the sling influences the strength of the pro-

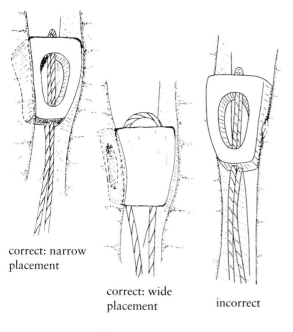

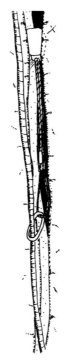

correct: narrow
placement

correct: wide
placement

incorrect

Figure 7-1. Curved Tapers in a Crack

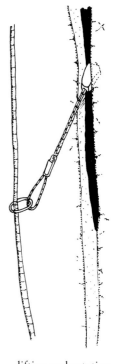

placement

lifting and rotation

*Figure 7-2. Lifting,
Rotation, and Failure
of a Wire Taper*

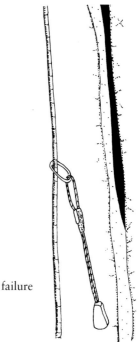

failure

tection. Formerly, tapers were slung with small-diameter round nylon webbing called *perlon*. The larger the diameter, the greater was the strength of the perlon, and each 1-millimeter increase in perlon diameter added about 1,000 pounds of breaking strength to the sling.

Also, since a perlon sling has some flexibility, you could often use a carabiner to attach the rope directly to the sling without fear that the nut would rotate out of the crack. If nuts rotate, they can fall out of the crack or slip deeper into it and become difficult to remove.

Most new small tapers come with wire slings, which are stronger than perlon. The stiff wire also acts as a handle that allows you to reach high to place the nut. Larger tapers come slung with 5.5-millimeter Kevlar threaded through drilled holes. Tapers with a wire sling are easily rotated by the movement of the climbing rope, causing the nut to dislodge (fig. 7-2). To prevent this problem, always use a short sling or *quickdraw* and make sure to attach the quickdraw to the wire with a carabiner (fig. 7-3A).

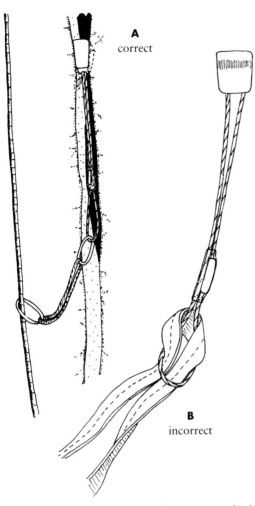

Figure 7-3. Slinging Tapers: A—*The correct method uses a carabiner to attach the nylon sling to the wired nut to prevent cutting.* B—*The incorrect method, without an intermediate carabiner, can lead to accidental cutting of the sling in a fall.*

The holding power of a modern taper—one without obvious fraying of the wire sling—depends on how well the face of the nut makes contact with the rock. Nuts with small faces have little contact with the rock and are at best marginal protection. Always look for frayed slings and friable rock around cracks.

The weakest point on the wire sling of an aluminum taper is where the wire bends sharply as it passes through the head of the stopper to form a loop. This weakness determines the lower size limit for wired nuts of this design. Small nuts also have less surface contact with the rock than larger nuts, so the force produced during a fall concentrates on a smaller area so that a small nut pulls more easily than a large one.

Brass and Steel Nuts

To overcome the above problems, you can use brass nuts with silver-soldered cables, which come in a range of sizes and shapes, including an offset shape designed for the chipped area where a piton was removed. Brass nuts deform rather easily and adhere well to tiny nubbins and irregularities, but they fail by shearing out of the crack.

Small steel nuts have a higher shear strength, and represent a second strategy to overcome the problems of small nuts. Steel nuts are made by injecting powdered stainless steel into a die under extreme direct pressure. The nuts are then drilled, and a steel cable is inserted and soldered in place.

Climbers commonly carry both brass nuts and steel nuts (fig. 7-4) and often use them with

Figure 7-4. A Steel Nut in a Crack and an Offset Brass Nut Compared in Size to a Penny

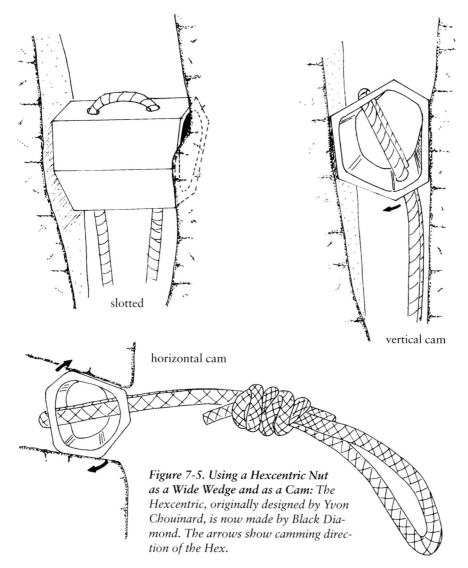

slotted

vertical cam

horizontal cam

Figure 7-5. Using a Hexcentric Nut as a Wide Wedge and as a Cam: The Hexcentric, originally designed by Yvon Chouinard, is now made by Black Diamond. The arrows show camming direction of the Hex.

a dynamic sling that absorbs energy by ripping apart to minimize the load on the nut.

Hexcentrics

Hexcentrics are larger nuts made of aluminum. They allow a number of placement possibilities, including camming and noncamming positions. They are desirable because they are effective, relatively inexpensive, and lighter than spring-loaded camming devices (discussed below).

You can place a Hex either lengthwise as a taper or sideways to cam in vertical cracks (fig. 7-5). The holding power of Hexes—and all nuts—is improved by having as much as possible of the surface of both faces in contact with the rock. You also enhance the placement of Hexcentrics, and all nuts, by slotting them as well as setting them in a camming position simultaneously. Use Hexcentrics as tapers in wide vertical cracks by placing them above a tapering section or as cams in a narrower parallel-sided crack. To achieve a good cam in a horizontal crack, place the sling so it leaves the nut near the roof of the crack.

Setting and Removing Tapers and Other Nuts

The leader sets a nut with a slight tug. Setting causes small crystals to bite into the metal of the nut and hold it in place. If you do not set a nut, friction from the rope may rotate and slot it deeper into a crack, or allow it to fall out of the crack. Oversetting, however, can make it difficult to remove. To remove a taper or other nut, the second must generally reverse the placement sequence after looking at the relationship of the protection to the crack and deciding whether the nut was purposefully placed or accidentally rotated. The leader can call down the information about how the piece was placed from above. Do not grab the sling and blindly yank because you could set the protection more firmly and bend and break the wire sling where it attaches to the nut.

Grasp larger nuts with your fingers and lift or rotate them from the placement. For smaller nuts, you may use a cleaning tool with a hook (fig. 7-6) that allows you to reach into a crack and behind the nut. The hook on cleaning tools should be narrow enough to fit behind the nut. You can grind hooks narrower on a grinder if the hook on your cleaning tool is too wide. Pad the palm end of the cleaning tool and hit it with your hand to free a sticky nut.

Sliders and Lowe Balls

Sliders and Lowe Balls (fig. 7-7) are spring-loaded two-piece tapers that expand to wedge into varying sizes of thin cracks. Sliders evolved

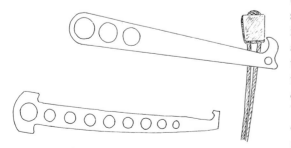

Figure 7-6. Two Cleaning Tools: One tool is shown hooking behind a taper.

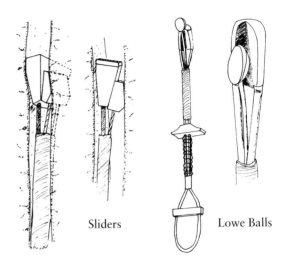

Sliders   Lowe Balls

Figure 7-7. Combined Spring-Loaded Wedging Nuts

from the early practice of stacking or combining two single tapers, one upside down with respect to the other, as a single unit to wedge into odd-size cracks. The Slider adds a spring to allow one-handed insertion.

The Lowe Ball is a logical and innovative combination of shapes to produce a wide range with firm holding power for a small nut. Its curved half-ball surface slides up a brass groove while its flat face orients itself to the rock surface and wedges. Place these small nuts in tapering slots so both faces are in full contact with the rock.

Lowe Tricam

A wonderful, innovative passive camming device, the *Lowe Tricam* (fig. 7-8) works in flares too small for most spring-loaded cams, piton scars, pockets, and horizontal cracks, as well as in places where spring-loaded camming devices also work. Tricams require attention and sometimes two hands to place properly. As a result, they are not as easy to place as a spring-loaded camming device when hanging on is difficult. You can use a Tricam as a passive nut or as a camming device, but you can usually cam it for additional protection any place that you can use it passively.

To prevent movement in the direction of pull,

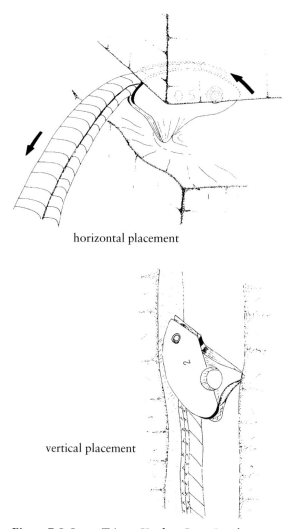

horizontal placement

vertical placement

Figure 7-8. Lowe Tricam Used as Cam: In a horizontal crack, you achieve a secure cam when the sling leaves the nut near the crack's roof, the nut is slotted, and a lip both prevents the beak from pulling directly outward and forces the Tricam to rotate forward and cam.

place the Tricam so that its beak rests in a depression or against a rock lip. Tricams work well in tapering or parallel-sided cracks. An outward or downward tug on the Tricam will start it rotating to produce the camming action. You get the best camming action in a horizontal crack when the Tricam's sling wraps around the top of the nut.

Tricam removal requires what is usually an obvious reversal of the camming direction and perhaps some movement to the side. You might have to rotate Tricams placed in pockets with large interiors and small openings 180 degrees inside the pocket before they come out.

SPRING-LOADED CAMMING DEVICES

Spring-loaded camming devices (SLCDs) work well in parallel-sided cracks, under down-pointing flakes, and in larger pockets. They come with either three or four cams and with one or two axes. Three-cam units (TCUs), which are used for protecting thin cracks, are small. They provide less friction and reportedly rotate more easily than four-cam units. The tendency to rotate increases in TCUs whose cams are close together and provide more of a pivot point. Devices with two sets of cams on two axes allow for greater contraction and expansion than four cams can on a single axis. Hence, camming devices with two axes fit a larger range of crack sizes than those with just one axis.

When you insert this type of protection into a crack, orient the stem so that it points in the direction that it would rotate if subjected to a leader fall. For vertical cracks, try to place the stem as vertically as possible. If you see a device with its stem protruding horizontally from a vertical crack, you know that the leader has made a bad placement that can be corrected by using the next-size smaller piece.

Try to size a spring-loaded camming device so that the cams are halfway retracted after you have inserted the device into a crack (fig. 7-9A). A device that is too small for the crack will open too far and possibly invert under load (fig. 7-9B). A device that is too large will be fully retracted (fig. 7-9C). It will be hard to remove because you cannot retract the cams any farther to make it smaller than the crack. Overcamming often occurs in the middle of a demanding lead, when you hastily pull an SLCD from the rack and shove it into the crack by pushing on the stem. In desperation you reason that the second

A—correct **B**—use a larger SLCD **C**—overcammed **D**—correct for SLCD with 2 axes incorrect for SLCD with 1 axis

Figure 7-9. Spring-Loaded Camming Devices: In each photo, the SLCD is located in the crack far enough from the edge to prevent the cams from popping out of the crack. **A**—*The SLCD has a rigid stem oriented in the potential fall direction. Its cams are properly contracted into the midrange.* **B**—*The crack is wide for this SLCD. The next larger size would be* a better choice. **C**—*The SLCD is overcammed and may be very difficult to remove because you cannot make it smaller than the crack.* **D**—*You can use SLCDs with two axes (shafts) fully open as passive nuts, but do not use a one-axis SLCD in this manner: it can fail if the cam inverts.*

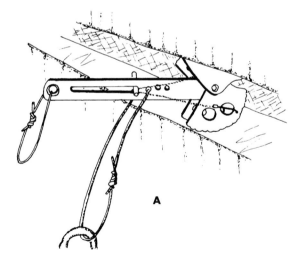

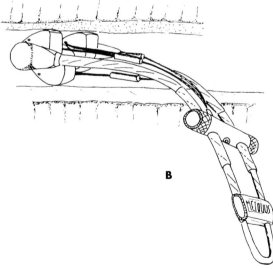

Figure 7-10. Two Ways to Safeguard SLCDs in Horizontal Cracks: **A**—*Tie a loop of Spectra cord through the hole in front of the trigger bar to prevent leverage. A safer placement for this crack would be a Tricam or* **B**—*an SLCD with a flexible stem.*

can deal with the problem. Yes, but a crowbar might be required!

An SLCD with two axes is strong enough to use as a passive nut in an open position (fig. 7-9D). Do not use the single-axis SLCD with the cams open: the cams can accidentally invert, and the placement will fail.

SLCDs are manufactured with flexible or rigid stems. The rigid stems are stronger but break when bent over edges, whereas the flexible stems can bend over edges but tend to fray and need replacing sooner.

A potentially dangerous placement occurs when the rigid stem of an SLCD protrudes from a horizontal crack. If the clip-in point of the device is at the end of a stem, a fall will turn the stem into a lever and the stem may snap. There are two ways to overcome this problem. Tie a small loop of Spectra cord (the current material of choice for slinging) through the stem holes forward of the trigger bar (fig. 7-10A). When the rope loads this sling, no levering action occurs on the stem.

Alternatively, you can use an SLCD with a flexible stem (fig. 7-10B). These stems are made of woven wire and may be single or doubled in a U-shape. The potential weakness of this design is that wire can fray and break strand by strand. Some manufacturers cover the wire with a stiff plastic designed to help shield the wire from abrasion. The wires controlling trigger bars also require routine replacement, which the manufacturer can do inexpensively.

Removing Spring-Loaded Camming Devices

Pressure from the climbing rope trailing behind the leader can make the device work—or walk—its way into the crack. The second might find it difficult to pull the trigger bar while pushing with the thumb in order to remove the protection. This situation is almost certain to happen when the leader places the SLCD in a crack at an overhang lip and the rope runs over it as the leader ascends. The easiest way to prevent this problem is to place a passive nut rather than an SLCD at the lip.

Special tools and ordinary nut removers, such

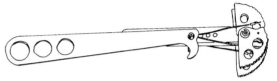

Figure 7-11. A Nut Remover Extracts Deeply Placed SLCDs

as the one sketched in figure 7-11, can help extract protection from these problem placements. The best special tool is an extended SLCD trigger bar called Friend of a Friend, designed by Ed Leeper. This device has hooks on one end to grip the SLCD trigger bar, and a trigger on the other end.

In an emergency, you can slip small wired nuts over both sides of the trigger bar and link them together with a carabiner (fig. 7-12). The carabiner allows you to pull on the trigger bar while you push with a nut remover on the stem. Executing this maneuver almost always requires you to hang from a rappel rope, a piece of protection, or a belayed rope from above, but usually results in success.

Camming Devices Placed behind Flakes, in Parallel Cracks, and Slotted

Camming nuts create outward forces that translate into friction to oppose the force of a fall. For a spring-loaded camming device, the outward forces are generated as the stem is pulled in the direction of the fall. Belayed falls with a body belay or mechanical plate create maximums of approximately 1,000 to 2,000 pounds of force, respectively, parallel to the stem of a camming nut. Cams may double this force as they transfer it to the walls of a crack. Because the energy of a fall is doubled and transferred to the rock, camming nuts placed behind flakes or loose blocks will push out and may break off the flake or block.

In general, SLCDs placed in parallel cracks hold as long as friction of the cams against the wall equals or is greater than the force on the cams in the direction of the fall.

SLCDs should hold in solid granite, but they might not hold in weakly cemented sandstone

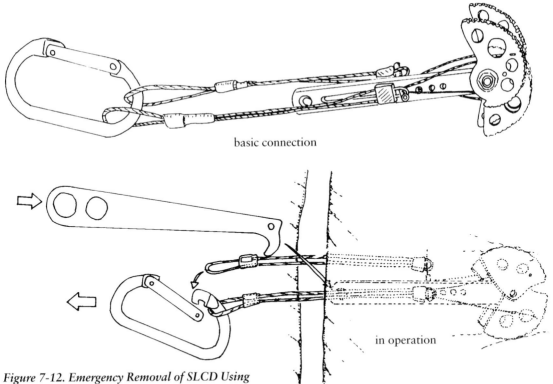

basic connection

in operation

Figure 7-12. Emergency Removal of SLCD Using Wire Tapers

or highly weathered rock. When the force of a fall does overcome friction of the cams, the SLCD slides, sometimes leaving behind grooves like ski tracks.

In irregular cracks you can improve the placement strength of a camming nut by slotting and camming the nut. In order for a slotted and cammed nut to come out, the nut would have to pull through the narrows of the slot in addition to overcoming the friction of the cam against the wall.

NUTS FOR OFFWIDTHS

Protection for wide cracks always has been something of a problem. Climbers used large pitons called *bong-bongs* in the 1960s. More recently, they used hollow aluminum tube chocks and, most recently, very large homemade spring-loaded camming devices that are now commercially available as Big Dudes (fig. 7-13A), Big

Trusting Fixed Protection

The move to all-nut free climbing in the early 1970s inadvertently created dangerous pitons. When nuts became the norm, any piton placed on a free climb was usually left in place as fixed, or *resident*, protection. Over the years, a layer of rust formed on the outer surface of the pins, and in some cases the rock itself slowly weathered, which resulted in loose pitons. Climbers cannot be certain of the quality of a resident pin placement without personally removing and replacing it. Always doubt the holding power of any pin found in place unless you have reason to believe it safe. Often, there are good nut placements nearby so you can set up an independent belay or at least back up fixed pins.

In densely populated climbing areas, local rescue groups often replace resident pins to protect climbers who have too much faith in pins. Check with the rescue group in your local area for its replacement policy.

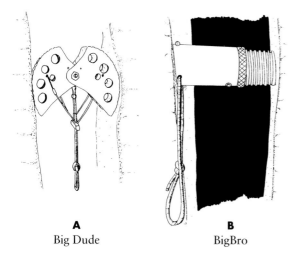

A
Big Dude

B
BigBro

Figure 7-13. Big Dude and BigBro Placements

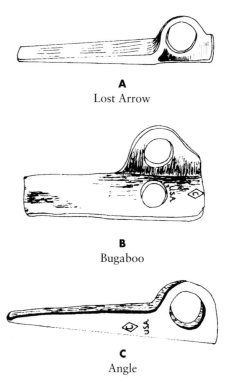

A
Lost Arrow

B
Bugaboo

C
Angle

Figure 7-14. Piton Types: Pitons may be blades (A and B) or angles (C).

Friends, or large Camalots. Added to the large-crack arsenal is the BigBro (fig. 7-13B), which features two tubes, one inside the other, that lengthen under spring pressure and lock open by means of a threaded ring. One-handed placement is possible for all of BigBro's four sizes, which fit fist-size to arm-bar-size cracks. A sling attaches to one end of the tube to help wedge or cam it into position above a slight constriction. The weight and bulkiness of large-crack protection usually means that most climbers go without unless they know ahead of time that they will absolutely require it.

PITONS

With the advent of nuts, many climbers are no longer familiar with the use of pitons. Pitons, however, are often fixed at belay stations on free routes and are still used for aid climbs and for winter climbs (when cracks are often partially filled with ice, preventing nut placements). As a result, there is still good reason to learn how to place pitons.

There are two types of pitons: *blades* and *angles* (fig. 7-14). Because the holding power of a blade comes from friction between the rock and the piton, you must drive these pins tightly into a crack. The holding power of an angle comes

from compression between the back and front of the piton, as well as friction.

Placing and Removing Pitons

Placing a piton requires the use of a heavy (20- to 25-ounce) hammer with a large, flat face (fig. 7-15) and a pick to help pry pitons during removal. You normally carry the hammer in a holster. Attach a keeper sling from your harness to the hammer's shaft so you will not lose the hammer if you drop it. The sling should be long enough to allow you to extend your arm fully.

Pitons should fit about three-quarters of the way into a crack to start and should produce a ringing sound that rises in pitch as the pin is driven. If the crack quickly bottoms out, the pin cannot be driven. If the crack widens inside, you will not hear the rising ringing sound, and the placement will be poor. Although piton placements in cracks at all angles can be excellent,

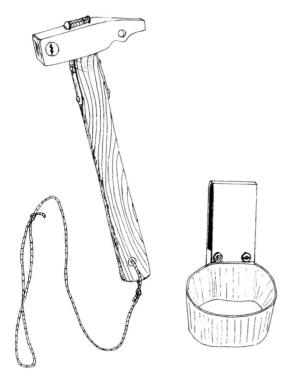

Figure 7-15. Piton Hammer and Holster

horizontal cracks provide an advantage in leverage over a pin in a vertical crack. Examine both the good and the bad placements in figure 7-16. Tie off pitons that are not driven (to the eye) with narrow ½-inch nylon loops, called *hero loops*, to prevent leverage.

To remove a piton, drive it back and forth several times as far as it will travel (fig. 7-17). Pull the pin out in the middle of its travel by using your hand or the pick on the hammer. Climbers often attach an old carabiner with a keeper sling to the pin so they do not drop the

Figure 7-16. Good and Bad Placements of Pitons:
A—A good blade placement with the blade horizontal or downward and with high friction between the rock and piton. B—Hollow and poor. C—Good: upward but high friction. D—Good friction with eye upward but poor placement of carabiner, which will both break the carabiner and lever the piton. E—A sling corrects this placement. F—Good if tied off with hero loop. G—Good angle with the back and front wedging opposite sides of the crack. H—Poor angle with the sides of the piton in contact with the rock.

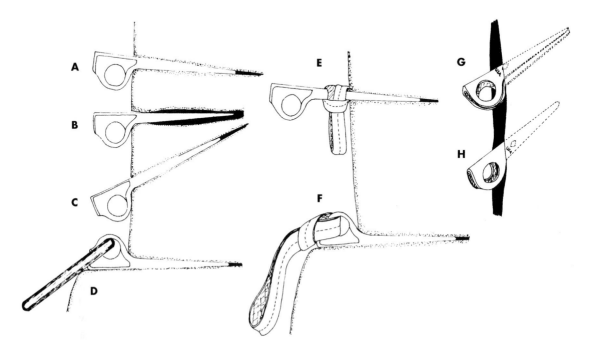

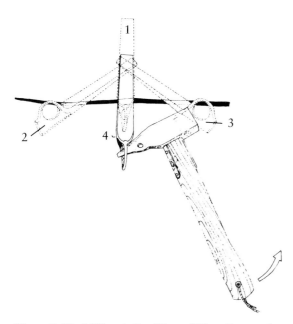

Figure 7-17. A Worm's Eye View of Piton Removal:
With the hammer, drive the piton, in position at site
1, back and forth in the crack as far as possible to
sites 2 and 3. Then, when it is back at site 4, use the
pick to lever the piton out of the crack.

pin and lose it. You will invariably pound on
and weaken the carabiner, so mark it and dedi-
cate it to piton removal.

Aid climbs often require piton placements
that are tied off by using hero loops to prevent
leverage. In advanced aid techniques, you can
stack pitons to fit larger cracks, although large
camming nuts lessen the necessity of stacking of
pitons. Small wired tapers, Tricams, and three-
cam units have lessened the need to use hero
loops on pitons that do not go into the crack
fully.

BOLTS

Bolts have been around for a couple of generations. Climbers accept bolts as long as the bolts
allow them to maintain the adventure and challenge of climbing. On Yosemite-size walls, a few
bolts linking short blank rock sections maintain
the challenge, whereas massive numbers guaran-
tee the climb. On adventure climbs, a single bolt

might turn a series of dangerously unprotected
moves into a long climb of exciting adventures.
On sport climbs, bolts allow climbers to create
gymnastic routes at the limits of their physical
abilities on otherwise unleadable rock.

Bolting was self-regulating as long as
climbers tediously placed the bolts by hand, but
the introduction of the power drill changed the
situation. The rate of placement has risen
sharply, numerous new cliffs have been developed, thousands of new climbers have entered
the sport, and gymnastic ability has increased
dramatically for practitioners of bolted sport
routes.

Another advantage of power drilling is that
the ¼-inch bolt has given way to the stronger ⅜-
inch bolt. Falls on bolts produce stress fractures,
temperature swings weather bolt holes, and
chemical reactions attack bolt metal, so examine
the quality of bolts and their placements carefully. Never hit a bolt with a hammer, and do not
trust a bolt showing signs of hammer damage.
Old bolts might hold a fall, but they might not,
so never trust these bolts alone for protection.

Bolt Types

Climbing bolts fall into three functional classes.
A hammer-in bolt is pounded into the hole; a
torque bolt is placed in the hole and torqued
with a wrench; and a glue-in bolt is a threaded
rod glued into an oversize hole.[5] This discussion
covers only the hammer-in bolt because it is frequently used and the problems it presents are
representative.

The 5-piece Rawldrive is a standard steel or
stainless steel bolt for hard rock, such as granite.[6] Use stainless steel in areas that experience
wet weather. For this bolt, a two-piece sleeve
with a nylon compression ring slips over the
bolt, which has a threaded cone on one end and
a hexagonal head on the other (fig. 7-18A and
B). Torquing the bolt in the hole pulls the cone
into the sleeve and expands it to exert an outward force against the walls of the hole. The
5-piece Rawl bolt depends on lots of friction
between the bolt and the rock, so it works only
in hard rock.[6] Older ¼- to ⁵⁄₁₆-inch-diameter

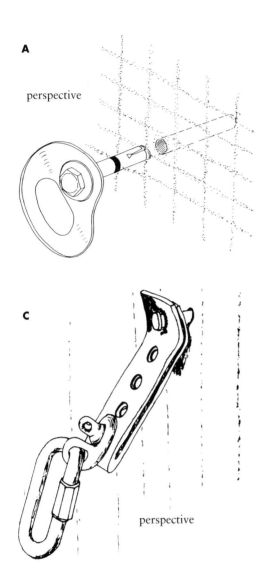

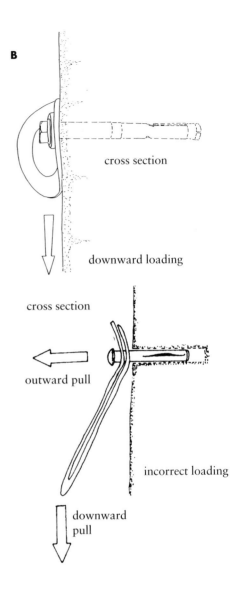

A

perspective

B

cross section

downward loading

C

perspective

cross section

outward pull

incorrect loading

downward pull

Figure 7-18. Forces Applied to a Bolt by Hanger Design: A—A perspective view of a 5-piece Rawldrive placed perpendicular to the rock. B—A cross-sectional view of a 5-piece Rawldrive bolt showing the strongest loading direction. Resistance to loading parallel to the axis is significantly reduced. C—Perspective and cross-section views of a poor homemade bolt design. This design creates an outward pull on the bolt shaft when a downward pull occurs on the bolt hanger. This bolt should not be used; it needs to be replaced.

Rawldrives predate modern bolting techniques. These bolts have a split shaft, slightly larger than the hole, that compresses when driven. These older split-shaft Rawldrives found on cliffs today should be removed.

Wedge-type hammer-in bolts include stud drives, machine bolts used as aid rivets (a scary technique used for some big-wall climbs), and ½-inch baby angles pounded into ⅜-inch holes that are used for anchors in soft sandstone. For soft rock, glue-in bolts are probably stronger and safer than ½-inch baby angles or Rawldrive bolts. The drilling required to place these bolts has become possible with the advent of power drills.

Placing Bolts

Place a bolt on a smooth rock face free from flakes, hollows, or natural drainage where freeze-thaw cycles will promote rock weathering. Bolts placed in natural drainage may be solid when placed but fall out when touched the following season. Gently chip away any protruding crystals so that the hanger can sit flush with the rock. Do not hit the area hard enough to fracture the rock.

The hole for a 5-piece Rawldrive should be perpendicular to the rock surface and about ¼ inch longer than the bolt (fig. 7-18A). Placing a bolt by power drill works well but is not allowed in many climbing areas. Hand drilling, laborous as it is, works fine. Twist the bit ¼ turn *between* hits while avoiding making a cone-shaped entrance hole. Once the hole is started, allow the drill to bounce slightly to help clear rock dust, which will cause the drill to bind. Dull bits will also tend to bind. Clear rock dust periodically by blowing into the hole with a piece of plastic tubing long enough to prevent your face from being attacked by the rock dust expelled from the hole. When drilling is completed, clean rock dust by blowing. Use a test-tube brush before you place the bolt to ensure that the hole walls are clean.

Once a bolt is in place, do not hammer on it because you can create internal fracture—a time bomb waiting to go off. You can recognize a bolt that bottoms out in the hole because the hanger spins freely or you can see the shank behind the hanger. Do not trust these bolts.

During the 1980s, many bolts were sealed with epoxy to prevent water infiltration. John Middendorf IV, reporting on research in *Machine Design Trade Magazine*, says that epoxy can corrode steel[7] and concludes that polyester resins are better in all respects for sealing bolts.

Commercial hangers for bolts made from stainless steel or chrome-moly steel come in various sizes. All rate at strengths of more than 4,000 pounds. These hangers apply force placed on the bolt perpendicular to the shaft—downward along the surface of the rock for a properly placed bolt (fig. 7-18B). Try not to pull a bolt outward along its axis because outward pulls work directly against the relatively smaller frictional resistance of the bolt shaft to the rock.

Outward pulls, such as those created by a fall under an overhang, produce torquing forces on many types of bolt hangers. Thus, when underneath overhangs, you should use bolts that are beefy and designed, if possible, with non-torquing hangers. A belayer leaning off a bolt at waist level at a belay station can also create outward pull.

Note that the principles that govern loading bolts are the same as those that govern loading ice pitons or screws placed in poor ice, discussed in chapter 13 under "Loading Ice Pitons and Screws Placed in Poor Ice."

Homemade anchors are often made from aluminum, angle iron, and scrap steel. You can guess their strength by evaluating how much material supports the load and to what degree leverage occurs. A poorly designed hanger will act to exert a pull away from the rock, as shown in figure 7-18B. The worst possible design places the force parallel to the shaft of the bolt, which is the direction required to pull the bolt straight out of its hole. Cold Shunts, hardware-store-variety links designed to repair or join chains, might or might not be welded closed to serve as climbing anchors. Not only do Cold Shunts protrude away from the rock so that a falling climber can hit them, but their strength is unpredictable. Tests[8] show that the strength of welded Cold Shunts varies by 70 percent, depending on initial thickness of metal around the eye of the shunt, the quality of the homemade weld, and the shape of the bend—angular bends concentrate stress and corrosion. Unwelded Cold Shunts hold minimal weight and should never be trusted. Climbers would not accept such a large variation in other climbing gear, for instance in carabiner strength, and should not accept Cold Shunts as climbing anchors.

Bolt Anchors

A bolt anchor consists of bolts, the webbing that links the bolts together, and an attachment point such as a rappel ring. Many of the webbing slings at rappel routes show signs of melting caused by friction produced as a rappel rope is pulled across the sling material. You can recognize friction melting in a smooth, blackened surface stripe on the nylon sling that corresponds to the position of the rappel rope. Do not rely just on such slings, which are reduced in strength. At frequently used rappel stations, a multitude of slings accumulates. Consider carrying a knife to cut away the oldest of these slings when they pile up; you may even want to leave behind a rappel ring to prevent friction melting of new sling material. Make sure that you rappel from the equalization point of the slings.

When you secure yourself to the webbing or chain, make sure that you will remain attached to the anchor even if one bolt fails. This usually means that you must clip the attachment cara-

Figure 7-19. Webbing Patterns for Connecting Bolts: A—A poor pattern for connecting two bolts. B—A good pseudo-equalized pattern. C—Good for a downward pull. D—An excellent self-equalizing pattern. The best choice is to do both C and D, using three slings. The angle Ø should be 60 degrees or less.

biner through a loop and not around two strands of webbing or a length of chain stretching between two bolts. Since undetectable structure and placement problems can exist with bolts, always insist on two or more bolts for an anchor. Three-bolt anchors are not uncommon. For the first person down a rappel, back up a bolt anchor with chocks where possible.

There are excellent and poor webbing or chain patterns to attach bolts together. Analyze webbing patterns to determine the loading sequence and directions of the bolts that make up the anchor: you want to see if the pull on the bolts is chiefly downward, as occurs when bolts are above each other, or whether rotational forces are applied to individual bolts. Before rappelling, check the entire rappel system, including the anchor. If you do not like it, change it until you are satisfied.

Figure 7-19 represents various configurations in which webbing can connect bolts. Diagram A is a common pattern of connecting two bolts with sling material that produces a complex and high-stress pattern on the sling, multiplying the load on both bolts and sling. This setup also produces rotation that turns the bolt away from a favorable downward pull. (Details of the stresses involved in this configuration are described in chapter 10; see the section explaining fig. 10-7.)

Diagram B shows that by placing one bolt almost in a vertical line with the other you form a two-sling anchor that will bear the load of the anchor equally. B and C represent patterns of

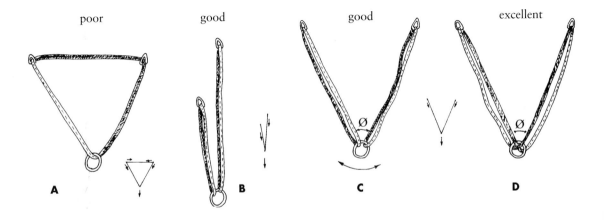

| poor | good | good | excellent |
| A | B | C | D |

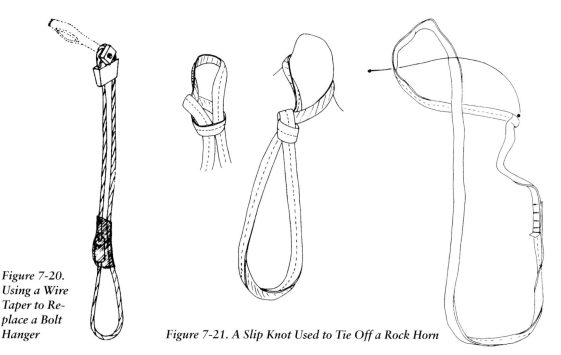

Figure 7-20. Using a Wire Taper to Replace a Bolt Hanger

Figure 7-21. A Slip Knot Used to Tie Off a Rock Horn

pseudo-equalization in which both bolts are loaded only in one direction or in a limited range of directions (indicated by the arc drawn below C). A *self-equalized* anchor pattern that directs the forces equally to both bolts through a wide range of arc is shown in D. Keep the angle Ø between the slings for all of these anchor patterns to 60 degrees or less to maximize the advantage of having two bolts. This placement will prevent load multiplication on the bolts and slings. (Load multiplication is also discussed in chapter 10.)

Allen Sanderson suggests that using three slings in a combination of patterns C and D is perhaps the best for connecting two bolts.[9] The one long sling of pattern D forms the primary load-bearing anchor because it is self-equalizing. The weakness of the pattern is that the entire anchor fails if this sling fails. To overcome this problem, use two slightly longer slings connected in pattern C to act as a backup that will not load the rappel point unless the primary sling fails.

If you anticipate establishing bolt anchors, you should be familiar with the simple physical principles discussed in chapter 10 and refer to the references listed at the end of this chapter.

Using Bolts with Missing Hangers

You might often find Rawldrive bolts with missing hangers on older routes. You need not pass these up; you can use them by slipping a small wire taper over the nut and sliding the nut head tightly against the bolt shaft, as illustrated in figure 7-20. This protection, at best, is insecure because it might fail if the wire taper rotates during a fall and the nut slips over the bolt's threads. Safeguard this marginal protection by using a dynamic sling, and by carrying a bolt hanger with you.

SLINGS ON HORNS

Slings around natural rock horns (sometimes called *chickenheads*), flakes, knobs, and similar features need to be snug at the base of the projection to prevent leverage and lifting by rope drag. You can secure slings on horns with a slip knot snugged up against the rock (fig. 7-21), and you can keep slings on flakes from lifting by jamming a knot, or the doubled sewn area, between the flake and rock wall.

BENT-GATE CONCERNS AND ENCHAINING CARABINERS

A carabiner used to clip into running protection normally has its gate turned out from the rock and downward to prevent accidental opening. Having the gate out and down on bent-gate carabiners designed for fast, easy clip-ins of bolted sport climbs can lead to accidental unclipping of the rope during a fall. Tests reported by Recreational Equipment, Inc., in 1990 show that "it is not the shape of the gate that presents this problem, but rather how far a carabiner's nose sticks out to 'catch' the rope, holding it against the gate and causing that gate—whether

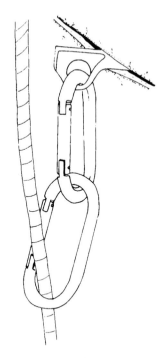

Figure 7-22. Enchaining Carabiners: Beware of passing the rope through the lower carabiner (backclipping) so that rope friction causes the lower carabiner to rotate against the upper one and unclip from it.

> ### Dynamic Slings
>
> Never use a dynamic sling to anchor a belayer. A belayer on a small ledge might very well be pulled off the belay stance as the sling lengthens by ripping apart. Also, a dynamic sling is better used on the piece that catches the fall. The impact force on this piece is about twice the force on the belayer.

---

straight or bent—to open." REI recommends avoiding "situations where the rope may cross back over any carabiner."[10] This is good advice if you can plan your falls ahead of time. But it would be better to avoid using these carabiners unless they provide a decided advantage for a specific climb. You might also remember that once you are clipped in, you may find it easier to stand in position, and you can place a second carabiner with reversed gate through the rope end of the quickdraw.

Enchained carabiners (fig. 7-22) are sometimes used to allow the rope to run freely through the protection where use of a full-length sling simply lengthens the distance of a potential fall. Enchaining is used most often on fixed pitons when climbs follow vertical lines. Always avoid enchaining where the rope produces a twisting force on the carabiners to produce a *backclip* because the carabiners can unclip from one another during the twisting. While enchaining can work in some situations, the use of a short quickdraw sling between carabiners avoids the disadvantages of enchaining and still keeps additional fall distances to a minimum.

QUICKDRAW SLINGS

Quickdraw slings are useful when you want a short sling to prevent nut rotation. You can fashion quickdraws out of a full-length sling, or you can purchase quickdraws. Figure 7-23 shows a technique for making a quickdraw from a full-length sling. This technique allows you to revert quickly to the full-length runner.

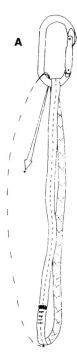

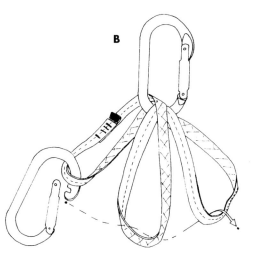

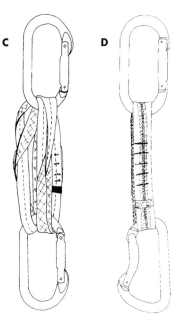

Figure 7-23. Quickdraw Slings: The sequence A–C shows how to make a quickdraw sling from a full-length sling. You can return the quickdraw to full length by unclipping one carabiner from C and placing it in one of the free loops in B. D is a commercial quickdraw.

Unclip a carabiner from one end of the quick-draw (C), clip this carabiner into one of the three released loops (B), and pull. Diagram D shows a commercially made quickdraw for comparison.

DYNAMIC SLINGS FOR MARGINAL PLACEMENTS

Until recently, forces created by the acceleration of gravity and friction in a fall have been absorbed by the rope, deformation of the climber's body, and the tightening of knots. The force ex-

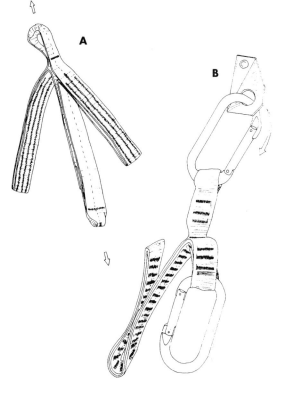

Figure 7-24. Dynamic Slings: A—The stitches of the Yates Screamer are parallel to the length of the sling to reduce carabiner gate vibration. The Yates Screamer is shown without the protective Lycra sheath supplied with it. B—An Air Voyager used on a ¼-inch bolt. After clipping in, rotate the carabiner so that the gate is down and facing out, like the bottom carabiner. Always use full-strength carabiners with dynamic slings and place them only on running protection, never belays.

perienced by a piece of protection is approximately twice the force experienced by the belay or the falling climber. Steel and brass micronuts are marginal placements that resist pulling out of a crack by means of the small amount of friction between their faces and the rock. They can pull in a fall because a well-placed micronut can have a resistance as low as 800 pounds, whereas the force tugging on the piece can be easily 1,000 to 2,000 pounds or higher. (Other marginal placements include most ice protection because of the uncertain quality of the ice, and perhaps fixed pitons and ¼-inch bolts.)

A *dynamic sling* (fig. 7-24) absorbs energy as its stitches rip apart, so all of the energy of the fall is not transmitted to a marginal placement.

Bill Forest introduced the Fall Arrest, the first commercially available dynamic sling. It was rather complex and expensive, and is no longer available. John Bouchard introduced a simpler design, the Air Voyager, made of folded and cross-stitched 1-inch webbing. It is also no longer available, but many Air Voyagers are still in use. In the Yates Screamer, the latest type of dynamic sling, folded webbing is stitched along the length of the sling.

Yates Screamers and Air Voyagers are ordinary sling material doubled over and sewn with thread. In the Air Voyager, bar tacks run perpendicular to the sling, and each bar tack absorbs energy once the process is activated at 700 pounds. Ripping apart one bar tack simply lowers the number available to rip, and the sling remains functional as a dynamic sling as long as there are other bar tacks. Once all bar tacks are ripped, it becomes an ordinary sling.

A potential problem with this design is that the periodic ripping of bar tacks can cause the carabiner that connects the sling to your rope to vibrate, and the gate might open and close. When the gate is open, the carabiner is weakened and could fail.

The lengthwise stitching pattern of the Yates Screamer, which activates at 550 pounds, minimizes gate vibration, but to ensure security you should use only full-strength carabiners; adding a lightweight locking carabiner on the rope end of a dynamic sling adds extra assurance against the gate opening. If you use the latter option, you will need to develop the habit of making sure that the gates are unlocked before starting off on a lead. Do not use lightweight hollow carabiners on dynamic slings.

REFERENCES FOR FUTURE READING

Cannon, Neil. 1985. Air voyagers. *Climbing*. 88:54.

Chouinard, Yvon. 1989. *Great Pacific/Chouinard equipment catalog*. Ventura, California.

Graydon, Don, ed. 1992. *Mountaineering: The freedom of the hills*. Fifth edition. Seattle: Mountaineers.

Jones, Chris. 1976. *Climbing in North America*. Berkeley, California: University of California Press for the American Alpine Club.

Leeper, Ed. 1980. *Alloy steel climbing hardware*. Boulder, Colorado: Ed Leeper.

Long, John. 1989. *How to rock climb*. Evergreen, Colorado: Chockstone Press.

McNamara, Chris. 1998. Anchors away. *Climbing*. 178:132–139.

Nagy, Shandor. 1997. Blind faith. *Climbing*. 173:114–119.

Lubben, Craig. 1989. Understanding your Friends. *Rock & Ice*. 33:76.

Middendorf IV, John. 1988. Drills, hangers, bolts: The dope for doing it right. *Climbing*. 106:103–108.

Peters, Ed, ed. 1982. *Mountaineering: The freedom of the hills*. Fourth edition. Seattle: Mountaineers.

Piana, Paul. 1988. Salathé wall. *Climbing*. 110:50–60.

Raleigh, Duane. 1989. Soft rock: the glue-in bolt solution. *Climbing*. 115:106–107.

———. 1992. Anchors away: The nuts of bolts, part 1. *Climbing*. 134:101–110.

———. 1992. Sticky business: The nuts of bolts, part 2: glue-in bolts. *Climbing*. 135:125–128.

Recreational Equipment, Inc. 1990. *Climbing 1990*. Seattle.

Robbins, Royal. 1973. *Advanced rockcraft*. Glendale, California: La Siesta Press.

Robinson, Doug. 1973. The whole natural art of protection. In *Chouinard equipment catalog*.

Sanderson, Allen. 1989. Rapper's delight: A safer method. *Climbing*. 116:122–125.

———. 1990. Chain rappel anchors: The non-degradable choice. *Climbing.* 121:94–97.

Stannard, John. 1973. Nuts in the Shawangunks. *The eastern trade.* New York: Tillson.

Webster, Ed. 1987. *Rock climbs in the White Mountains of New Hampshire.* Second edition. Eldorado Springs, Colorado: Mountain Imagery.

ENDNOTES

1. Carabiners were developed before World War II, but aluminum carabiners came after the war.
2. Webster, 1987.
3. Robinson, 1973.
4. Stannard, 1973.
5. See Raleigh, 1992, on glue-in bolts.
6. Rawl-Bolt is now Power-Bolt Anchor <http://www.rawl.com>.
7. Middendorf, 1988; McNamara, 1998.
8. Nagy, 1997.
9. Sanderson, 1989.
10. Recreational Equipment, Inc., 1990, 10.

Rappelling

INTRODUCTION

When you rappel, you run the rope around your body or a mechanical device to create friction, and this friction against the rope allows you to make a controlled descent. In a wider sense, rappelling includes the whole process of setting up an anchor, throwing the rope, setting up the brake, descending, and retrieving the rope. Many of these subjects are discussed elsewhere in this book, so this chapter concentrates on rappel brakes and descending.

Rappelling takes little skill, but it calls for great vigilance. You must concentrate on setting up the system and double-check it—and have your partner double-check it—before you back over the void. When you are fresh, concentration comes easily, but climbers often find themselves rappelling at the end of the day when they are tired and ready to head home. It is important to learn to rappel correctly and to practice the skill so it comes easily when you need it.

The brake should provide enough friction so that you can control your descent. When you

choose a brake, you should consider how steep the slope is and how much you weigh.

RAPPEL BRAKES

A rappel brake should provide the proper amount of friction required for you to use the force of gravity to control your descent. You need to match the amount of friction between the rope and rappel brake to your body weight and the steepness of the slope. The friction will produce heat as a by-product, so you need to take precautions to protect yourself and the rope from abrasion wounds or friction burns.

The Body Rappel

In a body rappel or *dulfersitz* you wrap the rope around your body to provide friction (fig. 8-1). This rappel is useful on short descents on gentle slopes. I use it, for example, to safeguard myself when I am setting up top ropes and need to clear ropes that have tangled in brush. Each time, the discomfort reminds me that I would

Impact Forces and Rappelling

When I was 17 years old, I horrified a group of matrons as I jumped off a bridge that spanned an almost dry creek. I went into free fall, wild with ecstasy, until I saw the creek coming up. I braked so hard that my body slid completely around in the rappel formed by wrapping the rope through my legs and over my shoulder. My descent abruptly arrested, I came to a stop in a fetal position, as I hung completely upside down in the creek's last remaining puddle. My embarrassment was offset by the expressions of wonder on the faces of the women on the bridge. On another occasion, I rappelled off a 40-foot-high pyramid-shaped training tower so fast that I swung back into its base and braked instantly when I reached the ground. Not once did I wonder about the safety of the anchor. Wiser now, I understand the errors that I survived.

Rappelling rapidly followed by rapid braking has something in common with a lead fall caught by a belayer. In both situations, dynamic impact forces have a shock effect on the gravity-accelerated rappeller or climber, belayer, anchors, and other elements in the system as you come to a stop. In a free fall of 15 feet followed by a sharp braking action, impact forces greater than 1,500 pounds, or far more than body weight, are transferred directly to the anchors on the tied-off end of the rappel rope, which more than likely is a tree or climbing protection in a crack. You might have seen this style of rappelling in old commercial advertisements that suggest you go around only once in life. How true! The anchors had better be good, or you are in for a ground fall.

Descending smoothly will keep impact forces nearer to your body weight, which can be held by a very small anchor (although most people want a beefy anchor for a large margin of safety). Look closely at that supposedly macho man in the old-time advertisements. You will see that he is tied in at the cliff edge and doesn't intend to go anywhere on rappel.

A rappeller on the way to disaster

not want to body rappel a full-length climb except in an emergency. That day has come and could come again, however, so it is worthwhile to know the technique.

To rappel using your right hand as your braking hand, straddle the rope, then pass it around your right hip, across your chest, over your left shoulder, and down your back to your right hand. To rappel left-handed, reverse the hip, shoulders, and braking hand. Do not make the error of braking with the hand that is on the same side as the rope as it goes around the shoulder (fig. 8-1B).

Both the body rappel and the arm rappel (following) are potentially dangerous because you are not tied directly to the rope. If you were to lose your balance during the descent, you could fall out of the rappel and get hurt. It is especially easy to fall out of an arm rappel.

An arm rappel is useful on exposed but low-angle slopes, such as slabs that you can walk down (fig. 8-2). Twist the rope around your arms so that it passes just below your shoulders. A small amount of friction is generated, which makes this technique more secure than walking down the rope hand over hand.

Figure-Eight Brakes

When you use a mechanical rappel device, you allow the metal surfaces to dissipate heat. They also allow for sharper bends in the rope, which

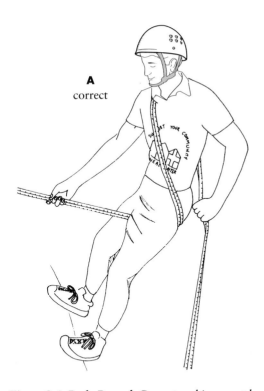

A
correct

B
incorrect

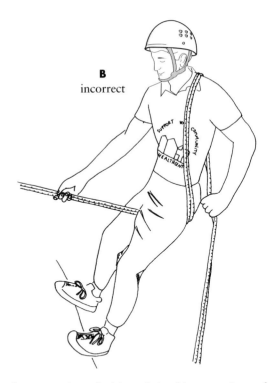

Figure 8-1. Body Rappel: *Correct and incorrect body rappels for a left-handed brake. Having your shoulder wrap on the same side as the hip wrap, as in B, is potentially dangerous because the shoulder wrap can come undone and you can fall out of the rappel. The danger is increased if you also brake with the hand on the same side as the hip and shoulder wrap. Instead, wrap the rope around the opposite shoulder (here the right) from the hip wrap, as shown in A, and brake with the hand on the opposite side as the shoulder wrap.*

makes it easier to lock off the rope during the rappel. The figure-eight descender (fig. 8-3) has long been used for general climbing. Several versions of the figure-eight are available. A figure-eight with an enlarged oblong attachment hole, for example, can double as a belaying device, and figure-eights with other modifications allow the brake to be used for rescue work.

To rappel, form a bight in the rope and slip it through the large hole of the device and over the outside of the smaller opening (rather than through it), as sketched in figure 8-4. Use a locking carabiner to clip through both the smaller hole and an attachment point on your harness (see Harness Carabiner Attachment for Rappelling photo page 56), to prevent the rope from coming off the brake accidentally.

Figure 8-2. Arm Rappel

Carabiner Brake

Many rappellers use a carabiner brake because it is effective and requires no gear other than the carabiners used as a normal part of protection-anchor systems. Oval and D-shaped carabiners work best; the shapes of offset D-shaped and bent-gate carabiners make it difficult to use them for this purpose. The brake can require up to six nonlocking carabiners (fig. 8-5); the labels in figure 8-5 help explain how to form the brake in figure 8-6.

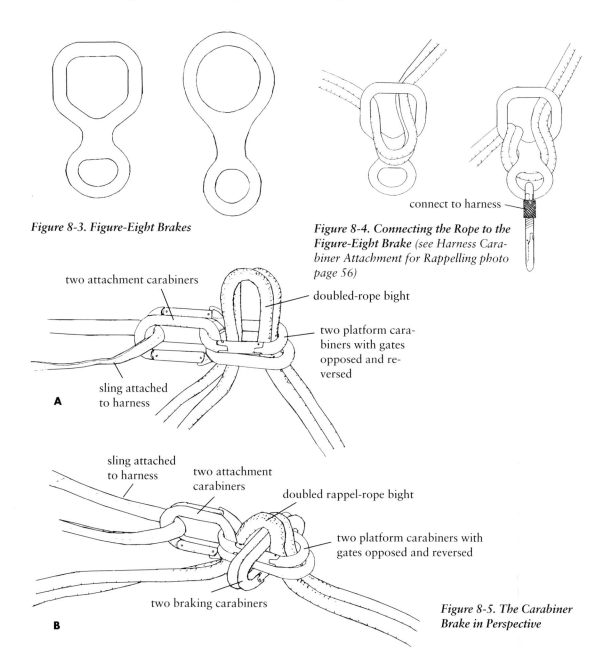

Figure 8-3. Figure-Eight Brakes

*Figure 8-4. **Connecting the Rope to the Figure-Eight Brake** (see Harness Carabiner Attachment for Rappelling photo page 56)*

connect to harness

A
two attachment carabiners
doubled-rope bight
two platform carabiners with gates opposed and reversed
sling attached to harness

B
sling attached to harness
two attachment carabiners
doubled rappel-rope bight
two platform carabiners with gates opposed and reversed
two braking carabiners

Figure 8-5. The Carabiner Brake in Perspective

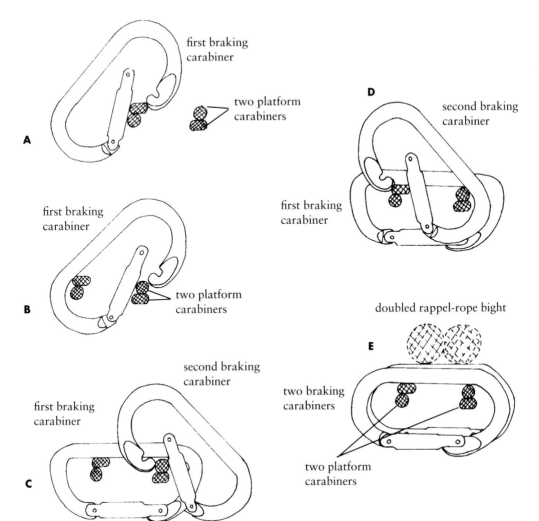

Figure 8-6. Weaving the Carabiner Brake in Cross Section: The completed brake shown in perspective view in figure 8-5B is also shown in cross-section view in figure 8-6E. The two attachment carabiners and attachment sling are shown in figure 8-5. For clarity, in figure 8-6, the doubled rappel-rope bight is not illustrated except in E.

A—Pass the first brake carabiner over the near side of the platform carabiners (cross-hatched) with the gate open and the carabiner's back angled at 45 degrees to the plane of the platform carabiners. Rotate the back of the first brake carabiner parallel to the plane of the platform carabiners, and the gate closes.

B—To pass over the far side of the platform carabiners, open the gate and again rotate the back of the first brake carabiner to a 45-degree angle to the plane of the platform carabiners.

C, D—Once across the far side of the platform carabiners, the back of the first brake carabiner rotates parallel to the plane of the platform carabiners and the gate closes again. If you use a second brake carabiner, start it from the opposite side so that you oppose the gates. The back of the second brake carabiner will be on the same side as the first to provide friction against the rope (C, D, and E).

E—This cross-sectional view of the complete carabiner brake is the same as the perspective view of figure 8-5B. When you finish this sequence, tighten the doubled-rope bight against the brake carabiners.

First, compare a cross section of the completed brake in figure 8-6E with the perspective view of figure 8-5B. The completed brake has two carabiners with opposed and reversed gates that form a platform that serves as a base for the brake. These platform carabiners are attached to the harness by means of two nonlocking attachment carabiners or one locking carabiner (see Harness Carabiner Attachment for Rappelling photo page 56). Friction in the brake is created by the solid backs of two opposed braking carabiners in contact with the bights of the doubled rappel rope, or of a single rappel-rope bight for a single-rope rappel.

To set up the brake, follow the sequence illustrated in figures 8-5 and 8-6. Attach two carabiners with gates opposed or a single locking carabiner to your harness, then attach two carabiners (to form a platform) with gates opposed and reversed perpendicular to the first carabiners. The opposed gates prevent accidental opening of the carabiners through side-loading of the gates. Next, form a bight in the doubled rappel rope and push it up through the platform carabiners. Weave one or two carabiners—the braking carabiners—across so that the doubled rappel rope comes to rest on the solid back of the brake carabiners when tightened. Whether you use one or two brake carabiners depends on the amount of friction required to control your rate of descent. You usually use two brake carabiners when rappelling with a single rope or when using a doubled rope on a steep drop. Rappels on gentler slopes might work with one brake carabiner.

BODY POSITION

A number of body positions are useful in rappelling when you are moving off the lip of a shelf, over overhangs, down slabs and faces, or down free drops. On most rappels, the most difficult physical (and mental) part is moving from a horizontal platform to a steep wall. Once on the steep wall, rappelling is usually easy and straightforward.

Before you rappel, tuck in all loose articles of clothing, hair, and equipment that could be acci-dentally drawn into the friction brake. To hook up the friction brake, face upslope, the direction that you will face during the rappel. This position prevents the rope from twisting as you attach it to the friction brake. For exposed starting positions, use a safety sling running from the anchor to your harness while you prepare to rappel. Unclip from the anchor only after you are attached to the rappel rope and begin the descent.

When you start backward on the horizontal platform, the brake usually provides too much friction, and it might be necessary to lift the rope to reduce friction. Walk backward toward the edge and continue to lift the rope until you go over the edge and need the additional friction to offset gravity.

The Edge Stance

At the edge, spread your feet widely to form a platform that keeps you stable (see photo below). Use this legs-apart position during the rappel to avoid swinging sideways across the cliff

Edge Stance

face. Push your midsection outward, tensioning the rope, so your legs are at an angle to the cliff face. This angle becomes greater as the cliff face becomes steeper and reaches an extreme on overhangs (see A in the photos at right). This position forces your feet against the wall and prevents them from slipping. Lean your upper body slightly backward, but stay upright enough to see foot placements clearly. This is the basic *edge stance*.

From this position, walk your feet down the cliff face, as you use whatever footholds are available while maintaining the edge stance. You can maintain this stance to the bottom of the cliff or assume one of the other stances described below, as the terrain and friction dictate.

Place one hand, the *guide hand*, above the friction brake, and the other hand, the *brake hand*, below the device (see photo previous page). The guide hand is usually the off hand (left hand for a right-handed person), which helps you balance. The rope passes smoothly through this hand during the rappel. You can also take your guide hand off the rope and use it to help push away from the rock or adjust your clothing.

The rappel braking hand acts like the belay braking hand and holds the rope against the friction brake. If you accidentally release the rope from your braking hand while rappelling, you will lose most of the friction it provided and lose control of your descent. For this reason, it is important to belay novice rappellers until they demonstrate competence. Even experienced climbers sometimes use safety backups, as discussed below.

You usually keep your braking hand below your body and wrap the rope around your hip

Face Stance. **A**—*A rappeller is in a modified edge stance.* **B**—*He swings into the rope's fall line as he* assumes the face stance to gain a better view and ease of rappelling.

Overhangs. A—Rappeller lowering his torso.

B—Stepping down with one foot.

for friction. The most comfortable position is to hold the braking hand against the crest of your hip bone. If you hold your braking hand high and away from your body, you increase the work that your biceps must do.

When you rappel on a single rope, pass the rope coming from the friction brake around your far hip and then around your back to your braking hand. Including the back of your hip and buttock as parts of the friction brake gives more control for rappelling.

The Face Stance

Once you have descended far enough for the rappel rope to contact the cliff edge, you can assume a *face stance* if the cliff is about 70 degrees or less. This position requires less effort. Rotate your body out of the edge stance so that an imaginary line connecting both hips is parallel to the rope and is in the fall line of the cliff. On lower-angle cliffs or on cliffs where there are abundant face holds, you can even rotate far enough to face down the cliff (see B in the photos on page 118).

The face stance might take a bit of adjustment, but it has two advantages. First, you can see where you are going and step from hold to hold as you descend, as though you were walking. You sacrifice lateral stability, so it is important to stay directly beneath the point where the rope passes over the edge of the cliff. This point marks the top of the fall line of the rappel and is the point underneath which you will swing if you slip. You can be out of the fall line and counteract the tendency to swing by pushing against face holds with your legs, but if you do slip you will swing back and forth like a pendulum before coming to rest in the fall line.

A second advantage of this position is that you can rest your braking hand against your hip, taking stress off your biceps. The face stance is definitely a faster and easier way to descend on less than vertical faces provided that you do not have too much or too little friction. You can quickly move back into an edge stance if you must pass over another lip during the rappel.

Steep Faces and Free Rappels

When descending a steep face, you usually stay in an edge stance with your feet almost perpendicular to the face. If the rappel is free, so that you hang directly on the rope and require additional friction for braking, you can obtain that friction by passing the rope from the brake down through your crotch and back up to your braking hand. This change in rope position adds the friction of the underside of your pants leg to the brake system. You can brace your braking hand against the bone structure of the upper outside surface of your leg to relieve the stress placed on your biceps.

As in all rappelling, you should descend smoothly and slowly. Avoid rapid acceleration followed by rapid deceleration because this motion produces forces that far exceed body weight alone and shock-loads your anchor.

Overhangs

To rappel an overhang, descend using the edge stance until the balls of both feet are on the lip of the overhang (see A in the photos previous page). Then slowly lower your buttocks well below the level of the lip until you can see the wall directly beneath the overhang. If the overhang is small, you can take one foot from the lip and brace against the wall underneath (see B in photos previous page), then follow with the second foot. Once both feet are on the wall, continue descending in the conventional manner.

If the overhang is wide enough to prevent bracing below the lip with your legs, your upper body and hands will swing back into the face above the lip. You want this to happen in the least painful manner. One method is to place your hip against the upper face of the overhang and descend slowly, being careful not to trap the fingers of your guide hand between the face and

the rope. Another method is to push off and descend rapidly; try to clear the overhang before you swing back in. Again, you must be careful not to injure your guide hand. This method stresses your anchor more than descending smoothly.

WORKING IN MIDRAPPEL

In order to stop in midrappel on lower-angle slabs to free a piece of protection, you can wrap the rope around your leg two to four times (fig. 8-7A). This position usually gives enough friction to allow the release of your braking hand so you can work. To add to the security of the leg wrap, you can also have someone on the ground tug lightly on the free end of the rope to give you a *ground belay*. (The ground belay is shown in fig. 8-8, where it is employed as an emergency belay.) On steep rappels, where you feel insecure about simply leaving the rope hanging as a source of friction, tie the free end of the rope around the standing end above the rappel brake (fig. 8-7B) or use a Prusik safety. Prusik safeties present their own problems, however, as noted in the following section.

SAFETY BACKUPS

There are four common ways to safeguard a rappel: double-check the entire system before you back over the edge, belay the rappeller, have the rappeller use a Prusik safety, and set up a ground belay. As noted at the beginning of this chapter, it is often desirable to safeguard rappellers, and safeguarding novices with a belay is mandatory (see "A Belaying System for Beginning Rappellers" under "Belay Systems for Groups" in chapter 17).

To set up a Prusik safety, place a Prusik knot on the rappel rope above the belay brake and attach it to your harness at the rappel attachment point. (The technique of tying a Prusik is explained in chapter 3, if you need a review.) The Prusik is useful for stopping in midrappel for extended periods, and—in theory—you can move the Prusik as you descend and it will catch you if you slip on

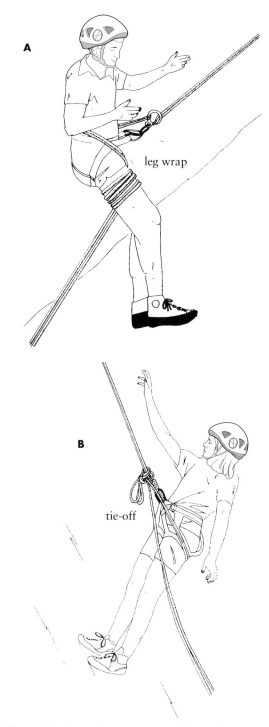

A

leg wrap

B

tie-off

Figure 8-7. Rappel Friction Wraps for Working in Midrappel

rappel device

brake hand

rappel device

leg-loop clip

AutoBlock Safety Backup

rappel. However, a number of problems make this system's use doubtful in an emergency.

The first problem involves overhangs. If the Prusik loop is too long, you can rappel below the overhang while the knot can tighten out of reach above it. Usually, the only solution is to use a pocket knife to cut the safety without cutting the tautly stretched rappel rope. The second problem is that the Prusik fails to tighten in many emergencies, and the friction of sliding down the rope partially melts the knot. It is easy to understand why this happens. The Prusik knot must be loose enough to slide but tight enough to stop a fall. The knot will not tighten automatically: it needs to be set (tightened and deformed) by the rappeller. In an emergency, rappellers hold the knot in a death grip and prevent it from deforming and catching. As a result, many Prusik safeties used on rappel fail.

If you set a Prusik knot to stop in midrappel

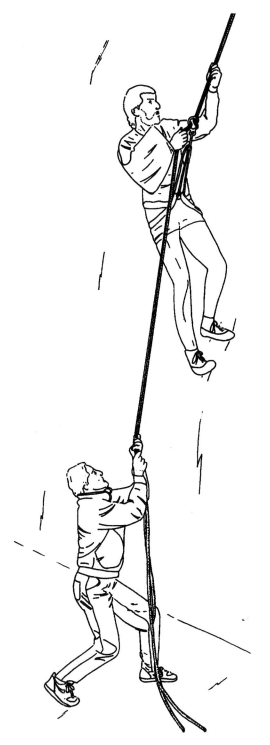

Figure 8-8. A Ground-Belay Safety Backup

—perhaps to remove a piece of protection that is stuck—you must loosen the knot before you can move on. Take your weight off the knot. Standing on a rock edge makes loosening simpler, but the stretched rope will tend to rebound when unweighted, carrying the Prusik knot upward and away from you. You can also bring your foot up fairly high and wrap the rappel rope around it a couple of times. Then bring the free end of the rappel rope up to your hand. Stand up and loosen the Prusik, thus allowing the rappel rope's free end to slip through your hand until the rappel brake loads fully and you can descend normally.

The AutoBlock (fig. 3-11) overcomes many of the problems presented by Prusik knots when used as a rappel safety. Set this knot *below* your rappel brake clipped to the leg loop on your brake hand side (see photo previous page), where it is prevented from getting caught in your rappel brake. When you rappel, hold the rope just above the AutoBlock with your brake hand to force it to slide as you feed rope through the brake; letting go should cause it to lock. You should test the AutoBlock at the top of the rappel before committing to the descent.

The ground belay is an emergency safety backup to use with injured rappellers and is controlled by a ground belayer who puts tension on the rappel rope (fig. 8-8). This tension increases the friction at the rappel brake. Do not use this belay routinely with beginners, who should be belayed with a top rope. The ground belayer can produce varying amounts of tension either by gripping the rope loosely or by sitting comfortably in a loop of rope. The belayer must be attentive in order to exercise control of the belay.

RAPPELLING SUMMARY

Because you usually rappel at the end of a hard day of climbing when you are tired, hungry, and dehydrated and have already spent physical and mental energy in the intense concentration of climbing, you are more likely to make mistakes than when you are fresh. Like all climbers, you tend to relax once you get to a large shelf that serves as a rappel station. As noted above, rappel anchors can be slings around marginal natural anchors, old fixed pitons with a tangle of rope-burned slings, or some other piece of gear that is not entirely safe. Add to this the fact that climbers do not wish to leave their personal gear behind, and the conditions are ripe for an accident. Gravity is a powerful force ready to accelerate the unwary to the ground.

Secure yourself at the rappel station, independent of the rappel rope and even the rappel anchor. Avoid being unfastened from anchors, and establish a backup anchor that will not be weighted unless the primary anchor fails. Examine the rappel anchors. Tie ropes together and have someone else check your knots before throwing the rope down, and also check the attachment of the rappel brake to you and your harness. Make sure your harness buckle is secure and that clothing and long hair are tucked in away from the rappel brake. Visually recheck the entire rappel system at the edge just before you lean back.

Set up a backup anchor and send down the heaviest person to test the system; then remove the backup and have the lightest person come last, descending as smoothly as possible. If you are not sure that the rope will reach the bottom of the cliff, tie a very large knot in each rope—a double figure-eight (fig. 8-9) or a single figure-eight with a carabiner through it that cannot possibly pass through a rappel device, even un-

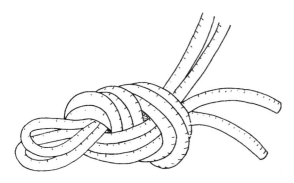

Figure 8-9. Double Figure-Eight Safety Knot to Prevent Rappelling Off the End of the Rope

der impact force, so that you cannot rappel off the end. More than one climber has rappelled off the rope end at the close of the day. The first person down should have Prusik slings available to ascend the rope if needed. Good habits can prevent accidents.

Rappel-Rope Retrieval

Climbers usually rappel on a single rope doubled around an anchor (for a half-length rappel) or two ropes tied together with a grapevine knot (for a full-length rappel). If you are rappelling the route you climbed, there should be no problem reaching each belay station with two ropes. The grapevine knot, however, can get stuck when you pull the rope unless you take precautions. When you set up the rappel rope, place the knot on one side of the anchor. Later, you will pull that side of the rope; if you don't, the knot could hang up in the anchor. Climbers routinely quiz each other about which rope to pull to focus their attention and impress the information on their mind. On multipitch rappels, you pull one rope after the first rappel, pull the second rope after the second rappel, and alternate thereafter. This system allows you to thread the lower rope (the end being pulled) through the lower anchor to expedite the process.

A second problem is that the knot joining two ropes can hang up at the edge of the rappel platform if the edge is a sharp lip. When there is a platform just below the lip, begin the rappel as usual, step down to the platform, and readjust the position of the knot so that it hangs over the lip. If you are rappelling on a red rope and a purple rope, for example, and you will be pulling purple, then feed red through the brake until the knot moves to where you want it. Remain attached to the rappel at all times, or attach yourself to protection pieces placed at the stance as you remove the rappel brake and adjust the knot position.

You can also prevent a knot from hanging up at the lip by changing the angle from which you pull it. If you are on the ground, seize the rope and walk directly away from the cliff, decreasing the 90-degree bend in the rope at the lip and thus

Memorable Rappels

With experience, rappels from small cliffs blend together and slip gently into recesses of memory. Memorable rappels are usually scary. I remember one from atop Mt. Asgard, just north of the Arctic Circle on Baffin Island. Topping out after a midnight-sun ascent, we saw clouds rolling in from Cumberland Sound. Realizing that our predicted 24-hour window of good weather was about up, we quickly started back down. Tom went last on the outrageous rappel from the top, but, from then on, it was my duty. Going last gave me time to reflect on just how far north and how isolated we were. By the ninth rappel, my mind began playing tricks. Fears that I had been holding at bay grew until another friend, Chris, took over the somber duty until we reached the exit snowfields below. Mental and physical fatigue arrived with the darkest period of the 24-hour day and forced us, euphoric with our success, to stop for a few hours before descending to our tents.

Another memorable rappel was done from poor anchors, established as though by Braille in the dark and used only because there appeared to be little other choice. Then, there was a long free rappel from the Maiden, high above Colorado's Eldorado Canyon, where I could overcome vertigo, induced by slowly twisting in the wind, only by closing my eyes.

I remember only one rappel with pleasure and a smile. When Gene and I climbed the North Face of the Grand Teton, we reached the summit just before dark and descended to a bivouac above the rappel station on the Owen-Spalding route. We snuggled deep into our lightweight, cold sleeping bags and awaited the first guided party to appear with a second rope needed for the rappel. When the party appeared, I brazenly asked if we could "have a ride down your rope." The guide, whom I recognized as a famous climber, agreed but told us to be careful because there were "loose rocks at the edge." Not wanting him to think that we came up an easy route, I answered that we had come up the North Face and had found plenty of loose rocks both underfoot and overhead. The guide's eyes opened wide. Extending his hand and introducing himself, he explained in friendly fashion and evident respect that he himself had not yet done the North Face. He spoke loudly to his clients: "Make way! Make way! These men have come up the North Face." With that wonderful proclamation in our ears, we backed out over the void.

---

reducing friction. (Some climbers rig up the rappel rope high in a cliff-side tree to reduce the angle. This procedure is not recommended, even with a large tree, because it produces a levering action that could pull the shallow root systems out of cliff-top soils and cause the anchor to fail.)

The rope itself can get caught if there are trees in the fall line of the rappel. To prevent this situation, walk away from the trees, parallel to the cliff base, to change the area in which the rope will fall. Just as the rope goes over the edge, give the rope a good jerk to pull it away from the trees. This technique is also useful if it appears that the rappel rope might hang up in a crack directly under the rappel point.

If the rappel rope does catch on a tree or in a crack, try pulling on the opposite rope to free the stuck point. You can also try walking away from the cliff or along the cliff to change the direction of pull.

To take a seemingly welded grapevine knot apart, see chapter 3, figure 3-7. Once one of the loops of the knot is loose, the knot comes apart easily.

When the Rope Gets Stuck

Sometimes, no matter what you do, the rope gets stuck firmly, and you must reascend the cliff to retrieve it. If you have a second rope, simply reclimb the pitch. If the rope is taut from the anchor to the ground and both ends of the rope are available, you can climb the rope safely with ascenders, Prusik knots, or Bachmann knots. If there is a lot of slack, you might be able to lead the pitch on aid by using the slack as a lead rope. If one of these strategies does not work, call for help and remember that, in most environmental conditions, a night out on the cliff will not harm you. On the contrary, it provides fodder for colorful stories you can tell your friends.

What remains are the desperate options that arise as you climb a stuck rope that can come unstuck under your weight. If you cannot secure help and if the weather or other conditions dictate that you must get off the route, your options are limited to potentially dangerous techniques. If only one end of the rappel rope reaches you, you might tie it off and Prusik up; frequently place nuts below you in case the rope suddenly comes unstuck. Tie into any slack below you with a knot attached to your harness by means of a carabiner. As you ascend, attach yourself to higher and higher knots in the rope and keep putting in the protection. Should the stuck end free itself, you will fall onto the rope that you are ascending, protected by the pieces that you placed, the Prusik, and the backup knot.

As a last resort, alpine climbers high on the mountain sometimes stretch a stuck rope as much as possible before cutting it and use the length salvaged for further descent. After the descent, these short lengths make great tie-downs.

Leading Rock

INTRODUCTION

This chapter explores leading, from getting started to getting down. It discusses ways to prepare for your first lead, outlines information you need to lead climbs on sight (without having climbed them before), and provides suggestions for racking gear, placing protection, and traversing. Even if you do not lead now, it is worth reading this material because you will better understand what goes on at the other end of the rope. This chapter also covers tying off a fallen climber, climbing with style, and getting down from a climb—information of use to both leaders and seconds.

STARTING OUT

Although climbing on a top rope can be physically demanding and give much satisfaction, there can be an even greater challenge and satisfaction in leading (see photo at right). The leader not only has to climb, but he or she also has to figure out where the route goes, place the

protection, and risk a fall. These activities can demand great mental and physical effort. The second, on the other hand, follows the route and takes out the protection while having an overhead belay.

Many climbers refer to leading as being on the *sharp end* of the rope because it can be dangerous to climb above protection. Making a major mistake can lead to serious injury. Once you start leading, however, it is hard to top-rope or follow exclusively. To lead well, you need solid movement skills, a high degree of concentration, and a realistic grasp of your ability to solve problems while on the climb. Given the penalties of making a mistake, how do you learn to lead safely?

Most people learn to lead by climbing with fellow climbers. This system works well if the other climbers are experienced, have empathy, and impart good safety habits. You can assess your friends' technical expertise by reading climbing books and watching other climbers. Also pay attention to how they talk about climbing, treat equipment, and relate to other people. But climbers may move well, treat their equipment well, and be considerate of others, yet be unable to teach you how to climb safely. Where does this leave you?

Many clubs provide instruction by experienced climbers. Indeed, the Sierra Club, Appalachian Mountain Club, Mazamas, and other organizations played an important role in the early development of the sport. College outing clubs also have a time-honored role in educating fledgling leaders. More and more colleges and universities offer semester-length climbing courses for credit as part of professional outdoor leadership programs (this book is to a large extent the outgrowth of one of these programs), and others offer climbing courses of shorter duration as a student activity.

Guide services offer basic, intermediate, and advanced climbing lessons. Guides generally are dedicated individuals who enjoy the sport so much that they climb for recreation as well as employment. Experienced guides who have worked with fledgling leaders can anticipate mistakes well before you make them. The American Mountain Guides Association accredits many guide services and individual guides in the United States. In Canada, the Canadian Guide Association is the accrediting body.

LEARNING TO LEAD ADVENTURE CLIMBS

To experience the sharp end of the rope, you may want to begin leading on bolt-protected "sport" climbs, where movement skills are more important than knowing how to protect. Indeed, a handful of short quickdraw slings with carabiners and a few longer slings for a bolted belay anchor are all that you need to protect yourself. *Adventure climbs* emphasize skills in route finding and protecting as well as skills in movement.

Before leading, you should have developed good movement skills by bouldering and following experienced leaders on roped climbs. You can learn a lot by placing protection and arranging anchors while standing at the bottom of the cliff. Start by experimenting with passive nuts, such as tapers and Hexcentrics; testing each piece in a variety of placements; and learning to slot, cam, and set to develop an "eye" for a crack. Then practice with spring-loaded camming devices (SLCDs). You will find that you can slot an SLCD and improve placements over simple camming alone.

When you have mastered placing protection at ground level, try the following strategies to prepare for leading a first pitch:

- Climb and down-climb a short pitch on a top rope. You can even climb with a small- to moderate-size pack as a handicap; when you climb without it, you will feel even more secure. If you can down-climb the pitch smoothly, you will be able to lead it.

- Ask an experienced friend to lead an easily protected climb, then pull the rope and leave

The Art of Leading

the protection in place; your friend then rappels or walks and belays you from below. Now you lead the pitch and clip into the protection as you go: your aim is to learn the moves. Climb a second time and concentrate on becoming familiar with the size, placement, and kind of protection. Next, strip the protection from the climb and lead the climb by using only these protection pieces on the rack. Finally, take a complete rack and lead the climb.

- To learn how to place dependable protection, lead a short crack on aid that takes nut protection easily. Choose a vertical crack that widens and narrows frequently, so that it is easy to place well-seated protection. After you place each piece, attach an *etrier* (a special short ladder made of flat webbing) and stand in it. The reality of putting your weight on the protection (*aiding*) will help you think carefully about whether each piece is well placed. You will also find out which placements actually work. Keep the climb short— 20 to 30 feet—because aiding takes time. You normally will drop only 2 to 3 feet in an easy aid crack if you do not commit gross errors that lead to pulling out all of the pieces. Oppose the lowermost nuts, as discussed later in this chapter, to counter this possibility.

Another advantage of aiding a crack is that you will get in the habit of placing protection at regular, close intervals. Some new leaders have a tendency to skip protection on easy sections because they "know" they will not fall. Protecting easy sections, however, develops your skills and also helps protect hard sections because protection is the total of all pieces.

Not everyone will want to follow these strategies. Some climbers want to jump on challenging climbs right from the start. But because there is the potential for accident (and even death) in adventure leading, you are well advised to learn step by step and develop solid skills in placing protection before you lead climbs that are at the limit of your climbing ability.

When you start leading, choose climbs that you have climbed before as a second, or toproped, so you know what to expect. A good first adventure lead is many grades beneath what you can follow or what you can lead when clipping bolts. Choose a climb that protects well, one with good cracks or flakes and one that has good stances so you can take the time necessary to sort through your gear rack to get just the right size nut to fit into a crack. Novice adventure leaders who are able to race up difficult climbs on a top rope or with bolted protection need to adopt a different pace in order to learn how to place protection on easy to moderate climbs. You should not be anywhere near your physical ability when learning to place protection. These early climbs should build a solid base for more difficult leads to come. An experienced leader can direct a novice leader to climbs that fit these requirements and give helpful hints while on the climb.

Choosing On-Sight Leads

Leading a climb with which you are unfamiliar is called an *on-sight lead*. Unless you are a very good climber, you will probably want to consult a guidebook to find climbs that are the right level of physical difficulty for you and that promise to be well protected. There are two types of guides: the descriptive style and the topographic (topo) style. Both types commonly use photographs to help describe the major rock features on a route. The descriptive guides, written as narrative, detail the general characteristics of a climb, such as its length, rating, and main features. For example:

Pitch 1. 120 feet, 5.8. Follow an overhang that diagonals up to the left for about 20 feet and then forms an inside corner. Climb this section with a delicate combination of lieback and friction. Above follow a crack with a small pine tree up to a birch. Reach a second birch and a belay stance after a short friction pitch.

The descriptive guide is useful if there are a limited number of climbs in an area, but it can be cumbersome if you want information, for example, about the 34-pitch Nose Route on El Capitan or the thousands of pitches in Yosemite Valley. The topo-style guidebook uses symbols as climbing shorthand, so that multipitch climbs can be described on a single page. Figure 9-1 is a topo of a typical climb. Topos contain notes about special features, for example, that a pitch is 180 feet long and sustained at its grade. The author might add comments, based on opinion or other sources of information about the climb—for instance, that the pitch is ugly.

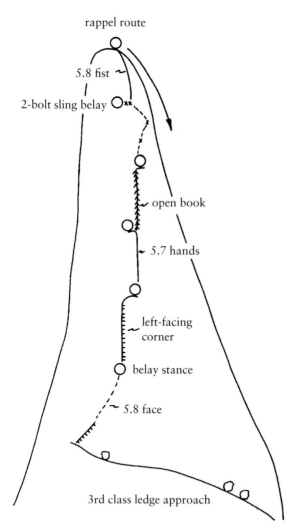

Figure 9-1. A Guidebook Topo

Labels in figure: rappel route; 5.8 fist; 2-bolt sling belay; open book; 5.7 hands; left-facing corner; belay stance; 5.8 face; 3rd class ledge approach

RATING ROCK

When you choose a climb, you may well ask: How hard is it? What techniques does it require—lieback, face, mantling, or crack? How long will the climb take? How difficult is it to protect? Is it a high-quality climb?

Yosemite Decimal System

The difficulty level of a climb is given as a *rating*. The initial rating system used in the United States was adopted by the Sierra Club from an early European system. At that time, the Sierra Club rated climbs from easy to very severe, the latter being a category that was undefined at the time. In the 1950s, a different system was introduced. Climbs were rated according to difficulty, ranging from class 1 (a scramble where hands are not needed) to class 5 (a climb that requires both rope and protection for safety). There was, however, no way to distinguish very easy from very hard class 5 climbs, a problem that showed up at Tahquitz Rock in Southern California, where most of the climbs were class 5. Climbers added decimals to subdivide the class, with 5.0 (read "five-o") being the easiest and 5.9 (read "five-nine") being the hardest.

For many years, the decimal subdivision system was closed; that is, no climb could be rated higher than 5.9. Then class 5.10 was added to represent what was considered to be the hardest possible free climb at the time. (Aided climbs are rated differently, A1 to A5, based on the difficulty of placing aid, the security of the aid once placed, and potential fall distance. Some aid climbs might later go free, thus changing the rating (e.g., an A2 crack might go free at 5.10.) The system, with modifications, was accepted for use in Yosemite and has become known as the *Yosemite Decimal System (YDS)*, the standard within the United States.

Usually, each area has a number of well-established climbs that serve as the standard of their grades. The best way to discover the nature of a 5.6 climb is, of course, to climb one. The problem is that cracks, faces, liebacks, mantles, or climbs requiring stemming might all be rated 5.6, but one will seem harder or easier than another to a specific climber because of the climber's particular skills. For this reason, climbers often classify climbs both as to level of difficulty and type—for example, a 5.6 crack. This gives information about the difficulty of applying specific techniques to the climb.

When you gain enough experience on different levels and types of climbs, the rating serves as a short description of each climb. If you have the skills to lead cracks where you must jam and protect at grades up to 5.8, but you can lead bolt-protected face climbs up to 5.10, you can easily choose climbs that are appropriate to your level.

Eventually, the YDS 5.10 grade contained climbs that were as different from one another as the original 5.7 was from 5.10. To accommodate new climbs that are harder than those previously established, the system currently uses the letters *a*, *b*, *c*, and *d*. A 5.10a is significantly easier than a 5.10d, though you might find 5.10b moves on a climb that is generally a 5.10a.

Some guidebooks use a three-tier system that grades difficult climbs as normal, plus, or minus: 5.10, 5.10– or 5.10+, but this system apparently is being slowly replaced by the four-tier letter system (a through d).

The 1970s saw a dramatic increase in hard free-climbing, which provided the stimulus to open up the grading system beyond 5.10, so some climbs are now rated at 5.11, 5.12, 5.13, and even 5.14 grades, each of which is in turn subdivided into a, b, c, and d levels. Further evaluation and definition of the grading system are possible and even probable, since climbing is demonstrably not a static sport.

The original YDS rating system graded the crux of a climb, but, in Yosemite, where climbs followed long cracks that demanded endurance as well as the ability to do a crux move, the rating became that of the entire climb. You might grade a crack 5.7 if there is a moderately difficult move or sequence of moves with easier climbing before and after. A nearby crack could have a succession of moves of the same difficulty as the crux of the 5.7 crack for the length of the climb. The second crack would receive a much higher grade—5.9, perhaps. Face climbs, on the other hand, are sometimes graded by their hardest move. Route topos often specify the individual grades of difficult sections, whether in a crack or on a face. There are many subtle variables in rating. One 5.9 might have moves that favor a short person, whereas another 5.9 might favor someone with a long reach. You will always find some climbs that are harder at their grade than others. Although they may be frustrating, savor these climbs: you can weave them into tales that you tell around the campfire.

Because climbers travel from area to area, the YDS has been applied in a relatively standard manner within the United States, with allowance for local peculiarities in the rock.

Commitment Grades

Commitment grades, denoted in roman numerals I through VI, describe the time that experienced competent climbers can expect to spend on a route, excluding the approach and descent. A grade III route in the mountains will take far longer to approach, climb, and descend than a grade III on a big roadside cliff. Expert climbers might be able to climb very much faster than even experienced competent climbers. Indeed, expert climbers have climbed two grade VI climbs on El Capitan in a single day; experienced competent climbers expect to spend two or more days on each of these climbs.

Table 9-1 shows the normal length of time required to climb various grades as well as the characteristic lengths of these grades.

Table 9-1. Table of Commitment Grades

Grade	Normal Time	Characteristic Length
I	1 to 3 hours	A few pitches
II	3 to 4 hours	2 to 4 pitches
III	4 to 7 hours ("short day")	3 to 8 pitches
IV	7 to 10 hours ("full day")*	6 to 12 pitches
V	1 to 2 days	10 to 18 pitches
VI	2 days or more	15+ ("big wall")

Quality and Danger Ratings

Some climbing guides use quality and danger ratings to give more information about specific climbs. Quality ratings commonly use one to four stars (*). A one-star route has at least one characteristic, such as a short sustained section with good rock, that makes it a better than average climb. Routes with the highest number of stars indicate that the route is one of the best in the area. Since quality is rated by the author of the guidebook, the determination is not standardized, but you will find it a generally good recommendation if you are new to an area.

Danger ratings, representing the author's opinion or local consensus, tell you how difficult it is to place protection on a climb. If a guidebook uses this rating system, the absence of a rating usually indicates that the route contains the normal protection possibilities for the area. An R rating indicates that protection is difficult to place or that little protection is available.

The most dangerous pitches are usually X-rated, and you should be extremely cautious; they are not suitable for an inexperienced leader. If you must climb one of these routes, try to find a local climber who has done it many times to guide you, but don't be surprised if you cannot. Many climbers take on X-rated routes once in a lifetime, if at all.

RACKING GEAR

It is the leader's responsibility to decide what to take on a climb. The collection of protection and slings that you take makes up the rack. Most climbers carry a general rack containing gear that will fit a range of possibilities, from thin to fist-size cracks. This gear can be racked on a runner-strength sling designed to slip over the climber's head and one shoulder, or it can be racked on harness loops, depending on both the climber's preference and the nature of the climb. An organized shoulder rack might contain three quickdraw slings for clipping fixed protection, a complete set of small wired steel or brass micronuts, three small wire tapers, four or five

A Rack for a Large Crack

larger wire tapers, two three-cam units (TCUs), the four smallest Tricams, SLCDs to fit a crack range, and a large Hexcentric; eight full-length slings to lessen rope drag, and one double sling for setting up an anchor. The micronuts fit on one carabiner and the wire tapers on another; generally each of the other pieces should have its own carabiner for ease of access. Three to five additional carabiners might be carried for use as needed.

If you know from inspection, a guidebook, or word of mouth that your climb is in an off-width crack, you can leave behind the micronuts and add large crack protection or be prepared to go without (see photo above). If your route is a bolted face climb, you can leave behind most of the rack and take only quickdraws and a few longer slings, plus perhaps a few Tricams to fit small pockets or micronuts for anticipated cracks. You would take quickdraws and a few longer slings.

How you place individual pieces on a rack, and their order, is determined by your need to take them off quickly with one hand. Most climbers consider nut size and type as well as the kind of climb in organizing their racks.

A single nut on a carabiner goes onto the gear sling with the gate up and against your body. When you rack a number of small nuts on a single carabiner, you can leave the carabiner on the rack, gate facing outward, to make individual nut removal easier, or you can remove the carabiner with all of the small nuts still attached and attempt to place one of the nuts. If you need the next size of nut, it is already in your hand and you can insert it directly into the crack. You would then put the carabiner and remaining nuts back on the rack and use a free carabiner to attach the nut placed in the rock to the rope.

During a climb, you may stop on a stance and estimate what gear you will need for the next few moves or section, then move this gear to an accessible position on the rack.

Tension can arise when two climbers organize their racks differently and swap the rack as they alternate leads. To avoid this problem, carry your own gear sling. When you are the second, as you climb, you can put gear for the climb on your rack the way you want it and obtain the unused gear at the belay stance. If you are not going to lead the next pitch, you can make the leader's job much simpler by reracking systematically and use the leader's arrangement.

When following, place each nut on a single carabiner and all nuts on a single shoulder-length gear sling. Take apart each sling created by the leader as you go and reduce complex configurations to single slings whenever stances permit. Shoulder-length slings will usually have one carabiner on them, and quickdraws will usually have two carabiners. With this method, when you arrive at the belay stance, you can reorganize the gear rack quickly with less likelihood of dropping gear.

If you climb overhanging rock or mainly use quickdraws on bolted climbs, you might find it more convenient to rack gear on the waist loops of your climbing harness, since a shoulder-length gear sling would swing backward. You might find that it is easier to clip carabiner gates out at the waist rather than in. Specialized chest harnesses are also commercially available to rack gear for big wall and overhanging free climbs.

To avoid dropping gear in the process of switching it from one person to another, make sure that both climbers are clipped to the anchor (to free up their hands). Remove one basic unit of gear at a time, such as a nut with attached carabiner, and pass that unit to the other person. Make eye contact: do not rely on a tug to tell you that the gear is secured. This process is similar to how a nurse hands a doctor a scalpel in the operating room over the table; like a knife plunging into the patient, a Hex plunging into the void will create problems. Often, you need only turn to one side so the other person can remove the gear from your rack, thus limiting the number of hands involved in the operation. You can hand all shoulder-length slings to the other person at one time.

If you are alternating leads and you led the last pitch, the rope is stacked properly and your partner is ready to climb. If you are to continue, the rope must be restacked. Your partner can restack as you finish racking.

PROTECTING THE BELAY

When you start a lead, place the first piece of protection to aim the belay and prevent the belay anchor from having to absorb high impact force if you fall. You place the first piece of protection early to protect the primary anchor, the belayer, and ultimately yourself. Additional pieces of protection also protect the belay by reducing potential fall forces on the system as well as shortening fall distances.

When the Belayer Is to the Side

When the belayer is not directly at the base of a climb, there is always the danger that the climbing rope will cause the first piece of protection to rotate so that it pulls out. Should this happen, subsequent pieces can fail, creating a domino effect that destroys, or *unzips,* all your protection. As a result, you need to make sure the first piece of protection is nondirectional so it will not pull out. The way to do this, if you are using nuts, is to oppose them.

Forces on Opposed Nuts

Use opposed nuts to prevent a nut from pulling out whenever there is potential for both downward and upward pulls. Situations where this might occur are at a belay and at the end of a traverse followed by a vertical section. Wired nuts in particular are prone to rotating out of the crack with even slight amounts of traversing. Do not create a pulley system that multiplies the load on the anchor, as illustrated in figure 9-2. If the climber falls, the resulting force is applied on the climbing rope in the vicinity of the first carabiner (fig. 9-2B), which would result in a doubling of the force. (This assumes that there is no friction in the system, including that of the rope sliding through the carabiner.)

The force on the upper nut will be approximately four times the force experienced by the falling leader because the whole nut-sling system acts as a pulley. First, the falling leader exerts a force that the belayer resists; the sum of these two forces tugs on carabiner 1 in figure 9-2B. Carabiner 1 then exerts a pull on carabiner 2 that is resisted by the lower nut (3); the forces of carabiner 1 and 3 tug on carabiner 2. As a result, carabiner 2 experiences a force twice that experienced by carabiner 1, which was already double that of the falling leader. As a result, carabiner 2 and the upper nut (4) attached to it experience an undesirable *load multiplication* of four times the impact force on the falling leader. The topic of load multiplication is covered in detail in chapter 10.

Avoid the pulley effect by fastening the sling of the lower nut directly to the carabiner (2 in fig. 9-2B) attached to the upper nut without slack, as shown in figure 9-3. Intermediate slings from the lower nut to carabiner 2 can be single, double, or triple. They can be wrapped one or

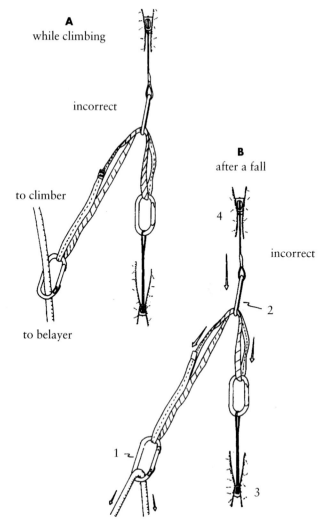

Figure 9-2. Creating Pulley Systems with Opposed Nuts: Both A and B are incorrect procedures.

more times around carabiner 2, in combination with doubling.

The clove hitch shown is hard to do in the field—you will need to use trial and error to some extent—because setting up opposed nuts often must be done one-handed while you are hanging on or in a precarious state of balance. If you can stand at the placement, use the clove hitch. If you need a simpler method, you can extend a sling from the lower nut through carabiner 2 as though you were going to create a

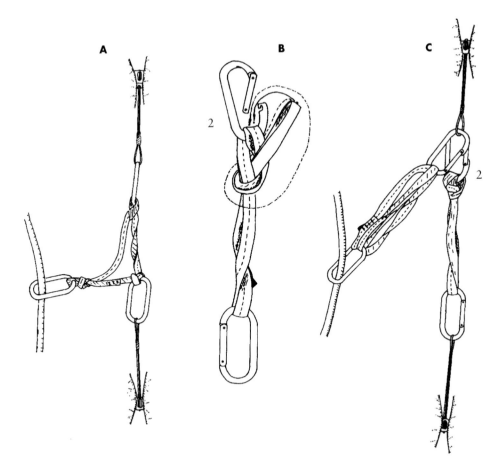

Figure 9-3. Avoiding Pulley Systems by Tying Off Nuts in Opposition: A—Clove hitches were used to connect the two nuts and join the opposed nuts to the rope. B—The trial-and-error method was used to make a taut connection between the nuts. A sling was wrapped around the carabiner twice in the process of doubling the sling. A separate sling was doubled and used to connect the protection to the rope.

pulley system. Then tie an overhand knot snugly against carabiner 2, and slip the free end of this sling over the gate end of carabiner two, as illustrated. This is not the ideal solution because shock in the knot might allow it to slip. But if you are hanging on with one hand, it presents a quickly realized solution of greater merit than the pulley system.

PLACING PROTECTION

Place protection often enough to keep yourself from hitting a ledge (see photo at right). With slack and rope stretch, you might easily fall twice as far below your last piece of protection as you were above it. You usually set protection, to prevent movement, by giving it a tug that causes rock crystals to bite into the nut faces. Be careful not to tug so hard as to make it difficult for your second to remove the nut. Sometimes you will place a piece of protection that you know is hung up on tiny crystals but would not catch a fall. Consider ahead of time what you will do when you are "maxed out." You might not fall, but if you leave inadequate protection, the thought of a long fall could inhibit your climbing—as well as keep you awake at night thinking about what might have been.

Placing protection correctly can allow you to relax and give you renewed energy that you did not expect so that you find you are not at your limit after all. And if you do rest on aid, you can always come back another day.

Clipping in with One Hand

When you lead free climbs where you can stand on two feet, you usually place protection as high as possible to give yourself a top rope for a short distance. The belayer pays out slack while you pull it overhead with one hand and clip into a carabiner that you stabilize with the other hand. This procedure requires two free hands. On difficult, or sustained, climbs you hang on with one hand and clip the rope with the other (see photo lower right and fig. 9-4); sometimes (as suggested by the name of a slab climb in Tuolumne Meadows, Too Thin to Clip In) you do not want to let go with either hand. Clipping

in can be the crux of a climb. As a last resort to prevent a fall on a sustained climb, hang onto your protection with one hand (using it as aid) while you clip with the other.

In a typical example of what you want to avoid when leading a sustained crack climb, you place protection overhead and start to pull up the rope to clip it in. In the process, the carabiner swings, inaccessible, into the crack. You sigh, drop the rope, move the carabiner out of the crack, and start anew. On the second attempt, you get closer. You hold the carabiner out of the crack as you lift the rope to the gate. The gate does not open, and the carabiner rotates against the rope to a position where clipping is impossible. In the meantime, you are trying not to fall off the climb.

How does a leader clip in? On sustained climbs, many leaders use bent-gate carabiners on the lower end of a quickdraw or on the sling

Place Protection Often

Clipping Protection Can Be Difficult

of a protection piece. Bent-gate carabiners are easier to clip than straight-gate carabiners because they help channel the rope into the gate, and their gate spring may be less stiff than that of a straight-gate carabiner. (On the other hand, straight-gate carabiners give added security that the rope will stay clipped.)

If you are using straight-gate carabiners with stiff springs, use the following method to clip in. Place the tip of your ring finger through the bottom of the carabiner and pull downward to stabilize it. The carabiner gate must face your thumb. If you use your middle finger, which is

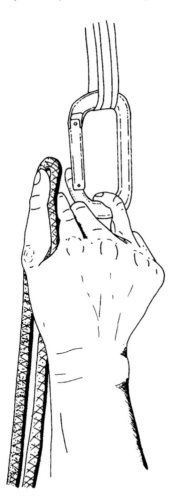

Figure 9-4. One-Handed Clip Using the Ring-Finger Pad: Stabilize the carabiner with the pad. Do not put your entire finger through the carabiner lest you fall.

larger, you will find that it is more difficult to slip the rope through the gate (fig. 9-4). Do not insert your entire finger into the carabiner, lest you fall and leave the finger behind. Finally, push the rope through the gate with your thumb and relax—you are clipped.

In another technique of one-handed clipping, you clip the rope near your harness tie-in point with a quickdraw, ask the belayer for slack, and then lift both the rope and quickdraw to clip the upper quickdraw carabiner to the protection.

You should learn to clip in with either hand. Practice clipping one-handed while sitting in your living room and on easy climbs, so you can do it quickly when you arrive at the "moment of truth" on a hard climb.

As a general rule on sustained climbs, place your protection low, somewhere between your waist and head. You will find it easier to clip and get positive protection, even if you do not get the security of protection above your head.

USING TWO ROPES

In *double-rope technique*, you use two ropes that are approximately 9 millimeters in diameter. This technique has several advantages, offset to some degree by the difficulty of managing two ropes. First, you can reduce rope drag by arranging both ropes in paths without sharp bends, and, second, you can reduce potential fall distance as you clip in (fig. 9-5). This system takes forethought as well as cooperation with the belayer. It helps if you use two different-color ropes. You use the left-hand rope, say, red, for protection on the left, and the right-hand rope, perhaps blue, for the right-hand protection. When you arrive at a piece of protection on the right, the belayer pays out slack in the blue rope without changing the tension of the red rope. If your belayer is out of sight, you might have to ask for slack on blue. This process is tricky with either a waist belay or a belay device, but it can be mastered with experience. It is important that you not negate the advantages of the double rope by twisting the two ropes together, which would produce sharp

bends, friction, and rope drag. A watchful belayer will help keep the ropes straight.

There is a second advantage to climbing on
double ropes. In figure 9-5, the leader is clipping the right-hand rope into protection and
has pulled up slack for this purpose. There is no
additional slack in the left-hand rope. Should
the leader fall while clipping in the right-hand
rope, the fall length would be twice the distance
from the leader to the last piece of protection
for the left-hand rope, plus rope stretch. In contrast, when you use a single rope, you pull up
slack in the rope that will catch the fall, thus
lengthening the potential fall distance. The fall
length will be twice the distance to the last piece
of protection, plus rope stretch, plus the
amount of slack needed to clip in, as well as the
stretch of the rope at the bottom of the fall.
Thus, if you fall while clipping using a single
rope, you can go quite a bit farther than with a
double rope.

A double rope is an advantage when you rappel: it gives you two ropes at all times with only
a slight increase in weight over a single rope.
You do have to manage the additional rope and
bear the cost of buying it, but these disadvantages do not outweigh the advantages of the
added strength.

In the UIAA test for double ropes, only one
of the two ropes is tested using a 50-kilogram
weight instead of the 80-kilogram weight for
ropes meant to be used alone.

As distinguished from double ropes, the
evolving *twin-rope* technique employs two
small-diameter ropes that are clipped through
the same protection pieces on separate carabiners, at least for the first few pieces where potential impact forces are high. (These ropes also
can have a wider diameter for the first few feet
and taper to a smaller diameter farther along on
the rope.) Higher on the climb, where potential
impact forces are lower, you can clip the rope
through separate protection pieces as you would
a double rope. The light weight of these ropes is
suited to extremely difficult gymnastic climbs
where you need the lightest possible rope that
has the advantages of a double rope.

ROPE DRAG

It is important to place protection so that it will
not create undue drag on the rope. An inexperienced leader might inadvertently create a problem of rope drag, as shown in figure 9-6, where
the leader placed two pieces of protection beneath an overhang and then climbed up to the
right.

The climber has produced two sharp turns in
the rope, which dramatically increases the

Figure 9-5. Double-Rope Technique

Figure 9-6. Rope Drag: A—The leader has inadvertently formed two nearly right angles in the rope and thereby created significant rope drag. B—Using longer slings, the leader straightens out the rope path to decrease rope drag.

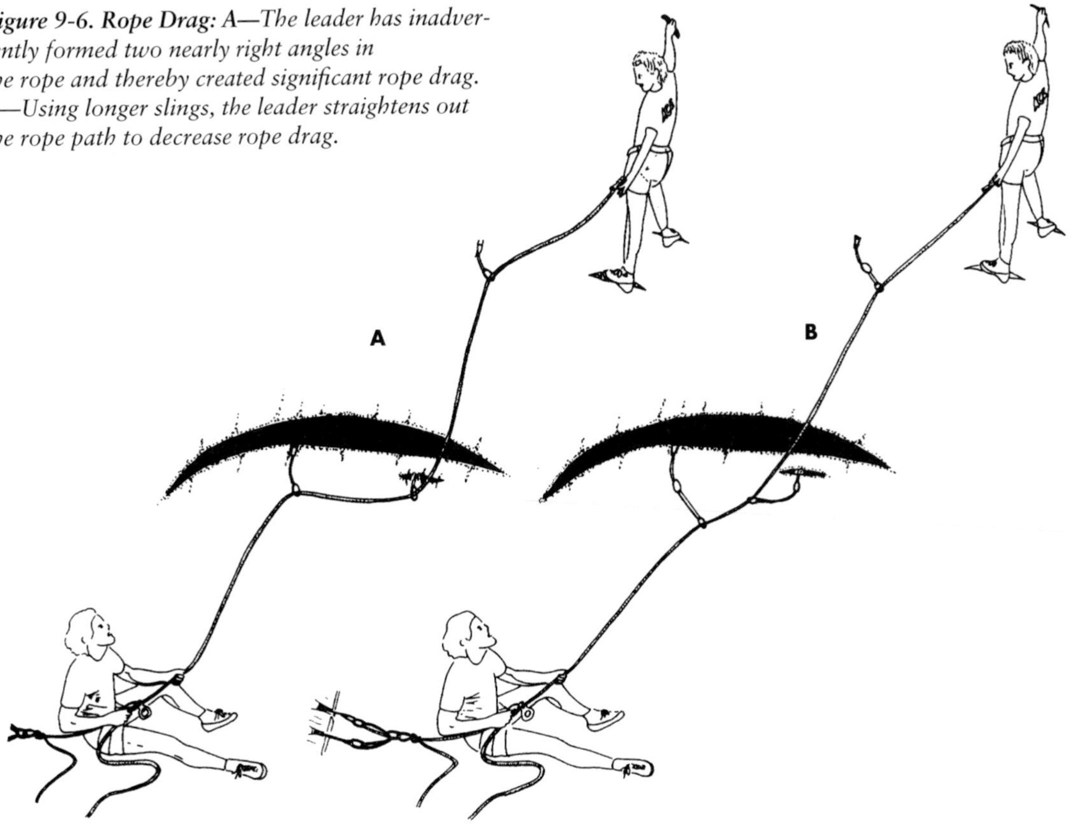

A

B

amount of friction in the system. Rope drag will cause him to spend almost as much energy in tugging on the rope as in climbing. In addition to causing balance problems and possibly a fall, rope drag can rotate and lift nuts from their placements.

You can easily keep the path of the rope straight by using full-length slings (fig. 9-6B). In some situations, it is appropriate to use double-length slings to prevent rope drag. The long sling could lengthen a fall, but it reduces rope drag and prevents an unopposed nut from rotating free of the rock.

TRAVERSING

Traversing (climbing laterally) presents problems for both the leader and the second. The general rule for a traverse is: *Always place protection before and after a hard move.* Protection before the move is for you; protection after the move is for the second.

In figure 9-7, the leader on the traverse has placed protection before doing a hard move across a steep slab. Because the remainder of the traverse was easy, he put in no more protection. The second has arrived at the difficult move and is removing the protection before attempting the move. If the second were to fall, there would be no more protection and the second would swing across the slab and hang beneath the leader. The leader should have placed protection just after the difficult move.

In practice, of course, you cannot always place protection both before and after a hard move. For this reason, both leader and second should be able to lead the pitch and perhaps be prepared, with knowledge and ascending equipment, to climb the rope after a fall. When protection is placed before a hard move but not

Figure 9-7. An Improperly Protected Traverse: After the second removes the protection, he can swing a long way if he falls. The leader should have placed protection before and after the crux to protect the second.

after, the second should be the better climber of the team or, at least, the person more willing to accept risk. The leader can also minimize danger to the second by choosing a higher belay stance to give the second more of a top rope during the traverse.

Three Climbers on a Rope— A Problem for Seconds

Figure 9-8 adds a third climber to the situation. The leader has led up a vertical crack and then followed a horizontal crack to the right. Should the second remove the protection on the vertical part of the climb? On the traverse?

If the second is inexperienced, the leader must anticipate this situation and, before starting out (especially if the second's progress is not within view), instruct the second as to what protection to remove or leave in place. Removing the protection on the vertical crack will not endanger the third climber, who will have a rope directly overhead. Clearly, the second should leave the protection on the traverse, unclip the lead rope, and clip into the protection the rope that trails to the third climber. If the third climber falls on the traverse, the remaining pro-

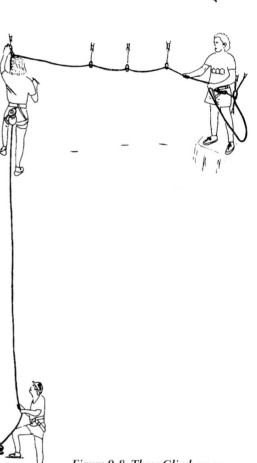

Figure 9-8. Three Climbers on a Traverse

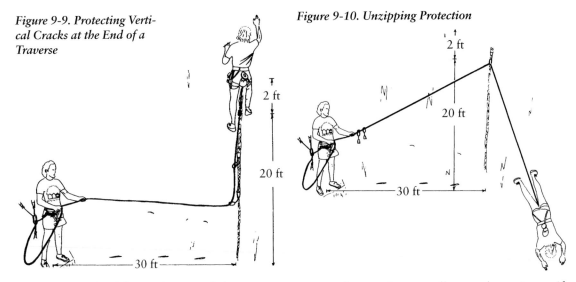

Figure 9-9. Protecting Vertical Cracks at the End of a Traverse

Figure 9-10. Unzipping Protection

tection limits the fall to a short pendulum.

In addition to the belay provided by the leader, the third climber can *back-belay* the second while on the traverse to prevent a swinging fall. To do this, the second ties into both ropes through the appropriate harness tie-in points and receives a belay from both the first and third climbers. This system prevents the second from swinging during a fall.

If the protection were removed from the traverse by the second, the rope would stretch diagonally from the climber on the ground to the leader on the belay stance. With no protection between the third climber and the leader, the third climber could pendulum across the cliff any time during the climb.

An Easy Traverse Followed by a Hard Crack

You often traverse from a belay ledge to a vertical crack. Figure 9-9 shows how an inexperienced leader can create a problem.

Here the leader has face-climbed horizontally 30 feet from the belay to the base of a crack. At the crack, the leader protects with a taper directed against a downward pull, then climbs the crack and protects the ascent with additional tapers. After ascending the crack for 20 feet, the leader puts in the last piece of protection, climbs 2 more feet, and falls off. How far will the leader fall? Think out this problem, which is a

matter of reasoning as well as mathematics, as if you were leading the pitch.

The Answer: In a traverse followed by a vertical crack, the lowest taper or other piece of protection tends to rotate toward 180 degrees and might pull out, causing the pieces above it to pull, and so on. Climbers refer to this sequential failure of protection as *unzipping* because it resembles the action of a zipper opening.

In this situation, the top piece has the best chance of holding because the force pulling on it still has a downward component. If the top protection piece holds in a fall that unzips all other pieces, the leader will still fall nearly 20 feet, plus rope stretch (see box on page 142). This situation is shown in figure 9-10. (I have seen scared leaders trying to put nuts in a crack overhead faster than the nuts below them could lift out.) If the last piece pulls out, the leader will fall twice as far as the amount of rope out, or 104 feet (2 times 52 feet) plus rope stretch.

There are ways, of course, to prevent tapers or other protection pieces from rotating and unzipping. At the end of a traverse, you have three safe choices before starting upward. First, you can break the traverse and vertical section into different pitches. Second, you can place opposed nuts at the end of the traverse to resist both upward and downward pulls. Third, you can use double ropes to minimize rope drag, although opposing nuts will still be necessary at the end of the traverse.

Increased Potential Fall Distance on Traverses

Recently, while leading the second pitch of a climb called Solid Gold in Joshua Tree National Monument, a friend of mine took a fall. He was not more than 6 feet from a good bolt that held, but three onlookers were surprised when he went several body lengths and broke his foot as he collided with an upsweeping friction ramp. The belayer wondered if she had made a mistake and was responsible for the injury.

The answer is no. When a climbing leader ascends vertically directly above the belayer, gravity directs the climbing rope downward. As a result, the total amount of slack in the climbing rope amounts to a couple of feet. The belayer attempts to provide just enough slack for the leader to move without belayer-applied tension, and no more. The leader will have to contend with the weight of the rope between himself and the belayer, plus whatever friction exists in the system.

Traverses present an additional problem to the belayer. The belayer still gives slack for the leader, but hanging loops form in the rope due to the pull of gravity on the rope itself (fig. 9-11). These loops represent additional slack that the belayer cannot completely control. The belayer cannot eliminate these loops because to do so would produce unacceptable tension on the leader. This situation is severe when there is a long, easy traverse at the level of the belay followed by a rising traverse. If the belayer can see the leader and loops, he normally pulls some of the slack out of the loops at the expense of slightly increased tension on the leader, but, if the leader is out of sight of the belayer, this slack tends to accumulate. My friend had moved horizontally away from the belay for quite a distance on easy ground. He was most of the way through the rising traverse and was attempting the crux when he fell.

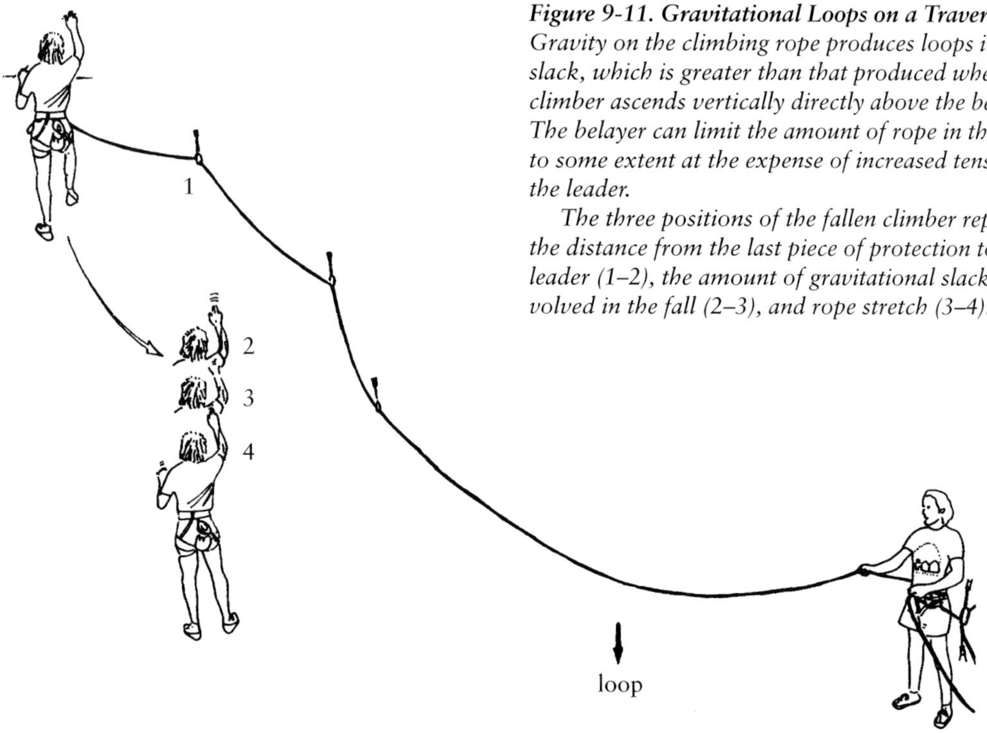

Figure 9-11. Gravitational Loops on a Traverse: *Gravity on the climbing rope produces loops in the slack, which is greater than that produced when the climber ascends vertically directly above the belayer. The belayer can limit the amount of rope in the loops to some extent at the expense of increased tension on the leader.*

The three positions of the fallen climber represent the distance from the last piece of protection to the leader (1–2), the amount of gravitational slack involved in the fall (2–3), and rope stretch (3–4).

A Surprisingly Long Fall

When the leader falls (see fig. 9-10) and unzips all but the last piece of protection, the fall is almost 20 feet. How can this happen when the leader was only 2 feet above the last piece? Before the fall, the leader had 52 feet of rope out—30 horizontal feet plus 20 vertical feet—plus the 2 feet above the protection. The leader essentially climbed the two legs of a right triangle with a 90-degree angle formed between the horizontal traverse line and the vertical crack. To find the length of the rope between the belayer and the remaining piece of protection (the hypotenuse), use the Pythagorean formula:

$$[c(\text{belayer to piece})]^2 = [a(\text{traverse})]^2 + [b(\text{crack})]^2.$$

$$c^2 = (30 \text{ ft})^2 + (20 \text{ ft})^2 = 900 \text{ ft}^2 + 400 \text{ ft}^2 = 1{,}300 \text{ feet}^2$$

We need the square root of 1,300 feet, so

$$\sqrt{c^2} = \sqrt{1{,}300 \text{ feet}^2}, \text{ and}$$

c = 36 feet (distance from belayer to the remaining nut).

Before the fall, there were 50 feet of rope from the belayer to the nut that held the fall. Unzipping the protection contributed 14 feet (50–36 feet) to the fall. In addition, the leader was 2 feet above the last piece of protection that held, making the total fall 16 feet (14 feet + 2 feet). Rope stretch due to 7 percent impact elongation might add about 3.5 feet (50 feet x .07) for a total of 19.5 feet. The leader thought that the fall would be only about 4 to 5 feet.

You need to understand that fall distances on a traverse are likely to be larger than you might suppose because of the gravitational slack in the loops. Three factors influence fall distance in a fall from a traverse. First is the distance from the nearest protection. The leader will swing directly underneath the last piece of protection for a distance equal to the amount of rope back to the last protection piece. The second component of fall distance is the slack accumulated in the loops, and the third component is rope stretch. When the leader is out about 100 feet on a traverse, gravitational slack normally will be about 4 to 6 feet compared to the 1 to 2 feet of slack that the belayer provides for a vertical pitch. The amount of gravitational slack can be considerably larger if the belayer is not concentrating or if the leader is out of sight. As a result, total fall distance for a traverse is potentially greater than for a fall from a vertical pitch directly over the belayer's head.

A partial solution to reducing fall distance on a traverse is to protect more often than you would on a vertical climb. This reduces the distance back to the last piece of protection. Certainly, this is important near cruxes. In retrospect, my friend's fall would have been considerably lessened had he placed protection in the thin crack at the crux. In addition, belayers need to be especially attentive to balancing the amount of rope in the gravitational loops with an acceptable tension on the leader.

CLIMBING UNROPED

Spur-of-the-moment unroped climbing is always dangerous.[1] Some climbers solo because they lose their way or because they attempt an exposed approach unroped. Climbers who do not intend to solo a route often unrope for convenience: At the top of a difficult lead climb, they might wish to cover quickly the low-grade third-, fourth-, or fifth-class terrain, where a fall over the exposure would be fatal. Other experienced climbers unrope near belay or rappel anchors without clipping in and fall to their death when they slip or when a ledge collapses. This spur-of-the-moment unroped climbing is dangerous, but most climbers have done it at one time or another.

Purposeful soloing is attractive to some leaders after they gain experience in leading difficult climbs, even though doing so is clearly dangerous. One famous early soloist was Paul Preuss, who had reached more than 1,200 summits at the time of his death from a fall at age 27.[2] He had done major climbs solo and advocated never climbing a route without being able to down-climb it. Nevertheless, he died in an accidental fall when a hold betrayed him. Soloing has come into the forefront recently and has been practiced by increasingly experienced, skilled, and trained climbers. In some regards, soloing takes climbing out of the realm of sport because each move is a life-or-death situation. Staying on the rock becomes life itself. If you are experienced enough to solo and can make a mature judgment concerning the safety of your own person, do not forget to consider family and friends who would be affected by your loss. Make sure that you are soloing for yourself and not for the envy of others.

GETTING DOWN FROM A CLIMB

Many climbing areas have one or more descent routes, which can range from walking down a gentle trail, to negotiating a steep gully, to rappelling. In alpine climbs, descending is often the second half of a climb and just as technical as getting up. Give as much, if not more, attention to studying the descent line as you give to the ascent line. Picking the right descent gully from the top can be a difficult problem.

Gullies are often filled with loose rock. Although it might not seem possible at first, you can learn to scramble down the gullies without starting an avalanche of rocks at each step. When two people descending encounter a particularly loose section, only one person should move at a time. The lower person takes cover around a bend from the fall line or behind a protecting rock.

Rappel descents on established multipitch climbs are often fixed and marked by a trail of old slings. One problem that occurs is that many climbers start down the wrong way and leave enticing footprints and rappel slings marking a false path. Be prepared to backtrack.

When you can see that both ends of a rappel rope reach the bottom of a rappel, your descent is assured. If you cannot see the bottom of the rappel, tie one or more knots in the rope end to prevent the rope from slipping through the rappel brake. A Prusik safety or AutoBlock can be used to safeguard a very slow rate of descent should the rope not reach. You must know how and have the gear necessary to reclimb the rope.

CLIMBING THE ROPE

Most free climbers do not set out to climb the rope but can find themselves in a situation where this is necessary, at least for a short distance. If you do set out to climb the rope, as you might on a big wall, you will probably take along specialized gear, including mechanical rope ascenders and special rope slings called *etriers* to stand in as you climb. Although you will not have this specialized equipment on a free climb, in an emergency, you can climb the rope with slings and carabiners that you are likely to have with you (fig. 9-12).

Place two Bachmann, Kleimheist, or Prusik knots on the rope (these knots are described in chapter 3). The upper knot attaches directly to the climbing harness, and the lower knot attaches to slings, formed from shoulder-length slings commonly used for running belays, that make stirrups for your feet. These are fastened together to the proper length for your body proportions. Making these slings the proper length is one of the most critical steps in setting up an efficient ascending system. You can adjust the length of foot stirrups by tying overhand knots in individual slings near the foot (fig. 9-12A). The climber is secured to the lower Bachmann ascending system with a short (dark) sling as a safety backup.

One of the advantages of the system shown is that you can comfortably rest for as long as desired in a sitting position. To stand, place your feet beneath yourself and pull up on the rope (fig. 9-12B). While standing, move the upper Bachmann knot up the rope and sit back down on your harness, which returns you to the position of A. Take your weight off the lower Bachmann knot and move it up the climbing rope as high as possible. The sequence starts over.

The Improvised Baudrier Chest Harness

If you plan ahead to climb a rope, you might want to take along a sewn chest harness of wide comfortable webbing, available from a number of manufacturers. If the need to climb the rope occurs unexpectedly, as when your partner leads

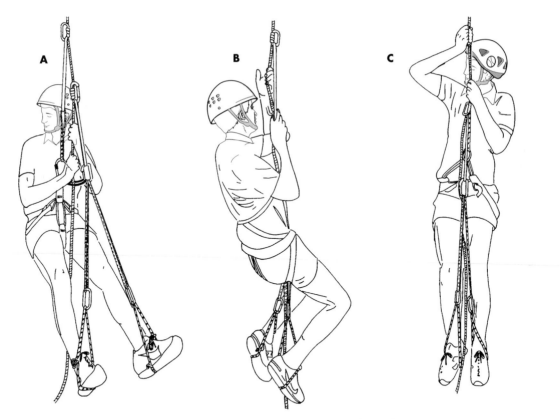

Figure 9-12. Improvised Rope Climbing System Using Runner Slings and Carabiners

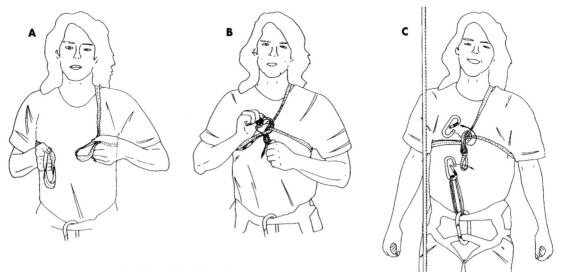

*Figure 9-13. An Improvised Baudrier Chest Harness
Tied with a Standard Double-Length Sling*

a 5.14 pitch, you can improvise a *Baudrier chest harness* in the field with runner slings that you have along for free climbing.[3] For short climbing distances, most people forgo improvised chest harnesses at the expense of added effort with their arms. During a full-length climb, however, the chest harness will help keep you upright and conserve strength and endurance.

You can make a Baudrier chest harness from a double-length runner sling by passing one arm through the runner and then behind your back. Now pull the doubled runner around to the opposite side of your body and bring it up under your armpit (fig. 9-13A). Tie a knot by passing the doubled runner around a bight in the far side of the sling to form a loop which is passed through the original bight (fig. 9-13B). Tighten the knot to complete the chest harness (fig. 9-13C).

Because this harness is improvised, it is probably not long enough to fasten to your seat harness. You make this connection by using a doubled single-length runner and a carabiner (fig. 9-13C). An additional carabiner passed around both the completed baudrier chest harness and the freestanding rope will allow you to lean back with some support as you proceed upward. A chest harness must not tighten enough to constrict your breathing, so always check it or any other harness before committing to the rope.

TYING OFF A FALLEN LEADER

A belayer might need to hold a fallen leader in the position of a fall if weather and other conditions permit and if lowering the leader would seriously aggravate injuries. Subsequent actions then depend on the belayer's ability to reach the climber or get help, but the belayer first must have some method of relieving the climber's weight from the belay brake, tying off the belay rope, and extracting himself or herself from the belay system. A Prusik tie-off (fig. 9-14) can be used in this situation. In all my years of climbing, I have never needed to do this, but it is wise to be prepared if the situation should arise.

If you use a body belay, you can wrap the climbing rope a number of turns around your leg and even step on the rope to lock the wraps in place to free both hands. Then fix a Prusik knot around the climbing rope leading to the fallen leader and attach the Prusik sling to the primary anchor by using a carabiner. Once you connect the Prusik, allow the belay rope to slip to the point where the Prusik grips and holds the weight of the fallen climber. Then you can unwrap the belay rope from yourself and tie it directly into the anchor with a figure-eight knot on a bight. Ordinary shoulder-length slings can serve as the Prusik sling for this emergency

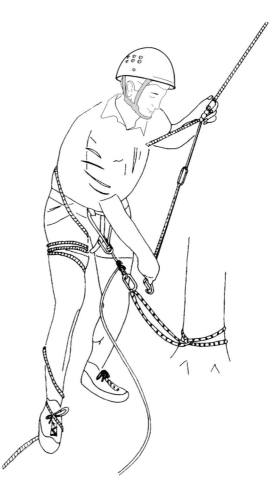

Figure 9-14. Prusik Tie-Off of a Fallen Climber from a Waist Belay

situation. It is important to make sure that your anchor system can counteract an upward pull, since transferring the leader's weight directly to the anchor will exert a direct upward pull.

If the belayer is using a mechanical plate, the extraction procedure is much the same as with a body belay. If the mechanical belay is being used directly off a primary anchor, then extraction is even easier. The belayer simply ties a knot in the belay rope adjacent to the belay device on the braking-hand side. This knot attaches to the primary anchor by means of a carabiner. The tie-off is completed. The belayer can then unclip from the anchor and help the fallen climber.

CONFIDENCE

Fear is very healthy—it keeps us alive. You need to judge whether your fear arises from real danger or from fear of the unknown. In climbing, the former is associated with getting hurt. It can come from a poorly protected climb, loose rock, or other environmental dangers. But fear also comes from normal self-doubts related to taking on challenges.

Even experienced climbers know that they will have to face fear, and controlling it can be one of the major challenges of climbing. Use guidebooks to help you avoid climbs that are too hard or unprotected; choose a climb at a level with which you are comfortable. Stretch your abilities on short climbs near the ground or by bouldering before attempting to stretch your abilities when far off the ground. Choose climbs that protect well, and make sure that cruxes protect well. You can do those long run outs on difficult terrain when you are an expert. Stretch and do a warm-up climb so that your body is functioning smoothly. Do that hard pitch soon afterward, before you get tired. Take rest days. As Winston Churchill said, "All men are cowards when they are fatigued." For backcountry climbs, maintain excellent physical condition so that you will be fresh after a heroic approach. Being properly trained for both strength and endurance will go a long way toward increasing your confidence.

One of the pieces of advice often given climbers is to relax. If you use energy in shaking, that is energy taken away from the concentration needed to climb. If you find yourself shaking, speak quietly to yourself and visualize your movements in the next section to focus your mind on climbing instead of falling off. This usually works when you are on climbs that are within your physical ability and experience. If, in desperation, you need to hang off protection, do so. With experience, you will wean yourself away from this aid. Climbing is a self-imposed sport with internal rewards. If you do not make false claims about the style in which you climb or alter the environment, most people do not really care about your style of climbing. They might have some fun with one-upping you, but you can handle that. People will respect you for your integrity far longer than they will remember a claim that you make about getting up some hard climb. If it is a false claim, they will remember that.

After picking a route that you can do, do not try to climb it all at once in your mind. Consider short segments of rock, from stance to stance or pitch to pitch. Take a second rope for rappelling, so that you are not committed to doing the entire route. You will be pleasantly surprised by getting up most of the routes that you attempt if you start with a positive attitude. Of course, on some routes you will retreat. When you do retreat, do it off secure anchors even if that means leaving gear behind. You will leave less gear if you have a few tied, as opposed to sewn, slings along that can be untied and retied around chockstones or trees.

Get an early start on longer climbs. Be ahead of the crowd, or choose an alternate route so you will not spend time worrying about someone dropping loose rocks on you. Be careful not to drop rocks on the party below. Consult the guidebook to see how long it should take you to do the climb. Giving yourself not only enough time to climb but to retreat or descend without bivouac will give you an extra measure of confidence.

STYLE

Style refers to how you do the route. Style is concerned with preserving the spirit of adventure. Getting up the climb by any means may be initially satisfying, but with experience you will care about how you did it. The best style is usually total free climbing without the direct aid of gear, such as nuts or slings. Using a piton or bolt for a hold, or even holding on to these while clipping in, is not considered to be in the best style. Pitons, bolts, and nuts are part of a system meant to safeguard a fall, not to make upward progress possible.

An ideal pure style would do away with shoes, chalk for your hands, ropes, and other gear and leave you to progress smoothly up the climb in total control. But climbers use universally accepted ropes and gear as safety items. A few have come closer to realizing the ideal by doing away with chalk and even climbing without shoes. Certainly, how you move your body is part of your style. There is an immense difference in how you feel getting up a climb in a jerking, hesitant manner as opposed to a smooth ascent in which you flow up the climb.[4] Obtaining this sense of flow where body and mind work in meditative harmony to solve problems presented by rock even can be a primary reason to climb.

In the final analysis, style is up to you so long as you do not alter the rock and are honest about the style in which you did the climb. This is doubly important for first ascents. The safety of subsequent parties is at stake because they will be attempting to do the climb in as good or better style than the first ascent party. If you need to grab a piton or rest on a nut to keep from falling off, do so. No one should get hurt to live up to a sporting standard, but come back later when you can do the climb totally free, and you will feel better about the climb and about yourself.

REFERENCES FOR FUTURE READING

Csikszentmihalyi, Mihaly, and Isabella Selega Csikszentmihalyi. 1990. Adventure and the flow experience. In *Adventure education*, edited by John C. Miles and Simon Priest. State College, Pennsylvania: Venture Publishing.

Gervasutti, Giusto. 1957. *Gervasutti's climbs*. Translated by Nea Morin and Janet Adam Smith. Seattle: Mountaineers.

Graydon, Don, ed. 1992. *Mountaineering: The freedom of the hills*. Fifth edition. Seattle: Mountaineers.

Horst, J. Eric. 1989. Happiness is a pair of big guns. *Climbing*. 116:118.

Long, John. 1989. *How to rock climb*. Evergreen, Colorado: Chockstone Press.

Meyers, George, and Don Reid. 1987. *Yosemite climbs*. Denver, Colorado: Evergreen Press.

Peters, Ed, ed. 1982. *Mountaineering: The freedom of the hills*. Fourth edition. Seattle: Mountaineers.

Setnicka, Tim J. 1980. Ascending techniques. In *Wilderness search and rescue, chapter 13*. Boston: Appalachian Mountain Club.

Smutek, Ray. 1978. Crevasse self rescue. *Off-Belay*. 40:2–8.

ENDNOTES

1. Meyers and Reid, 1987. Refer to pages 4–16 for a discussion of accidents in Yosemite.
2. Gervasutti, 1957.
3. Setnicka, 1980, 217; Graydon, 1992, 105. You can tie this harness with custom-length slings that allow a direct clip into the waist harness.
4. The concept of flow has been examined extensively by Csikszentmihalyi, who worked with many athletes, including climbers. Flow is a creative state in which a climber is totally involved with the challenge, uses appropriate skills, and receives immediate feedback. The climber does not stop, however, to evaluate the feedback. "Action and reaction have become so well-synchronized that the resulting behavior is automatic," says Csikszentmihalyi. In a more mystical sense flow occurs when you are "one with the rock." Flow is one of the primary reasons that people engage in an activity such as climbing that is without obvious external reward.

10

Anchor Systems

ANCHOR BASICS

At a belay stance, a climber places two or more protection pieces to form an anchor, and then uses slings to fasten or *tie into* the anchor against any potential pull. The ideal anchor system will distribute the load equally to all anchor points so as not to stress any single anchor point unduly. If one of the anchor points fails, the system as a whole should not fail.

There are two types of anchor systems: *self-equalizing* and *pseudo-equalizing*. Self-equalizing systems adjust automatically to share the load equally over a range of directions; pseudo-equalizing systems are those that share the load equally in only one direction. Self-equalizing systems apply more readily and for a larger number of situations than pseudo-equalizing systems, although climbers use both systems routinely.

The principles that guide the safe creation of anchor systems are relatively few. Systems that appear to be complex are made up of simple subsystems linked together. It is important that these subsystems and linkages be done correctly because climbing safely and stopping falls ultimately depend on a safe anchor. Once you gain an understanding of these principles, you can rapidly establish safe anchor systems, in familiar as well as new situations, with a wide variety of available slings and ropes.

SELF-EQUALIZING SYSTEMS

The basic self-equalizing anchor system is illustrated in figure 10-1. Twist a climbing sling and pass a carabiner, parallel to the axis of the sling, through the two loops formed and around the crossed section of the sling. In this way, each of the two loops of the crossed sling in the drawing on the top, labeled A and B, forms a complete circle around the carabiner. When you climb, these loops attach to anchor points, such as pitons or nuts.

Trace the path of the two sling loops around the carabiner in the drawing on the bottom and note how each loop encircles the carabiner inde-

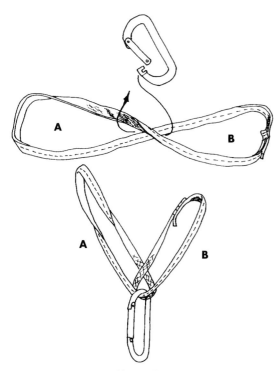

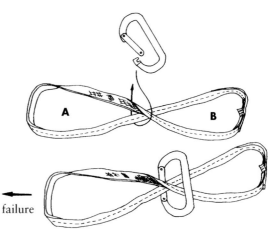

Figure 10-2. *Incorrect Attachment*

Figure 10-1. *Basic Self-Equalization*

pendently. If you pull the left-hand end of loop
A to the left, sling material will continuously
travel around the carabiner and loop B will get
smaller as loop A enlarges, until loop B is
wrapped tightly around the carabiner and loop
A cannot get any larger. Because loop B wraps
around the carabiner, the system as a whole will
not fail if the anchor point that loop B attaches
to pulls out.

If you incorrectly rig this system, as shown in
figure 10-2, it can fail if one anchor point fails.
Here, the load-bearing carabiner encircles the
crossed sling perpendicular, rather than parallel,
to its axis. It does not enclose the two loops of
the crossed sling: if the sling pulls to the left,
loops A and B will slide through the carabiner.
If either of the anchor points fails, the system
fails. Experiment with both the correct and incorrect attachments to see the difference in action.

In figure 10-3, a basic self-equalizing sling
connects two anchor points, a piton and a
nut. Because the anchor points are at different

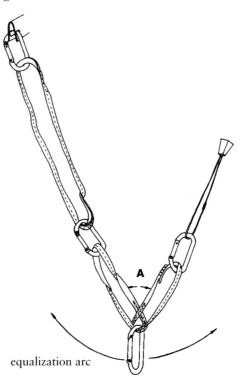

Figure 10-3. *Two Self-Equalized Anchor Points:* The
load-bearing carabiner can travel through an arc and remain equalized. This carabiner is physically limited in its
arc of travel by the length of the sling to which it is attached. Angle A determines load multiplication of the
system and should be less than 60 degrees; if necessary,
add slings to one or both anchor points to reduce the
angle.

heights, a second sling is needed to complete the system. The load-bearing carabiner is at the equalized position of the system. It can rotate through the equalization arc and still equally distribute the load on the two anchor points.

LOAD MULTIPLICATION

You have seen why it is desirable to connect two anchor points so that they share a load equally. You can offset the advantages of this sharing, however, if you do not understand the principles involved.

The angle, A, between the two sides of the equalized anchor, shown in figure 10-3, is very important in determining how the anchor points share the load. This angle should be no greater than 60 degrees because of a factor called *load multiplication,* which comes into play at larger angles. When the included angle between sides is 60 degrees or less, each

side of the equalized anchor holds approximately half of the total load. As the included angle increases, each side of the anchor carries an increasing load; combining anchors improperly can convert a potentially safe anchor into one that might fail.

Figure 10-4 shows an experiment that illustrates load multiplication. In A, the climber holds a 25-pound weight from an equalized sling. A spring scale like those found in an angler's tackle box is placed in one side of the equalized anchor system to record how much tension the weight exerts on this side and its anchor point.

With the ends of the equalized sling held together, the spring scale reads 12.5 pounds; that is, the weight is taken up equally by both sides of the sling. When the climber pulls the equalized sling apart to increase the angle between the sides, he applies force with his hands and arms. As demonstrated in figure 10-4B, the increased tension is recorded on the spring scale.

Figure 10-4. Tension in Anchor Systems

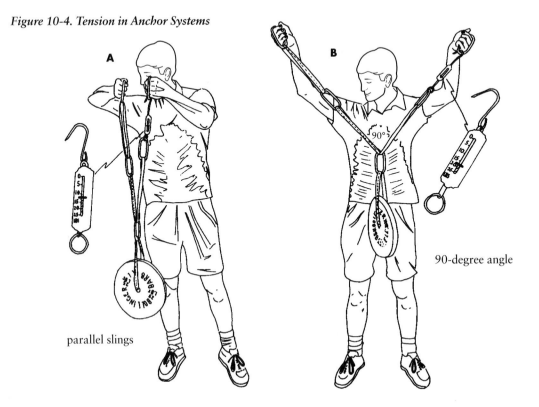

A

parallel slings

B

90°

90-degree angle

Table 10-1. Table of Load Multiplication

A°	T$_1$(150 lb)	(T$_1$ + T$_2$)	% Applied Load	Load Multiplication Zones
0	75	150	100	None
15	75.8	154.3	103	
30	77.6	155.2	104	to
45	81.3	162.6	108	
60	86.6	173.2	116	Moderate
75	94.6	189.2	126	Moderate
90	106.1	212.2	142	
105	123.2	246.4	164	to
120	150.0	300.0	200	High
135	195.8	391.6	261	High
150	289.6	579.2	386	
175	1704.6	3409.2	2272	to
180	∞	∞	∞	Extreme

Calculated for a static load of a 150-pound climber and expressed as a percentage (%) of the applied load. Zones of load multiplication are indicated.

T$_1$ and T$_2$ are the tensional forces in each side of the anchor separated by the angle A.[1]

When the sides of the sling are held at an angle of 90 degrees, nearly 18 pounds of force is exerted on one side of the sling (and therefore on the anchor point): an increase of nearly 50 percent. This result is somewhat unexpected, and the force grows as the angle between the sides of the equalized anchor becomes greater. Thus at an angle of 120 degrees, the spring scale will record 25 pounds of tension in one side of the equalized sling, for a total of 50 pounds of tensional force on both sides. (If you actually perform this experiment, you will find that your results will not be perfect because of friction and varying spring tension within the scale, but it is accurate enough to demonstrate the principle.)

Now imagine replacing the climber's arms with real anchor points. As you increase the angle between the slings, the load multiplies. The effects are summarized in Table 10-1, with load multiplication plotted as the tension, T$_1$ and T$_2$, on anchor slings as a percentage of an applied load of a 150-pound climber. Load

multiplication is divided into zones: None to Moderate, Moderate to High, and High to Extreme, based on the angle between slings. The desirable zone—None to Moderate—occurs when the angle between slings is between 0 and 60 degrees. Each sling in this zone bears approximately half the applied load. At the 120-degree end of the Moderate to High zone, a tensional force equal to the applied load is transferred directly to *each* of the anchor points, and the total anchor has to hold twice the applied load. This result negates one of the advantages of using two anchor points, which is to share the tensional force of the applied load between anchor points. In the High to Extreme zone, the anchor points would have to hold almost 12 times the applied load at 175 degrees and an infinite amount at 180 degrees. Such load multiplication is clearly undesirable and dangerous to the safety of your anchor points: attempt to keep the angle between anchor points to 60 degrees or less for nut or fixed anchor slings.

Static Load Multiplication on a Common Rappel Anchor

When two anchor points are connected in a triangle, as commonly happens with the two bolts of a fixed rappel anchor, you can inadvertently increase load multiplication even further[2] (fig. 10-5). The climber holds aloft a 25-pound weight with slings connected to a single sling, forming a 90-degree triangle. Now the spring scale connected directly to one anchor point measures the force applied to it at 32.5 pounds, or 130 percent of the applied load. This reading sharply exceeds the 18 pounds measured in figure 10-4B, where the angle was approximately the same. The triangular pattern not only increases load multiplication drastically, but, in addition, the applied load attempts to rotate the anchor points. Alternative desirable sling patterns for connecting anchors are described in chapter 7 under "Bolt Anchors."

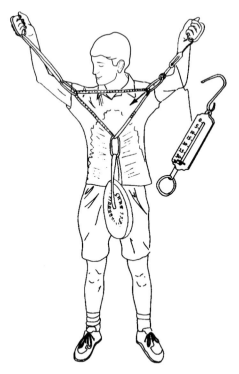

Figure 10-5. Load Multiplication Caused by Using a Triangular Sling Pattern. The lower angle between slings is 90 degrees.

EXTENDING THE BASIC SELF-EQUALIZING SYSTEM

You can use the basic self-equalizing system to distribute forces to three or more anchor points (fig. 10-6). Here, two of the anchor points are equalized as described above, and a second equalized system is integrated with the first. To analyze the force distribution, begin at the bottom carabiner, point C. This is the load-bearing carabiner for the system: the belayer connects to the anchor system through it. If you place a force of 100 pounds on this carabiner and the included angle A is 60 degrees or less, the two sides of the system, 1 and 2, share the 100 pounds approximately equally—each holds 50 pounds. On side 2, this 50 pounds of force is transmitted directly to anchor point D.

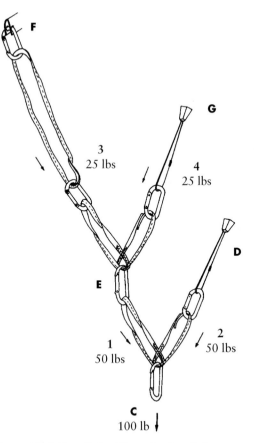

Figure 10-6. Equalizing Three Anchor Points

On side 1, the 50-pound force is applied to carabiner E, the load-bearing carabiner of a subsystem that equalizes anchor points F and G. At E, the 50 pounds is divided into forces of approximately 25 pounds each on sides 3 and 4. These 25-pound forces are applied directly to anchor points F and G.

Combining self-equalization systems for three anchors always causes two of the anchor points to share half of the applied force, while the third anchor point bears the remaining half of the applied force. You might use this system if one of your three anchor points is a large well-placed nut and the two other anchor points are small well-placed nuts.

Three anchor points can share the applied force equally, as described below in the section "Equalizing the Load on Three Equally Strong Anchor Points."

Connecting Four Self-Equalizing Anchor Points

An anchor system formed by connecting four anchor points using the basic system is illustrated in figure 10-7. To test your understanding of the system, there are blank underlined spaces for you to fill in the force applied at each point. Assume an initial force of 100 pounds. (The answers are given below under "Force Distribution in Figure 10-7.")

Force Distribution in Figure 10-7

If you apply a 100-pound force at carabiner C, the equalizing system distributes approximately 50 pounds of force along sling 1, on the left side of the system, to carabiner E, and an identical force along sling 2, on the right side of the system, to carabiner D.

Carabiner E is the load-bearing carabiner for a subsystem that distributes forces to anchor points F and G. The 50 pounds of force applied at carabiner E is distributed equally along slings 3 and 4 to anchor points F and G, which are therefore loaded with 25 pounds of force each.

Carabiner D is the load-bearing carabiner for the second subsystem, which distributes forces to anchor points H and I. The 50 pounds

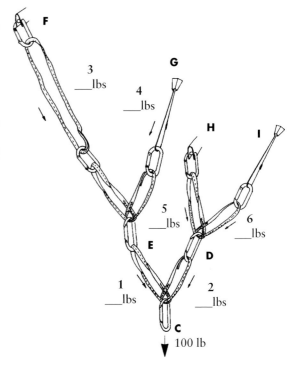

Figure 10-7. Combinations of the Basic System for Four Anchor Points

of force applied to carabiner D is distributed equally along slings 5 and 6 to anchor points H and I. Therefore, anchor points H and I are also loaded with 25 pounds each of the original 100 pounds of force applied at carabiner C.

Linking Basic Self-Equalizing Systems

To generalize the results of linking basic self-equalizing systems: when three or an odd number of anchor points are equalized in an asymmetrical manner, using combinations of the basic equalization technique, forces apply unequally to the anchor points. When two (or any even number of anchor points) are equalized in a symmetrical manner using combinations of the basic equalization technique, forces apply equally to all the anchor points.

At the end of a lead, you can quickly equalize two or even three anchor points using the techniques discussed above to make a very secure anchor. The three-anchor system is especially useful when you have three anchor points and one of them is significantly stronger than the other two because the two weaker anchor points can be combined into one anchor point with a greater combined strength that you then equalize with the remaining strong point.

When you set up top-rope anchors using combinations of the basic self-equalizing system, you will need a lot of slings and carabiners, especially since a fail-safe system for a top-rope anchor calls for locking carabiners or doubled carabiners with gates opposed and reversed. It is recommended, therefore, that you use longer slings in pseudo-equalized systems (see page 155), which can be made of sections of a retired climbing rope.

EQUALIZING THE LOAD ON THREE EQUALLY STRONG ANCHOR POINTS

To distribute the load equally to three anchor points of the same strength, use a double-length sling or a longer custom-length small-diameter rope (*cordelette*). Pass the sling through carabiners attached to all three anchor points, as shown in figure 10-8. Pull the sling between the carabiners down to form Vs, twist them, and pass the load-bearing carabiner through the loops they form and around the lower portion of the sling, as indicated by the arrow. The twists ensure that the sling is around the carabiner; if one anchor point fails, the carabiner will be still attached to the sling. Try failing each anchor point in turn to see how the remaining anchor points are affected in this setup. The method demonstrated is a general technique for connecting multipoint anchors if you have slings that are long enough.

Shock-Loading Equalized Anchors

The reason for creating self-equalizing systems is to share the load equally among anchor points. You begin with the assumption that individual anchor points will not fail, but that self-equalization will provide a measure of security if one of the anchor points should pull out of

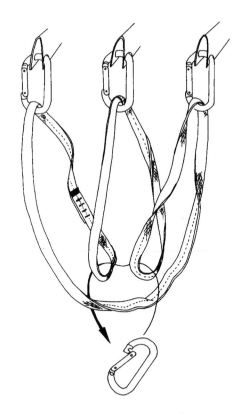

Figure 10-8. Connecting Three Equally Strong Anchor Points

the rock. If one of the anchor points does pull, however, the remaining anchor points could *shock-load* as the anchor-sling accelerates forward from the pulled anchor point to catch on remaining anchor points. The magnitude of shock loading is proportional to the distance the sling slides before it catches, in relation to the acceleration of the falling climber.

You can prevent shock loading by keeping the anchor sling from sliding. First, create a self-equalizing anchor system, and then aim the carabiner from which you belay toward the expected pull on the system (fig. 10-9). Take this belay carabiner and use it to tie an overhand knot or a figure-eight knot around all of the slings of the system (see photo at right). You have created a pseudo-equalized anchor system that will prevent shock loading while equally sharing the load in only one direction.

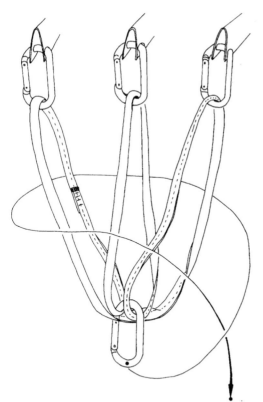

Figure 10-9. A Self-Equalizing Three-Point System

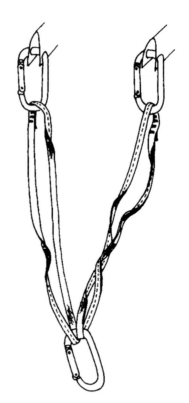

Figure 10-10. A Simple Pseudo-Equalizing Anchor

PSEUDO-EQUALIZED SYSTEMS

A pseudo-equalized system distributes a load equally onto two or more anchor points but in only one direction. An example of a pseudo-equalized system is shown in figure 10-10, where two slings tie two anchor points into a single carabiner.

Anchors for Slingshot (Social Belay) Systems

A *slingshot system* allows a belayer to give a climber a rope from above while remaining on the ground where it is easy to monitor the climber's progress. (To use this system on very difficult climbs, set up the anchor by walking to the climb's top along a trail, or lead an easier adjacent climb.) The climbing rope now runs from the belayer to an anchor set at the top of the climb—"top-roping"—and back down to the climber, who is starting from ground level.

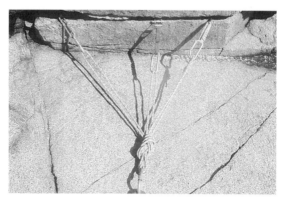

Pseudo-Equalizing the Three-Point System to Prevent Shock Loading

Hence the climbing rope forms an upward-pointing V, somewhat resembling the elastic band of a loaded slingshot.

In top-roping situations, climbers often fall,

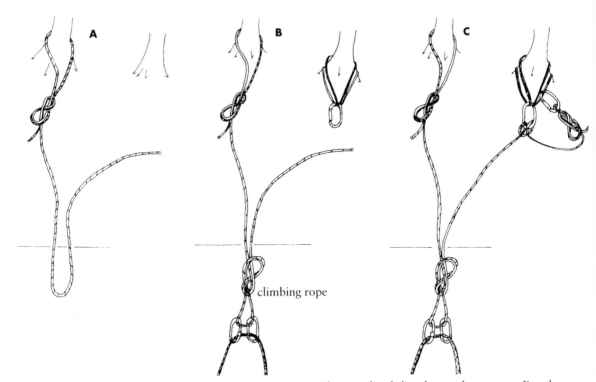

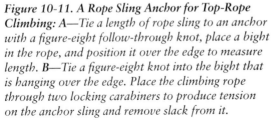

climbing rope

Figure 10-11. A Rope Sling Anchor for Top-Rope Climbing: A—Tie a length of rope sling to an anchor with a figure-eight follow-through knot, place a bight in the rope, and position it over the edge to measure length. B—Tie a figure-eight knot into the bight that is hanging over the edge. Place the climbing rope through two locking carabiners to produce tension on the anchor sling and remove slack from it.

C—The completed slingshot anchor system. Equal tension in the second anchor is achieved by using an easily adjustable clove hitch. Back this knot up with a figure-eight knot on a bight clipped into the anchor with a locking carabiner. You can use a single carabiner for both the clove hitch and figure-eight backup knot.

either because they are attempting routes that are difficult for their ability or because they are trying climbs of a high standard. Once climbers reach the top, they are often lowered (instead of down-climbing) back to the ground.

Falling and lowering subjects the anchor slings to repeated stretching and contraction, as well as abrasion where the rope passes over the edge of the cliff. You can pad the anchor sling, but you should also use two anchor slings over the side of a cliff to provide a safety backup if one of the slings is cut. A quick system for setting up two independent anchors that bear the load equally is illustrated in figure 10-11. (A

tensionless anchor, used for setting up rappel systems for groups, is described in chapter 17.)

Tie a sling made of rope to an anchor (tree) with a figure-eight follow-through knot. Secure yourself at the edge, drape the sling over the edge, and make a bight that hangs just below where you would like the knot to be when you have finished (A).

Next, pull up the sling and tie a figure-eight knot in the bight that was hanging over the edge (B). Place two carabiners, at least one locking, on the figure-eight knot; thread the climbing rope through the carabiners; and drop both ends of the climbing rope over the edge to provide tension on the tied-off anchor sling. This tension is essential. (You use two carabiners so that the rope does not bend as sharply as it would over one carabiner.)

Now, working at the second anchor, adjust the tension of the free end of the anchor so both ropes will bear the load equally. Place a webbing sling with a locking carabiner around a second anchor tree, as shown in C. Tie the free end of the anchor sling into this carabiner with a clove hitch, which can be easily adjusted, and adjust the tension on this sling so that both anchor slings are equally tight. Set the clove hitch as tightly as possible and back it up with a figure-eight on a bight that is clipped into a carabiner on the second anchor sling. Place the figure-eight backup knot as close as possible to the clove hitch without loosening the clove hitch.

This system allows you to adjust the tension on the two rope slings well away from the edge of the cliff, where it is easy to work in a relaxed manner.

Pseudo-equalized Anchors with Rope Slings

A leader normally carries eight to ten slings on a climb and sometimes must use these up on the intermediate protection pieces, which leaves none for the anchor. Equalizing two or three protection pieces for an anchor without slings sounds impossible until you realize that you can use the rope itself as a sling. If the pitch was less than a full rope length, the remaining length of 10 to 30 feet can be used to set up a pseudo-equalized anchor (fig. 10-12).

Step 1: Connecting Two Anchor Pieces with a Rope Sling:
After completing the lead, clip to a temporary anchor but leave room to maneuver. Go off belay and pull up as much slack as possible to use as a sling. Sometimes this means that the second needs to stand at the very start of the pitch, rather than away from it, to give all the slack possible. Place two pieces of protection in the rock and, taking enough rope to reach from the eventual belay position to the right-hand (or left-hand) piece of protection, tie into it with a clove hitch. Then make a V in the rope sling to create an equalizing subsystem and tie the rope sling into the second piece of protection, also by using a clove hitch. The angle between the sides of this subsystem should be less than 60 degrees to minimize load multiplication. Tie a figure-eight loop knot at the end of the V formed by the sides of the subsystem.

Step 2: Connecting the Third Piece of Protection:
After forming the first subsystem, tie the rope sling directly into the carabiner on the third piece of protection. Use a clove-hitch with a bit of slack between the two pieces of protection. If all three protection pieces are equal in size and placement, extend this last segment of rope sling directly to the V in the apex of the first subsystem and connect it there with a figure-eight loop knot and a carabiner. This will be the belay tie-in point. If the third piece is larger and better placed than the first two, a more general situation, form a second subsystem and tie another figure-eight knot. Note that the figure-eight knot at the apex of the second subsystem extends beyond that of the first subsystem.

Step 3: Tying the System Together:
Now fasten together the subsystems of the rope sling by using a carabiner to connect the figure-eight knots. The belayer attaches to the load-bearing figure-eight knot of the system with a carabiner. The free end of the rope leading to the second is used to belay.

Solving Problems:
If there is not enough rope to set up a three-point anchor when you use the climbing rope as a sling, an anchor based on two pieces of protection might be sufficient. You can use a carabiner to connect directly to the first V of Step 1 (fig. 10-12A).

Alternatively, you might have one or two slings at the end of the pitch. Use these to self-equalize the first two protection pieces. Then pseudo-equalize the anchor to the third protection piece if you use the rope as a sling in a manner similar to that described in Step 2. The first subsystem of Step 2 (in fig. 10-12B) would then be formed by self-equalized slings rather than the rope sling shown.

Then again, in the real world of climbing there could be no slings left at the end of a lead to hook up the anchor. Indeed, there might be only enough rope left to tie into one protection piece. Presuming that you are committed to the climb and cannot just walk off, this is a serious situation because one anchor point is not satisfactory to safeguard against a fall. However, you can temporarily strengthen one anchor with an aimed and braced body stance while the second climbs. After enough slack has accumulated and the second has gained a secure resting place, set up a rope-sling anchor system (fig. 10-12A and B).

There might even be a piece of protection on the ledge that the second can fasten to while the leader uses the accumulated slack to complete the rope-sling anchor. You will have to solve this kind of real-life problem by using your judgment—neither this nor any other book can do it for you.

Figure 10-12. Using the Climbing Rope to Pseudo-Equalize Anchor Points: A—Connecting the first two anchor points. B—The two upper arrows show connections made using a carabiner, while the lower arrow points toward the second.

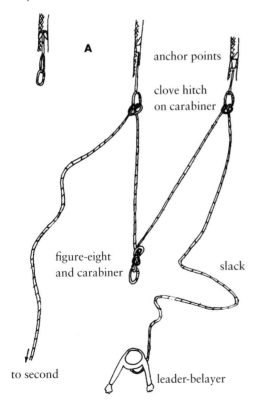

REFERENCES FOR FUTURE READING

Denise, Garet. 1987. Rappel stations—a bum rap: How safe are those slings. *Climbing.* 102:92–93.

Setnicka, Tim J. 1980. *Wilderness search and rescue.* Boston: Appalachian Mountain Club.

ENDNOTES

1. Load multiplication on anchor systems can be explored with some simple calculations that use static loads, simple geometry, and the trigonometric cosine function, which is defined below. Figure 10-13 shows the general setup of a basic anchor system and how loading stresses it. In A, the rappeller, who represents the load, is sitting quietly on the rappel rope. The anchors are connected by slings, and the rappeller's body weight pulls the slings downward to form angle A. (The forces are similar to those visualized in the illustration of the climber holding a weight with a spring scale, fig. 10-5.) Let us estimate the magnitude of load multiplication without direct, and possibly disastrous, experience.

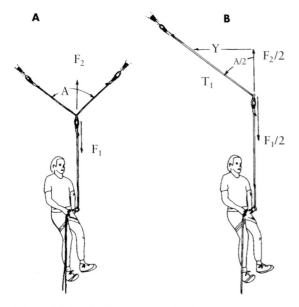

Figure 10-13. Static Forces on Anchor Systems. Modified from Setnicka, 1980.

When the system is at rest, the downward force due to gravity F_1 equals the opposing force F_2, which is an upward force. (If this were not so, the rappeller would continue down to the ground or, more unlikely, fly up into the sky.) The upward force is provided by the rope under tension, which in turn pulls on the nut anchors. How much tension is there in the rope and on the anchor system? For this calculation, we will work with one half of the system (as we did in fig. 10-5). When we have calculated T_1, the tensional force in the left-hand side of the rope, or half the total tension, we can double that force to get the tensional force for the entire system.

Solve for T_1 using the vector Y, which is the horizontal component of T_1. The vertical component of T_1 is the force $F_2/2$ and the angle concerned is (A/2). To simplify, use F/2 since $F_1/2 = F_2/2$.

$$\cos(A/2) = \frac{F/2}{T_1}$$

by definition of a cosine = adjacent side of a right triangle F/2 divided by the hypotenuse T_1 of the triangle; and then

$$T_1 = \frac{F/2}{\cos(A/2)}$$

by transposing

For example: a 150-pound person sits quietly on the rope and makes an angle A of 30 degrees.

$$T_1 = \frac{150 \text{ lb}/2}{\cos(30°/2)} = 75 \text{ lb}/\cos 15°$$

$$= 75 \text{ lb}/0.966$$

$$= 77.6 \text{ lb}$$

Since T_1 is one-half the total tension on the rope, or the individual protection point, the total tension on the rope and anchor points is twice this amount, or 155.2 pounds. This represents a load multiplication of 103.5 percent and demonstrates that total rope tension is greater than the downward force (F_1) of the climber sitting on the rope.

2. The increase in tensional force is directly proportional to the reciprocal of the sine function of the angle at the bolt. At 90 degrees, this increase is zero. It becomes infinite at zero degrees. For the plot of these angles, see Denise, 1987.

Fall Forces

FORCES AND SAFETY IN CLIMBING SYSTEMS

A popular T-shirt motto admonishes climbers to "Fight Gravity." This is good advice because gravity is very powerful, and it accelerates a fall earthward. To stop a falling climber, we construct an elaborate belay system that includes an anchor, a belayer, a belay brake, the rope, and protection for the leader. The anchor ties the belayer to the cliff; the belayer assumes a stance and tensions the rope; the belay brake provides enhanced tension; and the rope stretches to absorb energy. Advanced designs can make low-stretch ropes absorb energy equally as well as high-stretch ropes do. Additional energy can be absorbed as the rope slides through the belay brake and slides over carabiners on protection in the system. Because energy can be transformed but not destroyed, some fall energy is converted to heat and some goes into tightening knots and deforming bodies and harnesses. This chapter examines how the forces of a fall are absorbed and distributed, starting with simple concepts and ending with real systems.

THE FALL FACTOR

Climbers rarely want to fall, but, for obvious reasons, they must be prepared to fall. This is especially true because climbers recently have learned how to climb harder by repeatedly attempting difficult moves and falling, to the point that they have turned the rope into an active tool.

The *fall factor (f)*, which tells us something about the force that the rope experiences, is the ratio between the distance of the fall and the amount of rope out. It is calculated by the following formula:

$$f = \frac{\text{distance fallen}}{\text{amount of rope out}}$$

When the fall factor is large, we expect rope damage. If the fall factor is small, the rope does not experience much stress or damage.

A Roped Fall with No Fall Factor

Fall factor has no meaning if the climber is stopped by a ledge or the ground before coming onto the rope. An extreme case, along with probable injury, occurs when there is no protection between the belayer and the leader, and the climber hits the ground. This fall produces no effect on the rope; the fall factor in this situation is the same as if there were no fall. In other words, the fall factor is a simplified way to think about potential rope damage.

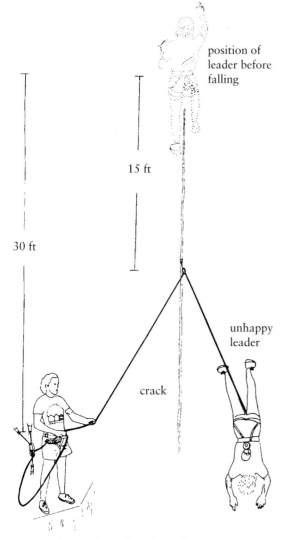

Figure 11-1. A Simple Fall from above Protection

Simple Falls

By examining a number of situations, you can see what each one means in terms of placing protection and strategies for leading.

In the simple but long fall shown in figure 11-1, the climber was 15 feet above his protection and then fell 30 feet:

$$f = \frac{\text{distance of fall}}{\text{amount of rope out}} = \frac{30 \text{ ft}}{30 \text{ ft}} = 1$$

A fall factor of 1 is a severe fall for the rope, the belay system, and the climber's body. The rope is suspect for future use after taking such a fall.

If the leader had placed protection more frequently, the fall factor could have been reduced. For example, if a second piece of protection were placed 7.5 feet above the first, the fall would have been twice 7.5 feet, or 15 feet onto 30 feet of rope:

$$f = \frac{\text{distance of fall}}{\text{amount of rope out}} = \frac{15 \text{ ft}}{30 \text{ ft}} = 0.5$$

This fall would have been easier on the rope, the falling leader, the belayer, the protection pieces, and everything else related to the climbing system. By placing protection often, you minimize the fall factor and safeguard yourself as well as the belay chain.

Falls in the Middle and End of a Lead with Intermediate Protection

A fall at the end of a lead is easier on the rope, protection, leader, and belayer than a fall of the same distance in the beginning or the middle of the same lead, as figure 11-2 shows. Consider two potential falls, each with a fall distance of 6 feet, onto different lengths of rope as indicated by the two sets of numbers in the illustration. For the first 6-foot fall, with distances indicated by number in boldface type, the leader climbs 10 feet above the belayer, places protection, and then continues upward 3 feet to the crux. At the crux, he falls the 3 feet back to the protection and then 3 feet below it, for a total fall of 6 feet,

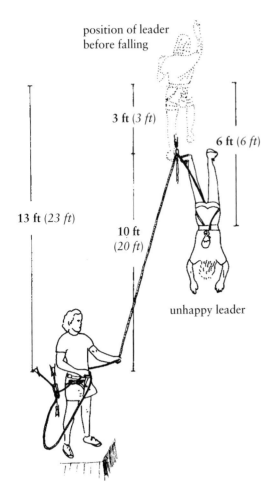

position of leader
before falling

3 ft (*3 ft*)

6 ft (*6 ft*)

13 ft (*23 ft*)

10 ft
(*20 ft*)

unhappy leader

Figure 11-2. Falls in the Middle and High on a Lead with Intermediate Protection: Distances for the separate falls are indicated by boldface numbers for the first fall and italics in parentheses for the second fall.

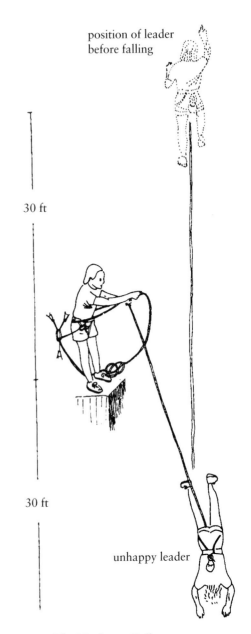

position of leader
before falling

30 ft

30 ft

unhappy leader

Figure 11-3. The Maximum Fall

with the 13 feet of rope between him and the belayer. The fall factor is 0.46 (*f* = 6 ft/13 ft) and is of moderate size. This produces moderate stress on the protection pieces, belay system, and leader.

If, however, the climber gets past the lower crux and falls at a higher crux on the climb (the distances indicated by the italic numbers in parentheses), the fall factor will be lower. In this higher fall, assume that the leader climbs 20 feet above the belayer, puts in protection, and climbs 3 feet higher before falling. There is now a total of 23 feet of rope to absorb the energy of the 6-foot fall, compared to 13 feet of rope in the fall at the lower crux. The fall factor for the second fall is *f* = 6 ft/23 ft = 0.26. This is a less severe fall.

Safety Tips for Minimizing Impact Forces

Harnesses
• Double-web back through any harness buckle to prevent accidental slippage, unbuckling, and resulting falls. Keep in mind the climber who did not have his buckle doubled back and told his guide that this was not a problem because the buckle would slip at about 350 pounds of force and he only weighed 150 pounds. Remember that your 150 pounds will produce a significantly higher impact force when you jerk onto the end of the rope in a fall.

Rappels
• Descend smoothly from anchors strong enough to hold potential impact forces. When you descend in a jerky or bouncing motion, you produce impact loading (it is like jumping up and down on scales). The impact force produced in a rappel, however, can rip out your lifesaving anchor.

Anchors
• Use two or more anchor points and an equalizing system, with the angle between slings at 60 degrees or less, to minimize load multiplication on individual anchors related to the geometry of the setup. Three anchor points provide greater assurance.

Running Protection
• Place the first piece of protection early to safeguard the anchor system and belayer. Because this piece is not designed to safeguard the leader, you should place it no matter how you feel about the difficulty of the climb. Additional protection safeguards lower pieces, limits fall distance, and reduces the length of time that an individual piece must sustain maximum impact force.

• Do not create pulley systems when hooking two nuts together, as they promote high impact forces and failure of the protection points.

Belaying
• Tie into the anchor and belay from your harness (see photo on page 76), rather than belaying straight off the anchor system. You will lessen the impact load on the anchor and help minimize the force on the protection pieces that catch the fall. Practice tying off a fallen leader and extracting yourself from the belay. (If you top-rope with a slingshot or social belay, then little impact force is expected and belaying directly from the anchor system is more acceptable.)

• A fall at the end of a well-protected pitch is easier on the rope, the climber, the belayer, and protection pieces than a fall of the same distance at the beginning because there is more rope to absorb the force of the fall.

• Belay after rather than before cruxes to minimize impact forces, and keep the belay as far as possible from the crux.

These two examples demonstrate that it is safer to fall higher on the climb than lower because as you near the end of a pitch there is more rope to absorb the fall energy. In general, to minimize the fall factor, do not set up a belay just before the crux even though you might desire the psychological satisfaction of having your belayer close at hand. To put it in a rule of thumb, *belay after cruxes rather than before them.*

The Maximum Fall Factor

The maximum fall factor of 2 experienced by the rope and climbing system occurs when the leader falls an equal distance below the belayer as he or she was above the belayer. This might happen as illustrated in figure 11-3, where the climber steps from a belay ledge to an exposed vertical climb with a lot of exposure. He climbs 30 feet without placing protection and then falls off, stopping 30 feet below the belayer.

This is a fall of 60 feet, or twice the length of rope between the leader and belayer; thus, $f = 60 \text{ ft}/30 \text{ ft} = 2$. The rope should be retired, and the leader should be suspect for failing to put in protection or putting it in badly so that it pulled out.

This example illustrates how important it is to prevent a fall directly onto the belay and why the most important piece of protection to safeguard the belay is the first piece. This first piece protects the belay anchor, the belayer, and the leader. Think of your belayer and your anchor and protect early.

Fall Factor and Rope Retirement

You should consider retiring a rope whenever it experiences a fall factor of 1 or more. As explained in chapter 5, many short falls have a cumulative effect on rope performance. The effect will be greatest if the climber repeatedly falls from the same point and falls on one segment of rope. The interior of a dynamic rope is made of braided strands that act like coiled springs to absorb energy. A fall will permanently stretch them, which makes them less capable of absorbing the energy of the next fall. In addition, a fall can abrade, cut, or otherwise damage the sheath.

IMPACT FORCE

When you fall, the energy of your falling body —the product of your mass and velocity at the time of braking—must be absorbed to bring you to a stop. Your velocity must be returned to zero. Your velocity at the start of braking depends on how long you have been falling. This, of course, means that the longer the fall, the more force is required to decelerate. The size of stopping force required to absorb the energy that you have acquired at the time of braking depends on the time during which you brake. A small force will do the job if you come to a stop over a long period. On the other hand, a large force will be necessary to stop the fall quickly. Most climbers want to stop quickly but also want to experience minimum impact force on their bodies. These opposing desires create problems for people who design the dynamic ropes used by climbers.

Impact Force and Rope Stretch

Ropes stretch to absorb energy. As the rope stretches, it exerts a continually increasing force until all of the energy of the fall is absorbed or until sufficient force is transmitted to the belay brake to overcome the friction of the brake and the rope slips. All belays are static, allowing the rope to stretch until they reach a certain limit determined by the belay technique and brake used, and then they allow the rope to slip and become dynamic. Once the rope slips through the belay brake, the amount of energy absorbed by rope stretch cannot get any higher; it levels off. Additional energy of the fall is absorbed by the friction of the rope slipping through the brake, around carabiners, and so forth.

The UIAA tests rope stretch or impact elongation in a totally static, nonslip belay using a procedure done on an engineered structure (see chapter 5, fig. 5-6). Rope stretch under these conditions usually measures approximately 20 percent of the rope length between the anchor and falling weight. In a real rock-climbing fall, however, impact elongation has been measured at only one-third of the rated percentage; during a fall a rope with a UIAA impact elongation of 21 percent was measured at only 7 percent.[1]

Static Impact Forces

If a belay is locked off (static), the belayer exerts a force that reaches a maximum when rope stretch reaches a maximum. This maximum force is the impact force (I) given by the equation:[2]

$$I = mg + mg \sqrt{\left(1 + \frac{2fM}{mg}\right)}$$

I can be expressed in ft-lb/sec^2 or in pound-force (*lbf*) by dividing ft-lb/sec^2 by the value of g, which is 32 ft/sec^2. We use *lbf* because it seems the simplest to understand intuitively:

I = impact force in ft-lb/sec^2

M = rope modulus in ft-lb/sec^2. Material constant depending on cross-sectional area of rope, fiber content, etc.

f = fall factor (distance fallen/amount of rope paid out)

m = mass

g = acceleration constant of gravity (32 ft/sec^2)

Because the rope modulus, mass, and effect of gravity will be constant for any one climber, the maximum force depends on the fall factor. Because fall factor is a ratio of the height fallen

A "Shocking" Near Miss

Todd led the crux pitch on Symmetry Spire and established a belay on a small shelf. His partner, Tom, fell while following. Expecting a 2- or 3-foot fall, instead he found himself plunging down the cliff, windmilling his arms as he dropped past holds that he could not grasp. When he stopped, he was back at the anchor point from which he began the pitch. He hastily clipped into the fixed anchor pitons now at his waist and began to collect his wits.

Todd, the errant belayer, had been pulled off the belay ledge and was hanging sideways—confused and disoriented—just below the ledge. He had partially lost control of the belay rope, so that it whipped around his waist during Tom's plunge down the cliff face.

Todd's anchor slings had been attached with too much slack, so the fall pulled him off the ledge and the impact force of the team's fall shock-loaded his three anchor nuts so hard that it broke a crack edge, which allowed one nut to pull out. He was hanging over the void from two rather small nuts. Needless to say, these nerve-shattered climbers rappelled off the climb without completing the route.

to the amount of rope out, this means that the impact force is independent of absolute height of a fall.

A second interesting result is discovered when the fall factor is zero ($f = 0$). This is the most gentle fall possible when a climber's weight settles onto a top rope with no slack between the climber and the belayer. The equation for impact force becomes:

$$I = mg + mg \sqrt{\left(1 + \frac{2fM}{mg}\right)}; \text{ or}$$

$$I = mg + mg \sqrt{1 + 0}$$

$$I = 2\,mg$$

This says that a 180-pound climber falling onto a top rope with no slack generates 360 pounds of force, which is perhaps twice what is expected. If the fall factor is 0.4, 0.8, 1.0, 1.4, 1.6, or 2.0, this climber generates an impact force of 1,137; 1,521; 1,676; 1,947; 2,067; or 2,288 pounds of force, respectively.

FALL SEVERITY

The severity of a fall is determined by the duration of time that impact forces must be resisted. Although a long fall and a short fall can have the same fall factor and resulting impact force, the longer fall will be more severe on the falling climber's body and the protection system because the impact force must be resisted for a longer period. The leader's body, the protection piece holding the fall, and the belay anchor might sustain impact forces for short periods without damage, but they might not be able to endure these impact forces for greater lengths of time. It makes sense to place intermediate protection pieces to limit fall distance.

IMPACT FORCES, THE BELAYER, AND THE BELAY

Above, we looked at impact forces for static belays, but, for leader falls, it is desirable to have the dynamic belays that are provided by most belay devices. This section examines the role of the belayer and the belay technique. If you simply grip the leader's rope in your hand without an additional friction surface, such as your waist, you might be able to hold a maximum of 50 pounds before the rope is pulled through your hand. You could also hold the rope loosely, so that it would run through your hand at a tensional force of less than 50 pounds. But as noted above, a falling climber generates forces of hundreds and even thousands of pounds.

No matter how strong you are, you cannot hold a fall statically—without the rope running—above limits imposed by the friction of the belay brake as magnified by hand strength. Once the force of a fall exceeds these static limits, the rope will begin to run dynamically through the belay brake. A few belay devices purposely lock the rope while other designs lock up accidentally; these lockups place maximum stress on protection and should not be used on climbs without bombproof protection.

The energy of the fall is absorbed first by rope stretch during the static portion of the belay and then by friction as the rope runs through the brake or over protection-system carabiners during the dynamic part of the belay. The impact force of a fall will reach a maximum when the rope stretches to its limit at the end of the static portion of the belay and will remain there until the fall is arrested.

What is the effect of the combined belay brake and hand strength on the maximum impact force that you can hold with different belay brakes? Many belayers use a Sticht plate without a spring and with the belayed rope passing around a single carabiner. This combination has a braking force of about 440 to 500 pounds when used with a dry rope. If a fall produces a greater tensional force, the rope will run dynamically through the plate until friction over carabiners in the rope system absorbs the excess force. Other belay devices work in a similar manner, although they have different maximum braking forces.

If you use a belay plate differently than described above, you can hold a larger maximum impact force. For example, the Sticht plate without a spring can hold a maximum of about 730 pounds statically if you belay using the plate with a dry rope, one carabiner, and a body belay. If you add a second carabiner, the additional friction increases the maximum force that you can hold to about 1,100 pounds. (In practice, there is little reason to use any belay plate in these combined modes because it creates too static a brake.) Note that if the rope is wet, the belay brake can hold about 200 pounds of force less for each of the belay methods described above before becoming dynamic.[3]

The maximum tensional force possible to hold, neglecting other sources of friction in the belay chain, is given in the following list for a number of belay brakes.[4,5]

Figure-eight descender in sport mode: 200 pounds

Waist belay: 180 to 240 pounds

Sticht plate with spring: 340 to 400 pounds

Sticht plate without spring: 440 to 500 pounds

Munter hitch: 290 to 590 pounds

Air Traffic Controller: 600 pounds

Grigri: 1,575 pounds

Of course, the leader usually puts in intermediate protection, which increases the amount of friction in the system. This additional friction, along with the tensional force provided by the belay brake, determines the maximum impact force experienced by a falling leader and the protection piece catching a fall. The running protection limits fall distance for the leader and works with the entire length of the rope and the entire protection system to absorb the energy of a fall.

Magnified Impact Forces in the Belay Protection System

If you use a mechanical belay plate, you might be able to hold a maximal tensional force of about 500 pounds before the rope begins to slip through the brake. This maximal tensional force supplied by the belay brake is magnified throughout the belay system by friction of the rope over carabiners and perhaps around rock corners. For example, as shown in figure 11-4, the initial 500-pound tensional force increases by about 40 percent, or 200 pounds, due to friction at the 90-degree turn in the rope at the first protection piece. By addition, this creates a 700-pound maximal force on the far side of the 90-degree turn. At the 180-degree turn, friction almost doubles the tension in the rope and adds 600 pounds of force, to make a 1,300-pound maximal impact force on the climber.

It is important to consider the tensional forces on the protection point that holds the fall. The belayer produces a tensional force on the protection piece directed back toward the belay, whereas the falling leader produces a tensional force on this same protection piece directed

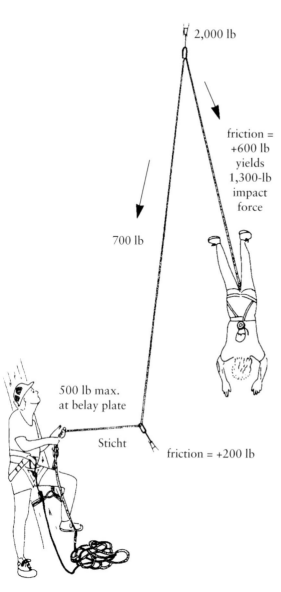

Figure 11-4. Tensional Forces in the Belay Chain:
Starting at the belayer, each time the rope turns
through a carabiner or runs over a corner of rock,
the tension in the rope is higher on the far side.
After Ed Leeper, 1980.

toward the falling leader. The sum of tensional forces on the protection piece holding the fall is approximately twice the force experienced by the falling climber. Thus, in figure 11-4, the protection piece holding the fall experiences maximal

forces of 1,300 pounds + 700 pounds = 2,000 pounds.

A similar analysis, using this simplified protection system, shows that the impact force on this protection piece varies widely for three common belay brakes. It reaches a maximum of approximately 1,000 pounds for a waist belay; 2,000 pounds for a slot plate, such as a Sticht plate; and about 2,400 pounds for the Munter hitch brake in its most static mode. These anticipated results generally have been validated by using a portable computer system to measure loads in simulated falls.[6]

Implications of Belay Technique

The lower impact force of the waist belay results from the fact that, first, rope stretch and, second, sliding friction absorb the energy of a fall. The falling climber travels farther down the cliff, however, before this energy is absorbed, with the added danger of hitting a ledge. If you use a belay that locks up in a severe fall, rope stretch without rope slippage is called on to absorb the energy of the fall. This force could rip out the protection piece holding the fall. Belay brakes that produce essentially static belays can also create obvious or hidden rope damage in a severe fall. For example, use of the Munter hitch has caused burned rope sheaths in test falls as short as 4 feet[7], and some belay plates can cut or damage the rope in a severe fall. On the other hand, most of the time, our belaying techniques and rope systems work and let us down gently. Belay plates, such as the Sticht plate with a spring, prevent lockup by design. You can prevent most belay plates from locking up by placing two carabiners on the rope between the plate and the belay carabiner. A clear advantage of the Munter hitch and belay plates is that they allow the belayer to control the rope easily during a fall.

The holding power of a nut used for protection depends on the area of contact between the nut and the rock, the breaking strength of the nut, the mechanical strength of the rock, and how well you place the nut. If the nut pulls out, fall length will be farther. With "average" protection, you would not expect it to pull out because of the belay plate, but the potential is there if you use marginal protection and take a big fall. Smaller pieces of protection used in competent rock or larger pieces of protection in less competent rock always should be considered marginal. Marginal protection also should be considered in reference to the maximal tensional force that you can apply at the belay. If you switch from a belay brake with a low static limit to one with a high static limit, you also need to reconsider your definition of what is marginal. You can use dynamic slings on marginal protection to limit the tensional force experienced by the protection piece holding a fall, as described in chapter 7. The Yates Screamer activates at 550 pounds of force as bar tacks rip, and no force applied to it can reach higher levels until all bar tacks are ripped out. This means that if you use a dynamic sling with a marginal piece of protection, the protection itself will not experience higher tensional forces as long as there are bar tacks to rip. Once all bar tacks are ripped, the sling behaves like an ordinary runner and directly passes tensional forces to the protection piece.

ENERGY ABSORPTION IN REAL PROTECTION SYSTEMS

So far, we have considered the belay brake and friction around system carabiners as absorbers of energy in climbing systems. There are more ways in which energy gets absorbed in a real fall. Some of the energy gets absorbed in deforming the belayer's body, and some of the energy goes into tightening the knot. In a simple system, without intermediate friction points and a static belay, the amount of energy that goes into knot tightening can be as much as 50 percent of the total.[8] This is why knots get so tight in a real fall that the leader needs help untying or, in extreme cases, has to cut away the knot. It also explains why you should untie and retie your knots after a fall, if it is safe to do so, to reconstitute this part of the shock-absorption system.

Undesirable accidental circumstances sometimes change the distribution of the energy ab-

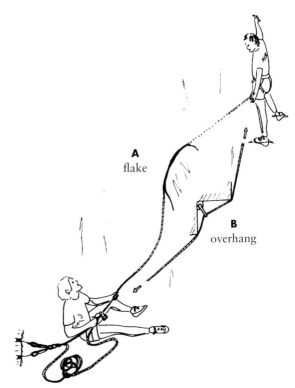

A
flake

B
overhang

Figure 11-5. Rope Drag and Tension: At A, the rope is stuck behind a flake; at B, the rope catches on the edges of an overhang and creates friction that can be eliminated by using a longer sling on the carabiner. The rope on the climber's side of the obstructions must absorb most of the energy of a fall.

sorption of the rope, belay brake, and protection system during a fall. For example, if the rope gets caught behind a rock flake or in a crack during a fall (fig. 11-5), this new point serves as the brake; the original belay brake is no longer effective. The force of the fall is taken up by rope stretch and protection between the point where the rope is caught and the fallen climber, rather than the belayer and the climber. Because there is now less rope involved, impact forces are correspondingly higher. The protection pieces might fail, and the rope might be cut. Rope drag on overhangs or corners produces a similar but less dramatic effect than a stuck rope. Rope drag adds friction to the system and concentrates the force of the fall in the rope and protection system on the side of the leader—clearly an undesirable situation.

REFERENCES FOR FUTURE READING

Cannon, Neil. 1985. Air voyagers. *Climbing.* 88:54.

Coats, Larry. 1990. Product interview with Dick Newell. *Rock & Ice.* 36.

Gadd, Will. 1993. Toys: Belay and descending devices. *Rock & Ice.* 54:106–108.

Graydon, Don, ed. 1992. *Mountaineering: The freedom of the hills.* Fifth edition. Seattle: Mountaineers.

Leeper, Ed. 1980. Belaying: Forces and stopping distances. *Summit.* 25(6):6–12.

Loughman, Michael. 1981. *Learning to rock climb.* San Francisco: Sierra Club Books.

March, Bill. 1977. The Sticht belay plate. *Summit.* 23(6):28–31.

May, W.G. 1973. *Mountain search and rescue techniques.* Boulder, Colorado: Rocky Mountain Rescue Group, Inc.

Microys, Helmut F. 1977. Climbing ropes. *American Alpine Journal.* 21(51):130–147.

———. 1984. A short course in rope physics—a rebuttal. *Climbing.* 85:61–62.

Nagode, P.E. 1999. Self-contained field computer lets REI quantify loads on climbing equipment. <http://www.somat.com/fieldstories/rei.html>

Peters, Ed, ed. 1982. *Mountaineering: The freedom of the hills.* Fourth edition. Seattle: Mountaineers.

Robbins, Royal. 1979. Climbing rope myths. *Summit.* 25(1):12–17, 23–25.

ENDNOTES

1. See Microys, 1984. The belay for this measured fall was a firm one and held up to 700 to 800 pounds of force before slipping. In a longer version of this article obtained from the author, the author quotes an example from Schubert (P. Schubert. 1982. "Zwillingsseile-Seiltechnik der Zukunft." *Der Bergsteiger.* October: 77–79), involving the most severe fall possible—15 meters of rope and a 30-meter fall. Rope slippage measured 5.5 meters. When combined with a 7 percent impact elongation (15 meters x 0.07 = 1.05 meters), the distance added to the fall by rope slippage and impact elongation was 5.5 + 1.05 = 6.55 meters. The total distance fallen was 36.55 meters.

2. The discussion here and in the section headed "Fall Severity" follows the work of Microys, 1977. Any errors of interpretation are mine.

3. See March, 1977, for Sticht-plate braking values.

4. Many of these values are taken from the Ontario Rock Climbing Association's *Rock Climbing Safety Manual* and are based on drop tests conducted by the association. Values for the figure-eight descender come from Gadd, 1993.

5. Beal Ropes lists braking forces as 550-pound force (200 daN) for a figure-eight; 677-pound force (300 daN) for the Italian or Munter Hitch; and 1,575-pound force (700 daN) for a Petzl Grigri on its Web site at <http://www.bealropes.com>.

6. See Nagode, 1999. REI engineers measured load data on protection, a belay, and a simulated climber during a fall. For this test, the rope passed through one piece of protection rather than the two pieces discussed in this text. As anticipated, a cam-lock static belay put the greatest load on the system at 2,215 pounds with loads experienced by the belay and climber of 839 and 1,382 pounds, respectively. A Trango Pyramid belay device, expected to catch a light load, expelled nearly 30 inches of a 10.5mm rope and produced a maximum load of 927 pounds; the loads on the belay and climber were 265 and 662 pounds, respectively. One of the firmest catches from a dynamic belaying device came from the HB Bigger Brake, which put a load of 1,227 pounds on the protection, 392 pounds on the belay, and 835 pounds on the climber.

7. See Leeper, 1980.

8. See Cannon, 1985.

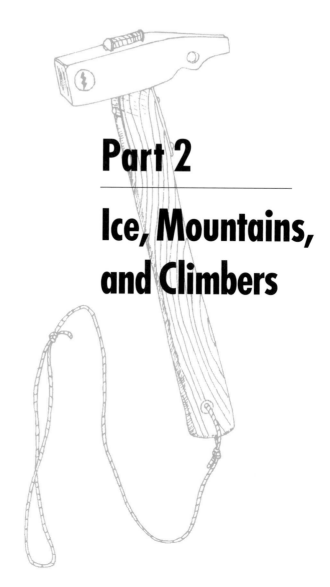

Part 2

Ice, Mountains, and Climbers

Movement on Snow and Ice

SNOW AND ICE CLIMBING BASICS

The part of this book devoted to ice climbing assumes that you know the basics presented in the previous chapters on knots, harnesses, belaying, and rappelling. Although skills learned in rock climbing are generally helpful, specific movement and leading skills on snow and ice differ from those on rock. In rock climbing, you adapt your body to the rock by using available holds, whereas in snow and ice climbing, you can use an axe to create holds where you want them. Snow and ice climbing takes place in a colder environment and requires greater attention to protective clothing. Protection for snow and ice climbing differs from rock-climbing protection, but linking protection into anchor systems and understanding the forces on these systems remain the same. If you take the time to master new snow- and ice-climbing skills, you will be able to move quickly through multipitch long sections of easy technical terrain (see photo above). Later on, mastery of these basics will

make climbing steep ice and even thin ice easier and will enable you to make a safe descent.

DRESSING FOR SNOW AND ICE CLIMBING

Snow and ice climbing takes place under environmental conditions that vary from very warm and moist to very cold and dry. What you wear is important because it can hinder or promote heat retention. You can adapt to the range of conditions by wearing layers of clothing. For the layer next to your skin, choose synthetic underwear tops and bottoms made of polypropylene or newer synthetic fabrics that do not absorb odors as much as polypropylene does. These fabrics wick perspiration, which is generated in even the coldest weather, to the next layer and eventually to the outside air. Cotton is a poor fabric for winter underwear because it absorbs moisture easily and cools as it conducts body heat away from your skin. Even wool, an old standby, conducts more body heat away from your skin than modern synthetics. The second layer can be synthetic or wool: synthetic pile is popular. Wear one or two layers of sweaters and a pair of pants. The outer layer should always be a wind shell; wind makes you feel colder.

Because snow and ice climbing requires active movement, three layers of clothing will keep you warm—and possibly even hot—at winter temperatures of 20 degrees Fahrenheit and below. To avoid overheating during the hike to the climb, wear only two layers. When you stop, you might even take off another layer for a few minutes to vent excess moisture before you cool down. Then dress warmly for the climb. You will feel colder while you stand around to belay, and it is difficult and can be dangerous to put on more clothes while on small stances. In very cold conditions, consider taking along a sleeveless vest that you can put on over your wind shell when you stop.

Most snow and ice climbers wear a hat and add a balaclava made of synthetic fabric when it

An Alpine Snow Climb

is cold. If you plan to go above the tree line, purchase a face mask that you can don without removing your climbing helmet. These masks cover the lower part of your face and fasten behind your head with Velcro, rather than going under your helmet and hat. Carry the mask in an outside pocket of your pack for those few but desperate times when you pop up into wind from a sheltered climb.

On long climbs, take along food to provide fuel for your body to keep producing heat. Do not expect to be able to sit down to a leisurely lunch in the dead of winter or even to stop to get into your pack during the climb. Carry food with a high fat content—such as a peanut-butter sandwich, nuts, or cheese—in your pockets so you can eat while belaying. You might also want something like candy, chocolate, or a granola bar to supply immediate calories. Do not forget to drink water: you will lose two to six quarts of water by normal respiration and sweating during a day of activity. If you do not replace this water, expect to experience dehydration, muscle soreness, fatigue, and general lassitude.

Helmets

A helmet helps to protect your head if you are hit by falling rock, ice, or equipment dropped by parties overhead.[1] (Helmets are discussed in more detail in chapter 4.) A survey of winter climbing areas indicates that alpine rock and snow and ice climbers accept the advantages of wearing a helmet.

It is almost impossible to avoid being hit by ice falling from above, whether it is knocked off accidentally by a climber or naturally. If you knock off ice from the climb, yell "Ice!" to warn those below. If you hear the call, look down, not up, so that the ice hits the top of your helmet and not your face. After you have been hit a few times, you will learn not to belay or stand underneath other climbers. For winter climbing, choose a helmet with a web harness and an adjustable headband that will allow you to wear a wool hat or go bareheaded underneath. Many models have ventilation holes to help make the helmet cooler.

A Clothing List for Snow and Ice Climbing

Head
- Balaclava—This hood covers the head and neck. A thin polypropylene balaclava is useful as a liner.
- Wool hat.
- Helmet—CEN/UIAA-approved for climbing, to protect yourself if you fall or are hit by falling ice.
- Face mask—The Masque brand has a Velcro fastener and goes on quickly in emergencies.
- Contact lenses—If you need corrective lenses, contacts give you better vision in a snowstorm (you do not want fogged glasses at a crux). In pleasant winter conditions, antifogging coatings keep eyeglasses from misting.

Upper Body
- Foundation undergarment—Underwear of synthetic fiber, such as polypropylene (polypro), or of wool for your upper body.
- Wool or polypro shirts or sweaters—One lightweight and one heavy, to wear over your underwear.

- Synthetic pile jacket or parka—To wear over the shirt or sweater.
- Windbreaker—To wear as outer layer. It should have zipper vents to regulate heat.

Hands
- Thin gloves (polypro)—These allow you manual dexterity in cold weather.
- Two pairs of light- to medium-weight wool or synthetic mittens—Wear one pair inside shells, and keep the other pair as a spare.
- Shell mittens—Medium-weight mittens keep your hands warm in most conditions as long as they are dry; shells help keep them dry. By wearing mittens and shells together, you should be able to grip an axe comfortably, and your hands will be protected if they strike the ice. Instead of mittens, you can use:
- High-tech gloves and liners—Made of synthetic material, designed for ice climbing.

Lower Body
- Long underwear—Made of wool or polypro, as a foundation garment.

- Wool or synthetic pile pants.
- Windproof pants—To wear over all. A full-length zipper allows you to don or shed them easily even when you are wearing crampons.

Feet
- Stiff-soled double boots—Designed for ice climbing, these are expensive but you probably should consider the $300 to $400 spent toward safeguarding your toes from frostbite a good buy.
- Gaiters—These keep snow out of your boots, insulate your lower legs, and hold in the bottoms of your pants so that you do not catch them with crampon points.

Packs
- Medium-size alpine climbing pack—Allows you to carry personal and team gear as you approach the climb and on the climb itself. The pack should be small enough not to inhibit climbing but large enough to store the gear that you need for a day without requiring a lot of time to tie it on. Many packs are designed specifically for ice climbing.

Mitts and Gloves

Climbing snow and ice can be hard on the hands because of the cold and dampness, and the tools have at least some metal parts that conduct heat away from your hands. Consider that, on steep ice, you are pumped with adrenaline and swing the axe with all of your strength. Your hand overgrips the tool, and your fingers and knuckles get smashed between the axe shaft and the ice. The water in the damp glove conducts heat away from your hand, and your wrist leash cuts off circulation. At the top of the climb, in a state of incipient frostbite, both blood and feeling painfully return to your hands. How do you avoid this un-

pleasant side effect of ice climbing?

Mitts and gloves must not only protect your hands from cold and damp, they must also serve as a cushion when you inadvertently smash your hands into the ice. Most climbers use a mitten or glove shell with a liner. There are a number of commercially available "dry" shells. Glove shells constructed to place your fingers in a curved position of function allow you to get a better grip on the shaft of an ice axe. Shells should be durable and preferably inexpensive, although technologically advanced shells, which work well, can be worth the money. Canadian Army leather shells are the best of the army surplus; after being broken in, they have a palm that grips the axe well. Liner mitts need not be very thick to protect you from the cold, but they do need to be dry. Wet liners conduct heat much more rapidly than dry liners. Carry spare dry hand coverings in an accessible place, such as the kangaroo pouch of a cagoule, and change liners when they are damp. This precaution is especially important for steep ice, where you might grip the axe tightly and accentuate heat loss by conduction. Belaying often squeezes water out of the climbing rope and into your mitt. Try belaying with a second set of liners or gloves to keep the mitt combination dry during belays and to give you added dexterity. You can switch hand coverings quickly and keep belaying gloves in the kangaroo pouch along with the spare dry pair of mitten liners.

CRAMPONS

English climbers began following snow climbs in lines of steps cut in the ice by guides with their ice axes while wearing nailed boots. By the end of the 1800s, climbers were using flexible 4-point crampons, and, in 1908, Englishman Oskar Eckenstein designed a flexible 10-point crampon, which evoked protests that it gave an unfair advantage to the climber. Once Eckenstein worked out the technique of flat-footing, there was no longer a need to cut steps. Today, flat-footing is called the *Eckenstein technique*, after its originator, or the *French technique*, after climbers who adapted it well to climbing.

Laurent Grivel, in the early 1930s, added 2 front points projecting forward to produce the flexible 12-point crampon. This innovation gave rise to the front-pointing technique that became identified with Austrian climbers, who adapted it to the hard ice of the eastern Alps. Climbers today can have the most fun and move most efficiently by using each of these techniques alone and in combination where appropriate. On any given climb, the technique used can change frequently and allow the climber to move in a more efficient manner in keeping with the terrain.

In the United States, Yvon Chouinard devel-

oped a rigid crampon to replace the flexible crampon. Rigid crampons, which underwent yearly refinement, reduced front-point vibration that shatters ice. To prevent breaking these crampons, however, it was necessary to wear them on boots that did not flex. In 1976, an ascent by Mike Lowe began an evolution of the Foot-Fang. There were "bolted to the bottom of his ski boots several jagged strips of chrome moly having needle-like front points that resembled nothing so much as the fangs of a pit-viper."[2] The Foot-Fang is an absolutely rigid crampon used by many to climb steep ice. Crampons continue to evolve, and current modular designs offer interchangeable monopoints and vertically oriented front-points.

When you start to climb on snow and ice, you have to learn to trust your crampons to provide security on ice. Just as you learn that rock-climbing shoes stick when you smear on a friction slab or edge on small footholds, so you learn how to use crampons for different kinds of footholds in flat, sloping, or steep ice. Figure 12-1 illustrates two crampons: the Lowe Foot-Fang and the Salewa flexible. Most crampons have 10 points perpendicular to the sole of the foot; some have shorter points in between for

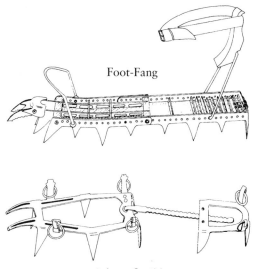

Foot-Fang

Salewa flexible

Figure 12-1. Rigid and Flexible Crampons

added security in snow. The 10 points are used in *flat-footing*, the technique used to walk and climb on flat to gently sloping inclines. The 2 points directed forward in the plane of the boot sole plus the two frontmost of the 10 points perpendicular to the sole are used in *front-pointing*, the technique used on steep ice.

SMC rigid and Foot-Fang crampons represent two different approaches to crampon design. Both are rigid crampons especially suitable for climbing steep ice. You must wear the SMC rigid design on a very stiff boot because any flexing of the boot will work-harden the crampon and break it. The Foot-Fang is very strong and rigid in itself and does not depend on the boot for its rigidity or strength. The frontmost points of the Foot-Fang are vertical (similar to the points of ice hand tools). In contrast, the frontmost points on the SMC crampon are horizontal. Some climbers prefer the horizontal orientation for mixed climbing—they place the front points on small positive edges of rock. Both kinds of crampons work well; try both, and choose the one that suits you best.

Think about weight, as well as rigidity, in choosing crampons. If you intend to climb alpine snow or ice, you might consider using a lightweight flexible crampon on a mountaineering boot that will flex as you walk. In alpine settings, approaches are often long, climbs are usually not as steep as modern roadside test pieces, and a lightweight flexible crampon and boot work well together.

Crampons are attached to your boots with straps that come in sets of two or four. They are commonly made of reinforced neoprene, which resists water rot. When the toe strap is one continuous piece, it begins on the outside of the instep, crosses the forefoot to the inside toe post, passes to the outside toe post, crosses to the inside instep post, and returns to the outside instep post (fig. 12-2A).

When you pass a strap through the toe posts, do so from the outside to the inside. After going through the post, pass the strap forward of itself. This technique will help prevent the strap

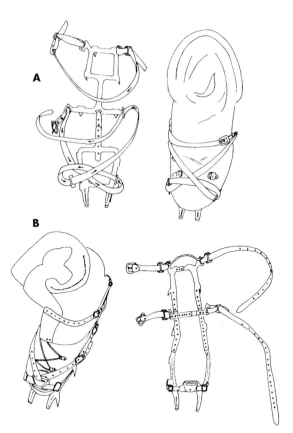

Figure 12-2. Adjusting Crampon Straps: A—One continuous toe strap. B—Speed straps.

from slipping forward over the toe when you front-point. If the strap slips, the slack can allow the crampon to fall off. This happened in the middle of my first ice lead and need not happen to you.

Feeding the crampon straps in such a complicated manner can be difficult at the best of times but is particularly difficult when it is cold and your hands lose the required manual dexterity. Wear thin polypropylene gloves to protect your hands without sacrificing dexterity. Better yet, use speed straps with prethreaded toe straps (fig. 12-2B). One long strap passes through a ring or plate in the middle of the toe segment to the instep post, where it fastens. This system significantly cuts time and reduces the effort required to put on crampons. The Foot-Fang shown in figure 12-1 has the quickest strap system. Toe and heel bails attach to solid boot flanges and act as step-in bindings.

Adjust new front points, as illustrated in figure 12-2, so that they extend in front of the boot approximately half their length—that is, half the distance between the end of the front point and the base of the first vertical point. This position should be correct for normal ice. You can make the front points longer for honeycombed ice and shorter for thin ice.

As the forward-directed front points wear, file them—on their upper surface only—to their original shape. Do not file the lower surface of these front points. Do not use a grinding wheel, which can easily destroy the temper of the metal. You cannot climb hard ice with dull points, so you should keep the points sharp. On the other hand, if you dull your crampons by walking on rocks and climb frequently, you will soon file them away if you sharpen for every climb. With a bit of experience, you will soon learn when it is critical to have freshly sharpened points. You can also file the 10 bottom points to their original shape.

Footwear

Modern ice-climbing boots largely prevent the cold-related injuries of previous generations, but the potential for cold injury remains. The boots have evolved from ski-boot technology and usually feature a hard nylon outer boot with a woolen or foam inner boot. Use the woolen inner boot in normal winter ice-climbing temperatures. A foam inner boot is very warm and is used for extreme cold conditions, such as climbing at high altitude. Most ice-climbing boots are stiff so as to form a stable platform for the foot as you climb steep ice or kick a step in snow. They are relatively high, to support the lower leg. The very features that make boots work well for climbing steep ice make them somewhat difficult to walk in: their stiff soles have only a small amount of curvature, which prevents the foot from rolling forward with each step. Some ice boots hinge to allow greater flexibility for walking.

Avoid walking directly on a climbing-hut floor in inner boots because water and abrasion will quickly damage them, and they are expensive. Take pile booties or sneakers for lounging in the hut or quick runs to the outhouse.

One of the chief dangers for snow and ice climbers is frostbite to the feet. Frostbite can be caused by cutting off the blood supply, for instance, by wearing too many socks under boots with flexible uppers or by tightening crampon straps too much. If the boot flexes while you are front-pointing, the straps dig into the soft upper with each placement and cut off blood to your toes. Crampons that do not use strap systems, such as Foot-Fangs, do not cause this problem. In extreme cold, you need to take care even with modern double boots. The microclimate surrounding your feet is more important than ambient air temperature—your feet can be at risk when you do not consider the temperature to be excessively cold at the level of your face or hands.

Conduction—heat loss produced by touching cold objects, such as metal—also causes frostbite. Crampons will conduct heat away from the foot just as steel-toed boots do. In very cold weather, insert a sole-shaped piece of Ensolite between boot and crampon to prevent some heat loss. Some crampons have a nylon plate for the same purpose; this plate also helps prevent wet snow from balling under the foot. Modern boot liners, particularly those of Aveolite foam, and overboots also prevent heat loss by conduction.

In otherwise fit individuals, two relatively common conditions, among others, can contribute to frostbite. Cardiovascular circulatory problems, either organic or drug related, can produce reduced blood circulation in the feet and toes. Twenty percent of the population has the condition called *Morton's foot*, in which the second toe of the foot is longer than the big toe. If the second toe touches the end of an otherwise well-fitting boot, it will get cold and can become frostbitten. If you have Morton's foot, choose boots made on a pattern that gives your toe plenty of room. Be aware of your feet: loosen crampon straps, stamp your feet, and take aggressive action whenever they begin to feel cold.

Raynaud's Disease

Most ice climbers, sometime in their climbing careers, find that their hands turn cold and numb, followed by a flood of pain upon rewarming. Once you have experienced this miserable condition, you will try everything that you can to keep your extremities warm: wearing dry gloves, warm boots, and a hat; drinking lots of water to avoid dehydration; eating high-calorie foods; and hanging from your wrist leash to avoid overgripping your axe on steep climbs because overgripping cuts off the circulation to your hands. Perhaps none of these measures will keep your hands warm. A few unlucky people experience cold-induced agony whenever they go ice climbing.

When most of us get cold hands, our sympathetic nervous system sends out a message to open up more capillaries and send more warm blood to the fingers. The capillaries of people with Raynaud's (pronounced "ray nose") disease never get this message and remain clamped down. Their extremities turn white, bluish, and numb; when the extremities warm up, they tingle, burn, and throb. If you have experienced this problem while your climbing partners show no sign of distress, you might have Raynaud's disease.

Raynaud's disease affects 5 to 10 percent of the total population, but women are five times as likely as men to suffer from it. People who subject their hands to stress—pocket-pulling rock climbers and knuckle-bashing ice climbers could certainly qualify—are more likely to develop the condition.

There is hope for longtime sufferers. The United States Army has done research on the subject and developed a 13-step program by which you can recondition blood vessels subject to Raynaud's disease. You can find further information in an article by Dorcas Miller in the October/November 1990 issue of *Climbing*. Dorcas explains the reconditioning program and describes how she successfully treated herself.

Flat-Footing (Eckenstein or French Technique)

To walk in crampons, you need to walk deliberately, picking up and putting down each foot carefully, even on flat ground. You can never shuffle because you could catch a point and fall. You cannot run in crampons without risking a broken ankle if a point sticks unexpectedly. I once saw a climber, relieved at having successfully descended an exposed gully, break into a run on flat ground. A crampon point stuck into a tree root, and I heard his ankle snap as his body raced forward of his stuck foot. Do not let this happen to you. Novice ice climbers always begin flat-footing sessions hesitantly but, in the course of a day, become very comfortable moving around on the ice. So confident are they that they forget ice is slippery when they take off the crampons.

Begin by walking on a nearly flat stream with a few gentle bulges or slopes. Flat-foot by placing all 10 crampon points perpendicular to the ice (fig. 12-3A). Stamp your feet to get the points in. Do not try edging, with only the uphill-side points in actual contact with the ice

(fig. 12-3B): the points probably will not hold, the crampon will skate, and you will fall. If you use crampons with parallel sides, such as Foot-Fangs, it may be possible to *hedge* (Jeff Lowe's term) by backing off from the traditional flat-foot stance by about 15 degrees. The idea is to get the uphill row of points all the way in while the downhill row rests on the ice. This position does not torture the ankles as much, but you can still skate. As you flat-foot on ice, your feet are farther apart than when you walk in street shoes on a rug. As you go up slight inclines, splay your feet outward like a duck (*en canard*).

There are two techniques for flat-footing on slopes. First, place your foot on contour, or parallel to the slope, so that both the toe and heel of your foot are at the same level and your body is sideways to the slope. Second, roll your ankle away from the slope. This movement rotates the bottom crampon points into proper position. In practice, consciously think about hip movement away from the slope because your leg, ankle, and foot are attached and must follow hip movement (fig. 12-3C). Flat-footing is similar

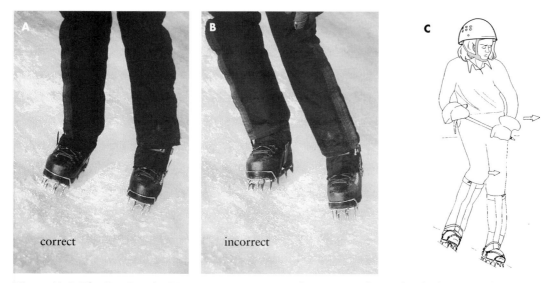

Figure 12-3. Flat-Footing: A—Ten points in contact. B—Trying to edge. C—Body posture while flat- footing on a slope. The climber is rolling his hip out to get all 10 points on each crampon into the ice.

both in body position and movement to traversing friction slabs.

You need *dynamic balance* for flat-footing, just as you need it for ordinary walking. When you flat-foot and when you walk, you ordinarily begin in a position of balance, move dynamically through a position of imbalance, and return to a position of balance. It is possible, as many beginners can attest, to stand on one leg, but this stance requires much effort on the part of your leg muscles. Moving through the imbalance position requires commitment so that there is enough momentum to get to the other side—the more commitment, the less leg energy required.

It is customary for beginners to have someone spot them with an outstretched arm, to try to protect the head in case of a fall. Spotters should beware of getting caught by the points of the crampons. (If you are spotting, stay off to the side or be ready to leap away from those crampon points. The best way to assist is to give feedback about whether the crampon is on contour. Remind climbers to roll their hips out in order to get all 10 points into the ice.)

The basic movement sequence of flat-footing on gentle slopes is to move directly up or down the slope in duck-foot fashion (fig. 12-4), a

Figure 12-4. Duck-Foot Walking on Gentle Snow and Ice Slopes

movement termed *pied en canard*. On water ice (see chapter 14), pure flat-foot technique—incorporating the use of an axe for balance—is most useful for moving efficiently over long stretches of low-angle ice.

Front-Pointing (Austrian Technique)

Front-pointing is the technique of moving with crampons on steeper ice. Although we often speak of two front points on each crampon, there are actually four points on each crampon involved in front-pointing, as you can see in figure 12-5: the two forward-directed points parallel to the boot sole and the two frontmost points most nearly perpendicular to the boot sole. When all four of these points are well planted in the ice, they will not shear out, and they form a stable platform on which to stand. In order to keep these points in the ice, you must keep your heel down so the sole of a rigid boot is horizontal.

Front-pointing involves short, gentle swing-

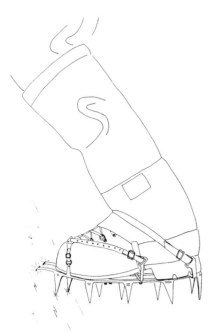

Figure 12-5. The Four Front Points: Hold the crampon horizontally by focusing on heel elevation in relation to the front points. Chip small platforms for the two forward-directed points; the two frontmost bottom points contact the ice.

Front-Pointing

"I looked back, down our endless ladder of steps. Up it I saw the New Era coming at express speed; there were two men running—and I mean running, not climbing—up it. Admittedly, practiced climbers can move quickly in good steps, but for these two to have reached this point quite early in the morning was positively amazing. They must have bivouacked last night on the lower part of the wall; it hardly seemed possible that they had only started up it today. But it was, in fact, the case.

"These two were the best of all the 'Eiger Candidates'—Heckmair and Vorg—wearing their twelve-pointed crampons. I felt quite outmoded in my old claws."

Heinrich Harrer, *The White Spider*

---

ing kicks in a motion that chips small platforms for each of the front points. To kick a platform, swing your leg in a normal manner directly in front of you at a selected target. If there is a natural foothold, use it as long as it does not pull you out of balance. Do not choose the platform position at random. Take advantage of any ripple in the ice, even one as small as a fraction of an inch, to enlarge as a front-point platform. Hard swings tend to work-harden, or embrittle, the crampon points as they bounce off the ice and to break away the small front-point ice platforms formed by a previous swing. When you climb on thin, iced-over rock, delicately attached ice columns, or steep ice, the ability to chip platforms for the front points becomes critical. These platforms allow you to get weight onto your legs and off your arms. Find a gentle bulge that is not too high and see how much force you need to form these platforms.

When climbing on front points, balance is important. If you boulder without hand tools, you will need to take small steps in order to stay in balance. This movement is very similar to the balance and small steps required on rock when only small holds are available. If you have large handholds on rock or use hand tools on ice, you can always lean back on these and take larger

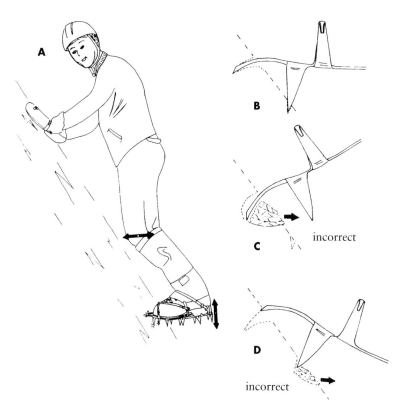

Figure 12-6. Front-Pointing on Moderately Angled Ice:
A—Push your upper body away from the ice and hold the bottom of your boot and crampon horizontal. Arrows show that rotation of the knee causes the boot heel and crampon to lift or drop.
B—The front points and crampons positioned correctly in a horizontal plane.
C—Front-directed horizontal points shear out of the ice when the heel lifts, and the climber falls.
D—The horizontal front points leave the ice, and the frontmost bottom points shear when you drop your heel. The climber can fall again, but this rarely happens in practice.

steps. The analogies with rock climbing go further. You must keep your body upright and away from the ice. On low-angle ice, push your upper body away from the ice much as on a low-angle slab climb on rock (fig. 12-6A).

Knee position helps to keep the sole of the foot and crampon horizontal (heel-down position) because your knee is connected to the top of the lower leg and in turn to the ankle and foot. Bend the knee slightly toward the ice surface to keep the foot horizontal (fig. 12-6A and B). If you consciously focus on your knee to gain the heel-down position, your foot, ankle, leg, and knee rotate in a natural way to keep the front points in proper position.

Climbing with a lifted heel can produce a fall (fig. 12-6C). Initially, the two frontmost bottom points on each crampon lift from the ice, which reduces the stable platform. With further rotation, the two forward-directed points of each crampon will shear away the small ice platform on which you are standing (fig. 12-6C), and you

will fall. Alternatively, if your heel is too far below the front points, the two forward-directed points can lose contact with the ice and the two frontmost perpendicular points will shear from the ice (fig. 12-6D). In practice, it is somewhat difficult to lower your heels this far. Experiment with the various positions—heel-up, heel-down, and heel very low—to get an idea of when your points will shear and when they won't. Of course, practice only a few inches above the ground so that you will not get hurt when the points shear.

To down-climb with front points, you extend your leg and kick, stiff-legged, as though you were kicking a football. If you want to move your right foot downward, extend the entire right leg and swing the leg as a unit without flexing the knee too much. At the same time, keep your upper body upright so you can see what is happening to your foot.

Climbing with front points requires what at first might seem to be strange body positions.

The two forward-directed front points of many crampons follow the curve of the boot, which makes it necessary to angle your feet to place the front points perpendicular to the ice. Even parallel-sided crampons require similar, but less extreme, positions.

How you hold your feet varies with the geometry of the ice surface. For flat vertical surfaces, you must move your heels apart and assume a slightly duck-footed stance; this stance brings the knees together. This strange knock-kneed position becomes pronounced when you climb steep, sharply curved convex bulges, which are among the most strenuous ice climbs. It is harder to stand in balance on front points, and more effort has to go into hand-tool placements and upper-body strength.

On concave surfaces, bring your heels together to maintain the proper front-point angle with the ice; this position will seem relatively natural. The heel-together stance becomes more pronounced as slight concave surfaces turn into right-angle corners, which are climbed by stemming from wall to wall. Stemming allows you to get more weight over your feet and generally makes these climbs less strenuous.

The next time you approach an ice climb, look for a surface that curves inward. Only a few degrees of curvature make a line up this surface less strenuous than a dead-vertical wall. Avoid surfaces that curve outward unless your objective is to pump out on ice. Indeed, top-roping outward curving bulges is a good workout.

Front-pointing, once mastered, feels very secure. However, it has some drawbacks. In the front-pointing position, the points act as a fulcrum around which the body rotates. If the crampons are flexible ones on flexible boots, you resist this rotation largely with your calf muscles and to a lesser extent with your foot muscles. The more rigid the boot-crampon combination, the less muscular effort required to resist rotation, but if the crampons are absolutely rigid, they will be heavier and call for more work by your upper leg muscles. Thus, although manufacturers have attempted to close this gap, you must choose among boot-crampon combinations that emphasize low weight versus high rigidity. Your decision might be influenced by whether you climb steep ice by the roadside or hike long distances to do alpine climbs.

Whether you are learning to front-point or helping someone also to master the technique, here is a checklist of principles to remember:

- Kick the ice with short, not overly hard, swings to form front-point platforms.

- Take short steps.

- Form a horizontal platform by keeping your boot heel down. Keep your upper body away from the ice. This position will help prevent front-point rotation in a vertical plane and allow you to see the position of your heel in relation to the front points.

- Bring your heels together or push them apart. The front points need to be perpendicular to the ice surface in a horizontal plane. An insecure placement results if only the front points on the inside or outside of each crampon are in the ice.

- Down-climb with a rigid leg and an upright body position that allows you to see all four front points and heel.

Combined Technique (Pied Troisième)

Combining flat-footing and front-pointing takes advantage of the strengths of both techniques. The photo at right shows a climber using the combined technique. His right foot is in the flat-foot position; his left foot is front-pointing. His arms are pushing his upper body away from the ice to keep his weight over his feet. On his next step, he can alternate and flat-foot with his left foot to give his left calf muscle a rest.

You can flat-foot when the incline of the ice varies from low angle to near vertical, and when there are one-step bulges. On low-angle ice, alternating flat-foot technique with one foot and front-pointing with the other is efficient. You accomplish changes of direction by going onto front points with one or both feet. On moderate ground, the combined technique allows you to

Combined Technique: *Flat-footing and front-pointing simultaneously.*

Ice Axe: *The axe shown has interchangeable picks.*

move fast with security and without tiring the calf muscles. On steep ice, you can rest calf muscles by flat-footing on the top of small bulges. You can overcome short walls (those slightly taller than one step) with the following sequence. Stand flat-footed at the base of the wall. Front-point with one foot halfway up the vertical section, and finish by picking up your lower foot and placing it on top in a flat-foot position.

ICE AXE

The ice axe long has been the hallmark of the mountaineer. The axe, along with the skill to use it and a pair of good boots, make up most of what you need to climb long snow slopes. During the late 1960s and the 1970s, the axe underwent a radical evolution that enables climbers to climb even steep frozen waterfalls with a sense of security.

The parts of the ice axe are shaft, spike, and head (see photo above). The spike and shaft connect at the ferrule. The head has a pick on one end and an adze on the other. Use the adze for cutting steps in snow and ice. Use the pick to provide traction in hard steep snow and ice and for self-arrest on snow. Use the shaft for snow belays.

The shaft of the axe was originally made of wood, a natural material that was lightweight but not very strong and susceptible to dry rot. I have seen at least one wooden-shafted ice axe, left outside a tent overnight, that suffered the ignoble death of being consumed by porcupines. (Presumably the animals wanted the salt left from the climber's hands.) Metal-shafted axes were stronger but cold to the touch and devoid of aesthetic appeal, even when the metal was wrapped. Yvon Chouinard introduced laminated bamboo shafts to provide strength and

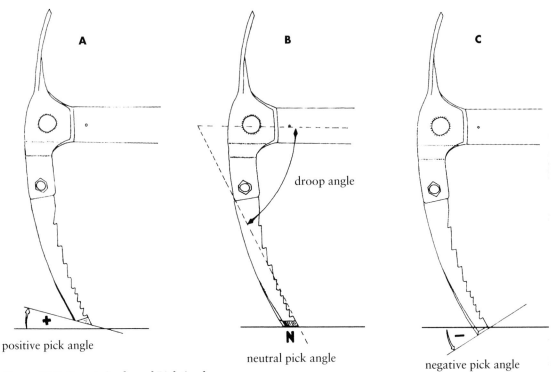

Figure 12-7. Droop Angle and Pick Angle

low weight combined with good looks. The best modern axes use high-tech carbon-fiber compounds, which are strong, lightweight, and well crafted.

The proper length of the ice-axe shaft depends on your height and its intended use. Traditionally, a 70-centimeter axe is the choice for general alpine climbing. The alpine axe is often the single tool that aids movement on low-angle ice and snow, as well as providing direct aid, termed *piolet traction* (*piolet* is French for axe), on steeper climbs. For steep climbs, a long shaft actually interferes with climbing because the spike hits the ice at the start of a swing. The increased leverage of the longer shaft also makes it more difficult to wield the axe high overhead. Generally, therefore, a 45- to 55-centimeter axe is recommended for steep climbing. On the steepest of climbs some climbers prefer shafts of hammer length, which can be as short as 20 to 30 centimeters. In sum, there is no rule about length, and

climbers have used axes of every size to ascend the steepest of climbs.

Droop Angle and Pick Angle

Pick *droop* refers to the angle between the pick blade and the axe shaft (fig. 12-7B) and is determined by the manufacturer. A pick with its blade perpendicular to the shaft has no droop. Droop increases as the pick blade bends (droops) toward the axe shaft. The pick blade can be either straight or curved. Modern ice climbing began with the introduction of radically drooped pick blades that hold well on steep ice.

Pick *angle* is the angle formed between the end of the pick blade and a snow or ice surface. Although picks on new axes come with a fixed angle, you can change this angle with a file. Pick angles can be positive, neutral, or negative (see fig. 12-7). A positive pick angle produces a sharp point that penetrates snow and ice easily, which is an advantage when climbing hard ice but might

The Radical Curve

"On a rainy summer day in 1966, I went onto a glacier in the Alps with the purpose of testing every different type of ice ax available at the time. My plan was to see which one worked best for *piolet ancre*, which one was better at stepcutting, and why. After I found a few answers, it took the intervention of Donald Snell to convince the very reluctant and conservative Charlet factory to make a 55-centimeter ax with a curved pick for the crazy American. In those days a 55-centimeter ax was crazy enough—but a curved pick! I had the feeling that modifying the standard straight pick into a curve compatible with the arc of the ax's swing would allow the pick to stay put better in the ice. I had noticed that a standard pick would pop out when I placed my weight on it. My idea worked, and a few years later Rob Collister wrote in *Mountain*, 'The development of a curved pick for axes and hammers was an event in ice climbing history comparable to the introduction of crampons in the 1890s, or the use of front points and ice pitons in the thirties. It could prove more revolutionary than either. Since it makes for both greater speed and greater security, it will encourage those who have previously been deterred by the need to choose between the two.'"

Yvon Chouinard in *Climbing Ice*

penetrate too rapidly during a self-arrest on snow. Axes dedicated to snow are often ground with a negative pick angle to slow penetration and give greater control during self-arrest.

Hammers

Ice hammers (fig. 12-8) are shorter and heavier than axes. You commonly use them in your off hand when climbing steep ice. Hammers have an anvil head in place of the axe's adze. The added weight of the anvil and short length give you additional momentum and control that result in more penetrating power and compensate

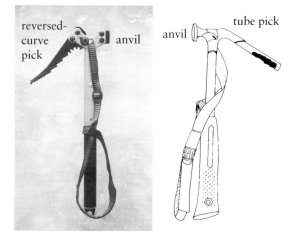

reversed-curve pick   anvil   anvil   tube pick

northwall hammer   Hummingbird hammer

Figure 12-8. Hammers

for any lack of strength or coordination present in the off hand.

Hammers commonly have a reverse-curve pick that droops at an angle of 55 degrees. The reverse curve evolved from the straight pick of the Terrordactyl developed by Hamish Mac-Innes. You place Terrordactyl picks with a chopping motion, and you can even hook them onto rock ledges or into preexisting hand-tool placements. These radically drooped straight picks work extremely well when in place. However, they encourage smashing your knuckles into the ice; "Terrordactyl knuckle" has become a term to describe enlarged, deformed knuckles. The reverse-curve pick overcomes this problem to a certain extent, as do newer designs with curved shafts. Reverse-curve picks allow a more natural swinging motion that spares the knuckles somewhat, and they are just as secure.

One of the problems with striking the pick of an ice axe is that the pick tends to shatter the ice. You get around this complication by striking repeated targeted blows to remove brittle ice from the surface and to get at more plastic ice underneath. Lowe Alpine Systems introduced a hollow tube called a *Hummingbird pick* that allows ice to expand inside the pick and minimizes external ice shattering. Axes with hollow picks probably work better than other designs in very brittle ice. Interestingly, the tube can both be secure and rotate, thus simultaneously allowing the climber to move up or down in a lieback off the axe. Most other axe designs require the axe to be more directly overhead to remain secure, since the flat pick cannot rotate.

ICE-AXE TECHNIQUES

The Cane (Piolet Canne)

If you climb low-angle snow or ice slopes, you can use your ice axe as a cane. Grip the head of the axe with your hand, and cover the adze with your palm (fig. 12-9). Direct the point forward in the line of travel. Place the spike into the ice with the shaft held vertically. As you step up, push down on the axe head with your palm to get an upward assist from your arm muscles.

It is important that when you supplement crampons with hand tools, you continue to use the crampons properly. In the cane position, the ice axe is simply an aid to balance: almost all your balance and progress come from proper use of your feet. Each new technique introduced here requires greater concentration, when first added to crampon technique, than the one discussed before.

Stepkicking

To climb snow, you kick steps with a stiff boot. The best boot for kicking steps is one designed for general mountaineering that has a relatively flat sole. You usually kick steps straight uphill on soft snow that is not too steep. As the snow hardens and the angle increases, you kick steps on a rising diagonal.

In soft snow, a good step will be the size of

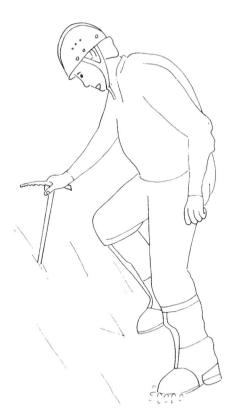

Figure 12-10. Stepkicking and Piolet Canne

your forefoot. As snow hardens you might be capable only of using the edge of your boot to kick a narrow platform. Then you will reach a point where you will either have to cut steps or put on crampons.

You usually kick steps with an ice axe in hand. Begin by using the ice axe as a cane to assist in walking (fig. 12-10). Always hold the axe on the uphill side when traversing. When you change directions, you switch the axe to the new uphill hand.

Piolet Manche

On steeper snow slopes, you can gain security by using the axe as a self-belay by plunging it into the snow and using it as a stake; this technique is called *piolet manche*. Grip the head of the axe, oriented parallel to the snow slope, with both hands, palms on top of the pick and adze (fig. 12-11A). Plunge the axe shaft verti-

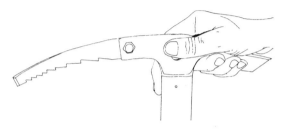

Figure 12-9. Hand Position for Using the Axe as a Cane (Piolet Canne)

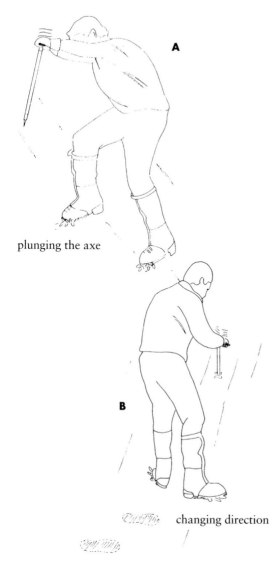

plunging the axe

changing direction

Figure 12-11. The Stake (Piolet Manche)

Cutting Steps

You will need to cut steps when the snow becomes too hard to kick steps efficiently. In the evolution of winter climbing, the earliest climbs on low-angle slopes were done entirely without the use of crampons by cutting steps. With 10-point crampons (no front points), cut steps allowed ascents of slopes greater than 40 to 50 degrees. With the advent of front points, rigid boots, wrist leashes, and modern technique, stepcutting has become mostly a lost art. But lines of steps are still useful on short alpine slopes where it is faster to cross in steps than to put on crampons.

You normally cut steps in snow with the adze. A flat sharp adze will do a better job than a curved dull one. The classic pattern of stepcutting is an ascending diagonal, but as the slope gets steeper, the line of steps turns uphill. On low-angle firm slopes, only the inner edge of

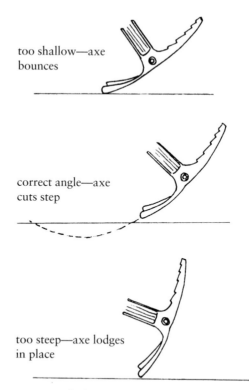

too shallow—axe bounces

correct angle—axe cuts step

too steep—axe lodges in place

Figure 12-12. Slash Step: Cut in hard snow for the inside edge of the boot.

cally into the snow. To progress upward, you bend and place the axe forward and then kick steps up to the axe. Gain balance in the step, remove the axe, and start the process over again. In the stake position, the axe provides a secure handhold. This handhold, which gives added security at the turn, can replace that provided by *piolet canne* when you change direction while traversing in zigzags (fig. 12-11B).

your boot need be on a flat surface. In this situation, a step cut with a single slashing blow might be all that you need. As you cut the *slash step*, swing the axe at an angle so that it neither bounces nor sticks in the snow (fig. 12-12). Instead, the axe should continue the arc of the swing to remove enough snow to allow your inside boot edge to rest on a cut platform.

As the firm snow slope becomes steeper or harder, you use more effort to remove snow for a *side step* (fig. 12-13). The side step is large enough to hold your entire foot. Swing the axe in a near-vertical plane and use the inside corner of the adze. As you remove the axe, flick the axe to remove the cut section. Begin cutting the step near the end of the step that will be closest to you, and make the next cuts away from yourself. In general, you can cut a side step with three blows. If you cut the bottom of the step so that it slopes inward, you will gain an added sense of security as you stand in it. Stand in the next to last step, and use the last step as a handhold while you cut a new step. You can also cut a parallel line of steps to use as footholds and handholds. These will not only enhance security on the way up, but make descents by this line of steps secure as well. Instead of cutting a second line of steps, you can plunge a second axe shaft into the snow above the step and use it as a handhold.

Pigeonhole Steps

As the slope of hard snow becomes steeper, you can cut *pigeonhole steps* directly up the slope (fig. 12-14). Because you use these holds for positive handholds as well as footholds, you cut a lip on the inward-sloping hold. You cut these steps with the axe adze, but, in hard ice, you will have to shape the interior of the hold with the pick. Cut a line of holds for each foot. The overall pattern will be a uniform zigzag of holds going up the slope, spaced a step apart, rather than a series of paired left and right steps. Because you place only the toe of the foot in a pigeonhole, your calf muscles might begin to fatigue. To rest, cut an occasional long horizontal platform that you can stand on with both feet.

Figure 12-13. Side Step: A—Schematic to cut in steep hard snow to hold the entire foot. B—Cutting the step.

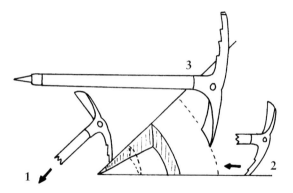

Figure 12-15. The Slab Step: Make cuts 1 and 2, then pull off a piece of slab with the adze, 3.

snow with the axe pick held vertically (fig. 12-15). Second, make a slit starting upslope with the pick held vertically. This second slit should cross the first slit at an angle of 45 degrees. Third, cut out the snow between the two slits with the adze.

Stepcutting in Ice

You will need the pick to cut steps in ice. Cut a series of vertical incisions into the ice, and then cut horizontally with the pick. You can level the bottom of the step with blows of a sharp adze. Cutting steps in ice is hard work, so you will probably want to cut only the occasional step as a rest or to place protection while climbing in crampons. When cutting ice steps, use whatever natural platforms exist to save energy. You can find natural handholds and footholds where ice separates from rock, at the top of a bulge where snow sits on the ice, or at the base of ice columns.

Cutting the occasional step can turn an otherwise desperate ice climb into an interesting problem. For example, when you leave a platform beneath a vertical or overhanging section, cut one or more front-point-size steps overhead. This maneuver will allow you to use more balance and less arm strength as you climb. On climbs where ice is at foot level and rock is overhead, small steps cut to the side in the ice allow a balanced traverse. On thin or fragile ice, a series of light chipping blows will do the job while preserving the ice.

Figure 12-14. Pigeonhole Steps

Stepcutting on Windslab Snow

When you encounter snow that breaks off in slabs, you cut steps in a different fashion than in hard snow. First, make a horizontal slit in the

MORE ICE-AXE TECHNIQUES

Bracing with the Axe (Piolet Ramasse)

Piolet ramasse is the technique of using the ice axe as a counterbalancing or bracing tool on moderate slopes to assist balance while flat-footing (see photo below).

Place the axe across your body about shoulder height. Hold it by the head with the adze under your palm and the pick directed away from your body. Your other hand holds the axe on the ferrule just above the spike. You can lean into the axe and press with shoulder and arm muscles on the head in a direction parallel to the shaft. This pressure helps to keep the axe in the ice so that it will not pull out and provides a third point of contact, in addition to each foot, for resting. When you move from this position, you can use the axe as a handhold by pulling downward with the second hand at the top of the ferrule. Having this hand close to or touching the ice prevents leverage and allows you to pull fairly strongly.

This bracing technique is commonly used with *pied troisième* (discussed earlier in this chapter), in which you flat-foot with one foot and front-point with the other in order to change direction.

Resting in Balance on a Steep Slope (Pied Assis): You can rest on relatively steep slopes of hard snow or ice by sitting in balance over your crampons in the position called *pied assis* (fig. 12-16). Stabilize this rest position by using the axe in the cross-body brace (see photo at left). *Pied assis* is one of many positions that you can assume during a day of moving about on snow. It is the fluid and appropriate use of each of these techniques that makes an accomplished ice climber.

Cross-Body Bracing (Piolet Ramasse)

Figure 12-16. Resting in Balance (Pied Assis): To stabilize this position, use the axe in a cross-body brace.

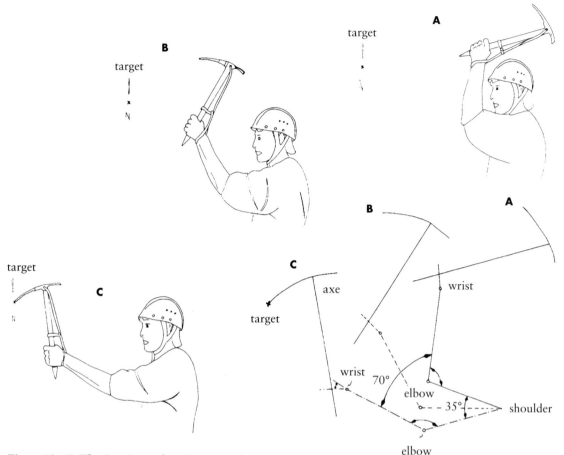

Figure 12-17. The Axe Swing from Upper Right to Lower Left

Piolet Ancre

Piolet ancre is a technique in which you use the pick as an anchor. How you place the pick depends on axe design and your own physical limitations. Hold the axe above the ferrule at a point that seems natural for swinging—it will vary depending on the length of the axe. When you swing an axe with an alpine pick, the axe head should follow the arc or droop of the pick—that is, the curved line extending from the shaft to the pick (fig. 12-17). This means that you swing the axe from your shoulder by using the upper, as well as the lower, arm. One common mistake novices make is that they swing with only the lower arm. Do not bend your wrist during the swing or when the pick strikes

the ice. Some expert climbers claim that they flick their wrist as the axe point enters the ice, but this is not necessary or even desirable for most of us. The length and strength of the swing vary somewhat, but start with the shaft angled away from the ice, nearly vertical. You can use considerable strength in swinging but not at the expense of control. Begin with swings of modest strength.

If you examine the axe swing in the lower right drawing of figure 12-17, you see that the upper arm pivots about the shoulder joint through an angle of about 35 degrees, whereas the lower arm pivots twice as far, or about 70 degrees. The elbow joint opens up as the arm swings forward, but wrist and hand position relative to the lower arm does not change throughout the swing. If you are using a reverse-curve pick, modify the swing to a chopping motion.

Swing the axe so that the pick strikes the ice perpendicular to the surface. In water ice, do not expect the axe to stick on the first swing. Instead, pick a target and hit it repeatedly. Expect the axe to stick on the second to fourth blow, depending on ice quality and your technique. You will observe experienced climbers, even on very steep ice, looking over the ice to pick a specific target. (This process relates to the nature of the ice, discussed in chapter 14.) Place the axe directly above your shoulder so that you can balance underneath it.

The actual penetration of the ice surface presents difficulties to the novice. If the axe turns in your hand or you flex your wrist, the ice will shatter when the axe strikes its surface, and placements will not be secure. At first, it seems that your hand and wrist are not strong enough to control the impact force of the axe pick against the ice. Strength might not be the problem, however, as most climbers learn to control the wobbly axe after a number of hours or perhaps on the second day.

There are a couple of things to look for if you encounter this problem. First, choose an axe with a shaft diameter that fits your gloved hand. Some axes have a very large cross section that requires a large hand to control it. Also, the glove combination must not be so thick that you cannot grip the shaft. Second, smooth-shafted axes are designed to be slippery so that they penetrate the snow pack, thus giving security. This slipperiness makes it difficult to keep the axe from rotating in your hand when you hit hard ice. Wrap the lower part of the shaft with the nonslip tape sold in hardware stores for bathtubs. Third, as noted above, the length and weight of the axe have an effect on your ability to control it. Long axes with heavy shafts require more hand-wrist-arm strength.

Shorter tools, northwall hammers, or axes

Using the Axe to Anchor (Piolet Ancre) While Flat-Footing

with added weight concentrated in the tool's head build up momentum during the swing. This momentum carries the moving axe into the ice at the angle directed and requires less hand-wrist strength. When climbing steep ice with two hand tools, you normally use a tool with added head weight in your weaker, off hand to gain added momentum.

When placed, the axe should be capable of holding at least a short fall. First-time climbers often want to move up on axes that wobble. You might be able to do so if you are on a moderate slope, if you are top-roping, or if you are balanced well on your crampons. On steeper ground or when leading, it becomes more critical to have good placements. These placements require perseverance, and you should never move up without a solid placement unless you are prepared to fall. With a bit of experience, you learn to *hear* good place-

Figure 12-18. Mantling on the Axe

ments, even from a distance, as well as *feel* them.

The design of the curved pick locks the blade in place by lifting the shaft away from the ice. (This design seems to go against your natural desire to rest the spike against the ice.) Releasing a well-placed tool is sometimes difficult. First, push the spike against the ice and try lifting the shaft. If this does not work, try lifting the pick out of its hole by the head. You might try enlarging the pick hole by pulling out on the shaft, and then releasing by pushing in and lifting the head. This process can succeed, but, if done forcefully, it will torque the pick and might break it.

The Ice-Axe Anchor: A climber moving across a slope with one axe can use it in the anchor position (*piolet ancre*) as an aid to balance, as shown in the photo at left. You place the axe pick and use it as a counterforce to your body to move across the slope; pull up on the handle to lock the pick, and then lean from the axe to move. After moving, balance over your crampons, remove the axe, and place it again to continue.

Mantling on the Axe: On a steep slope of hard snow or ice, you can mantle on the axe to push yourself upward. Place the axe well overhead and front-point up on crampons while holding onto the axe shaft with one hand (bottom of fig. 12-18). Place your other hand on top of the axe and then begin to mantle onto the axe top (center). At the top of the mantle, balance over your front points, remove the axe, and place it higher (top). In this way, you can move quite high in one placement. Maintaining balance during axe removal is easier if you can use a natural handhold or finger hold as an aid.

Piolet Panne: *Piolet panne*, or daggering, is a technique using two axes that works well on long alpine gullies that have the consistency of Styrofoam. Grip each axe with a palm on top of an adze, as shown in figure 12-19. Place the picks by thrusting them like a dagger. You usually dagger on moderately angled slopes of about 45 degrees, in combination with front-pointing and the odd flat-foot move to change

Figure 12-19. Daggering (Piolet Panne)

directions. When conditions are right, daggering is a very enjoyable way to gain height quickly.

Piolet Rampe: You can use the axe as a banister in the *piolet rampe* technique to descend short bulges or sections of ice to 45 degrees by a single axe placement (see photos below). Place the

axe well in front of you and duck-walk down the slope while using the axe as a railing. Pull up on the axe shaft to lock it in position, and allow your hand to slide along the shaft until it comes to the head. At this point, move your feet and body well downslope of the axe head so that you reach back to hold onto it. Then, gain balance over your crampons and remove the axe. Repeat the sequence as necessary.

DESCENDING SNOW SLOPES

Descending snow can be fun, but it also can be dangerous. In ranges where rock climbing is the prominent technique used for ascending, such as the Grand Teton Range of Wyoming, many accidents occur when climbers descend on snow. An initial slip turns into a runaway toboggan ride that ends with a crash into rocks below. Low- to moderate-angle snow slopes require specific, practiced techniques to descend. Practice slopes require a good run out, free of rocks, at the bottom. J-lines, described on page 198, are used to safeguard self-arrest practice.

Glissading

Glissading is a method of sliding down a moderate snow slope without crampons. You need a

Descending a Short Ice Slope (Piolet Rampe) from Right to Left

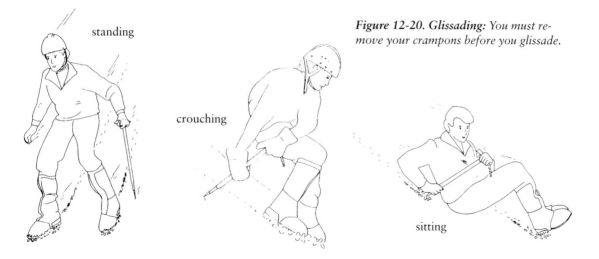

standing

crouching

Figure 12-20. Glissading: You must remove your crampons before you glissade.

sitting

slope with soft surface snow and harder snow underneath. These conditions often occur on summer afternoons at elevation, in alpine areas, as long as the sun is on the slope. When the slope is in shadow, the snow quickly turns to ice, and you might need crampons for descent.

Done properly, glissading can be one of the most exhilarating aspects of mountaineering. You can quickly cover great distances. I once descended almost 3,000 feet with a heavy backpack and took only a few minutes for each 1,000-foot section. This descent was the reward for all the effort required to get that weight uphill.

You can glissade in a standing, crouching, or sitting position, as shown in figure 12-20. The standing position is similar to skiing and requires practice to learn. Stand crouched forward in balance, with your feet flat to the slope and pointing downhill. Hold the axe as a cane with the pick pointing away from you. Bend your legs at the knees and balance over the balls of your feet. If you wish to slow down, you can shift weight back onto your heels or turn to traverse the slope.

By crouching lower you can use the ice axe as a rudder and emergency brake. Hold the axe with one hand on its head and the other well down the shaft, with the pick pointing away from you. Digging the spike into the snow on your side acts as a brake when combined with a

weight shift onto your heels. This is a slower method of descent. Your center of gravity is closer to the snow and not far away from the self-arrest position.

The sitting glissade places your heels and lower body on the snow, thus increasing the surface area of contact. It is useful when you cannot maintain your balance in a standing or crouching glissade or when you would descend too rapidly. If the surface is soft, sitting will keep you on the surface and allow you to slide. Sliding in rough wool pants can slow you. Slick nylon wind pants or a full-length cagoule decreases surface friction and will speed your descent. You can still use the ice axe as a brake, and you will be ready to roll over into a self-arrest. Remember to remove your crampons for the sitting glissade, or you will probably end up with a sprained or broken ankle or punctured leg.

Plunge Steps and Hand Grips

If you do not feel good about sliding down a slope, the plunge step is a workable alternative. Plunge-stepping uses body weight to produce a step. You descend facing outward, as shown in figure 12-21; step off with a stiff leg, land on your heel, and drive your heel down into the snow. This technique requires boldness because it takes the weight of your body to drive the step. Your "falling" weight decelerates as the

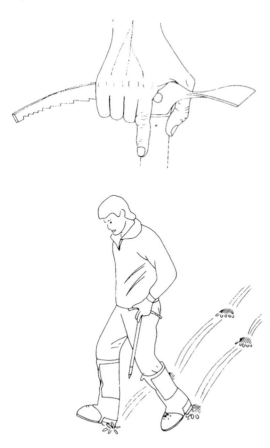

Figure 12-21. Plunge Steps and the Self-Arrest Grip

snow compacts in the step, so you might feel more secure if you make your own steps rather than using someone else's steps.

While plunge-stepping, hold the axe in a modified cane position and be ready to plunge it into the snow below your foot should you lose balance. Instead of holding the axe with the pick forward (see fig. 12-9), turn the adze forward. Hold the axe with your thumb around the adze and your fingers wrapped around the pick adjacent to the shaft. This position allows you to self-arrest almost immediately without reorienting the axe.

If plunge-stepping makes you feel insecure, descend by turning around so that you are facing uphill. Kick steps while using the axe in the stake position.

Self-Arrest

Self-arrest provides an emergency brake if you lose control while descending. You can self-arrest with or without crampons and, although the technique is usually done with a hand tool, it is possible to self-arrest without one. You need to practice the technique to learn it and should practice it periodically to keep the skill sharp. Practicing on slopes with safe run outs or using a J-line (as described on page 198) will provide a safeguard and allow you to have fun while learning or renewing the skills.

The aim of self-arrest with an ice axe is to get your body weight over the pick and force it into the snow to act as a brake. In the arrest position, hold the axe across your chest so that the pick is about shoulder high and the spike somewhat lower (fig. 12-22). Arch your back between your shoulders and toes if you are not wearing crampons; arch between shoulders and knees if you are wearing crampons. There is a real danger of breaking your ankles and lower legs if crampons catch on brush or snow during a fall.

To enter the arrest position, roll onto the pick (fig. 12-23A). If you roll toward the spike, you could lose the axe, pole-vault it, or—worse—force the pick into your body.

Because you usually self-arrest when you are sliding unexpectedly, your body might not be in the best position for the arrest, and you might

Figure 12-22. The Final Position in Self-Arrest, with and without Crampons

have to obtain and maintain the arrest position. This movement requires practice, thought, and coordination. It is easiest to do quickly, before momentum builds up and carries your body down the fall line of the slope and away from the dug-in axe. To prevent the axe from being

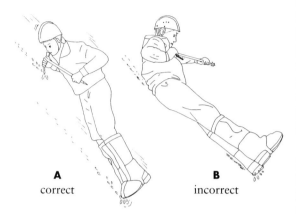

A
correct

B
incorrect

Figure 12-23. Roll Toward the Axe Pick, Not the Spike

pulled above your shoulder where it cannot arrest the slide, aggressively arch your back and use your muscles to pull yourself back over the axe.

Arrest Sequences: There are four basic starting body positions for a fall. You can be on your front or back, with your feet downhill or uphill. If you fall face down, with your feet downhill, you are almost in the arrest position, and simply need to put the axe across your chest and arch your back. If you fall face up, with your feet downhill, roll toward the pick and arch your back to get the shoulder-high pick firmly dug into the snow (fig. 12-24).

If you are headfirst and face down, plant the pick out in front of you downslope and across your body (fig. 12-25). The axe pick acts as a pivot and allows your body to rotate around it until both feet are below the axe. You must pull yourself over the axe with an arched body to come to an effective stop.

Figure 12-24. Arresting with Feet Downhill on Your Back

*Figure 12-25. Arresting Face Down
with Head Downhill*

If you are headfirst on your back, plant the pick out to the side, as in figure 12-26. The pick again acts as a pivot point for your body, so your feet will soon be below the axe. Again, you pull your shoulders over the axe and you arch your back. This position seems very strange at first, but you will soon see that is effective.

You can also self-arrest without an ice axe or crampons by radically arching your back and digging in with well-gloved hands and with your toes. This technique is more effective than you might first think possible, but you must do it immediately or it will not work.

J-lines: Whether you are a novice or an experienced climber, you should practice self-arrest, preferably on a slope that has a clear run-out zone at the bottom, void of rocks and other obstacles. When this is not possible, you can use a J-line. Construct the J-line with a climbing rope attached to solid snow anchors (described in chapter 13) offset from each other so that the rope takes the shape of the letter J (fig. 12-27). Position anchors at both ends of the J and fasten the rope so that it hangs in a loop below the lower anchor. Use a nylon sling and carabiners to attach yourself. Should you lose control during practice, the J-line stops downward progress with an abrupt deceleration applied by rope stretch. Before using the J-line, make sure to test each anchor individually by using the efforts of a number of people to pull on it.

*Figure 12-26. Arresting Face
Up with Head Downhill*

It is best not to have a leash of any kind attached to your ice axe so that it will not bounce wildly about should you lose control of it.

You can make the practice of headfirst self-arresting easier by cutting one or more large steps or platforms at the top of the J-line. These platforms are for you and two assistants. After attaching your safety leash to the J-line, your assistants hold you by the legs, in the head-down position, until you give the signal to let go. After a bit of practice and a gain in confidence, you can launch yourself with vigor and success from this unlikely position.

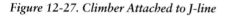

Figure 12-27. Climber Attached to J-line

REFERENCES FOR FUTURE READING

Blackshaw, Alan. 1973. *Mountaineering: From hill walking to alpine climbing*. London: Penguin Books.

Chouinard, Yvon. 1978. *Climbing ice*. San Francisco: Sierra Club Books, in association with the American Alpine Club.

Harrer, Heinrich. 1976. *The white spider*. London: Hart-Davis, MacGibbon.

Lowe, Jeff. 1979. *The ice experience*. Chicago: Contemporary Books, Inc.

———. 1981. *Technical manual*. Lowe Alpine Systems: Broomfield, Colorado.

March, Bill. 1973. *Modern snow & ice techniques*. Cumbria, England: Cicerone Press.

Miller, Dorcas. 1990. Raynaud's disease: Can it be controlled? *Climbing*. 122:109.

Williamson, John E., and J. Whitteker, eds. 1989. Statistical tables, in *Accidents in North American mountaineering*. New York: The American Alpine Club, and Banff: The Alpine Club of Canada.

ENDNOTES

1. The 1989 *Accidents in North American Mountaineering* (Table III) indicates that lack of a hard hat was a contributing cause in 10 to 13 accidents per year between 1951 and 1988. However, John E. Williamson, editor of that publication, states in a 1993 personal communication, "Helmets are *primarily* to protect against falling rocks or objects. Leader falls *with* helmets can result in basal skull fractures *because* of the helmet."

2. Lowe, 1981.

13

Protection on Snow and Ice

SNOW PROTECTION

Snow and ice continually form, change character, and melt, requiring climbers to be alert to current conditions. Over the years, climbers have developed a variety of techniques and tools suited to particular conditions. Ice screws and ice pitons are screwed or pounded, respectively, into the ice. Climbers can cut posts, called *bollards*; drill holes for an hourglass anchor; or bury axes or special plates, called *deadmen*, to form stable anchors. There are also many ways to use an ice axe to contribute to safety.

When you climb snow, you can protect on a step-by-step basis by using the ice axe. If you take a wobbly step, use the ice axe to regain balance by quickly plunging it and hanging onto it as a stake. If you do lose your balance completely, use the techniques of self-arrest described in chapter 12 to come to a stop. These techniques are for individuals and do not safeguard a team. A team requires some type of anchor that works effectively on snow for belaying.

You cannot self-arrest on water ice. At the beginning of a fall, a quick, desperate, and lucky swing might lodge a pick and prevent a fall. Once the fall begins, however, you need bombproof anchors to stop it.

Ice-Axe Belays

You can belay on your ice axe. Plunge the axe into the snow, shaft vertical, all the way to the axe head, as indicated by the arrow in figure 13-1. Orient the pick blade perpendicular to the fall line and use it as an anchor. Stand in a kicked platform downhill of the axe and attach yourself to it by a sling clipped through the carabiner hole. Then push the axe shaft into the snow until you bury the head, to prevent leverage on the shaft. This belay anchor is only as strong as the weakest layer of the snow, which is usually at the surface. When the force of a fall applied perpendicular to the axe shaft causes the axe to rotate through the upper weak snow layer, it fails as an anchor.

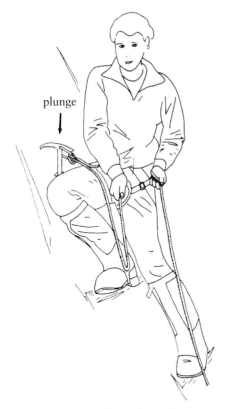

plunge

Figure 13-1. Ice-Axe Belay: Plunge the axe to its head and orient the axe blade across the fall line.

Boot-Axe and Hip-Axe Belays

On moderate slopes, the boot-axe belay (fig. 13-2) overcomes some of the problems of the ice-axe belay. Drive the ice axe into the snow, shaft vertical, upslope and adjacent to your uphill foot. Orient the head of the axe perpendicular to the fall line. Push it into the slope but stop just above boot level so that you can wrap the climbing rope around the axe shaft. The rope passes from you around the upslope side of the axe shaft, underneath both the pick and adze, and then around the downslope side of the boot. The downhill side of the boot provides most of the friction to arrest a fall; the axe acts to reverse the direction of the rope. During the belay, keep the axe in place in the snowpack by pushing downward on the head. You can prevent the shaft from rotating by bracing it against your boot just in front of your ankle. Stamp down the snow beneath the axe and your boot to make this brace more effective.

When the snow slope gets steeper or softer, it is no longer possible to use a boot-axe belay. A hip-axe belay (fig. 13-3) can serve. You form a platform in the snow with your body weight and stamp out foot placements to use as a brace

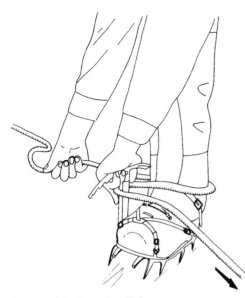

Figure 13-2. Boot-Axe Belay

Figure 13-3. Hip-Axe Belay

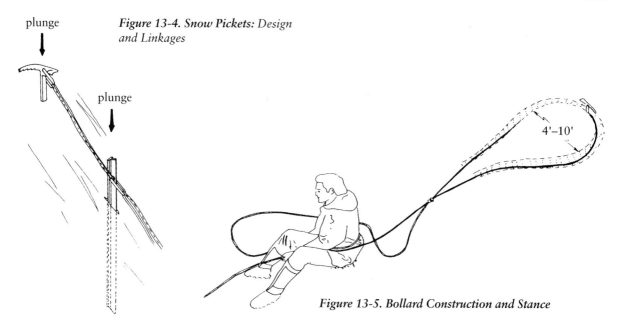

plunge

plunge

4'–10'

Figure 13-4. Snow Pickets: Design and Linkages

Figure 13-5. Bollard Construction and Stance

for your legs. Drive the axe in next to your hip and hold it with downward pressure from your hand and arm. Then pass the rope around the axe shaft and around your body to your braking hand. Because your glove and the rope are down in the snow, both are likely to be snowy and slippery. If you need more friction, wrap the rope around your wrist.

Snow-Picket Belays

A snow picket (fig. 13-4) has a T-shaped cross section that resists shearing out of hard-packed snow much better than the oval shape of an ice axe. Larger in cross section, the snow picket can make a more effective belay anchor than the ice axe. You can purchase pickets or make them from stock T-shaped aluminum. Under consolidated snow conditions, individual pickets can be used as running protection for moderate-angle snow slopes. When you tightly link snow pickets or ice axes with connecting slings placed through carabiner holes in the picket tops, they make excellent anchors in firm snowpack.

Linked in this fashion, the lower picket serves as the primary anchor and the upper picket, or axe, as its safeguard. To pull out, the lower picket would have to rotate through a large arc in the snow. It is prevented from doing so because it is linked to the upper picket, so the upper picket must rotate and fail before the lower picket does. You can substitute long snow axes for snow pickets, but axes have less holding power because of their smaller cross section.

Bollard Belays

Bollard is a nautical term for the mushroom-shaped post used when tying a ship to a dock. You can use an ice axe to cut a similar post in snow to serve as an anchor for belaying or rappelling. Use the adze of the axe and cut a symmetrical trench into the snow slope with a circular arc on the uphill side, coming to a point on the downhill end (fig. 13-5). Cut the bottom of the trench about 1½ feet deep on the uphill end. Allow this trench to rise to the undisturbed snow surface at the lower point. This excavation leaves a raised island of snow in the center of the trench. The uphill end of this island should have a little overhang to prevent the rope from slipping out of the trench; the remaining sides are vertical. Pass a rope around the island. Position yourself well downhill of the bollard to ensure a downward pull, and sit in a braced stance composed of a kicked seat and foot braces that will absorb much of the energy of a fall. As in rock climbing, the stance safeguards the anchor by limiting the energy that the anchor must absorb.

The strength of a bollard depends on its size in relation to the consolidation and structure of the snowpack. Bollards in firm snow with well-bonded layers can be as little as 3 to 4 feet across, but in less firm snow they should be up to 10 feet wide. It is a good idea to make and test a bollard on the slope that you intend to climb before starting out, where there is a safe run-out zone. Get several people to pull statically on the rope to duplicate the dynamic impact forces that can come onto the bollard.

You can strengthen a bollard by driving your ice axe into the trench on the uphill side, between the anchor rope and the snow island, where shearing forces are greatest. Line the trench with sweaters and jackets to distribute shearing forces over a wider surface. If you rappel from the bollard, use twigs, branches, and flat rocks rather than leave your gear behind, and do not multiply the load by bouncing when you descend. It is best to practice cutting bollards and test them before you try to rappel on them.

Snow Flukes

A *snow fluke*, which is an aluminum plate with a steel cable (fig. 13-6), is designed to be inserted into a T-shaped slot in the snow. Snow flukes provide belays on hard, homogeneous snow, typical of summer alpine or glacier ice.

You must place the fluke in the T-slot (fig. 13-7A) at an angle of 40 degrees to the snow

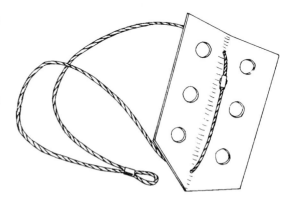

Figure 13-6. Snow Fluke

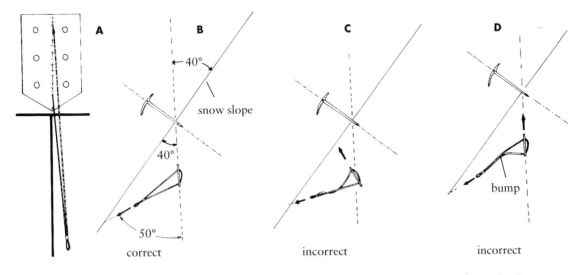

Figure 13-7. Snow-Fluke Placements: A—The T placement (front view). B—Estimation of the 40-degree angle (cross-section view with axe indicating direction perpendicular to snow slope). C—Incorrect angle (cross-section view). D—A bump along the cable path (cross-section view).

Figure 13-8. An Improvised Ice-Axe Deadman in Perspective and Cross Section

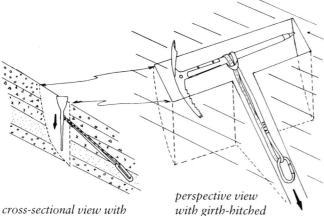

cross-sectional view with
undisturbed snow layers

perspective view
with girth-hitched
axe

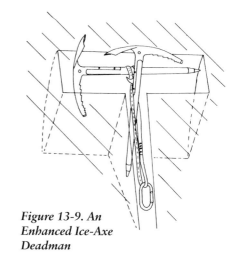

Figure 13-9. An Enhanced Ice-Axe Deadman

surface. To find this angle, place your ice axe perpendicular to the snow surface (fig. 13-7B). If you bisect the angle between the axe and the snow surface, you will have a 45-degree angle; if you lean the snow fluke slightly—5 degrees—toward the upper snow surface and insert the fluke, it will be at a 40-degree angle to the snow. (Many flukes have a cable stop that sets the angle between the plate and the cable at 50 degrees, the desired angle.)

Hammer the fluke plate a foot or so into the crossbar of the T-slot and place the fluke cable into the cutout stem of the T-slot, which takes a direct line downhill to the belayer.

The snow fluke can fail if you place it at the wrong angle or dig the cable slot incorrectly. As the drawing of a snow fluke at an incorrect angle shows (fig. 13-7C), a pull on its cable will cause the fluke to pop up through the snow and the belay will fail. If the fluke cable rides over a bump in the cable slot, an upward pull on the fluke occurs and again the fluke pops out of the snow (fig. 13-7D).

The belay stance you assume with the snow fluke is critical. On steep slopes, you need to sit well downhill of the fluke to ensure that the fluke and its cable pull at the proper angle. You can use snow flukes to belay on horizontal surfaces above steep slopes. Here you need to sit

well in front of the fluke but also back from the edge; you should not sit on a *cornice*, an unsupported overhang of snow.

Ice Axes as Deadmen

Snow flukes belong to a general category of buried objects used for belaying called *deadmen*. You often need to belay on snow without having such specialty items as snow flukes along. Ice axes placed in horizontal trenches make improvised deadmen, as shown in figure 13-8. Girth-hitch a sling around the center of the horizontal axe and pass it to the surface through a vertical slot you have dug perpendicular to the trench. It is important that the T-shaped trench and slot disturb the natural snow structure as little as possible in order to retain the snow's original strength. Placing the axe forward in the trench against the undisturbed front wall maximizes the strength of the placement. Take a stance well downslope of the deadman to ensure the proper angle of pull on the attached sling and deadman.

You can strengthen the axe-deadman belay by inserting a second axe into the trench vertically through the sling and in front of the horizontal axe (fig. 13-9). By penetrating beyond the surface and into deeper layers of the snow, this axe resists forward motion of the horizontal axe.

Under special circumstances, you can even use a short hammer as a deadman. I once needed to safeguard bridging a deep and wide moat, or *randcleft*, between a glacier and a rock wall. I buried a short hammer while I was braced in a sitting position and attached the hammer to my climbing harness with a tight sling. The hammer itself became frozen in, as I later discovered when I attempted to retrieve it. This is an example of successful improvisation, based on sound principles, that is often necessary in real climbing situations.

ICE PROTECTION

With the advent of modern tools and experience, climbers are tackling steeper ice with minimum amounts of intermediate protection. As a result, the old saying that the leader must not fall is still good advice. On the other hand, modern ice protection that is properly placed in good ice should catch a fall. The tubular, hollow-core ice screw, such as that manufactured by Black Diamond Equipment, Ltd., with threads having large surface area, is a strong design. Shown in figure 13-10, this design minimizes fracturing of the ice because the displaced ice moves up into the core of the screw. A good example of ice-screw design, it has four cutting teeth and a conical interior. The tip of the cone is the toothed end of the screw. As ice enters the cone, it can expand. The core fills with ice chips that are easy to clean out by tapping the screw against a hammer or axe head. The outside diameter of the screw, which is the load-bearing surface, is larger than that of an older Salewa ice screw and should be harder to pull out of the ice. The older Salewa design had two cutting teeth and an interior with parallel walls that produced a solid ice core. To remove the core, you had to melt it with body heat and ream the partially melted core with a stiff wire. Cleaning the screw was the second's job, so the leader had a good reason to lead. Possibly, this duty was the mother of invention that led to modern ice screws. Salewa has designed a newer tubular screw along the lines of the Black Diamond model.

> ### Protecting Ice Climbs
>
> "In the end, there are absolutely no absolutes in assessing ice quality. I find this to be one of the appeals of ice climbing, wherein the art of the sport lies. Protection on a typical ice lead will still run the gambit of Spectr's, tied-off icicles, pins, positive angled screws, negative angled screws, and, most important, the confidence and experience to climb through unprotectable sections sans pro. Prudence, trust in gut feeling, and experience are the requisite essentials for leading and protecting ice safely."
>
> Alex Lowe—thinking about the results of ice screw strength and angle test—in a letter to Black Diamond Equipment, Ltd.

Lowe Alpine Systems produces a hollow, pound-in ice piton with small threads called the *Snarg*. The small threads allow the Snarg to be screwed out after a bit of initial chopping. The pound-in design was developed so that the protection could be placed from small or precarious

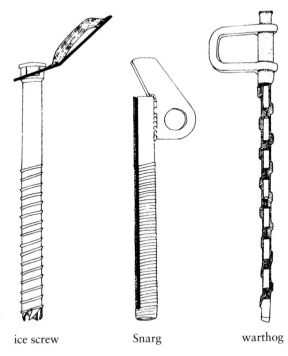

ice screw   Snarg   warthog

Figure 13-10. Ice-Protection Designs

stances. Snargs have replaced an older solid pound-in design typified by the warthog. Once the leader has started a pound-in, he or she can hang onto it for balance while driving it. For this reason, Snargs play an important part in safeguarding modern steep ice climbs. (Although warthogs are discussed here, they are largely of historic interest and do not belong on a modern climbing rack. They shatter the ice excessively and are not strong. Snargs, which are almost as strong as ice screws, have replaced these primitive pound-ins.)

Snargs have a much larger load-bearing surface than solid pound-ins and they displace the ice core inward. As a result, there is very little shattering of the ice surrounding the screw. The Snarg gives reasonable protection at minimal stances on steep climbs, a compelling reason to have them on your rack. They are also useful to safeguard you when you are tired at the end of a long run out before you chop out a stance and set up a belay with screws.

Establish your belays with tubular ice screws to take advantage of their design strengths. The tubular ice screw with an uninterrupted cylindrical shape fails by bending. In water ice, it must first bend approximately 45 degrees across the length of the screw before it begins to pull out of the ice. The Snarg pound-in is not a complete cylinder; it has a slot in its side to allow for ice expansion and removal. The Snarg fails by breaking at this slot.

It is important to place both screws and Snargs all the way into the ice, so that they rest against the eye flange to resist bending.

The older warthog pound-ins, which are not as strong as tubular screws or Snargs, have to be hammered in all the way. Because they shatter ice extensively, they have to be placed well away from other pieces of protection.

Another disadvantage of the warthog is that it is difficult to remove. You might need to chop out a warthog for at least a third or half of its length. This is an exasperating and tiring experience for the second. The Snarg, on the other hand, might need a little chopping in the beginning but turns rather easily once started because

---

The Birth of the Snarg

"In the first years of the last decade, Mike Weis and I had long contemplated doing an extended climb of a steep frozen waterfall. But from experience on short routes we had discovered just how difficult it is to stop on a vertical pitch and place a tube screw. We also had found that solid-shafted pitons would most often completely destroy the ice of these climbs. My brother, Greg Lowe, provided us with the solution to the problem. He had made half a dozen chrome-molly tubes, about 9 or 10 inches long with the tips beveled to the inside. These tubes gave Mike and [me] the confidence to lead out on pitches of brittle, vertical, and bulging ice. A new world had been opened to us. . . . These ancestors to the Snarg were crude beasts."

Jeff Lowe on the Origin of the Snarg, Lowe Alpine Systems, Inc., *Technical Manual*

---

of the threads milled on its exterior. After a few turns, you usually can pull it straight out. Tubular screws screw out for most of their length. This is normally not difficult. The leader puts the screw in originally and does most of the work of setting the screw and providing a space to turn it. The newest tubular screws have flanges with some movement separate from the screw shaft, which simplifies removal as well as placement.

Ice protection placed optimally in high-quality ice is relatively secure. You can improve the margin of safety by placing a dynamic sling on each ice screw or pound-in used as an intermediate protection point. Dynamic slings, discussed in chapter 7, rip apart and lengthen fall distance as they absorb the force of the fall. Most ice climbers use between one and four intermediate protection points per pitch. You can easily carry four dynamic slings on an ice-climbing rack.

Starting Ice Screws

Placing an ice screw requires that you understand the quality of the ice and judge its solidness at the location of each placement. There is no one way to place an ice screw that meets all conditions so that it will be safe; the attentive ice climber is constantly alert to changing ice conditions on a climb, as well as possibilities of placing high-quality rock protection on an adjacent rock wall. Solid ice often appears as slabs where the ice takes on a uniform density without internal fractures and is clear blue or green in color; it is not hollow, slushy, aerated, cauliflowered, or dinner-plated, nor does it have water running under it (see chapter 14 for a discussion of ice quality). Look for flat or concave surfaces of solid ice. Solid ice usually requires that you use the ice-screw flange as a lever to place the ice with a bite against consistent resistance as you turn the screw. The ice of vertical and overhanging climbs, where more difficult climbs lie, is often less than solid.

Once you select solid ice, clear away especially brittle or rotten surface ice with a few axe blows and start a hole in the ice underneath with the axe pick. Older conventions recommend that ice screws be placed at an angle of 15 to 25 degrees to the ice surface *above* the screw, but tests on Black Diamond screws with aggressive threads indicate that they be *angled down* 15 degrees *in the direction of loading*[1] (fig. 13-11). In solid ice, these screws rely on the "bite" of the screw threads in the ice rather than the resistance of the tube material to bending or shearing through the ice. In less than solid ice, where the resistance of the tube material to bending or shearing through the ice is important, angle the screw up in keeping with the classic convention. Always angle pound-in ice pitons up with their very low thread relief. Modern screws with very sharp teeth usually start by hand even in the hardest and coldest ice, but, if they are resistant to catching, tap the screw in the hole with a light hammer blow and give it a quarter to a half turn. Repeat the process of turning and pounding a few times until the screw teeth catch. In warm, wet ice, this process can clog the screw with slush and prevent it from initially catching. Clear the clogged screw of ice and repeat the process; this time, because you will penetrate deeper into the hole and into drier ice, you might succeed.

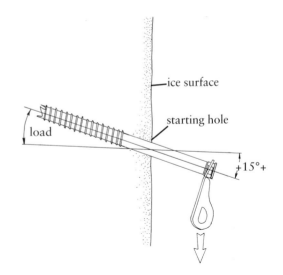

Figure 13-11. Starting an Ice Screw: The new convention sets ice screws 15 degrees with the direction of the anticipated load.

The pressure of the screw melts the surrounding ice, thus providing lubrication and allowing the screw to turn easily. (In the same way, when you ice skate, the ice beneath your blades melts and you are able to glide.) In extremely cold weather, the pressure of the lever-turned screw is not sufficient to melt the ice. Without lubrication, the screw will be hard to turn and will make disturbing chattering noises.

Manufacturers now make ice screws with large diameters, which resist *shearing* through the ice. These screws logically would work better in less than solid ice, but comparative tests have not been reported. Modern screws have more and sharper cutting teeth that cut more easily and might have built-in ratchets that allow easier placement. Placement entirely by hand is now possible in some ice conditions.

Placing Ice Screws

Ice screws tend to shatter the ice as they enter it. The surface ice, in contact with very cold air, shatters more readily than the ice beneath the surface, which is more plastic (fig. 13-12A). If you do not remove the shattered surface ice, it easily breaks away when loaded and leaves

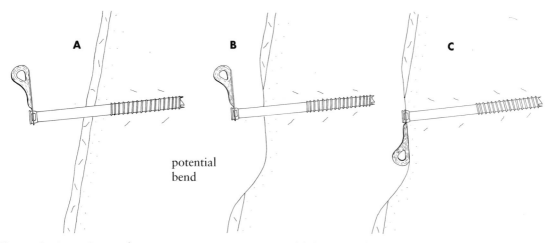

potential
bend

Figure 13-12. Ice-Screw Placement (Cross-Section View): A—The brittle surface ice will not support the ice screw and allows the screw to bend in the fall line and fail. B—The brittle surface layer is removed. C—The flange comes to rest on the solid ice interior. The placement will resist fall-line bending and failure.

the ice screw vulnerable to being bent at the point where the screw protrudes from the ice. When you place the ice screw, remove the surface ice and turn the ice screw into the bottom of the prepared hole until the flange of the carabiner clip-in rests against the ice.

Loading Ice Pitons and Screws Placed in Poor Ice

Imagine an ice piton without threads in solid ice. The load-bearing surfaces on the piton are the outside surface of the tube and the bottom of the carabiner flange (fig. 13-13A). The piton has no threads, and its "bite" plays a minor part in holding the load. In less than solid ice, place an ice screw and load it in the same way as the ice piton, so that the screw's tube bears the load rather than the "bite" of the aggressive screw threads.

Therefore, you need to pay attention to the flanges of the ice piton or screw. The flange, to which you clip, is an important part of the load-bearing surface. It needs to rest against the ice and point downslope. There should be no clearance between the flange and the ice; clearance might allow the piton or screw to rotate in a vertical plane and reduce ultimate holding power.

When you load an ice screw, in any type of ice, screw length is important. A screw should be short enough to allow the flange to rest against the ice. A traditional practice among climbers is to tie off screws that bottom out against rock and prevent full-length placement. Recent tests of screws with aggressive threads indicate that a tied-off screw will flex and bend, which causes the sling to slip to the head of the screw, and result in high leverage. Failure is generally caused by the sling being cut by the edge of the hanger. Limited data on screws with aggressive threads indicate that you should clip to the hanger if they have less than 2 inches sticking out of the ice. These tests indicate that they might still catch a fall that produces a moderate load on a screw.[2] Tied-off ice screws, with or without aggressive threads, will never hold as well as fully placed screws. Attempt to place a shorter screw that fully penetrates the ice, or look for rock protection in a nearby rock wall.

When you load an ice piton or a screw in less than solid ice, you need to pay attention to ice irregularities or a belay stance that affects how the screw is loaded. In less than solid ice, avoid loading the screw to apply force along the shaft, as shown by the arrow in figure 13-13B. Place screws in less than solid ice so that the load will be applied parallel to the screw flange and

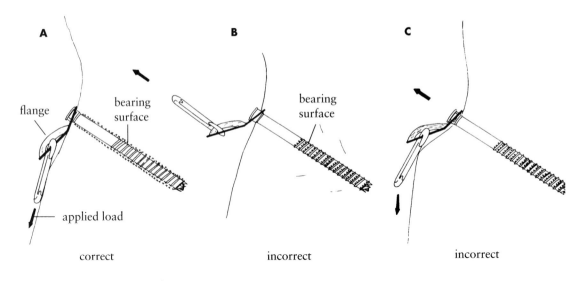

Figure 13-13. Loading an Ice Piton or a Screw in Less than Solid Ice: A—The piton or screw is loaded correctly (marked by Xs on the shaft surface) in a direction perpendicular to the main load-bearing surface. B—The screw is incorrectly loaded parallel to the screw shaft and only the screw threads (Xs) *bear the load in less than solid ice. C—An ice bump beneath the attachment carabiner produces leverage and an outward force along the screw axis. This position incorrectly loads the screw threads (Xs) in this less than solid ice. The bump should be chipped away until the carabiner lies as in A.*

perpendicular to the shaft of the screw (see fig. 13-13A).

Also, chip away any ice bumps left beneath the attachment carabiner until the carabiner lies flat and produces a pull perpendicular to the screw axis. If the carabiner is not flat, it can lever the screw, forcing it out (fig. 13-13C).

Ice Screws and Bulges on Water Ice

Note, that to be effective, screw placements described in this section require firmly frozen and structurally solid winter water ice. Screw placements that work better in softer ice at warmer temperatures or where pressure melting can occur are described in the next section.

Bulges on water-ice climbs present problems when you are placing ice screws. You naturally want to place a screw before attempting to climb the bulge. If the bulge is waist to chest height, you will most likely place the screw in the convex part of the bulge. In doing so, you will create large fractures in the brittle surface

and you might break off large *dinner plates* (fig. 13-14A). If this happens, courtesy and safety demand that you trap the plates between the ice and your body and methodically break them up into small pieces before allowing them to fall.

If you place screws above a bulge for an anchor, you must place them far enough apart so that their fractures do not intersect, totally shattering the ice (fig. 13-14B). Usually, at temperatures below freezing in water ice, a 3-foot separation is sufficient. The screws also need to be far enough behind the bulge to prevent fracture in the bulge (fig. 13-14C). Again, the specific distance depends on ice conditions, but 3 feet is usually sufficient.

Optimum Screw Placement

On softer alpine ice or on steeper water ice, pressure melting will more likely occur under loading (as in a hanging belay) as temperatures approach or move above freezing. To strengthen placements and counteract this melting, place

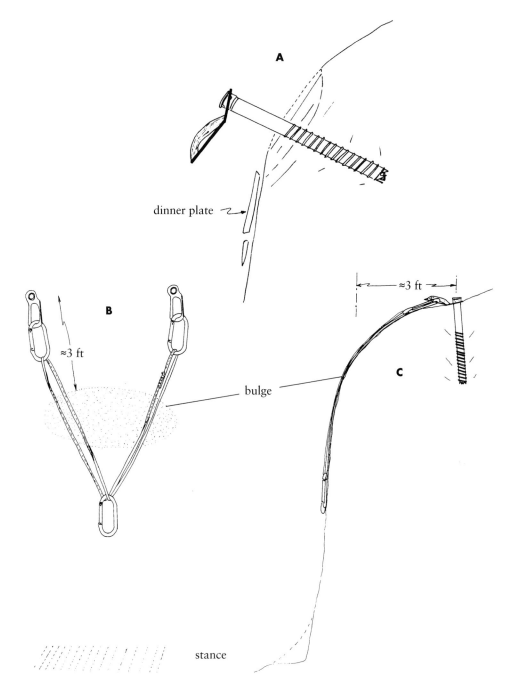

Figure 13-14. Ice Screws and Waist-High Bulges:
A—A screw placed in the apex of a bulge will cause the bulge to dinner-plate. B—Front view of a naturally formed belay stance just below a bulge. The screws are placed well above the bulge and far enough apart so that fractures from one screw do not intersect those of the other screw. C—Side view of screws behind the bulge far enough to prevent shattering of the bulge.

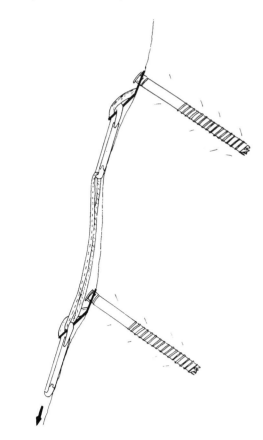

Figure 13-15. Belay for Steep Ice to Offset Pressure Melting: The upper screw must rotate from its position before the lower screw can bend and fail. The belay anchors to the lower screw.

screws one above the other, as shown in figure 13-15. Angling the shaft of the screw upward is intended to counteract rotation induced by pressure melting. The top screw connects to the bottom screw by a tight sling, and you clip into the lower screw. The lower screw must rotate downward through the ice to fail, but the upper screw resists this rotation. A force applied to the lower screw transfers directly to the upper screw, which must rotate through the ice before the lower screw can move. With this type of anchor, a friend of mine successfully caught a 300-foot fall when the leader was pushed down a steep Canadian glacier by a falling cornice. The top

screw pulled out about a quarter of an inch during the fall, but the bottom screw holding the fall did not move. (This is a good recommendation for the anchor but not for climbing under a cornice.)

An independent screw placed slightly above and off to the side of the belay as a first protection point for the next pitch will prevent a fall directly onto the anchor and help safeguard it. Use a dynamic sling on this protection point.

Ice-Screw Placements in Thin Ice

Placing screw anchors in thin ice is never satisfactory, but, if you run out of rope and have a few inches of ice, you can set up screws as shown in figure 13-16. Turn each screw in its hole until it hits rock, and promptly stop turning. If you turn any farther, you will either bend the teeth of the screw or strip the small ice ridges formed by the screw threads. Tie off the upper screw with a loop of small-diameter webbing (a hero loop) next to the ice to prevent levering, or preplace a wire taper on the screw in a manner similar to that used for bolts without hangers (see fig. 7-20). Tension the hero loop or wire taper to the top of the lower screw by using an adjustable sling. Next, tie off the lower screw next to the ice surface. Clip into the lower hero loop or wire taper for your belay. The lower tie-off minimizes leverage on the lower screw. This lower screw must rotate to fail, but the tight sling attached from the top of the lower screw to the upper screw prevents rotation.

If you are climbing and belaying on thin ice, it is a good idea to take along pitons and nuts to use in cracks that have been cleaned of ice. Tied-off tools, as discussed in chapter 15, and a good stance can also enhance your belay.

BOLLARD AND HOURGLASS RAPPELS FROM ICE

You can usually have confidence in rappel anchors placed in rock walls bordering climbs. Sometimes, however, you might be forced by circumstance to rappel from ice. If you leave screws behind, you will leave behind a small

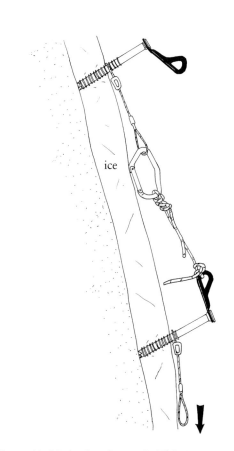

Figure 13-16. Anchor Screws in Thin Ice

fortune, and it is possible that you might not have enough screws available when you need them. Climbers facing this problem before have come up with a number of solutions.

Ice bollards are identical in shape to snow bollards, but they can be smaller because of the greater structural integrity of ice. On well-consolidated glacier ice, a bollard can be roughly 18 inches across and 6 inches deep on the upper side, which you in-cut slightly to prevent the rope from popping off. You can cut bollards in water ice, but this requires laborious controlled chipping with the axe pick to keep the bollard intact. Less chipping is required if you drape a double sling over the bollard as a rappel anchor rather than cutting deeper grooves to accept the thicker rope. Because of the work involved, most rappellers will seek a different anchor.

The Abalakov hourglass provides a secure rappel anchor that you can construct relatively quickly. To form this anchor, place two ice screws 22 centimeters or longer in a horizontal plane so that they point toward each other and intersect inside the ice (fig. 13-17). The optimal distance between screw entrance holes is 8 inches, and each screw is angled at 60 degrees from perpendicular to the ice. Next, remove the screws and clean the holes. Pass a 7-millimeter cord into one empty screw hole, and catch it with the end of a flexible cable inserted into the second screw hole to pull it through. Finally, tie off the cord or use it to pull a sewn sling to form a rappel anchor. The plastic string used in weed-whackers or plastic-coated wire makes a very light cable loop. For emergencies, you might be able to improvise a threading cable using small

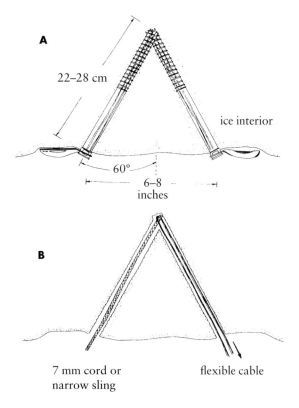

Figure 13-17. Cutaway of the Abalakov Hourglass Rappel Anchor (Viewed from Above)

wire tapers. Tie the cord to one wire stopper and push it headfirst into a clean screw hole. Use the back end of the second stopper to grip the head of the first stopper to pull it through.

Abalakov hourglass rappel anchors, tested in glacier ice by the German Alpine Club, were found to fail at about 2,000 pounds with a 6-inch span between holes. Murray Toft and Joe Josephson, Canadian ice climbers, conducted tests in water ice, first in moist plastic ice and later in colder brittle ice. They found that the best placements, obtained by placing entrance holes 8 inches apart, failed at 2,900 pounds of force in moist ice at above-freezing air temperatures of 41 degrees Fahrenheit (5 degrees Celsius). In warmer ice, the 7-millimeter rappel sling failed by slowly shearing through the ice. In cold brittle ice at 14 degrees Fahrenheit (−10 degrees Celsius), with entrance holes 8 inches apart, the 7-millimeter sling failed at 3,250 pounds of force without the ice breaking. In the moist 41-degree Fahrenheit conditions, failure rates were lower when the entrance holes were placed at 6 inches, but still were an impressive 2,250 pounds of force. Clearly, the hourglass creates a strong rappel anchor.

You will want to practice and test this technique, as I have, by using a mechanical-advantage system powered by three climbers, to gain confidence in it and to be efficient in creating, cleaning, and threading before you need to use it. As in any rappel, back up your anchor as you send the heaviest member of your party down first to test the need for the backup. When you become confident in the rappel anchor, you can remove the backup. The lightest member of the party should rappel last and slip as smoothly as possible down the rope.

REFERENCES FOR FUTURE READING

Harmston, Chris. 1997. *Myths, cautions, and techniques of ice screw placement.* Black Diamond Equipment, Ltd.
Lowe, Jeff. 1981. *Technical manual.* Broomfield, Colorado: Lowe Alpine Systems.
Luebben, Craig. 1997. The cold truth: How strong is ice protection? *Climbing.* 172:106–113.
Toft, Murray. 1991. Getting down on a shoestring. *Climbing.* 124:100–101.

ENDNOTES

1. See Harmston, 1997, and Luebben, 1997. Tests in 1992 by REI Engineers in glacier ice, by Craig Luebben in Ouray and Boulder Canyon ice in 1997, and by Chris Harmston in 1997 under laboratory conditions challenged conventional wisdom of placing ice screws and placed greater emphasis on adapting placement angle to ice quality.
2. See Harmston, 1997. Limited data indicate that bending typically occurs at a load of around 1,500 pounds followed by failure in the 2,000- to 3,500-pound range. The possibility exists that further testing will change conclusions.

The Nature of Ice

INTRODUCTION

There are many kinds of ice, and their environmental characteristics influence the season, or even time of day, that a climb can be attempted in a reasonably safe manner; differences in local ice properties affect the safety of anchors and tool placement once you have begun a climb. The expert climber on a steep water-ice climb will hang from one tensed arm while aiming the second ice tool to a specific ice patch that will take tools better than the ice immediately adjacent. You need to know the types of ice, their behavior during tool and anchor placement, and seasonal transformations for greater safety and enjoyment, and to gain skill at the sport.

The four major varieties of ice are *glacier ice*, *alpine* or *couloir ice*, *rime ice*, and *water ice*. *Freezing rain*, supercooled water drops that freeze when they contact cold surfaces, occasionally produces unique ice climbs.

GLACIER ICE

New snow can be dry or wet. Dry, or powder, snow is made of well-formed hexagonal crystals (fig. 14-1). If the wind blows hard enough to transport the snow, the arms of these crystals break and a densely packed *windslab*, prone to avalanching, can form on lee slopes. If the new

Ice Fall on Bugaboo Glacier Range

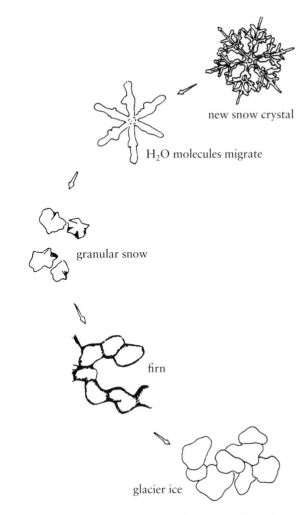

new snow crystal

H_2O molecules migrate

granular snow

firn

glacier ice

Figure 14-1. Metamorphism of Snow to Glacier Ice:
New snow crystals become rounded as water mole-
cules migrate from their pointed extremities to con-
cavities and eventually form grains. These grains
connect to each other and, by eliminating most of the
entrapped air, crystallize into glacier ice.

snow crystals settle with arms intact, and if the
snowpack has the same temperature at top and
bottom, then water molecules migrate from the
pointed tips to concave areas between the arms.

The snowpack undergoes transformation as a
result of heat exchange. Heat moves from the
ground to the atmosphere during the coldest
parts of the winter, and from the surface down
during the summer when the sun is warmer than

the ground. After the snows of winter collect,
the warming days cause the snow to melt during
the day and freeze at night. This melt-freeze cycle produces *corn snow*, the loose, granular
snow so often encountered during the spring.

By the end of a season, individual grains
bond firmly together through repeated melting
and freezing to form a complex network. This
processed snow forms a dense snow structure,
or *firn*, that becomes part of the permanent
snowpack. It can be very hard at night or in
shadow, and turn into slush when the sun
strikes it during the hottest part of the day.

Eventually the firn becomes compressed under
subsequent layers of firn and undergoes further
changes to form glacier ice in layers that represent hundreds to thousands of years of accumulating and metamorphosing snow (see photo
page 215 above left).

Glaciers gain snow and ice during the winter
and lose it during the summer, both by melting
and evaporation as the ice turns directly into
water vapor. As the glacier loses snow and ice
(ablation), *ablation surfaces* form: these areas are
marked by accumulations of dirt (fig. 14-2) present in the snowpack but diluted enough during
the winter that the snow appears white. Thus,
glaciers take on a structure of white winter accumulation layers separated by summer ablation
surfaces. If a summer or series of summers is
warm enough for the glacier to melt intensely, an
unconformity structure of ablation layers trun-
cated by more recent ablation layers forms. This
situation often produces an angular contact between older and more recent accumulation layers.

ALPINE ICE

Alpine ice forms in gullies, or couloirs, high on
the side of mountain peaks, such as the Enclosure Ice Couloir (see photo at right). In shadowed alpine gullies, surface water percolates
down through the snowpack and can transform
it. By late summer to early autumn, the gully
can become packed with hard *crystalline ice*.
Black ice is old gully ice mixed with dirt and
rock that has fallen down from above.

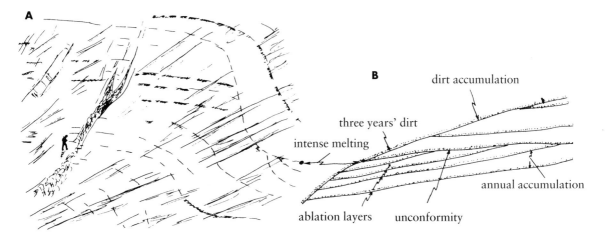

Figure 14-2. Glacier Structure: A—The Middle Teton Glacier. Horizontal bands are ablation layers; diagonal lines are water grooves. B—Cross section of A *showing annual accumulation layers, ablation layers, and an unconformity produced by a period of intense melting.*

RIME ICE

Rime ice forms when droplets of supercooled water impinge on rocks, snow, or other objects in their path above tree line and build exotic *ice feathers* that extend into the wind on rocks exposed to wet, cold winds on treeless summits. In Scotland and Patagonia, entire climbs can be on rime ice.

WATER ICE

The characteristics of a given section of water ice depend on whether it evolved from running water or from snow on ice (fig. 14-3). Climbers find water ice tenacious and difficult to penetrate, so it is sometimes called *hardwater ice.* An observant climber will note that different types of water ice have formed adjacent to each other, within inches or feet, at the same time and on the same ice climb. On a particular climb, hand tools might easily penetrate the wet *plastic ice* formed where water is running over the surface, but ice screws placed in the same ice would probably not hold a fall. Only a few feet away, colder and more solid ice can take screws well but shatter when struck by the axe. Pockets of ice formed from snow on ice will either allow

Ice Originating from Snow in the Enclosure Ice Couloir of the Grand Teton

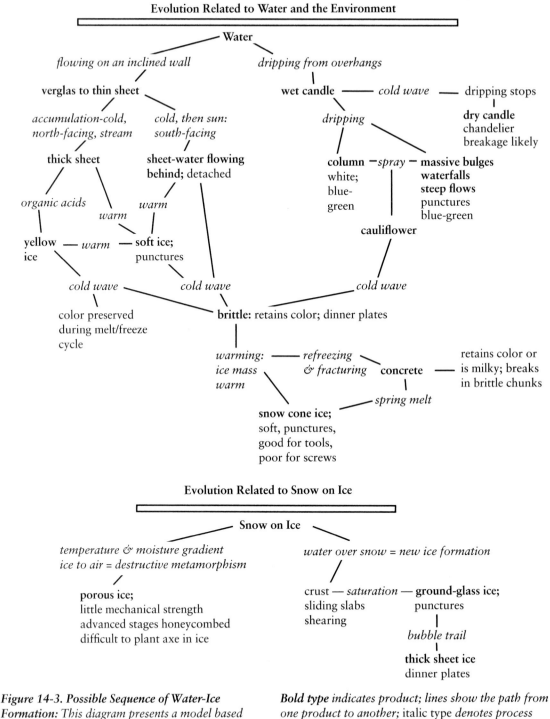

Figure 14-3. Possible Sequence of Water-Ice Formation: *This diagram presents a model based on observation of ice formation; it is subject to redefinition with further investigation.*

Bold type *indicates product; lines show the path from one product to another; italic type* denotes process *along the paths; and plain type describes the mechanical behavior and color of the ice.*

hand tools to shear through the mass or hold the tools well, depending on its state of transformation.

Water-Ice Evolution and Running Water

Running water can form a glaze over rock, called *verglas*, which might eventually become thin—and then thick—sheets of water ice. Water dripping from overhangs can form stalactite-like candles, with rounded stalagmites below.

Ice can be transparent, white to milky white, blue-green to blue, or yellow. It can be brittle or plastic, and it can break into blocky pieces of *concrete ice* or into thin sheets called *dinner plates*. Alternating warm and cold weather can transform ice to a brittle concrete structure; longer spring days can make *snow cone ice*. Figure 14-3 provides a summary of water-ice evolution.

Water ice often begins to form as water flows from a groundwater seep over a cliff face. This situation occurs most readily if there is a snowpack above the cliff and if the air temperature is warm enough or the sun is strong enough for the snowpack to melt. Thin sheets of verglas form on the rock (you can see the rock through the ice) as the temperature drops. If accumulation continues, either during very cold weather or on a north-facing cliff, thick sheets of ice can form. If the cliff faces south and the sheets remain thin, the sun might warm the rock behind the ice and melt it. This melting becomes more pronounced as the days grow longer and the sun rises higher in the sky later in the ice-climbing season. As a result, thin ice that is climbable early in the day, before the sun strikes the cliff, could have water running behind it later in the day. This ice becomes detached or hollow and cannot be climbed safely.

If the cliff has a small overhang, stalactites of ice begin to form, eventually meeting an ice bulge that started to form below. Many small stalactites or candles of downward-hanging ice might form. The individual candles are transparent to white, and the overall mass of the ice is also white. When forming, *candle ice* is wet, but in a cold period it dries out and becomes brittle. In either case, a significant part of the candle-ice mass consists of air pockets. It is relatively easy to bury an ice axe or ice hammer up to the head in wet candle ice, but climbing this mass is precarious because of the constant possibility that the tool may shear through the mass. When the mass is brittle, a hand tool or crampon shatters the candles with the tinkling sound of a breaking chandelier. You can sometimes climb candle ice by kicking tenuous footsteps or by breaking through the outer layer of candles if there is a more substantial mass of ice underneath.

Beneath the dripping candles, rounded masses of ice similar to stalagmites begin to grow upward, and eventually the two growing ice masses join to form *columns*. Associated with columns and dripping overhangs you find *cauliflower ice*, which results when water spray forms as dripping water strikes the lower surface. Cauliflower ice is rounded, resembling the vegetable for which it is named. Since it usually forms on a ledge, it often incorporates snow into its structure, while an ice crust forms on its outside.

During the spring, an ice mass begins to warm and takes on a surface texture with the appearance and consistency of a snow cone, while the plastic ice of the interior gives good hand-tool purchase that might tempt you to climb. Climbing would be dangerous, however, because ice screws do not hold well in the soft plastic ice, and running water between the ice and the cliff will have partially detached the ice.

Concrete ice is formed when ice warms and fractures as it freezes again. When warm, this ice is fun to climb because it is very plastic and ice tools stick with little effort. After a cold wave, concrete ice, which is milky white, is extremely brittle and breaks off in blocky chunks rather than in dinner plates when you hit it with hand tools. Crampons, unless recently sharpened, tend to skate even on low-angle concrete ice unless you work very hard. You can climb concrete ice, but it is difficult to do so because of the effort involved and the insecure tool placement.

Ice Color and Consistency: Ice color, which can vary on a climb, provides information about evolution, consistency, and potential response to tools. Yellow is the easiest color of water ice to understand, although its color is related to an external agent and not the nature of the ice itself. Yellow ice forms from seeps that have run over slabs beneath cedar bushes or other vegetation. Organic acids derived from the vegetation give the ice its pronounced dingy yellow color.

Transparent ice, white ice, milky white ice, and blue or blue-green ice take on their color because of interactions with and filtering of light as it passes through the ice. These colors do give some indication of how the ice will respond to tool placement.

Thin ice is transparent, but as it gets a little thicker it appears white. This white color is the mixture of all of the colors or wavelengths of visible light reaching our eyes, where they are mixed and then interpreted by the brain as white. As water continues to run over the ice surface and freeze, the ice thickens and begins to turn first blue-green and then blue. Blue ice appears blue whether you look at it in direct sunlight, shade, or even under a gray blanket of cloud and illuminated by the *incident* (scattered) light of the sky. John Tyndall, the nineteenth-century British scientist and climber, discussed the appearance and origin of the blue-green and blue colors of ice in his delightful book, *Glaciers of the Alps*.[1] Tyndall concluded, "When the rays of light pass through a sufficient thickness of ice the longer waves are, as in the case of water, more and more absorbed and the final colour of the substance is therefore blue." That is, the ice acts as a filter that only lets through light that we perceive as blue in color (fig. 14-4).

Blue ice is ice without internal fractures, but you might create some when you swing your tools. If it takes hand tools without much internal fracturing, it is plastic ice, but blue ice can become very hard and brittle on the outer surface as the air temperature drops. This surface shatters when struck, and dinner plates, with razor-sharp edges, break off. These are a threat to the belayer who, more often than not, is below in the line of fire. The lead climber can help by trapping and breaking up the dinner plates into small pieces before allowing them to fall. Often, the more brittle ice is next to the surface, and you can find more plastic ice underneath into which you can securely sink your hand tools.

The milky white color of concrete ice apparently originates in the interaction of sunlight with many fractures formed in the ice as it freezes again after warming. All wavelengths of light, reflecting from these surfaces, come to our eyes, and our brain interprets them as white. Snow crystals that are individually transparent take on a white color in the snowpack because of similar reflections from crystal faces.

Snow Alteration of Water Ice

Snow sitting over ice transforms the ice's appearance and properties. In a destructive *metamorphic* process, snow insulates the ice from the outside air, which is usually colder than the ice itself, causing a temperature and humidity gradient between the ice and the outside air, similar to that found in a winter snowpack. Moisture moving from the ice to the air results in a porous ice mass that holds climbing tools and ice screws poorly. This situation is unfortunate because it means that you cannot use low-angle ice areas for practicing or teaching in heavy snow years, even if you go to the effort of clearing snow from the ice. It also means that as you exit from a vertical, difficult climb onto a snow-covered ledge, you might find porous ice with little integrity and will have difficulty getting good hand-tool placements over the top.

Ice crust (fig. 14-5) is formed when snow sits on ledges and adheres to steep surfaces. Water flows over the top, freezes, and forms a crust over the snow. When this crust occupies a large area at the bottom of ice bulges, it is a potential danger. It will perhaps support your weight, but more likely it will break and you will fall into the snow on the ledge and might continue falling from the ledge. It is best to break the crust purposely rather than to have it break unexpectedly. You also need to recognize ice crust because it sometimes has enough integrity for you to place ice screws but does not provide

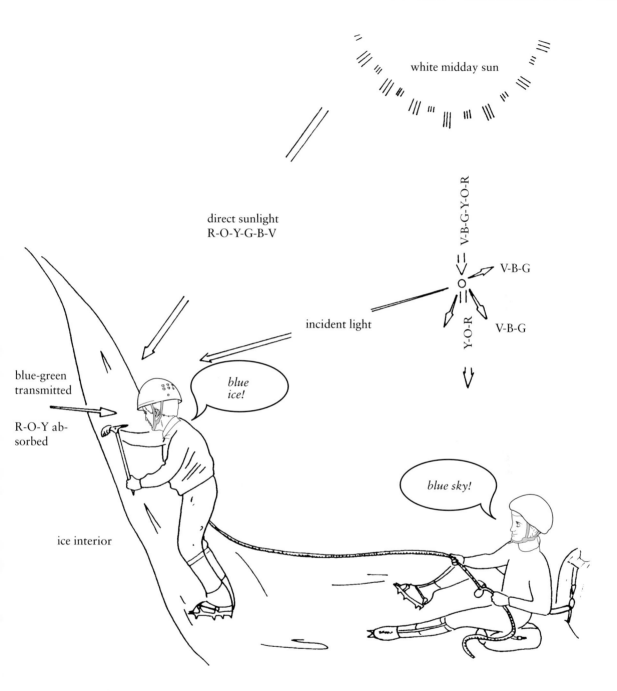

Figure 14-4. Blue Sky and Blue Ice: *When either direct sunlight or incident light hits ice, the ice absorbs (filters) longer wavelengths of red, orange, and yellow light and transmits wavelengths of blue. The light coming to our eyes from the ice is predominantly blue-green to blue, wavelengths to which the human eye and brain are especially sensitive. R = red, O = orange, Y = yellow, G = green, B = blue, and V = violet.*

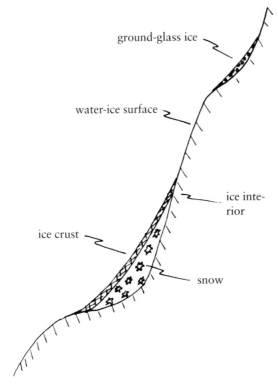

Figure 14-5. Formation of Ground-Glass Ice and Breakable Crust

enough shear strength to prevent the screws from pulling out when loaded.

Where the crust forms over a few inches to a foot or so of snow, the snow can solidify as water percolates through. This situation produces *ground-glass ice*, which as its name implies, is an opaque white mass easily distinguished from the clearer brittle white ice surrounding it. As ground-glass ice turns into water ice, only a thin bubble trail might remain as evidence of its process of formation. Ground-glass ice holds ice tools far more easily than the brittle ice surrounding it, and recognizing it can save you untold amounts of energy while climbing relatively steep sections.

REFERENCES FOR FUTURE READING

Bentley, W.A., and W.J. Humphreys. 1962. *Snow crystals.* New York: Dover Publications, Inc.

Daffern, Tony. 1983. *Avalanche safety for skiers & climbers.* Seattle: Cloudcap Press.

Plummer, Charles C., and David McGeary. 1991. Glaciers and glaciation. Chapter 12 in *Physical geology.* Dubuque, Iowa: Wm. C. Brown Co.

Post, Austin, and Edward R. Lachapelle. 1971. *Glacier ice.* Seattle: Mountaineers and University of Washington Press.

Tyndall, John. 1860. *The glaciers of the alps: Being a narrative of excursions and ascents, an account of the origin and phenomena of glaciers, and an exposition of the physical principles to which they are related.* London: John Murray.

———. 1896. *The forms of water in clouds and rivers, ice and glaciers.* New York: D. Appleton and Company.

ENDNOTES

1. Tyndall, 1860. The famous scientist John Tyndall did many interesting ascents of peaks, including the third ascent of the Matterhorn, during the golden age of alpine mountaineering. He solved various puzzles about glaciers and was the first to understand why the sky is blue.

15 Steep Ice

RATING ICE CLIMBS

Because modern ice ratings are more or less internationally accepted, an ice climb of a given grade is recognizable wherever you find it, within the context of local conditions. Ratings take into account average overall angle and length of the climb, the length of sustained vertical sections, and average ice conditions. Pluses and minuses are added to the rating to show variations in degree of difficulty. For example, at one time in New England, the relative shortness of climbs limited the upper end of the grading scale to 5⁺ in comparison to longer western Canadian climbs, such as Polar Circus, a 6. A current trend to push the limits on "horror show" ice has raised the upper limit to grade 6⁺ or even 7⁺ on big climbs. In addition to the ice rating, a commitment grade, similar to that used for rock, indicates how long the average competent party can expect to take to complete the climb.

Mixed routes involve both ice climbing and rock climbing (in rock portions, climbers hook reverse-curve tools and place crampons on nubbins—dry tooling). In this realm, ratings have quickly risen to 8 or 8⁺ with the introduction of "sport" ice climbing, which employs hooking moves with axe picks on small holds, gymnastic hanging transitions from rock to ice stalactites, and ascending thin ice smears, all within short vertical distances. Jeff Lowe has suggested incorporating the Yosemite Decimal System, commitment rating, and technical difficulty of rock climbing into a coherent system that would serve for pure rock climbs, pure ice climbs, or mixed climbs.[1] This method gives detailed information about climbs, which is particularly desirable when you are new to an area. A system for the mixed "sport" climbs now popular on small cliffs gives ratings of M1 to the current limit of M8⁺. As an example of how this system works, an M6 feels like 5.10 climbing, where you place the blades of ice axes to torque and you must dry-tool to climb. An M7 climb requires this type of tool use to proceed, and the climbing well might be overhanging so that it feels like 5.11 rock climbing. The

Ice Ratings

Grade 1: Low-angle (less than 50 degrees) hardwater ice, or long, moderate snow climbs requiring a basic level of technical expertise for safety.

Grade 2: Low-angle hardwater ice routes with short bulges of up to 60 degrees.

Grade 3: Steeper hardwater ice of 50 to 60 degrees, with short 70- to 90-degree bulges.

Grade 4: Short, vertical columns interspersed with rest on 50- to 60-degree ice. Fairly sustained climbing.

Grade 5: Generally multipitch ice climbs with sustained difficulties and/or strenuous vertical columns with little possible rest.

Grade 5+: Multipitch ice routes with a heightened degree of seriousness, long vertical sections, and extremely sustained difficulties, but not as long as grade 6.

Grade 6: Multipitch ice routes with a heightened degree of seriousness, long vertical sections, and long, extremely sustained difficulties.

Grade 7: Multipitch ice routes, with an extreme degree of seriousness, long vertical sections, and extremely sustained difficulties involving tenuous ice.

Based on the Scottish System, the New England Ice Ratings, and longer climbs of western Canada. See Wilcox, 1982 and 1992.

system continues as it is open ended.[2]

After gaining experience in a locale, you might find that the relative ratings—easy, moderate, and hard—tell you all you need to know about a climb. But with ice, the climb can vary enormously in difficulty—depending on the season, the day, the weather, the amount of ice, and its quality—no matter what system is used.

CLIMBING STEEP ICE

Climbing steep ice is a relatively new sport. It began during the late 1960s when drooped picks, rigid boots, and ice hammers were developed. Previously, climbers boldly cut steps up steep ice and experimented with insecure ice daggers to maintain a precarious balance. The new tools allowed rapid front-point ascents of climbs that had previously taken several days.

Scout vertical ice before you attempt to climb it. It could contain concave sections with corners, grooves, or chimneys that allow stemming to take weight off your arms. The most strenuous section of vertical ice to climb will be a convex section that places you on the outside of a long bulge. Your arm muscles and arm bone structure have to do much of the work of keeping you on the climb. You might prefer long sections of uniform steepness that are not quite vertical to sections that start out at lower angles but require pulling over a bulge higher up.

When climbing vertical ice, you must place two hand tools very well indeed if they are going to provide security. Target a spot and keep hitting the target to get proper placement. The first blows might simply remove brittle or fractured surface ice but reveal better ice below.

Use the tool with the heaviest head in your off hand to provide momentum to penetrate the ice. Place the two hand tools above your shoulders and directly above your feet to maintain balance. Placing the hand tool well off to the side of the body provides little aid in balance unless you plan to move your feet underneath. Place the two tools at full arm extension well above your head. In this manner, you can move up to the tools and take them out while maintaining balance. If you move very high on the tools before taking them out, you will lose balance and fall backward. A good rule of thumb is to climb no higher than eye height on the tool heads. Placing the hand tools will take effort and concentration. It is essential to remember to use your crampons properly in the manner that you learned on less strenuous ice.

PIOLET TRACTION

Piolet traction is a technique used when ascending steep ice and bulges and when traversing. The technique involves placing an ice tool's pick above your head, gripping the shaft near the spike, and pulling down on the shaft to provide a handhold. Climbers normally add wrist leashes to hang on to the axe.

Wrist Leashes

A *wrist leash* is a sling loop, attached to the ice tool, that you wear over your wrist. A well-designed leash leading from the axe to your wrist helps to prevent fatigue on long vertical sections. Without a leash, you would have to hold on to the shaft of your ice axe very tightly to support your body weight, and your arm muscles would soon tire. With a leash, however, you can put body weight on the wrist loop, and the bone structure of your arms, rather than the muscles, will bear the weight.

A leash also allows you to retrieve and grip a dropped tool one-handed, slide your hand into position for use on snow and low-angle ice, and free both hands by hanging from an elbow to place an ice screw. The leash should also hold onto you, rather than requiring you to hold onto it, if you tire near the top of a long, strenuous climb.[3] If you use your ice axe on slopes of different angles, do not use the wrist leash on low-angle snow slopes because doing so prevents you from transferring the axe to your uphill hand.

Wrist leashes that do all of these tasks are commercially available. A custom leash for a 60-centimeter tool (fig. 15-1) uses approximately 5 feet of ½-inch supertape. A 50-centimeter tool requires about 4 inches (10 centimeters) less tape. You can replace the overhand knots with bar-tack stitching to produce a less bulky leash. The wrist loop should be sized so that when you twist it once or twice around your mittened or gloved hand, your hand will be at the proper position on the shaft. For more comfort, slide a piece of 1-inch tubular webbing over the wrist loop. The wrist loop should allow your arm to slide through it up to the elbow, so that you can use your elbow for balance while you are placing an ice screw with your hands (see fig. 15-6). The shaft loop might not slide on a rubber-coated tool, so you may wish to eliminate this loop or tie it larger. Minor adjustments in posi-

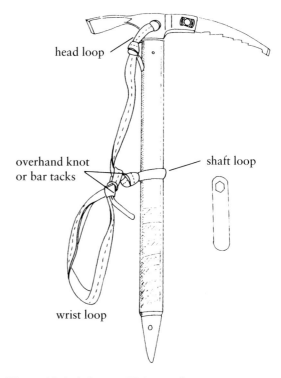

Figure 15-1. A Custom Wrist Leash

tion of the grip are possible by altering the length of the head loop.

Normal Ice Traverses

Traverses on steep water ice are somewhat harder than on rock because of the difficulties of balance when a tool is off to the side, and because of the properties of picks that are blades (as opposed to picks that are tubes). An ascending diagonal line is always easier than a direct horizontal traverse, but many steep climbs require a few direct horizontal moves.

When you traverse, you need to place the axe above and off to the side, and the easiest way to do so is to use a diagonal cross-body swing. This diagonal placement, however, is undesirable. While a cylindrical pick would rotate, a bladed pick might bend as you step under the axe (you will feel as though you are holding onto a spring) and might shear from the ice or break altogether.

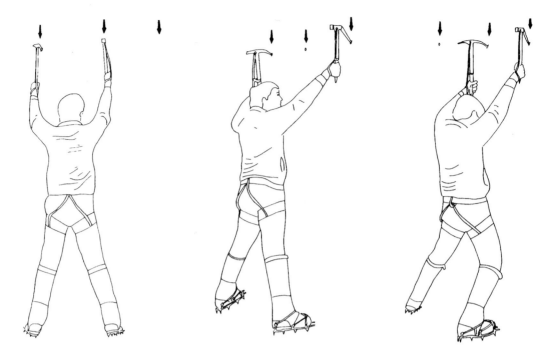

Figure 15-2. Traverses on Ice with a Bladed Tool (from Left to Right)

To avoid this problem, orient the axe so that the shaft is parallel with the fall line. You must not place the axe very far off to the side (fig. 15-2). Instead, you must make a series of short axe placements, and then move your crampons underneath the newly placed tool. When you start to move, shift your weight in much the same manner as you would in traversing rock, but do not make long reaches. Put one foot out to the side and then shift your center of gravity over your foot before attempting to stand. (Refer to figure 1-7 if you need a reminder.)

Because they rotate when securely placed in ice more than 1 inch thick, hollow tube picks allow you to lean farther and make cross-body placements with the shaft diagonally oriented to the fall line (fig. 15-3). The axe and hollow pick simply rotate as you traverse. Once you make a placement, shift your weight from left to right front points while doing a lieback on the axe with a straight arm. You can extend this technique to reverse steep ice pitches.[4]

Figure 15-3. Traverse on Ice with a Hollow Tube Pick. After Lowe, 1981.

An Unusual Traverse on Ice

In its usual thin condition, the Black Dike of New Hampshire's Cannon Cliff requires a series of unique moves to pass the crux. After roping up beneath the narrow cleft, you ascend an easy 65-degree ice flow on ice thin enough to show the black rock of the dike below. This thin warm-up pitch brings you to an aerie high above the glacial trough of Franconia Notch and sets you up for the crux.

Leaving the belay, you venture left onto a rock buttress marked by two vertically stacked ledges, each large enough for one foot. From the upper ledge, you notice that the steep wall overhead has no holds for hooking the reverse-curve blade of the axe. Off to the left, a long arm's length away, a thin ice smear plunges vertically from a platform down a narrow chute. It does not seem that you can get to the ice from your tiny ledge, since there are no holds overhead and no ice thick enough to take your axe. You are at the crux traverse!

This traverse does not yield to normal technique. It requires that you hook a waist-high rock flake on your right side and lean left on it. Leaning from the axe, you take little hop-steps to get as far left as you possibly can in order to make room for your right foot on the hold. While still lying away off the axe, you throw your left foot across the void to a platform large enough for one set of front points. With a new stability, you lean left as far as possible and plant your blade in thin ice to give a minimal point of balance. Now stand on your left front point and do what you can with your right crampon and right ice axe to help you step up to the platform. Congratulations, you have passed the crux. Now protect and climb the steep, ugly black ribbon overhead to a wildly exposed belay.

Ice Bulges

Ice bulges too high to step over are a challenge and can be more difficult than a steep wall. A bulge between waist and chest height presents much the same problem as the top of a nearly vertical ice climb. In order to pull over an ice bulge, reach over the top of the bulge as far as possible and place the ice axe securely. You must stand as close as possible to the ice so that your feet almost touch the base of the bulge. A common mistake is to leave space between yourself and the ice. This space limits how far forward you can place the axe. If the bulge is not vertical, do not try to place the axe too far forward, or you will lean enough to rotate your front points and cause shearing.

Place your axe well enough to hold a short fall and lean back on it, as shown in A in the photos next page. In this manner, you commit your safety to the axe. Leaning back ensures that you can see your front points and that you force them into the ice. If you lean forward, your front points will shear out and you will probably fall. In this committed but secure lieback position, walk your feet higher and higher.

The top of the bulge (see B and C in the photos next page) requires the most care and commitment to the axe. Continue to lean back with your posterior hanging out over space until you plant one foot on top of the bulge. Then step up, smoothly shifting your weight onto the upper foot.

Note the role of your hands during this sequence. You begin gripping the axe with your hand in the leash's wrist loop. Place the other hand on the shaft of the axe, and slide it up the shaft as you climb higher. When possible, put the palm of the second hand on top of the axe to assist you as you mantle up onto the top of the bulge. Your wrist-loop hand will also slide up the shaft as you get higher. Stand on the top of the bulge (see D in the photos next page) and take out the axe. You are now ready to move on. (Sometimes it helps you to stand if you remove the axe and use it as a cane.)

Bulges at the top of vertical ice climbs can be very troublesome if the top is horizontal, particularly if you are climbing with two reverse-curve tools. These tools are very difficult to place on a horizontal surface while you are front-pointing on a vertical surface. On the

Clearing a Waist-High Bulge: A, B, and C show a climber clearing a bulge. Between C and D, the climber uses the axe as a cane to stand on top of the bulge.

other hand, you can easily plant a tool with a normally drooped alpine pick, thus securing an easy exit. Some climbers use hand tools with reverse-curve picks in both hands for steep ice and reserve a third tool with an alpine pick in a holster until the exit.

Using a Short Ice Axe to Brace—Piolet Ramasse:
Piolet ramasse is the technique of moving over low-angle ice at the bottom or top of a steep climb by bracing with a short ice axe. The 45- to 50-centimeter axe that works best on steep ice is not the best length for cross-body bracing on low-angle ice. It would be nice if we could always depend on having the right ice axe for a particular slope, but, in the absence of the perfect tool, we can adapt our technique to the tool at hand. This way, after ascending a long, steep ice column, you do not have to bend over awkwardly and continue using steep-ice technique on a 30-degree slope.

To adapt your bracing technique to a short axe, hold the shaft vertically instead of in the cross-body position while stepping over short bulges (fig. 15-4). Keep your hand on the ferrule and spike next to the ice surface, and press vertically down on the head of the axe. This position will give you additional security in those final few feet of the climb.

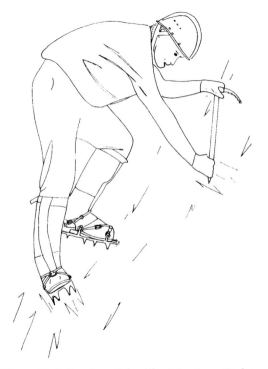

Figure 15-4. Bracing with a Short Ice Axe—Piolet Ramasse

The Monkey Hang

On very steep ice where you cannot stem, move in a specific progression called the *monkey hang* (see photos at right). The object of the monkey hang is to transfer weight from your arm muscles to your bones.

If the base of the ice has an ice slope leading

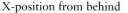

X-position from behind   rest position   stand   tensed left arm

The Monkey Hang: A—Start in an X-position with your feet about shoulder-width apart. Reach up high and place the hand tools slightly off to the side to avoid getting hit with ice chips during placement (view from behind climber). B—Move both feet up to waist height. This unlikely position is a rest position: you are hanging mostly from bone structure rather than muscle. C—Stand slightly to loosen one axe (here, the right) while maintaining balance with the other arm tensed. D—Stand to full extension, place the loosened (right) axe higher, and then loosen the second axe and place it higher too. E—You have returned to the X-position and the beginning of the cycle (view from the side).

X-position from side

up to it, balance to the top of this starting slope by using crampons and whatever natural hand-holds you find. In this way, you can avoid three or four hand-tool placements and save your muscles for what lies ahead.

Place your right-hand tool as high as possible, then your left-hand tool. Seen from the rear, your body makes an X, with your arms and legs forming the crosspieces of the X (see A in the photos above). Now bring both of your feet up to midthigh level so that you are in a squatting position on the vertical wall (see B in the photos above). This position minimizes the effort of your arm muscles because most of your weight hangs from your arm bones and tendons. If you chip small platforms with your crampons, your front points will not skate down the ice. When

you are secure in the squatting position, stand up (see C in the photos above).

First, loosen your right-hand tool in its hole without removing it. Then stand partway up while hanging off your bent left arm (see D in the photos above). This position is strenuous because your biceps are taking much of your weight. Remove the right-hand tool, reach as high as possible, and place the pick securely. Transfer your weight to your straight right arm and loosen the pick of the left-hand tool. Remove it, reach up as high as possible, and place the pick. You are back in the starting X-position (see E in the photos above).

If preexisting pick placements are available, producing a kind of ice pegboard, you can save much energy by using them. Sometimes you can leapfrog the height of hand-tool placements rather than having both hand tools at the same level during the sequence. Experiment on a top rope and learn what works best.

FANGING

Climbing steep ice with no hand tools, sometimes called *fanging*, can be an entertaining way to perfect technique or to keep in practice. You use handholds in the ice—flakes, pockets, etc.—as you would on rock. The technique requires excellent balance. Try it when the ice is dry but not too cold. (If the ice is wet, your gloves will get wet, resulting in rapid heat transfer. If it is too cold, you would have to use thick mitts that would hinder dexterity. Very thin gloves do not hinder dexterity.) Practice fanging on a tight top rope, but use the technique in leading when a move or two is actually easier without hand tools than with them—for example, on some thin-ice moves. Read the ice for the best line, and look for flakes, columns, and pockets to lieback; shallow concave surfaces and corners to stem; and one- and two-finger pockets to hook.

You will be amazed at what you can climb less strenuously than when you use hand tools. For difficult moves, however, you spend a bit more time making secure front-point platforms than you do when using hand tools. Even overhangs yield to fanging, particularly if you can follow a corner that you can stem. Your balance will be more like that of rock climbing, and you will come to think of the ice-climbing movement in much the same way as you think of movement on rock.

LEADING ON STEEP ICE

Climbers have developed different strategies for leading ice than they have for leading rock. These strategies have changed with tool evolution because ice climbing is tool-dependent. The fact that water-ice climbing takes place during short days and in cold temperatures also affects the choices because climbers have a limited amount of time in which to finish a route, and they do not want to get too cold doing so. Un-

like rock, ice is renewable and usually repairs itself in a day or two. An ice climb can change from being desperate to moderate or easy during the course of a season. Climbers routinely report the conditions under which they made an ascent, and wise climbers wait until the climb is "in shape" before setting out.

As long as it seems reasonable, you should attempt to move from one resting point to another and place protection at good stances. Many kinds of ice climbing require you to concentrate on good technique and to accept long run outs between stances. Pound-in ice pitons and the latest ice screws, coupled with good balance, allow you to place intermediate protection from front-point positions without resorting to direct rest or hanging from the hand tools. Climbers sometimes rest directly on ice tools, or purposefully aid from them, when climbing long stretches of steep ice. The first ascents of a number of now-classic long, steep ice climbs were done using *aiders* (slings in which to stand) attached to three Terrordactyls to make progress. As tools have evolved, more confident climbers have climbed longer and longer sections without hanging from the tools other than by wrist loops.

The ice leader can form holds to make the job of leading less strenuous and precarious. For example, it is often desirable to cut steps or enlarge natural footholds on steep climbs where you want to stop and place an ice screw. On climbs that are less than vertical, you can cut footholds or toe holds overhead with the adze of one axe while hanging on with the other. You can then move up to stand in the new hold. When starting a vertical section, it is sometimes helpful to chip front-point platforms overhead before leaving a stance. These chipped holds reduce the amount of muscle power needed and convert a strenuous climb into a balance problem.

Protecting Yourself While Leading

When you use the rope to secure balance while placing protection, as in figure 15-5, you can place it around the axe next to the ice to prevent leverage. The belayer then takes slack out of the

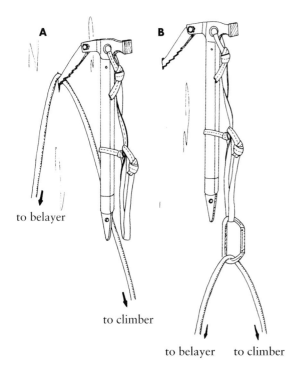

to belayer

to climber

to belayer   to climber

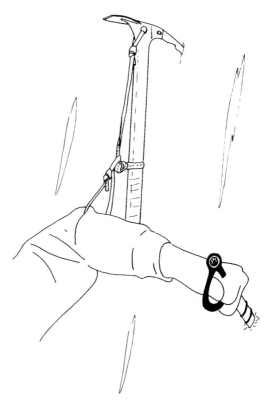

Figure 15-5. Temporary Belay with a Hand Tool:
A—The rope drapes over the ice pick next to the tool
to prevent levering. B—The rope attaches to the wrist
loop with a carabiner.

Figure 15-6. Using the Wrist Leash to Place an Ice
Screw while Balancing on Front Points

rope to aid balance. Alternatively, attach a cara-biner to the wrist loop of the ice axe and run the climbing rope through it.

You can also attach the secured hammer directly to the harness with a runner sling (or a keeper sling, described below). The wrist loop is not a good attachment point if you plan to hang directly from it because you will stretch the loop flat and make it difficult to reinsert your wrist. These attachments provide security while you stand balanced on one foot or on slightly larger stances, as you place an ice screw or pound-in for more reliable protection.

When the ice steepens to around 70 degrees, you can still balance on front points while placing an ice screw, but you will want to remain firmly attached to your axe. Use a wrist loop that opens up enough to allow your arm to slide up to the elbow (fig. 15-6) so you can use the

axe for balance and your hand to help start the screw. Some steep-ice climbers use hero loops permanently attached to the screw to allow them to clip the rope when the screw is partway in. As the screw turns deeper into the ice, the security of the screw increases.

Keeper Slings and Cows' Tails

You use *keeper slings* and *cows' tails* in order to rest on steep ice or as an emergency technique should something go wrong. A keeper sling (fig. 15-7A) is a permanently attached sling extending from an axe's spike hole to the rope-attachment point of your harness. If a rest becomes necessary, you can plant the tool firmly and hang from the keeper sling. In addition, hand tools with keeper slings are useful for safeguarding you when you set up a screw belay, and for backing up the belay. A cow's tail (fig. 15-7B) is

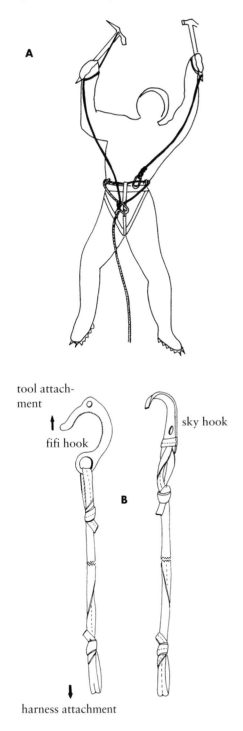

tool attach-
ment

fifi hook

sky hook

B

harness attachment

Figure 15-7. Keeper Slings and Cows' Tails:
A—Keeper sling. B—Cows' tails.

a removable sling used whenever you want a rest. One end attaches to your harness, and the free end has a *fifi hook* (a metal hook shaped something like a question mark) or a *sky hook* (a metal hook with a sharp bend) that you tuck away until you need it to connect to the axe. Carabiners do not work as well as hooks when you want to get out of an attachment to the hand tool because of difficulties caused by trying to open the gate while you are hanging from the tool.

Hanging from either a keeper sling or a cow's tail frees both your hands so you can place ice screws and gain a complete physical rest on very steep ice (although you may not mentally relax enough to enjoy it). To enhance your sense of security, make a two-headed cow's tail to distribute your weight to two hand tools firmly planted in the ice. Equalize a rappel ring in the middle of a loop that has fifi hooks or sky hooks attached to both ends. Tie a short sling directly to the rappel ring and make a loop in its free end. This loop attaches to your harness with a locking carabiner, and the fifi hooks attach to firmly planted ice axes. Commercial versions of this rig are available.

The length of keeper slings and cows' tails can present a problem on low-angle ice and snow. For steep ice, slings should be long enough for you to place the hand tools overhead at full arm extension but no longer. If the sling is too long, you would lower too far below the tool when resting, so the tool might be out of reach. Then, in order to grip the tool, you would need to use a second tool to climb back up. On low-angle ice, however, a keeper sling dangles underfoot and threatens to trip you at every step.[5] Avoid this problem by clipping up the slack with a second carabiner or by running a piece of elastic inside a tubular nylon sling that contracts and shortens the sling when it is not in use. You can also put the tool and keeper sling away and climb with a longer tool that is more appropriate for low-angle ice. Remove keeper slings on snow as they prevent you from transferring the axe to your uphill hand.

As with any technique you have not used be-

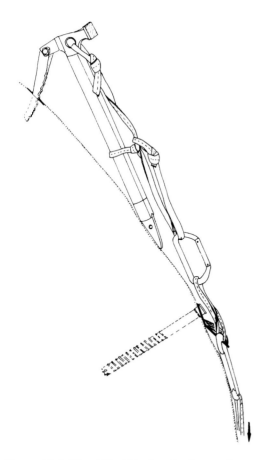

Figure 15-8. Hand Tool Used as Anchor Backup

fore, experiment with keeper slings and cows' tails to determine what is suitable for your particular climbing style and needs. To experiment with these slings, find a column of steep ice placed so that you can stand at the bottom of it. Place your hand tools in the ice at full-arm extension. Then slowly lower your body weight onto the keeper sling or cow's tail in such a way that you can quickly stand up again if the technique is not working.

Reinforcing Ice Screws at Anchors

To supplement ice screws at a belay, attach a runner sling from the ice-tool wrist leash to the screw, as shown in figure 15-8, or directly to your harness. When you are setting up a belay on thin ice, a driven hammer provides more se-

curity than the screws. When driven into the frozen mud found in cracks on thin-ice climbs, the tool gives you a sense of security, and perhaps some real value.

Depending on the tool and its placement, you can optimize the strength of a tool belay by tying off the pick with a hero loop next to the ice like a tied-off piton. The security of a hero-loop belay is based on pick curvature, the presence of tie-off holes in the pick, the nature of the ice, and other factors. When you use a tool anchor of uncertain strength, make sure that your stance is secure enough to take the impact of a fall in order to reduce force on the anchor.

You can use ice hammers and axes as temporary anchors while placing more permanent protection or to supplement screw anchors. When you arrive at a marginal stance, bury the pick of an axe or hammer in the ice. Northwall hammers work very well. If you carry an additional hammer as a third tool—and many climbers do—then use it to place the northwall hammer (fig. 15-9). Some hand tools also have a raised

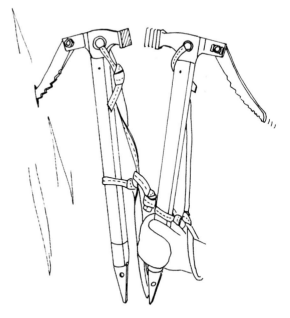

Figure 15-9. Securing a Hand Tool with a Hammer: Some tools have a flange on the tool end of the pick to hit and drive the tool into the ice. Protect your eyes from flying ice chips.

flange at the head of the pick that you strike to drive the pick into the ice. The first few blows should be relatively gentle ones to set the hammer so it does not bounce out of the ice under a misguided blow. If you set the hammer too deeply, you will need to chop it out when you want to remove it. Note that hitting one tool with another will produce flying ice chips, so you will need to protect your eyes with sunglasses or goggles or by looking away as you strike one tool with another.

REFERENCES FOR FUTURE READING

Barry, John. 1987. *Snow and ice climbing*. Seattle: Cloudcap Press.

Cinnamon, Charles. 1981. Hanging oneself. *Summit*. 27(4):4–7.

Cinnamon, Jerry. 1980. A versatile leash for hardwater ice tools. *Summit*.

Lowe, Jeff. 1979. *The ice experience*. Chicago: Contemporary Books.

———. 1981. *Technical manual*. Broomfield, Colorado: Lowe Alpine Systems.

Wilcox, Rick. 1982. *An ice climber's guide to northern New England*. North Conway, New Hampshire: International Mountain Equipment, Inc.

———. 1992. *An ice climber's guide to northern New England*. Second edition. North Conway, New Hampshire: International Mountain Equipment, Inc.

ENDNOTES

1. Lowe, 1979.
2. This explanation of mixed climbing is posted on the Web site of Doug Millen at <http://www.NE-ice.com> under the heading How Hard is it?
3. Cinnamon, 1980.
4. Lowe, 1981.
5. See Cinnamon, 1981, for things that can go wrong with axe keeper slings.

16

Avalanches

AVALANCHE VICTIMS

There are about 25 avalanche fatalities per year in North America, and the survival statistics are sobering (see fig. 16-1).[1] One out of 10 people caught in an avalanche dies, and a person who is completely buried has one in three chances of surviving. The deeper a victim is buried, the smaller the chance of surviving: 46 percent survive when buried from 1 to 2 feet, 32 percent from 3 to 4 feet, 21 percent from 5 to 6 feet, and none when buried deeper than 7 feet.[2]

Two thirds of the victims die of suffocation, one third die of internal injuries including head and neck injuries, and about 1 percent die of hypothermia. About one half of avalanche victims die if they are not recovered within 30 minutes, and realistic longer-term rescues of live victims appear to be in the range of 2 hours.[3]

Avalanche-related deaths can be reduced only if backcountry users avoid avalanches and if the avalanched party executes a rapid self-rescue. Although it is important to educate backcountry users so they can avoid avalanches, attitude is

crucial: many victims are knowledgeable but choose to ignore obvious warnings.[4] Self-rescue becomes more significant in backcountry situations, where 44 percent of the fatalities occur. These backcountry accidents involve climbers and others who, once caught, have trouble getting help fast enough to carry out an effective rescue. Recent innovations, such as an air filtration vest to assist a victim's ability to pull air from the snowpack, promise to give searchers time to execute a rescue.[5]

Despite these deadly statistics, it is imperative to initiate a rescue. Even after 6 hours, approximately 1 victim in 40 is found alive. There is one documented case in which a victim lived after being buried under 5 feet of snow for 25½ hours. He had defied all odds; an airspace the size of a washtub around his head saved his life. Similar examples from the Alps indicate that survival times can vary, "so rescuers and victims should never give up hope."[6]

Dan, whose experience with an avalanche is featured in the box on page 238, made several

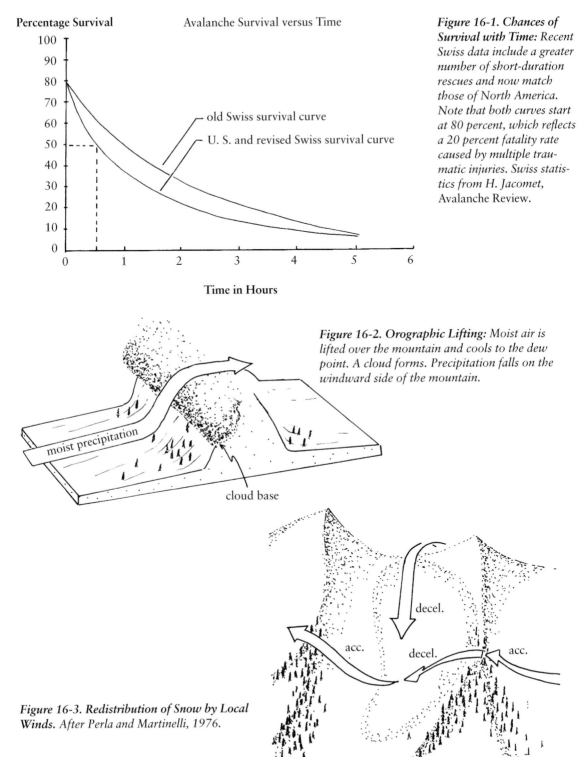

Percentage Survival

Avalanche Survival versus Time

old Swiss survival curve

U. S. and revised Swiss survival curve

Time in Hours

Figure 16-1. Chances of Survival with Time: Recent Swiss data include a greater number of short-duration rescues and now match those of North America. Note that both curves start at 80 percent, which reflects a 20 percent fatality rate caused by multiple traumatic injuries. Swiss statistics from H. Jacomet, Avalanche Review.

Figure 16-2. Orographic Lifting: Moist air is lifted over the mountain and cools to the dew point. A cloud forms. Precipitation falls on the windward side of the mountain.

moist precipitation

cloud base

decel.

acc.

decel.

acc.

Figure 16-3. Redistribution of Snow by Local Winds. After Perla and Martinelli, 1976.

mistakes. He was climbing early in the season, when the late autumn snowfall had not had time to bond well to the ice of the glacier. He was on the climb late in the day, when the snow-ice bond was weakened, and he set off the avalanche that then threatened to bury him. Like other lucky victims, he rescued himself, and he took out two health policies after his experience—traditional insurance to pay medical bills, and an educational policy to learn how to avoid avalanches.

MOUNTAIN GEOGRAPHY AND AVALANCHES

A mountain range triggers its own snowfall by the process of mountain, or *orographic*, lifting of moist air (fig. 16-2). The moist air cools as it rises over the mountain until water vapor forms snow that eventually falls. Warmer air can hold more moisture and give rise to heavier snowfall.

Once on the ground, snowfall is distributed by local winds (fig. 16-3). It scours in some places and accumulates in others as wind speed and direction change in response to local ridges and valleys. Scouring occurs on the windward side of mountain ridges and leaves behind eroded slopes that are generally avalanche free. *Sastrugi*, a fluted snow surface formed by wind etching, often marks these eroded surfaces. The eroded snow is taken up to the ridgeline, where it is deposited as cornices, or transported to lee slopes, where it is deposited as an avalanche-prone windslab.

AVALANCHE CLASSIFICATION

Avalanches are classified by type, trigger, size, and sliding surface (fig. 16-4).[7] You can recognize powder or *loose-snow* avalanches by the

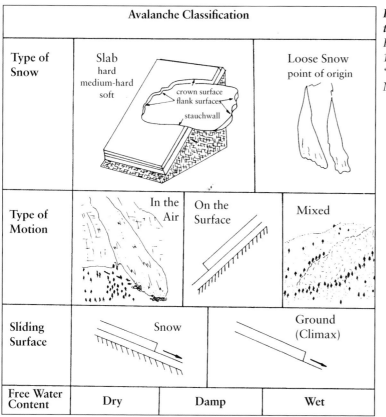

Avalanche Classification			
Type of Snow	Slab hard medium-hard soft crown surface flank surfaces stauchwall		Loose Snow point of origin
Type of Motion		In the Air / On the Surface	Mixed
Sliding Surface	Snow		Ground (Climax)
Free Water Content	Dry	Damp	Wet

Figure 16-4. Avalanche Classification. Based on The Avalanche Handbook (Perla and Martinelli, 1976) and the National Ski Patrol "Circle A" Avalanche Course Notes (Damon, 1986).

Tobogganing the Tyndall Glacier

Dear Jerry:

I was climbing the Tyndall Glacier in Rocky Mountain National Park and was about 40 feet from the top when the whole thing slid. There was around 4 or 5 feet of wind-packed snow covering the ice, around 50 degrees or so and maybe a little steeper as it topped out on a ridge between two peaks. The glacier is probably around 1,000 feet high and has a large basin at its base, which I had to climb down into to get to the glacier. It looked so beautiful, this huge expanse of smooth steep snow, I just had to climb it. I really didn't think I had to worry about it sliding, even though it was wind-pack, because it was so early in the season (Nov. 9).

It was right around 2:00 P.M., just enough time to top out, maybe bag one of the peaks, and then blaze on down and out to the car. I had to climb right up the center of the slope at the top because the sides were blocked by cornices. I was really close to the top and figuring that I'm home free even though it's getting steeper and all

of a sudden something feels weird. I tried to self-arrest but I was going so fast and the ice was so hard, my axe just flew out of my hands. I knew I didn't want it dangling from my wrist so I tried to reach for it, or at least thought to do this, but it was futile. Then I remembered I had my crampons on and thought I should bend my legs; again this was futile. Then I remembered you're supposed to swim to try to stay on top but again, well, you guessed it. I was flying along the ice with a million tons of snow pummeling me. I was completely disoriented and everything was dark so I just went with it, pretty much my only option. It was weird. I really don't remember being scared or knowing if I was getting hurt or not.

After a while the snow started slowing down and I began to see light. Then all of a sudden I just sort of rolled to a stop and there I was, only halfway buried. I just lay there and freaked out for the longest time. Then I looked down at my body as I pulled myself free, and, amazingly, I was intact. My axe was dangling from its leash and my crampons (clip-on) . . . had been torn off and were all bent up! . . . I stood up and my whole left side

was hurting. My ankle, hip, and elbow were really sore but I could just put some weight on the leg. I thought my arm was broken because it looked like hell and I couldn't move it. I turned around and was horrified to see that the whole glacier was no longer a beautiful white snow slope but an ugly green and dirty ice field. The snow had fractured right above where I had been and then the fracture line stepped down and around the whole glacier. The basin at the bottom, where I now stood, was filled to overflowing; the whole landscape had changed.

I knew I had to get out of there fast because I was alone, so I took a bunch of Advil and hobbled out. . . . No broken bones, just lots of bad bruises and two sprained ankles. A park ranger . . . and the doctor agreed that I was probably the luckiest person in the world that day. I have since ordered new crampons . . . and am more psyched than ever to head for the hills. I also got a health insurance policy . . . and signed up for an avalanche class.

Take care,
Dan

---

fact that they release from a point on a slope and spread out in a fan downslope. There is little cohesion within the snow.

Slab avalanches usually occur in an accumulating snowpack that undergoes internal changes or metamorphism. These changes relate to settling as well as temperature and humidity gradients in the snowpack: some layers of individual snow grains are bonded together, whereas others become cohesionless. A slab or layer of consolidated snow forms that is poorly connected to underlying layers. A *windslab* is a particular type of slab that forms from the accumulation of broken snow crystals that pack densely during and following a storm when wind speed exceeds 5 meters per second. The broken crystals do not interlock well with older snow and leave the slab less stable.

As the slab sits on a slope, it *creeps* downhill under the influence of gravity. Because different parts of the slab creep at different rates, tension builds up and can be released by cracking within a slab and by failure of cohesion between slabs, which result in a slide. During the slide, the coherent slab breaks up. Climbers who start out on the surface can quickly become buried in the moving mass. Slab slides are recognizable after the fact by a vertical fracture line, the *crown surface*, that runs across the top of the slide. Broken-up pieces of slab often appear at the bottom of the slope.

Slabs are classified into *hard* or *soft,* depending on their resistance to probing with skis and how well they survive lengthy trips downslope without disintegrating. Slab avalanches initiate at a crown surface and often have saw-toothed side boundaries, or *flanks*. They slide on a *bed surface*. The downslope fracture, called the *stauchwall*, is often difficult to identify because it is usually overridden and obliterated by the sliding blocks.[8] A trigger, which is usually the victim in accidents involving people, disturbs the connection between these layers, and gravity pulls the slab downhill. Other triggers involve natural release, as well as various kinds of purposely controlled ski or explosive releases. The surface on which the slab slides can be either an old snow surface or the ground. Avalanches vary in size from snow sluffs to whole mountainsides, but the average fracture (in a study of Colorado avalanches from 1951 to 1991) is 300 feet across with a fall of 700 vertical feet. Soft slabs accounted for 67.5 percent and hard slabs 26.2 percent of fatal episodes. Very large avalanches create an *airblast*, which is a strong and potentially destructive wind that can extend well out in front of the avalanche itself.

Small snow sluffs called *spindrift* are also of interest to climbers. Spindrift is small loose snow that slides down steep slopes during a snowstorm. Spindrift can be a problem if enough loose snow builds up on a climb to force climbers backward off their stance. A quick rush of spindrift can also cause a lead climber to lose balance and fall. Of course, spindrift fills openings in clothing with cold snow and blinds climbers for short periods of time. When spindrift accumulates on gentler approach slopes below a climb, it can build up slabs that avalanche. Because most avalanches occur within 24 hours of a storm, the presence of much spindrift indicates that climbers are endangering themselves by climbing at that time, especially if the rate of snowfall is heavy—exceeding 1 inch per hour—and if the temperature rises as the storm continues. A warming trend, common to most storms, indicates that wet, heavy snow might be sitting on a layer of loose, unconsolidated powder, thus producing the conditions in which a slab of new snow can slide.

AVALANCHE DANGER SCALE

The avalanche danger scale below is used by avalanche centers in the United States[9] and, with minor changes in terminology, in Canada and Europe:

Low (green)—Natural avalanches are very unlikely. Human-triggered avalanches are unlikely. Generally stable snow; isolated areas of instability. Travel is generally safe. Normal caution is advised.

Moderate (yellow)—Natural avalanches are unlikely. Human-triggered avalanches are possible. Unstable slabs are possible on steep terrain. Use caution in steeper terrain on certain slope orientations (aspects).

Considerable (orange)—Natural avalanches are possible. Human-triggered avalanches are probable. Unstable slabs are probable on steep terrain. Be more cautious in steeper terrain. Be aware of potentially dangerous areas of unstable snow.

High (red)—Natural and human triggered avalanches are likely. Unstable slabs are likely on a variety of aspects and slope angles. Travel in avalanche terrain is not recommended. Safest travel is on windward ridges or lower-angle slopes without steeper terrain above.

Extreme (black)—Widespread natural or human-triggered avalanches are certain. Extremely unstable slabs exist on most aspects and slope angles. Large destructive avalanches are possible. Travel in avalanche terrain should be avoided, with travel confined to low-angle terrain well away from avalanche path run outs.

Figure 16-5. Cornice Structure in Relation to Wind Direction. Modified from Perla and Martinelli, 1976.

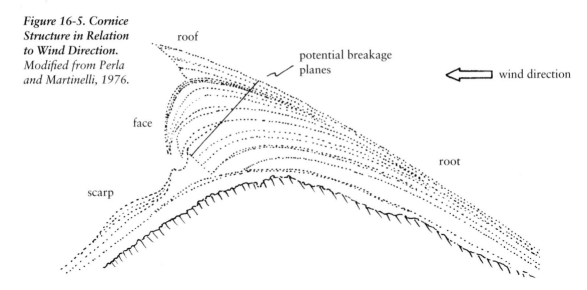

roof

potential breakage planes

wind direction

face

root

scarp

CORNICES

Cornices (fig. 16-5) form at the crests of ridges. They blend with the mountain slope on the windward side but overhang steep, snow-laden slopes and are unsupported on the leeward side. Cornices form as the wind decelerates after passing over the crest. Angular ridgelines produce a more rapid wind deceleration than rounded ridgelines and tend to promote the formation of cornices. Cornices are formed of broken crystals packed together so well that they create a density of about half that of glacier ice; new snow is usually much less dense.

Cornices are under tension and can fracture on the windward side well back from their crest. They are a danger for at least three reasons. First, climbers approaching them from the windward side can wander onto them and cause them to break. The literature of mountaineering is filled with near-accidents, and the disappearance of a number of famous climbers is attributed to falling through cornices.[10] Unsuspecting climbers might not know that they are on a cornice until their ice axe or foot plunges through into open air below. Second, cornices can fall on climbers coming up leeward slopes. If the cornice does not fall during an ascent, it might break as climbers tunnel through the cornice to

exit the climb. Third, a falling cornice can trigger a windslab avalanche on the slope below.

SLOPE STEEPNESS AND LENGTH

There is a relationship between slope steepness and the potential for avalanche. Slopes steeper than 60 degrees will sluff snow continuously. *Slopes 45 to 60 degrees will avalanche and should always be suspect.* Slopes of 25 to 45 degrees *can* avalanche and present the greatest danger because their stability is unknown.

Slopes less than 20 degrees are low enough in angle that they might not slide during the winter. If there is a steeper slope above, however, there can be a problem. One 1991 case involved three sledders on an 18-degree slope overlain by a 40-degree slope. The shallow-angled slope settled beneath the sledders and released the snow on the steeper slope above.[11]

People have a difficult time in judging slope steepness and usually have to rely on clinometers (fig. 16-6A) or other measures. A simple observation of the angle between an upright ski pole and the slope will help give a realistic idea of the slope's steepness. If you mark one ski pole with tape and stand it vertically and use the second pole horizontally (fig. 16-6B), you can ap-

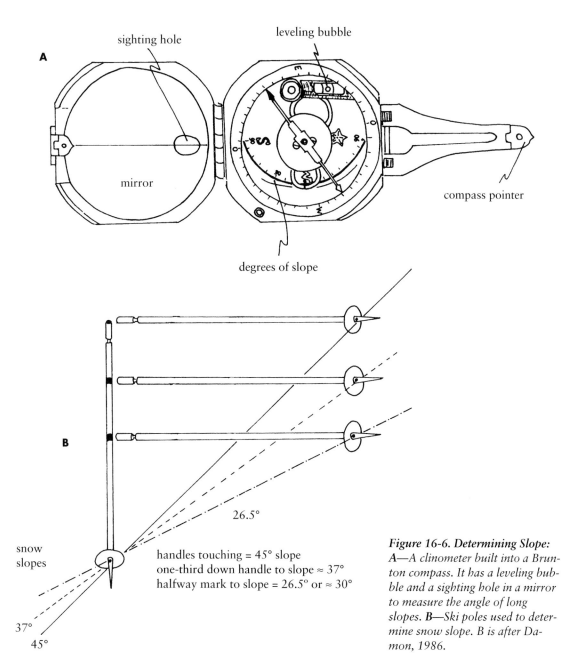

Figure 16-6. Determining Slope: A—A clinometer built into a Brunton compass. It has a leveling bubble and a sighting hole in a mirror to measure the angle of long slopes. B—Ski poles used to determine snow slope. B is after Damon, 1986.

handles touching = 45° slope
one-third down handle to slope ≈ 37°
halfway mark to slope = 26.5° or ≈ 30°

proximate the steepness of the slope.

Short slides kill as effectively and as frequently as long slides. Many victims (8 percent) are caught in slides of less than 100 feet, with the most frequent fatal slide falling 300 to 400 vertical feet (18 percent). Fully half (53 percent) of fatal avalanches fall less than 500 feet. Interestingly, in the Colorado statistics from which these figures are taken, there were no avalanches on slopes of 1,300 to 1,699 feet, but almost 14 percent of the fatal avalanches occurred on slopes greater than 1,700 feet long.[12]

Cornice Fall and Survival

Dear Jerry:

The final 800 feet of the 3,000-foot-high hanging glacier looked like an easy romp up a narrow chute, but it was already 7 P.M. and darkness was pressing. To get to this point we had started at first light and soloed steep ice early in the morning. In the midday we had climbed four pitches of unprotectable disintegrating rock around an overhanging section of the glacier. With that crumbling vertical horror behind, we could see the top and hoped to beat darkness and undergo a cold bivouac near the summit. The chute started from the crevasse where Dan later landed at the end of his 300-foot fall.

At the end of the second lead Dan belayed in the middle of the ice groove that obviously channeled all falling things. There was good ice in the groove for an an-chor and we would quickly be out of the line of fire when I led through. No rocks or ice had fallen off earlier in the day. We thought that if cornices were going to fall, they would have done so in the heat of midday. In retrospect, our reasoning was flawed; thick clouds and smoke blowing over the mountains from fires raging out of control in British Columbia combined to prevent normal cooling. It was too warm.

A section of the cornice the size of an 18-wheel tractor-trailer rig broke off. Giant blocks fell on top of Dan and pushed him down the slope like a hydraulic ram. An an-chor carabiner broke, his ax keeper slings ripped out, and he unzipped the 32 bar tacks of a dynamic sling on a piece of protection before pulling the screw and finally collapsing a snow bridge over the crevasse that stopped his fall. This was a good landing place that provided dynamic deceleration. The tightly stretched rope cracked my ribs but did not completely cut me in two. After regaining consciousness, I rappelled down to Dan and we made our way to where we thought a helicopter could land or hover, because by now we knew that we needed help to get out alive. Dan's legs were not functioning and, in a freak side effect of the accident, I had lost most of the skin from my back and quickly became hypothermic. Dan's faith and activity kept us going throughout the cold night on the glacier. An alert warden realized that we had not signed back in from our climb and initiated a rescue the next day. Dan eventually quit climbing because of his damaged knees. Whenever I get near a cornice the scarred skin on my back starts to itch.

Take care,
Jim

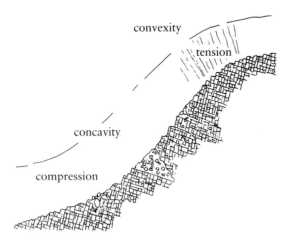

Figure 16-7. Slope Profile and Fracturing: Compression occurs on a concave slope, and tension cracks appear in the middle of a bulging or convex slope. After Perla and Martinelli, 1976.

CONCAVE AND CONVEX SLOPES

Snow slabs can be relatively rigid, and their tensile strength is affected by the slope profile (fig. 16-7). A concave slope tends to place snow in compression so that the maximum stress builds up at the base of the slope. This slope will release by sliding from the bottom. Convex snow slopes are in tension and tend to fracture in mid-slope where the release occurs. A uniform snow slope is more or less in tension throughout its length and can fracture at any point.

ATMOSPHERIC CONDITIONS

Atmospheric conditions are very important when you are considering travel in avalanche country. Most avalanches take place within 24 hours after a storm. Heavy storms that have a snowfall of greater than 1 inch per hour are

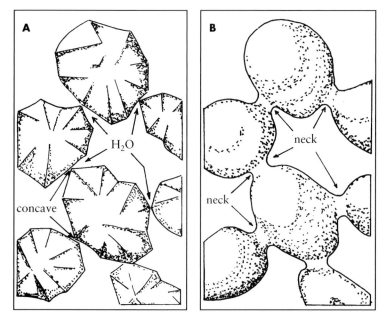

Figure 16-8. Equitemperature Metamorphism: A—The weight of the snowpack presses ice grains together. If the temperature in the snowpack is equal, water molecules migrate into the concavities from convex regions. B—This process, which rounds grains and joins individual grains together into a skeleton, is called sintering. After Perla and Martinelli, 1976.

more likely to create unstable conditions rapidly. High winds—greater than 15 miles per hour—transport snow and form unstable windslabs on lee slopes. Rising temperatures during the storm will place a layer of heavier snow on top of lighter, less dense snow, which creates an unstable situation. Rain will increase the weight of the snowpack and increase the influence of gravity to promote sliding. Ample water from rain or sun melting can descend through the snowpack to a potential sliding surface, lubricate it, and promote detachment and sliding.

CHANGES WITHIN THE SNOWPACK

The snowpack will undergo three types of change during a typical year: *equitemperature metamorphism, temperature-gradient metamorphism,* and *melt-freeze metamorphism.* Each change affects snowpack stability.

Equitemperature Metamorphism (ET)

Equitemperature metamorphism is a slow change that takes place when the temperature from the bottom to the top of the snowpack is uniform. Mild days, with nights not much colder than freezing, promote this type of change.

If you examine individual grains of snow, you will see that angular, newly fallen crystals rapidly lose angularity and become more rounded. Water vapor migrates away from sharp points and convex bulges to the sharp valleys formed where individual grains touch or to concavities. Because of lower vapor pressure in the valleys, water vapor deposits in the solid form, thus filling and strengthening the bond between particles. Equitemperature metamorphism creates strength and stability in the snowpack (fig. 16-8).

Temperature-Gradient Metamorphism (TG)

The top of a snowpack is in contact with the air and exists at the prevailing atmospheric temperature. The bottom of the snowpack sits on ground. Small amounts of heat from within the earth, as well as heat retained in rocks and soils, are sufficient to keep the bottom of the snowpack around 32 degrees Fahrenheit (0 degrees Celsius).

In a thin snowpack during a cold snap, there is a very large difference between the temperature at the bottom and at the top of the snowpack (fig. 16-9). This temperature gradient

Figure 16-9. Temperature Gradient in a Snowpack: In temperature-gradient metamorphism, water vapor is deposited on the grains, leading to an increase in grain size and decrease in overall strength of the ice skeleton. Depth hoar develops, forming hollow cup-shaped crystals seen here in side view. After Perla and Martinelli, 1976.

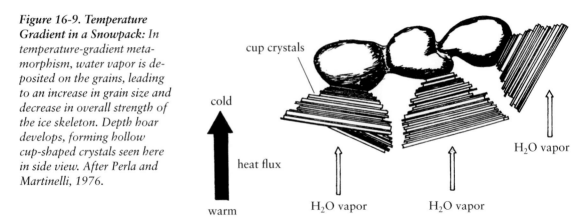

cup crystals

cold

heat flux

warm

H_2O vapor

H_2O vapor

H_2O vapor

drives water vapor from the warm bottom to the cold top. As moisture leaves the bottom of the snowpack, the remaining snow becomes less dense. Snow crystals change, or metamorphose, to produce *depth hoar*—crystals that are not well bonded to their neighbors. These crystals might look like sugar to the unaided eye and appear as cup-shaped crystals under magnification. Depth hoar often forms directly on the ground or on an ice crust.

Because depth hoar has little structural rigidity, its formation destroys the bonds to the snow slab above and creates a sliding surface. A significant thickness of depth hoar can form overnight under very cold conditions in a thin snowpack. One investigator observed a more than 12-inch thickness of snow converted to depth-hoar crystals overnight in a 24-inch-thick snowpack at temperatures of −40 degrees Fahrenheit (−40 degrees Celsius).[13]

Equitemperature and temperature-gradient metamorphisms produce radically different results in the snowpack. ET metamorphism tends to stabilize the snowpack, and TG metamorphism tends to destabilize it. The temperature difference across the snowpack and snow density determine which type of metamorphism predominates. A loose, low-density snow allows vapor to flow easily, whereas higher-density snow reduces vapor flow. Higher elevations, shadowed north slopes, and very cold temperatures tend to promote temperature-gradient metamorphism. Climbers should keep track of

storm and temperature patterns throughout the winter; early snowfall followed by cold periods will produce TG metamorphism. Thus, subsequent snow accumulation will be supported on an unstable foundation.

Melt-Freeze Metamorphism (MF)

The melt-freeze process operates on the snowpack during spring and summer. Snow that survives into the summer, either on the ground or on glacier ice, continually melts during the daytime and refreezes at night. It is a simple process, with the grains becoming ever larger. It can, however, lead to deep instability because each grain in the melt cycle is surrounded and lubricated by water. A sudden shower or snow squall can add enough weight to initiate a slow-moving avalanche of very wet, heavy snow. Early in the morning, beware of a deep melt covered with a thin skin of frozen snow.

On the other hand, the melt-freeze cycle promotes stability of the snowpack in the frozen state because melting destroys weak depth-hoar layers produced during temperature-gradient metamorphism. Indeed, the melt-freeze cycle is the only process by which temperature-gradient crystals are converted to a stable form.

Surface Hoarfrost

If moist air moves over a snow slope and cools at night to below freezing, *surface hoarfrost* can form. This deposition is similar to that of dew during the summer except that thin ice crystals, rather than dewdrops, are deposited. These hoarfrost crystals can persist during the daytime on shaded slopes or in gullies, where they form a beautiful sparkling surface. The hoarfrost layer is essentially frictionless and can act as a sliding surface if covered by new snowfall. If surface hoar is incorporated into the lower part of a snowpack, it becomes a weak layer that is difficult to detect because it is usually only a few millimeters thick.

INDICATIONS OF SLOPE INSTABILITY

There are certain signs to look for to determine quickly if a snow slope is unstable. Examine nearby snow slopes that have the same orientation as the slope in question for current or prior snow sluffs or avalanches. If avalanche debris is present on these slopes, then the slope in question can be unstable. Avalanche debris from a slab slide accumulates at the base of the slope as broken-up blocks of the former slab. The slab leaves behind both a sliding surface and a crown surface at the top of the slope.

If cracks run across the slope, then the slope is under tension. If the cracks are deep, stay off the slope. Shallow cracks involving only the thin upper layer suggest caution and further tests. Snow that emits a hollow sound or settles with a "whumphing" noise, which results from a rapid expulsion of air, is unstable.[14] You might also encounter hollow areas if you probe with an ice axe or ski pole. Cartwheel-shaped snow structures called *sunballs* rolling down the slope indicate that the layers involved are wet and unstable. Any open slope between the angles of 25 and 60 degrees should be suspect. If you know that a slope has a slide history or if you observe trees uprooted or with broken-off trunks or without branches on the uphill side, you should consider the slope potentially dangerous.

Hasty Pits

The direct way to test a snow slope is to dig a *hasty pit*. This means that backcountry travelers must carry a shovel large enough for digging and keep it accessible, so that it actually will be used rather than simply carried. Dig hasty pits to ground level, if possible, or at least down to old snow surfaces. The pit will have vertical walls on three sides far enough apart for the tester to get into and perform a shovel shear or compression test, or a wedge-compression test, described below. Dig the first hasty pit on a smaller slope that has the same orientation and elevation as the questionable slope or at the edge of the questionable slope. (The process of digging the hasty pit could trigger an avalanche.) You can dig subsequent hasty pits in the suspect starting zone of the slope in question if conditions allow. This can be a dangerous procedure, and you should consider precautions, including safety lines to trees.

Once you dig the pit, you can carry out a number of tests. Bring out the *stratigraphy* of the snowpack by brushing the vertical rear wall of the pit with either a paintbrush or an evergreen bough. Brushing accentuates the differences in hardness of the individual layers and makes them more apparent. Ice crusts will stand out in relief, and softer layers will recede. Remember that significant layers, such as surface hoar or sun crust, might be only a few millimeters in thickness.

You can determine the hardness of the individual layers by probing them in a direction perpendicular to the back wall. Hardness increases as you progressively use a fist, a finger, a pencil, or a knife to penetrate an individual layer. A particularly soft layer might indicate depth hoar, whereas particularly hard layers could be sun crust.

If you carry thermometers, you can test temperature gradients in the hasty pit between the ground and surface layers. This information will give a good indication of current temperature-gradient conditions, although it says little about past conditions.

You can examine the individual layers with an 8- to 10-power hand lens for faceted grains or "stepped" hoar temperature-gradient crystals, which might be the cause of any weak layer discovered in the hardness examination. You might first suspect these crystals to form at ground level in the snowpack, although a thorough examination can reveal them at any level in the pack.

Shear and Compression Tests

You can test the overall structural integrity of the snowpack with a shovel test or by means of the shear-wedge (Rütschkeil) and shear-block (Rütschblock) tests described below. All shear tests take advantage of the downward-sloping layers of the snowpack to find weak layers. To carry out the shovel shear test, dig a pit as deep as possible and make a column of snow detached on three sides (fig. 16-10). As you

Figure 16-10. The Shovel Shear Test: Insert the shovel vertically until shear occurs on the weakest layer. As you insert the shovel, pull it downslope to reveal weak layers in the snow. Easy shear, particularly in the topmost layers, indicates that you should be cautious.

continuously insert the shovel vertically at the rear of the column, weakly bonded layers will shear off.

You can test the bonding between each successive individual layer by inserting the shovel only to the depth of the topmost layer and pulling the shovel toward you until the layer slides. As you pull, be careful not to rotate the handle of the shovel and "pry" the block loose. After pulling off the current topmost layer, you then test the strength of the next layer and so on until you reach the bottom of the pit.

If, during your investigation you find that temperature-gradient metamorphism has formed a layer of depth-hoar crystals, you can use a shovel compression test to determine the compressive strength of the layer. Do not cut the back wall of the column, but bear down with the flat of the shovel or a ski on the upper surface of the column. The amount of force needed to collapse the TG layer gives an indication of the compressive strength of this layer.

For the shear-wedge test, dig a hasty pit and place a snow probe or upside-down ski pole equidistant from the side walls and about 6 feet behind the rear wall (fig. 16-11A). Now pass a length of avalanche cord, 5-millimeter kernmantle rope, around the ski pole to form a wedge-shaped pattern. To help this cord cut through the snow, you can tie overhand knots in it about 1 foot apart to act as cutting teeth. Then jigsaw the cord down through the snow the length of the ski pole. This process cuts out a wedge-shaped block, which might spontaneously release, extending to the ski pole from the rear of the hasty pit.

The shear-block test is similar to the shear-wedge test except that you cut a rectangular snow block rather than a wedge (fig. 16-11B). Start by digging a hasty pit somewhat wider than a ski length. Next, dig trenches back into the snow perpendicular to the hasty pit wall for about the same distance. The remaining wall of the block is cut free by jigsawing the avalanche cord.

The shear wedge or shear block might release spontaneously as it is cut. This indicates ex-

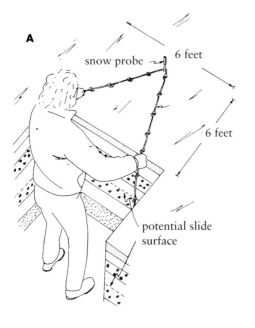

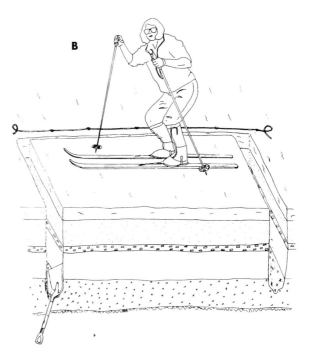

Figure 16-11. The Shear-Wedge and Shear-Block Tests: A—An avalanche cord is used to jigsaw through the back wall of a hasty pit to form a wedge that will be increasingly weighed to check for potential slide surfaces. The avalanche cord has overhand knots tied in it about a foot apart to act as cutting teeth. B—Cut three sides of the sliding block with a shovel and the remaining wall with the avalanche cord. From Damon, 1986, and Munter, 1985.

treme instability in the snowpack. If there is no spontaneous release, test the compressive stability of both the shear wedge and shear block by stepping very gently onto the upper surface. If the wedge or block does not release, weigh it more heavily by rapidly flexing both knees to transfer energy into the snow. If the snow still does not slide, jump onto the block. If this does not release the block, take your skis off and gently weight the block with one foot and then both feet. Finally, jump easily and then vigorously. Any weak layer will fail at some point during the testing and slide into the pit. If the layer does not break until you are jumping up and down on both feet, the slope is quite stable. If failure occurs somewhere between easy and very difficult, you must estimate the safety of the slope based on experience and the need to cross it. Needless to say, a spontaneous release signifies maximum hazard.

ROUTE SELECTION IN AVALANCHE COUNTRY

Potential avalanche slopes are stable much of the time, and many backcountry travelers ski and cross them without incident. To cross safely over a long period of time, you need to be attuned to microchanges in snow conditions and travel when the snowpack is stable. It is best to learn the skills of snow travel from an experienced backcountry traveler, but there are guidelines that you can follow.

Avoid going out for the first few days after a storm because this is the time when most avalanches occur. Watch and probe the snow as you look for changes in slope and snow conditions that suggest instability. Travel between rocks or in dense timber stands, if possible. Be wary on sparsely timbered slopes that probably do not anchor the snow sufficiently. Dig hasty pits if you are suspicious. Pits do not take long to dig and provide critical information.

If you must cross suspect slopes, it is better to stay high on the slope above *starting zones* (zones of potential fracture) or to keep to the side if you must climb the starting zone. Move quickly across the slope and travel one at a time, in the same track, in order to disturb less snow. Never violate the rule of traveling one at a time, and give the person ahead of you plenty of time to reach a safe island before you start out. Even if many members of the party have crossed safely, stay alert because slopes can slide during the passage of the second, third, or tenth member. Many killer avalanches are relatively small —less than 100 meters in length and somewhat narrower. You might belay a person crossing these slopes. If you do have to cross a suspect avalanche slope, go directly uphill and downhill. Do not crisscross or switchback the slope, and do not ski above another person lest you set off a slide.

Travel Zones

In traveling through avalanche terrain, it is useful to think in terms of travel zones related to wind direction, valley slope, and ridge lines (fig. 16-12). Travel in V-shaped valleys is dangerous and probably a path of last resort because of the steep slopes on either side. Higher up on the

slope, wind might have scoured the snow away, leaving behind a good crampon surface. However, in deeper snow, this slope can develop depth hoar and become hazardous. Near the ridge line, but behind potential cornice fractures, is a relatively safe zone of travel. This area is above most of the snow, and the slope may flatten out at this point. The most dangerous zone lies on the lee side of the cornice. This is where a decrease in wind velocity deposits much snow, and it is directly beneath cornices. The degree of safety increases downslope on the lee side, and travel becomes fully safe only when you are well away from the possible run out of spontaneous cornice falls and avalanches.

Crossing Suspect Snow Slopes

When you cross suspect slopes, button up your clothing and put on a hat and gloves. Activate avalanche cords and beacons as discussed below. Have snow probes ready for use. Loosen ski bindings, pack belts, and safety straps in case you need to jettison the equipment. Remove ski-pole wrist straps so you can drop the poles. Skis are a mixed blessing when an avalanche occurs. On skis, you might be able to

Figure 16-12. Travel Zones Related to Wind Direction for V-Shaped Valleys and Ridges.
After Daffern, 1983.

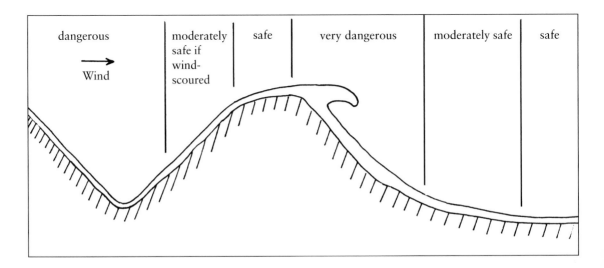

move to the side, or your skis might stick up through the snow to indicate your position if you are buried. On the other hand, skis limit mobility and prohibit swimming motions, which have proved effective for many victims of avalanches.

Interviews with avalanche survivors indicate that those people who tried to swim were somewhat successful. They tended to be able to control their movement upward in the snowpack. One survivor said, "I recall I was able to swim and did so as naturally as one would were he trying to surface in a pool of water."[15]

Martin Epp, a European mountain guide, feels that rolling is a better technique. "Although the passage of an avalanche can be compared to the flow of water, the analogy of swimming out is less effective . . . than rolling like a cylinder or a bottle. Swimming tends to flatten you at the bottom of the avalanche. You will quickly be unable to move or breathe. But you can sometimes roll faster than the snow is moving."[16] Initially, he says, you should try to ski out to the side at a steep 45-degree angle, but if you are caught, begin to roll. Get rid of your skis and poles but retain your pack, since it gives you a greater volume per weight and helps bring you to the surface. (Retaining your pack is contrary to the advice usually given for attempting to swim because the pack restricts the swimming motion.) You should initiate the roll around your body's axis at a 45-degree angle to the path of the avalanche. As the momentum of the avalanche slows, try hard to remain on top. This technique should allow your nose and mouth to remain free of snow and allow you to breathe.

Whether you attempt to swim or roll, it is clear that you need to abandon skis and poles. Members of the party not caught in the avalanche and standing on the side of the avalanching slope can try helping victims to initiate action by calling for them to swim or roll.

Most victims of avalanches suffocate because the moisture from their breath freezes in the snow around their mouths and cuts off further oxygen supply. To help increase air supply, you should get your hands out in front of your face and try to make an airspace as you are coming to a stop. In addition, keep your mouth shut so it does not fill with snow and prevent breathing. Smutek noted a number of instances of survivors who had created an air pocket. He also noted that a snow ranger, who survived because he was found within two minutes of being buried, had tried to form an air pocket with his hand, but "the piling up snow forced it away."[17]

A few victims of avalanches owe their lives to having a hand above the snow. As the snow is coming to a stop, victims should attempt to thrust their hands toward the surface. "I noticed that it seemed lighter above me. I punched violently upward with my left hand and my fingers broke through the snow. It was this hand movement which was seen from the chairlift and led to my being quickly dug out by the rescue crew," said one survivor.[18]

Once the avalanche comes to a stop, the snow hardens and makes it very difficult to create a breathing pocket or to dig out victims.

If someone gets caught and buried in an avalanche, the remainder of the party activates a hasty search. Before initiating the search, however, safeguard the remaining members of the party so they do not get involved in further avalanches. Then, record the victim's fall line and starting location; the location of hats, packs, gloves, or skis that might have been dropped; and the last sighting of the victim. A person who has been caught by an avalanche will tend to follow the fall line in a direction determined by the terrain, as indicated in figure 16-13. The victim might come to rest in corners or on benches, as well as in the toe of the avalanche.

AVALANCHE BEACONS

Avalanche rescue beacons have proved effective in rapidly uncovering victims. Recovery time and survival using all beacons depend upon a searcher's training and facility at rescue gained by practice. All members of a team of backcountry travelers must have beacons tuned to transmit to the same frequency of 475 kHz, which

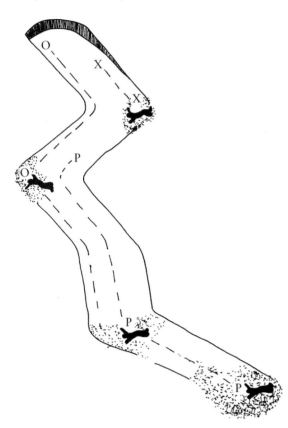

Figure 16-13. Fall Line of a Victim: Avalanche victims tend to follow the local terrain and stop in corners like figures X and O, or on a bench or in the toe of the avalanche like figure P.

was adopted January 1, 1996. An earlier North American standard frequency was 2,267 Hz; for a period of time, dual-frequency beacons were sold that operated at both the 2,267 Hz and the 475k Hz frequencies. Beacons operating on only the 2,267 Hz frequency should no longer be used. When a backcountry team member is caught in an avalanche and buried, with the beacon transmitting, the remaining members of the party switch to receive and become searchers. All beacons should be checked at the trailhead to ensure that they are transmitting properly.

All avalanche beacons transmit and receive inaudible radio analog signals, but older and newer models process the signal differently. Older analog beacons convert the inaudible radio signal of the transmitting beacon into an audible tone, echoing the strength of the original, pulsed signal. Newer digital transceivers sample the received signal digitally, process it, and then output visual *and* audio signals. The most significant difference between analog and digital beacons can be the learning curve involved with using them effectively. Recreational users of digital beacons might achieve good results in a search with less practice than required by analog beacons. Well-practiced individuals will probably achieve better results in using either type of beacon. Digital beacons should evolve quickly and present the promise of even faster and more effective searches for victims.[19]

If a victim is swept up in an avalanche, the remaining members of the party should stay out of the avalanche area while they switch their transceivers to receive, mark the last-seen area of the victim, post a guard to watch for additional avalanches, and prepare to switch back to transmit if there are new avalanches. If multiple searchers enter the search area, they move directly downhill or uphill until someone detects a faint beep.

Modern avalanche beacons with external speakers and light-emitting diode (LED) indicators, or numerical readouts, allow for several search patterns. The classic search pattern is a grid. Grid search can be used with all beacons. This is the method of choice with dual-frequency beacons that have only an earplug for audio output, with all beacons when the search becomes confused, and when in the immediate vicinity of the victim to pinpoint location. To begin, a single searcher can more effectively cover ground by running directly uphill or zigzagging down. Initiate the search this way unless the location of a victim is confined to a narrow slide path, or you can start from the last known location of the victim or from the location of a victim's hat or glove. In a narrow slide path, walk up or down the path center. Ranges to pick up initial signals vary from 20 to 30 meters for some receivers under field conditions to 80 meters for others under good conditions. After detecting the initial beep (position 0 in fig. 16-14), the searcher stops and turns the hand-held transceiver in three dimensions to its loudest position, with the volume control all the way up. This position is maintained with respect to the geographic area—not the searcher's body—as the searcher moves but is reoriented at stops as the search area narrows. At the first beep (0) the searcher begins tracking and backtracking (0 to 1, 1 to 2, 2 to 3) along a line and listens for volume changes; volume increases as the searcher nears the victim and fades as the searcher moves away. After discovering the loudest position (4) along the initial line, the searcher stops, reorients the transceiver for loudest volume, reduces volume setting, turns at right angles to follow a new line, and listens for volume fade (4–5) or increase (5–6) until fade begins (6–7). The searcher backtracks (7–8)

beyond and returns to the loudest position (9) along this line. Here, the searcher reorients the transceiver, decreases volume to its lowest setting, and moves slowly at right angles (9–10) until passing the loudest position on the line, at which point a backtrack brings the searcher to the victim (11). During the last phase of tracking and backtracking, the searcher can remain in one spot with feet planted wide apart and move the transceiver back and forth in the search line just above the snow surface to pinpoint the victim's position.[20]

If you have a single 475 kHz transceiver with an external speaker or LED light readout, you might be able to conduct the middle part of the search faster by using the tangent to the electromagnetic induction line emitted from the buried transceiver. By this method, when you first get the signal, orient the beacon in a horizontal

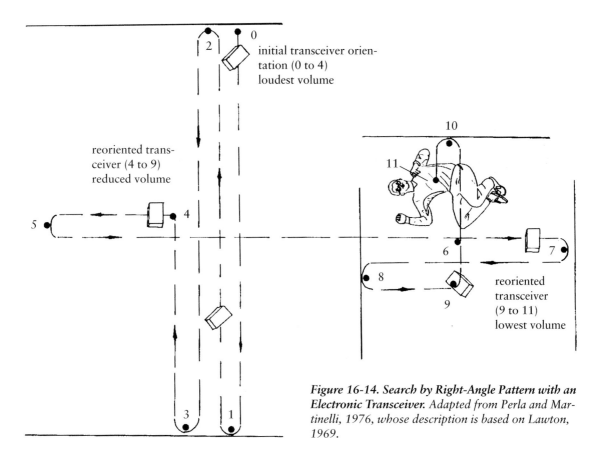

Figure 16-14. Search by Right-Angle Pattern with an Electronic Transceiver. Adapted from Perla and Martinelli, 1976, whose description is based on Lawton, 1969.

plane and search for the loudest signal. Head off in this direction; if the signal weakens, backtrack and head off in the opposite, 180-degree, direction. The signal strength will increase as you head toward the buried transceiver. While moving, sweep your beacon from side to side 45 degrees to the left and to the right to determine the middle of the track where volume is loudest. You are following the tangent of a curving induction line. As signal strength increases, turn down the volume. If you have been following a strong signal and it stops, keep going. The lack of a signal could indicate that you have passed beyond the buried transceiver's range or you could be directly over it, in the null point, with the transceiver pointing perpendicular to the surface. If your signal returns within a few feet, you were at this point. If the signal does not return, you are out of range and the signal has faded.[21]

A digital avalanche beacon has a narrower receive range than that of an analog beacon. A searcher might have a more difficult time in picking up an initial digital signal, but once a signal is picked up, it is easier for inexperienced searchers to get within the vicinity of a victim than with an analog signal. To pinpoint a victim's location, a grid method might be best for both analog and digital beacons. A digital beacon with two antennas, because of its greater ability to stay on a signal line, allows a practiced searcher to follow the signal quickly to the victim by refining directional aim. You probably will be able to pinpoint the burial location of a victim quicker by probing than by using a beacon when you get within a 2-foot-square search area.[22] Success in searching for buried victims is based on practice that is aimed toward rapid recovery times. Studies show that practiced individuals find avalanche victims quicker than nonpracticed searchers, consistent with a professional rather than a recreational approach to traveling on snow, and achieve a higher success rate at live recovery.[23] It is worth noting that finding the victim quickly might not be of much value unless you have shovels. Avalanched snow is extremely dense and difficult to penetrate even with shovels.

Wearing an avalanche transceiver does not automatically provide a greater degree of safety because people wearing a transceiver sometimes take more risks, and many survivors of avalanches are in a state of shock that considerably diminishes their ability to search and rescue. Only 35 percent of those completely buried while wearing an avalanche transceiver are rescued alive.[24] Obviously, the success of a transceiver is related to a high degree of training and the ability to function under stress. The transceiver clearly does not replace the judgment necessary to avoid avalanche terrain in the first place.

AVALANCHE PROBES

If there are surface clues, such as a hat, a limited number of probers can probe in likely spots immediately below the clue, hoping for a rapid recovery. However, probers will probably need to organize into lines and probe for long periods that will tax their strength and endurance. A line captain should see to the creature comfort of probers—water, food, and rotation with shovelers who dig all "strikes" by probers. Probing calls for discipline and concentration, and probers do nothing but probe, keep to the line, and listen to the line captain's commands without distraction. Strikes are investigated by shovelers who stand behind the line; stuck poles are left behind while the prober steps to the line with a new probe if possible. Ideally, probers use poles of rigid tubing 10 to 12 feet long, but you can use ski poles without baskets or other makeshift probes for shallow burials. It is critical to handle the probes with gloves to keep them from warming and icing. Icing will prevent the probes from penetrating the snow or cause them to become stuck in warmer snow.

Probes are either *coarse* or *fine*. A coarse probe, with which you begin, has about a 70 percent chance of striking a live victim. Completing a second coarse probe before initiating a fine probe significantly increases the chance of finding the victim and is faster than a single fine probe. Fine probes are more closely spaced but

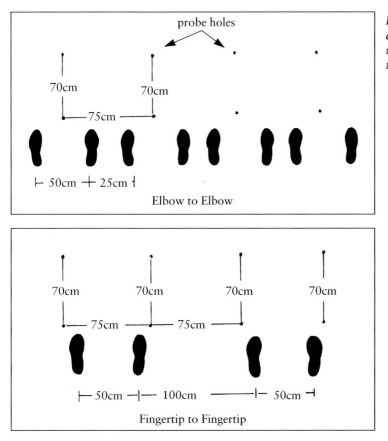

probe holes

70cm   70cm
—75cm—

⊢ 50cm + 25cm ⊣

Elbow to Elbow

70cm   70cm   70cm   70cm

— 75cm — — 75cm —

⊢ 50cm ⊣— 100cm —⊢ 50cm ⊣

Fingertip to Fingertip

Figure 16-15. Two Methods of Executing Coarse Probes: Methods used whenever live rescue is expected. After Perla and Martinelli, 1976.

are too slow to expect live victim recovery, although they ensure almost 100 percent recovery.

Organize probe lines at the base of the avalanche slope, and work uphill after first making sure that the working area will not undergo further avalanching. In organized probing, a line captain, aided by assistants at both ends, has the job of keeping line movement organized and straight. The line captain also observes the depth of the poles plunged by the line members. A pole that strikes a body will not go as deep into the snowpack as other poles and will feel very different from a pole that strikes a rock or ice layer.

You judge spacing for the coarse probe to a certain extent on the number of probers present and the area that you need to cover (fig. 16-15). Probers stand in a line, feet apart, elbow to elbow, and hands on hips to determine sideways spacing. You insert the probe once at the center of your straddled span. Then, on a signal from the line captain, line members together take one step upslope. Another signal initiates probing. When the number of probers is limited, you use fingertip-to-fingertip spacing. You insert the probe first on one side of your body, say the left, and then on the other. You organize fine probing to insert the probe every 10 to 12 inches over the field that you wish to search.

Some experienced avalanche workers feel that individuals within a line can speed up their work by probing their sections at their own pace. This method gives probers a chance to push in their probes as often as they can without waiting for commands.[25] Members of the probing line must be experienced enough to maintain the line as it advances. It is critical that there are shovelers to follow up sites that show resistance to probing. Areas already probed should be marked to prevent later confusion.

AVALANCHE SCENARIO

The situation that follows illustrates the problems and decisions that you might make while traveling in avalanche country with a group of fellow climbers. You can work through the simulation by yourself, or gather two to four climbers[26] plus a moderator. The moderator should be someone who understands the information presented in this chapter or has had field work with avalanches.

The situation: You are completing a day climb or ski tour. Because of travel and routefinding problems, the trip has taken longer than expected. It is 45 minutes before sunset. In an attempt to be out before dark, you have deviated from the planned route and taken a shortcut that will allow you to reach your car in 30 minutes. In so doing, you have ventured into unfamiliar terrain. You have come to a slope that you fear might be unstable and prone to avalanches.

What information do you need? Review this chapter, and discuss appropriate questions. Write the first question on a sheet of paper. The moderator will give you the answer; use the answer to ask a second question. After you get the second answer, ask a final question.

To conclude this simulation, use all three questions and answers to decide on a group plan. If you chose your three questions wisely, you should have enough information to make a sound decision. If you need more information, you can ask the moderator additional questions. Write out your plan on a piece of paper and discuss it with the moderator.

Answers to Questions Your Group Might Ask

- "Do we have the equipment to survive a night out?"
Answer: You have what you would normally have for skiing or climbing in the backcountry. This means that you should be prepared to spend a night out.

- "How are we currently situated?"
Answer: You are situated in an extensive stretch of trees on the edge of a suspected avalanche slope. The slope, out in front of you, is about 2,000 feet high at an angle of 45 degrees. A cornice overhangs the suspect slope, but your current position is out of the fall line of the cornice.

- "Is there an alternative route?"
Answer: If you backtrack for about a mile, you will ascend a safe slope that will put you onto a ridge. You can follow the ridge out in about three hours. It will be difficult to follow the trail until you start up the correct slope leading to the ridge.

- "What is the current weather?"
Answer: Currently it is snowing very hard. Visibility is low, with snow blowing horizontally.

- "Are there any signs to suggest that the slope is currently unstable?"
Answer: There are no cracks, "woomfs," or avalanches to suggest that the slope is currently unstable.

- "What do we find if we dig a hasty pit?"
Answer: The hasty pit reveals an extensive zone of depth hoar about 3 feet down. A shovel shear test produces sliding without much applied force.

- "Are we expected back before dark?"
Answer: Your friends expect to see you about one hour after dark.

Possible Plans of Action and Probable Results

1. Travel directly across the slope.
   You reason that the slope shows no obvious surface signs of sliding even though it is at a 45-degree angle and a cornice overhangs it. The snowfall, apparently at more than 1 inch per hour, seems to have produced no effect on the slope. Your friends will be worried if you are late, and you have only 45 minutes of light left, so you want to get out quickly. The slope is too wide to belay, but

you figure that you can protect yourself by moving one at a time. Everyone checks that their avalanche beacons are turned to transmit, and the first person heads out across the slope.

This reasoning will lead you across a dangerous slope that is rapidly becoming more unstable as the storm progresses. Your party would probably trigger the slope. A hasty pit would have revealed an extensive sliding surface of depth hoar, and the shovel shear test would have shown easy sliding conditions. At least one member of the party and perhaps the entire party would probably be caught in a big avalanche.

2. Climb up the side of the slope, traverse beneath the cornices, and head out.

You reason that the climb uphill will be tiring, but at least you will be above the avalanche slope. You decide to take a chance that the cornice will not fall off during the brief time that you are under it.

It is almost dark, however, and visibility is low, with snow blowing horizontally. You might easily wander onto the suspect slope. The climb uphill would have been exhausting. Even if everything else worked ideally, you would have to pass beneath the unstable overhanging cornice. Even if you were to reach the other side, you would face unknown difficulties in descending to a safe area.

3. Retreat immediately.

You decide that you will be safest if you return to your original route.

However, it is almost dark and visibility is low, so it would be difficult to follow the trail. You would likely get lost.

4. Stay where you are until morning.

This promises to be a cold experience, but it probably is the wisest choice. Being in the trees, you would be somewhat protected from both wind and avalanches. You would have the necessary equipment to spend the night out as you are routinely prepared to do this when climbing in the mountains. In the morning, visibility would be better. You could then backtrack, ascend the safe slope to the ridge, which would be swept free of snow, and walk out. Your friends would have been worried, but they would have been greatly relieved that you chose the safe option.

REFERENCES FOR FUTURE READING

Armstrong, Betsy R., and Knox Williams. 1992. *The avalanche book*. Golden, Colorado: Fulcrum Publishing.

Atkins, Dale. 1998. Companion Rescue and Avalanche Transceivers: The U.S. Experience. *Avalanche Review*. December.

———. 1991. White death: A review of fatal accidents in Colorado, 1950–91. *Avalanche Review*. 10(1).

Brown, Belmore. 1956. *The conquest of Mt. McKinley*. Boston: Houghton, Mifflin Company.

Couche, S. 1977. Avalanche awareness survey. *Mazamu Journal*.

Daffern, Tony. 1983. *Avalanche safety for skiers & climbers*. Seattle: Cloudcap Press.

Damon, Roger. 1986. *The "Circle A" avalanche course notes*. The National Ski Patrol.

Diemberger, Kurt. 1991. *Summits and secrets*. Trans. by Hugh Merrick. Seattle: Mountaineers.

Dostie, Craig. 1999. Avalanche science. *Couloir Magazine*. 11(5).

Epp, Martin, and Stephen Lee. 1987. *Avalanche awareness for skiers and mountaineers*. London: The Wild Side.

Lawton, John G. 1969. *Instruction manual: Skadi III avalanche search and rescue system*. Buffalo, New York: Lawtronics.

Meiklejohn, Brad. 1988. Warm and dead. *Avalanche Review*. 7(2).

Perla, Ronald I., and M. Martinelli, Jr. 1976. *Avalanche handbook 489*. Forest Service, U.S. Department of Agriculture. Washington, D.C.: Government Printing Office.

Setnicka, Tim J. 1980. *Wilderness search and rescue*. Boston: Appalachian Mountain Club.

Simpson, Joe. 1988. *Touching the void*. New York: Harper & Row.

Smutek, Ray. 1977. Portrait of an avalanche survivor. *Off-Belay*. 36:8–12.

Soles, Clyde. 1998. A quicker fix? Straight talk on digital avalanche beacons. *Rock & Ice*. 89: 114–117.

Steger, Will, and Jon Bowermaster. 1991. *Crossing Antarctica*. New York: Laurel-Dell Books.

Williams, Knox. 1975. *The snowy torrents: Avalanche accidents in the United States 1967–71*. Forest Service, U.S. Department of Agriculture, General Technical Report, RM-8. Washington, D.C.: Government Printing Office.

———. 1977. Portrait of an avalanche victim. *Off-Belay*. 36:5–7.

ENDNOTES

1. Statistics are maintained at the Colorado Avalanche Information Center and are available in graph form at <http://www.caic.state.co.us> under the U.S. graphs category.

2. Williams, 1977.

3. Williams, 1975.

4. Atkins, 1991. The portrait of a modern avalanche victim emerges from a study of 40 years of Colorado avalanche data. "The typical avalanche victim is a 30-year-old male, who is an advanced skier, either a tourer or out-of-bounds lift skier, and who has had some avalanche training. The accident is most likely to happen on a January day. . . . The accident happens as the skier is traveling on a north-to-east-facing slope near or just above tree line. He triggers a slab avalanche on a 38-degree slope. The avalanche fractures 300 feet across, failing on a weak, old snow layer 3 feet below the surface. The slide races down the mountain, falling 700 vertical feet. Some victims survive the ride, and some do not. Most of those who do not are buried just over 4 feet deep in the debris."

5. The Avalung by Black Diamond Equipment, Salt Lake City, Utah, is a filtration device that draws air from the snowpack.

6. Epp and Lee, 1987.

7. Williams, 1975.

8. Perla and Martinelli, 1976.

9. From the Colorado Avalanche Information Center at <http://www.caic.state.co. us>.

10. Perhaps the most famous fall through a cornice is that of Hermann Buhl when he was on Chogolisa. This accident is detailed in Diemberger, 1991. In 1988, Joe Simpson described how his partner, Simon Yates, fell along with a cornice that broke off 40 feet back from the crest and produced a break-line of vertical snow nearly 30 feet high.

11. Atkins, 1991.

12. *Ibid.*

13. This is an observation by Roger H. Damon, to whom I am indebted for critiquing this chapter.

14. Steger, 1991, describes encountering "snowquakes" in which areas the size of a large lawn or football field would suddenly collapse and produce a loud noise that startled his dogs. The physical cause of this collapse was not explained in the text.

15. Williams, 1975.

16. Epp and Lee, 1987.

17. Smutek, 1977.

18. *Ibid.*

19. Dostie, 1999.

20. Perla and Martinelli, 1976, give a detailed description of the search techniques, in Lawton, 1969.

21. A good discussion of the tangent method by Michael G. Smith can be found at <http://www.gearworld.com> under the heading Avalanche Rescue.

22. Dostie, 1999.

23. Atkins, 1998. The complete paper is available at <http://www.caic.state.co.us/Atkins_beacons.html>.

24. Epp and Lee, 1987.

25. *Ibid.*

26. This simulation was created by Roger Damon of the Eastern Division of the National Ski Patrol and is based on a similar simulation presented by Doug Fesler at the National Avalanche School. Damon's simulation was presented at the 1993 advanced avalanche course held at Pinkham Notch, New Hampshire.

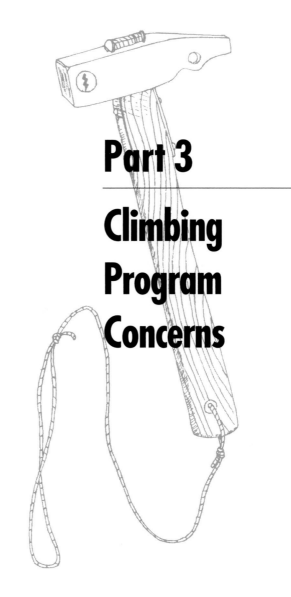

Part 3

Climbing Program Concerns

17

Top-Rope Site Management for Groups

INTRODUCTION

This chapter explores the problems and concerns of organized climbing programs for groups. Most of the climbing techniques used in programmatic climbing, such as anchor construction, are the same as those used by recreational climbers, although a few specific techniques have evolved for use with groups. What makes the management of a top-rope site different for groups than for individuals is that institutions must consider liability and risk management; they need to develop strategies for instructors who work with up to six beginners per instructor; and they should be concerned with methods of formally processing the experience.

Knowing how to make the climbing environment as safe as possible is also a part of site management. For this reason, it is also useful to know something about cliff formation.

LIABILITY IN CLIMBING PROGRAMS

Climbing and mountaineering are not in themselves a cause of liability, and you do not need to avoid them simply because they might be dangerous. Liability arises when you teach climbing, thereby assuming the obligation to provide a safe environment by following accepted professional practices, and an injury occurs. Teaching beginners requires the most care because they have the least understanding about what they are getting into and are least capable of being responsible for themselves.

The structure of the program affects the degree of liability. Liability might be less for a loose cooperative adventure (emphasizing individual choice and group cooperation in decision making) and greater for a highly structured program, such as a credit-bearing course with instructors.[1]

If you run a climbing program or if you teach in one, you also must be concerned with product liability. This liability involves the design of a product—a design that makes it hazardous—as well as defective workmanship or materials that cause an injury. Generally, unless you make, distribute, sell, lease, or rent the product, you need not be concerned with product liability so long as you use only equipment that is in good repair and designed for the activity, and use it in the manner specified by the manufacturer. In practice, this means that climbing programs should use only ropes, helmets, harnesses, and other equipment that are approved by the CEN/UIAA, an international organization of alpine clubs, and maintained in good condition. Equipment made for other purposes, such as construction helmets or yachting ropes, should not be used for climbing.

If you run an organization that sponsors climbing or other adventure activities, you should be familiar with the concepts presented here and consult an attorney concerning specific state laws and your individual situation. More detailed information is available from the references listed at the end of the chapter.

Owning a recreation site introduces separate liability concerns not discussed here. Many states have laws that protect the landowner who exercises ordinary responsibility toward the public. In general, you are not responsible for natural hazards, such as a cliff, but you may incur liability for hazards resulting from negligence, such as a poorly maintained or unsupervised climbing wall. Learn the laws of your state if you own a recreational site or wish to work with the owner of one.

One of the basic tenets of liability is *duty owed*. If you take individuals climbing, you are responsible for providing a safe environment. This responsibility exists whether your organization is for profit or nonprofit, and whether you are paid or unpaid. The duty owed is to provide a *standard of care* that has three major aspects: *supervision*, *conduct of activity*, and *environmental conditions*. The standard of care "is that of a 'reasonable and prudent professional' and asks what are the best practices (requires up-to-dateness) and what others who are knowledgeable and expert in the field do?

By accepting a leadership role, a person holds himself to be competent."[2]

Supervision

The site leader becomes the focal point of safety management after preliminary work is done and participants are at the cliff. Site leaders should be able to identify dangerous conditions and anticipate dangerous situations. They should provide for the proper rendering of first aid and know what to do in an emergency. They should have more experience than required for the activity at hand. They should be trained both in technical areas and in overseeing others. This additional experience gives them a cushion of knowledge and skill to prevent accidents and to handle the situation if anything should go wrong. They should observe the overall condition of participants and take specific steps to reestablish safe conditions if necessary. Just having experience in cooperative-adventure climbing does not qualify you to be a general supervisor of an organized climbing trip. However, there is every reason for individuals with good technical skills to contribute to the overall success of the trip under the leadership of individuals with broader experience.

Conduct of Activity

Climbing or mountaineering in itself cannot be considered the cause of injury or liability. Whether you are deemed liable is determined by the manner in which you conduct the activity. Thus, it is reasonable to take a group climbing, provided that you meet certain standards: you must be capable of analyzing the skill level and performance of participants to enhance skills through a teaching progression and match these skills with challenges appropriate to their maturity, physical condition, and ability. Participants need to understand how rules relate to safety.

Environmental Conditions

You should know the specific environment in which you are going to operate, either through personal visits or by talking to other leaders who have operated there recently. Visiting a cliff, cleaning loose rock annually, and inspecting for loose rock on each trip are aspects of meeting the environmental conditions portion of the standard of care. Program participants should have appropriate safety devices and protective clothing, including helmets and harnesses that are designed for rock climbing and that are in a good state of repair.

Participants' Responsibility

Participants also bear responsibility for their own safety. In litigation, courts look to see if a "plaintiff's conduct under the circumstances was that of a reasonable and prudent person exercising ordinary care for his own safety."[3] It is important, therefore, that participants be informed about the nature of the activity that they are going to undertake.

It is also important to discuss the inherent risk. Discussions should be specific and might take place each time you introduce new elements. Briefing sessions just before you enter the cliff area and when you change areas or activities provide good opportunities. You can present general information, such as slides of a previous group in action. Even commercial climbing videos are useful to the extent that they help people understand what they will be doing. The object is to inform participants as fully as possible. As a participant becomes more experienced and skilled in an activity, he or she assumes a greater share of the risk.

Assumption of Risk, Liability Release, and Medical Forms

Assumption-of-risk forms help to inform participants (and parents, if the participants are minors) of the nature of the activity and provide the climbing program with acknowledgment that participants have been informed about conditions, demands, and dangers of the program. Specifics are better than generalities. For example, rather than simply saying that climbing is dangerous, state that there is danger of falling rock and falls from rock, as well as other spe-

cifics. The assumption-of-risk form should also set out the program's rules and regulations and inform participants about the consequences—which may include expulsion from the program without refund or failure—of using drugs or alcohol, or not following reasonable instructions while on the trip. To ensure that participants understand the form, go over it verbally if possible, and have them (or their parents, if the participants are minors) read it and sign it. The assumption-of-risk form informs participants but does not relieve the program of its duty to meet the standard of care.

The *medical form* requests pertinent medical information, such as prior injuries or frostbite, allergy, and other conditions related to the participant's ability to perform the activities in the program. It does no good to ask for this information, however, if you do not examine it and discuss potential problems with participants.

A *liability release* is different from an assumption-of-risk form. The release is a contract that excuses the provider of a recreational service from the duty owed—that is, the responsibility to protect the participant. These releases have been upheld when the signer is of majority age, when there are viable alternatives available to potential participants (including not participating), and when the release is signed voluntarily.[4] Viable alternatives might be similar but less strenuous activities, such as a less strenuous hike below tree line rather than a more strenuous and exposed hike above tree line; scraping and painting a building does not provide a viable alternative to the exposed hike.

RISK-MANAGEMENT PROGRAMS

Organizations that sponsor climbing programs can reduce the potential for accidents by undertaking a risk-management program.[5] All program personnel—including the board of trustees, president, program directors, small-group leaders, logistics and equipment personnel, site leaders, instructors, and assistant instructors—have a role to play in promoting safety in all actions of the organization. Safety begins with establishing policies that are taught and implemented in hiring and training staff; purchasing, maintaining, and issuing equipment; scheduling; cleaning sites; and instructing.

All members of the organization should be involved in establishing written policies that undergo periodic review at all levels of the organization. "Any departure from specific safety policies must only be in emergency situations to significantly enhance safety, and involve a carefully developed, rational, and defensible plan."[6]

Safety should be subject to ongoing in-house reviews and periodic external reviews. Reviews should examine the integrity and effectiveness of the entire range of program components beginning with a statement of philosophy, goals, and learning objectives through staff training, staff/participant ratios, and health care procedures, among others. Guides to conducting safety reviews are provided by *The Safety Review Manual* by Ian Wade and Michael Fischesser, and *Safety Practices in Adventure Programming* by Simon Priest and Tim Dixon.

QUALIFICATIONS FOR CLIMBING INSTRUCTORS

If you are a climbing site leader or instructor working with a group, you must have the same general qualifications as any instructor of experience-based adventure programming (i.e., you must be competent in a broad range of skill areas).[7] You should be skilled in the techniques of climbing and know how to promote safety in a climbing program. You must be vigilant not just during the climb but at the time of assembly, during travel to or from a climbing site, and when camping. To do this properly, you need to be physically and mentally fit enough to cope with the stresses of the program, and sometimes more fit than the participants. You need to be trained in first aid and cardiopulmonary resuscitation. You should teach low-impact methods of camping and traveling in the natural environment.

In addition to teaching climbing techniques, safety, and protection of the natural environment, you should also provide participants with an experience of general value that can be used in other settings. Instructors facilitate group debriefing at the end of an activity to help participants to clarify and learn from an experience.

Other responsibilities of the instructor include planning and budgeting, organizing food and equipment, and arranging transportation.

When you teach, you must be able to break down skills into basic components. When you initially teach climbing systems and procedures, you might want to use a *ground school*, run on flat ground, instead of placing participants on or near the cliff while they are learning. You must be capable of developing teamwork and cooperation among participants, and be skilled at crisis intervention and conflict resolution to deal with problems that arise in the stressful environment of climbing and group effort. This means that you can work with people and respect their rights, standards, styles, and values. The structure of the entire program and the focus of individual instructors must allow participants to attempt a particular climb or defer it if they feel ill at ease. You work with these individuals in a supportive manner, but you should not coerce them into attempting a particular climb. You must be mature, skilled, and confident, as well as approachable, honest, and fun-loving.

You need to be able to communicate well with other instructors, as well as with participants; give and receive feedback in a constructive, unthreatening manner; solve problems while under stress; and demonstrate a flexible leadership style that suits participants' needs under different conditions. In summary, climbing instructors need to be broadly experienced and demonstrate good judgment.

PROGRAMMATIC PRACTICES

Site leaders have the job of organizing trips and supervising the climbing site and gear. For many programs, the site leader (1) inspects the site for loose rock at the beginning of the season and before each use; (2) selects and inspects gear, makes sure that gear is in good condition, initiates repairs, and orders new gear; (3) sets up and oversees all climbing-rappel systems and instructs course instructors in their use; (4) briefs instructors and students about the events of the day; (5) oversees the climbing progression; (6) debriefs the group at the end of the climbing day; and (7) oversees the dismantling of all climbing systems and return of gear to a storeroom at the end of the climbing day.

As with safety policies, every organization should establish its operating procedures in writing. Among the items covered might be:

There is a maximum of _____ (commonly six) participants to one instructor.

If there are two or more instructors, one should be designated the site leader.

Unroped climbing is prohibited.

First-aid material, including litters and backboards, must be available on site.

Helmets are required for organized groups at climbing sites because of safety and liability concerns. Both instructors and students must wear helmets when climbing or when in designated areas at the base of a climb.

Safe-zone rest areas must be established well away from potential falling rocks, so that people can take off their helmets.

All safety rules apply to all climbers, including instructors. In addition to providing personal safety, course instructors are professionals who serve as role models for novices.

Helmets and harnesses used for climbing should be manufactured specifically for climbing and must be approved by the CEN/UIAA and carry the CE/UIAA mark.

CLIMBING SITES AND LOOSE ROCK

Cleaning the Site

Inspect top-rope sites thoroughly at least once a year for dangerous loose rock. Freeze-thaw action during the winter could have loosened previously stable rocks. There are at least three categories of rocks of concern. First is the gla-

cial material consisting of angular rocks called *erratics*, as well as finer till material dropped by a melting glacier. This material forms the soils and many of the large blocks on cliff tops in northern latitudes. Second are the exfoliation flakes that parallel surfaces of granite domes, and third are jointed blocks bounded by cracks.

Clean loose rock only when the cliff is secure, so that passersby or workers will not be hit by falling rock. Communicate clearly with fellow workers to avoid misunderstanding. If you are doing the cleaning, do so on belay or while tied in, and remain uphill of the loose rock at all times. If you find high potential for an accident during cleaning, abandon the site and pick a different climbing area.

Granite Exposure at the Surface by Uplift and Differential Erosion

It is helpful to know a little about how granite cliffs form. The process starts with the cooling of granite perhaps a mile underground. After cooling, very large regions of land, perhaps the size of New England, lift up above sea level as global-scale sections (plates) of the earth move. Stresses related to regional movements and their relaxations often give rise to parallel sets of fractures or cracks called *joints*.

In elevated land areas water weathers and erodes the land surface. As weathering proceeds, rock types surrounding the granite are often removed more readily than the granite itself, which results in elevated granite hills or mountains as shown in figure 17-1. In northern latitudes, glaciers have a dramatic effect upon these elevated lands with exposed granite outcroppings and transform preexisting rounded peaks and valleys into a pronounced angular landscape.

Exfoliation: As a granite body in the earth uplifts the rock above, the rock surface erodes and releases a tremendous pressure from the granite. This phenomenon, called *unloading*, allows the granite to expand upward, as shown in figure 17-2. The outer part of the granite expands more than the inner part, and cracks called *sheet-joints* develop parallel to the outer surface.

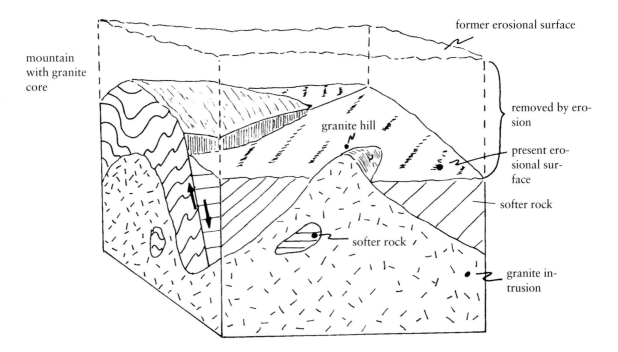

mountain with granite core

former erosional surface

granite hill

removed by erosion

present erosional surface

softer rock

softer rock

granite intrusion

Figure 17-1. Differential Equations and Isolated Granite Hills: A granite body undergoes regional uplift and differential erosion. Rainwater, weathering, and erosion remove the more easily eroded rock above the granite and expose the granite as rounded hills.

A

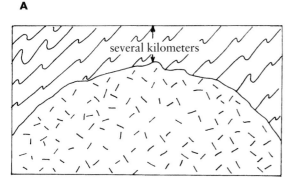

several kilometers

B

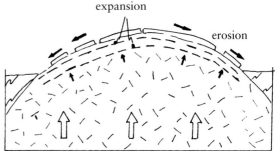

expansion

erosion

Figure 17-2. Exfoliation: A—Granite intrudes into existing rock as a liquid, cools, and hardens several kilometers underground. B—Regional uplift sets in motion erosion; erosion removes the rock over the granite, which releases pressure on the granite body and allows upward expansion. Exfoliation occurs along sheet joints that are closely spaced at the surface (where expansion is greatest) and more widely spaced at depth. Modified from Plummer and McGeary, 1991.

On cliff sides, gravity can cause the rock between the sheet-joints to break loose in concentric slabs or flakes from the underlying granite mass. Most climbers have routinely encountered these flakes and have been correctly concerned about the possibility of their breaking away, or *exfoliating*. Where exfoliation flakes have broken away, fresh gray rock that is surrounded by more highly oxidized rock of a red or pink color is often exposed. The expanding flakes found on many climbs are exfoliation flakes, and these flakes can be pried loose with camming devices. Rounded domes such as Half Dome of Yosemite Valley are rounded due to exfoliation.

Perched Granite Blocks on Cliff Edges: Glaciers that covered large valleys, whole mountain ranges, and entire continents during the last ice age had a major hand in creating cliffs in northern latitudes. These glaciers quarried the cliffs along planes of weakness and carried material down-ice, forming the cliff. Glaciers also picked up, carried, and then deposited blocks and finer material called till. After the glacier had vanished, other blocks came to rest on the till as they broke off nearby walls during frost expansion along joint cracks. The blocks fell on till soils containing pebble and fist-size angular rocks set in a matrix of fine-grained ground-up rock. Granite blocks ranging up to many tons sometimes sit on top of till at the edge of an out-sloping cliff (fig. 17-3A).

Over a period of years, rain and frost expansion in the soil remove the finer-grained ground-up rock particles (soil) from the till beneath the blocks, which leaves the blocks supported by fist-size rock "rollers" (fig. 17-3B). These massive blocks sit poised, ready to go over the cliff edge without very much force, as described in the accompanying box. Although you will not encounter them every day, these blocks are not rare. I have dislodged two, one that wiggled every time climbers stepped on it as they exited a popular top-rope climb, and the other at the top of a new route.

The easiest way to dislodge these blocks purposely, for site management, is carefully to pick out the rock rollers one by one from beneath the block as you attempt to push it over the edge. Both the person working with the block and

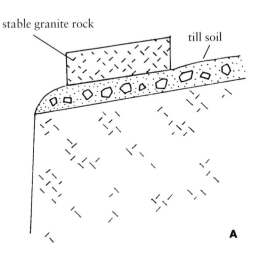

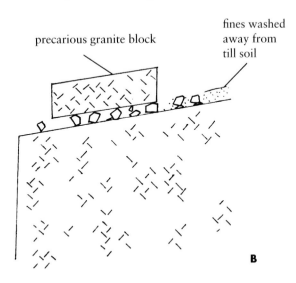

Figure 17-3. Perched Granite Blocks on Cliff Ledges: A—A granite block has been broken off along joints by frost wedging and has fallen on top of glacial till soil on a cliff ledge. This block also could be a glacial erratic. *B—The fine particles of the soil washed away, leaving the block precariously perched on angular rollers at the edge of the cliff.*

anyone below must be extremely careful. *The best course of action might be to leave the block alone and just stay away because you can never be completely sure of safety while dislodging a block.* A site leader who has all pertinent site information will have to assess the situation and decide the best course of action.

An additional danger related to till soils (covered under "Belaying on Glaciated Cliffs" in chapter 6) is that trees growing in these soils on cliff ledges are not deeply rooted and should be suspect as belay anchors without rock protection backup.

TOP-ROPE SITE PRACTICES

Top-Rope Site Geography and Safety

The ideal top-rope site can be approached from the bottom; has a flat, boulder-free platform where climbers and belayers can belay and climb; is less than a rope-length high; and has good anchor locations near the cliff edge. It is also convenient to have a staging area, away from potential pebble-fall, which can be used for rest and lunch. The cliff itself should be free of loose rocks and pebbles. The top of the site should be flat, with a trail leading away from the cliff edge by which climbers can return to the bottom.

Because ideal sites are not always available, you might need to manage your location to make it safe. If, for example, climbers need to rappel to the base, as at a seaside cliff, then you must safeguard participants at the cliff top and give extensive help to climbers as they get to the bottom and back to the top. If the top of the cliff is rounded, with loose pebbles underfoot ready to act as ball bearings even after a reasonable amount of cleaning, you must make sure that participants do not slip over the edge.

Use control ropes for safety when groups are at the top of a cliff or on starting ledges above drop-offs. A couple of experienced climbers out on a cooperative adventure might be able to manage themselves safely in these situations, but the presence of inexperienced individuals in a group mandates ropes. Whether experienced or inexperienced, people clustered together on a cliff can bump into one another or react unexpectedly to a thrown or dropped object. Group behavior and reaction to events are very different from the behavior and reaction of an individual person.

There are two kinds of control rope. One type is simply a barrier to prevent access to the edge of the cliff (fig. 17-4). You can use this method when the top of the cliff is relatively flat and you establish a staging area at the top, or when a trail runs near the cliff edge. Climbers on the cliff side of the control rope are tied in at all times, while group members behind the control rope are free to walk around cautiously.

The second type of control rope safeguards traverses from the top of a climb, above ex-

Figure 17-4. Barrier on a Cliff Top

Figure 17-5. Traverse Line: A novice climber, who is traversing right to a safe zone and descent trail, has clipped into a traverse line with a sliding attachment. A climbing specialist, on the left, is coiling a top rope and will throw it back to the ground for the next climber. The climbing specialist can oversee the top of a number of climbs as indicated by the two slingshot systems shown.

posed out-sloping slabs, to a safe descent trail (fig. 17-5). The novice often climbs on a slingshot setup and unties from the rope at the top. The novice needs to be clipped into a safety traverse line by means of a sling and carabiner attached between the climbing harness and traverse line. A climbing specialist usually sets up the control lines and ensures that novices attach to the line. You can also use the traverse control rope when the starting area is exposed above a drop-off and participants are standing in an exposed position at the base of the climb.

Leashes for Cliff-Top Management

When a number of slingshot systems are being operated with the belayers at the cliff base, a climbing specialist usually controls the cliff top. The specialist either helps climbers exit the climb to safe areas or works with rappellers. If belaying is done by instructors at the top of the cliff, away from the edge, the specialist serves as a communicator between the top belay and bottom tie-in points.

Instructors who are working in exposed positions also must be clipped to an anchor. A simple sling connection to the traverse line can suffice (see fig. 17-5) when the top of the climb is within a few feet of the traverse line. If the top of the climb varies from zero to many feet away from the traverse line, however, you need a leash of variable length. Figure 17-6 shows how to make a variable-length leash from a length of climbing rope. You can tie to the leash directly with a knot. For greater mobility, attach by means of a mechanical ascender backed up with a knot tied at the end of the travel path of the ascender. Mechanical ascenders grip the rope with teeth that set into the outer rope sheath and release by means of a trigger, making it relatively easy to

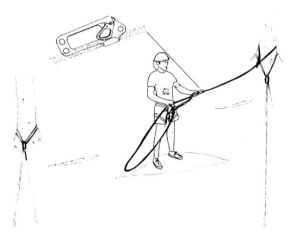

Figure 17-6. Variable-Length Leash with Mechanical Ascender: The enlargement shows the ascender used to grip the rope. The climbing specialist ties the leash into his or her harness, and the tie-in serves as a backup to the ascender.

move the ascender. Only one ascender is required for the leash. How much mobility you need depends on cliff geography and the number of climbs you are overseeing.

Climbing programs often make use of low-angle cliffs, but participants still often get stuck, unable to climb up and unwilling to back down. If instructions and encouragement from below fail to help, you can rappel to the climber on a tied-off single-strand rope, safeguarded by also tying into the rappel rope. You can calm, instruct, and encourage the novice, then ascend by using the rappel rope and one or more mechanical ascenders; clip your harness into the ascenders as well.

Ground School

Ground school provides basic instruction in climbing on flat ground where mistakes have little consequence. It can be part of a progression of instruction and is particularly useful in working with groups of beginners. If boulders are available, they can be incorporated into ground school to teach climbing movement. Ground school should address the various types of climbing movement and body position involved in liebacks, mantles, stems, and other basic moves.

Ground school should familiarize participants with the climbing system, preferably by duplicating on the ground the system to be used at the cliff site. Set up a belay anchor at a tree and then have the "climber" move away from the belay to simulate climbing. You can use top and bottom anchor points and either slingshot or top belays. With groups, locking carabiners provide the best security. Practice tying into the climbing rope and into anchors; belaying and giving climbing commands; clipping into a safety traverse line; lowering someone from a climb; and executing other safety procedures. Beginners who have practiced on the ground will be more comfortable in dealing with exposure or movement problems on rock. Ground school can last two or more hours and commonly occupies the morning hours before lunch, followed by actual climbing.

Belay Systems for Groups

The belay system used for a group depends on the goals of the group. Groups that use belaying for a number of different elements, such as climbing and ropes courses, might wish to standardize belaying techniques. Often these groups will use either a waist belay or a mechanical belay plate that is consistent with the program goals. If the climber lowers back to the ground, as in a slingshot climbing system, a mechanical belay brake might be preferred over a waist belay to prevent friction burns. If you wish to focus on movement skills, you might consider having instructors do all belaying, while participants concentrate on climbing. However, as participants become familiar with basic movement skills, they often want to take part in belaying. This is a normal progression of learning, and you can teach belaying under close supervision as individuals are prepared to learn.

The novice backup belay shown in figure 17-7 gives responsibility to as many participants as possible and teaches belaying in a more structured progression. The primary belayer, a novice, gives a waist belay that is backed up by a safety belay provided by a second novice. An instructor oversees the two belayers and climbers. The primary belayer provides a normal waist belay and

Figure 17-7. Novice Backup Belay

is fastened with a locking carabiner to an anchor. The rope is prevented from lifting from the primary belayer's waist by a carabiner. The backup belayer stands on the helping-hand side of the belayer with the rope in her hands, but not necessarily around her back. She allows enough slack, a few feet, so that she does not interfere with the primary belayer's manipulation of the rope. If the primary belayer forgets to brake the rope during a fall, the backup belayer can simply tighten the rope around the body of the primary belayer. The backup belayer can serve as apprentice to the primary belayer and become the new primary belayer when the former primary belayer climbs.

A Belaying System for Beginning Rappellers: When you work with inexperienced rappellers, you must take into consideration that they might not retain control of the braking hand. You can protect the rappeller by setting up a belay. The rappeller ties in with a bowline on a coil. If you attach the rope to an independent anchor, the belay system will be completely independent of the rappel anchor and the harness.

Stuck Rappellers: A belay can prevent out-of-control descents, but it does not help when a rappeller is stuck. Rappellers can become physically entangled in the rappel when a loose article of clothing, such as a shirt, or long hair is pulled into a mechanical rappel brake. Help rappellers to prevent these problems by reminding them to tuck in clothing and hair. Traditionally, these problems are solved by cutting away the offending shirt, hair, or knot with a knife, while taking care, of course, not to cut the main rappel rope, which will part easily under the tension of the rappeller's body weight.

Stuck rappellers might also become more stuck if they use a Prusik safety that is too long and becomes locked above an inaccessible overhang as they rappel. The AutoBlock knot (see chapters 3 and 8) used below the brake is far less likely to become inaccesible than the Prusik used above the brake.

There is a simple solution if a rappeller must be lowered. Place a figure-eight rappelling device on a sling around a tree (fig. 17-8). (For single-rope rappels, you can also form a Munter hitch on a pear-shaped carabiner in place of the figure-eight brake.) Pass the rappel rope, either single or doubled, through this device and tie it to a second tree with a tensionless anchor. Wrap the doubled rope around the tree several times to gain friction, then pass the bight (formed in the wrapped end of the rope) around both segments of the rope to form an overhand knot; secure it with a locking carabiner. As long as there is sufficient rope between the figure-eight rappel device and the tensionless anchor, the entire rappel system, including the stuck climber, can be quickly lowered to the ground. Once on the ground, the rappeller can easily release himself or herself from the rappel device.

Top or Bottom Belays for Safeguarding Rappelling: Are top or bottom belays better for rappelling? The choice depends on program goals. It is clear that top belays using an anchor separate from that of the rappel provide the ultimate in safety for a novice rappeller. The bottom belay, applied by tensioning the bottom end of the rope and thereby adding friction in the belay brake itself, needs to be applied continuously and instantly if the rappeller loses control. Momentary inattention on the part of the belayer renders the belay ineffective because the amount of braking force applied by this technique is small. This is not true of the top belay, where lapses in feeding out the rope simply prevent the rappeller from continuing. In addition, the top-rope belay system can be backed up by tying the novice to the belay rope with a bowline on a coil. This provides a separate tie-in from the rappel harness, the rappel brake, and the rappel rope itself. Programs that use rappelling to promote personal growth and character development as a main goal would be safer to choose a top belay for rappelling.

Military programs often use a bottom belay

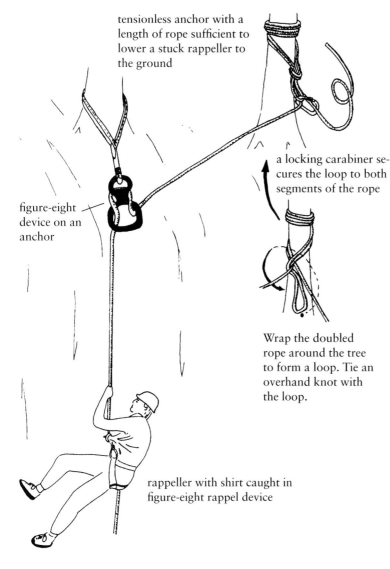

tensionless anchor with a length of rope sufficient to lower a stuck rappeller to the ground

a locking carabiner secures the loop to both segments of the rope

figure-eight device on an anchor

Wrap the doubled rope around the tree to form a loop. Tie an overhand knot with the loop.

rappeller with shirt caught in figure-eight rappel device

Figure 17-8. A Rappel Lowering System for Groups: The rappel rope, either single or doubled, passes through a figure-eight rappel device and attaches to a tensionless anchor. The rope on the far side of the rappel device must be long enough to lower the rappeller and rappelling rope to the ground. Novices are usually given a top-rope belay using a bowline on a coil tie-in, and the belay is often done by using an anchor separate from that of the rappel rope. This belay is not shown here.

for rappelling when a top belay, as from the platform of a helicopter, might not be possible. In addition, much military training is designed to simulate wartime situations where speed during a descent is essential for the safety of the mission. Here a bottom belay or no belay might be appropriate. Bottom belays are also used upon occasion by experienced recreational climbers to safeguard each other when rappelling from overhanging lips or to assist an injured climber when they anticipate that control will be difficult.

EQUIPMENT LOGS

It is important to record the history of each piece of climbing equipment used in a climbing program because hidden damage can occur from a number of causes. If various instructors use the same equipment, the history of the equipment cannot be stored in a single person's memory. Use a logbook to keep track of equipment and to document proper maintenance.

Ropes are the most likely piece of equipment to suffer invisible damage, and most benefit is gained from keeping a rope log. Give each rope a number and catalog historical data, such as date of purchase, use, purpose, hours used, falls taken, and date of retirement. To keep track of individual ropes, attach a numbered tag that corresponds to the log number to each rope before storing.

Because ropes retired from climbing are often useful for other purposes, such as tie-downs, you should store them separately and mark them so that you do not mistakenly use them for climbing. Dipping the ends of the rope in black paint is an effective marker for ropes dead to climbing.

PROCESSING THE CLIMBING EXPERIENCE

Climbing enriches our lives in many ways. It gives a sense of physical well-being and of challenges met. It takes place in some of the most scenic spots on our planet. Experienced climbers consciously know that they renew themselves each time they touch rock. As instructors, we can help first-time climbers absorb their experience by reflecting on it. This allows individuals to be conscious of what they learned and to interpret and pattern events to give meaning.[8]

Using Metaphors to Help Process the Climbing Experience

Throughout the actual climbing experience, there are many opportunities for learning by drawing parallels from past and present experience. The learning can be unconscious or part of a structured experience. For example, a novice might be fearful before and during a climb but be elated at the top because he or she has achieved a difficult task. A climber who draws parallels with similar life experiences can generalize this learning and transfer it to real-life situations, such as writing a paper required for school. Similar parallels can be drawn between the cooperation required between the belayer-climber team members and that required between people in real life. Stephen Bacon calls this type of learning *metaphoric education*.[9] Metaphors work best when the metaphoric ex-

perience closely parallels, at least symbolically, the real-life experience.

A structured program can provide metaphoric experiences throughout the activities. In fact, in therapeutic programs, skilled therapists sometimes draw extensive metaphors for all aspects of the climbing experience.[10] These might take the form of narratives and anecdotes that accompany experiences. Stephen Bacon relates that he once asked his assistant instructor to tell two tales about his personal climbing experiences in great detail. One tale dealt with the fear, trembling, sweat, and turmoil that he experienced on a difficult climb. The second tale dealt with details of a successful climb in which everything went well. These stories were *isomorphic* (had the same form) with the experiences that the students were about to face and provided an opportunity for them to validate and examine their own feelings just before climbing.

Quotes selected from the instructor's favorite sources are useful in providing parallels between adventure and real life. For example:

> *Let go and grow—*
> *To climb, one hand must go*
> *above the other.*
> *So in life we succeed not by hanging fearfully*
> *   to the old,*
> *but by reaching out,*
> *taking new handholds,*
> *mentally accepting, welcoming,*
> *adapting new and better ideas.*
> *Hold fast—we fail.*
> *Let go—we grow.*[11]
>
> *Author Unknown*

Other readings might not necessarily draw the parallels so tightly, but, like the following, they will be obvious to adventure participants:

> *When you get into a tight place and everything goes against you, till it seems as though you could not hang on a minute longer, never give up then, for that is just the place and time that the tide will turn.*[12]
>
> *Harriet Beecher Stowe*

Gather your own quotes or draw on published collections, such as the Hurricane Island Outward Bound School's *Readings*, which explores self-reliance, challenge, wilderness, education, and leadership, or Project Adventure's *Golden Nuggets: Readings for Experiential Education*, which contains material on commitment, community, journey, leadership, and values with humor, one-liners, and songs.

Debriefing

Debriefing is a good way for small groups to learn from their experiences. (Other teaching strategies and instructional processes are discussed by educator David Cockrell in *The Wilderness Educator*.) Debriefing is a verbal form of processing experience that works within a sequence of levels of thought—knowledge and comprehension, analysis, synthesis and evaluation, and transference:

- Knowledge and comprehension.[13] This level stresses concrete information and detailed recall of events. Questions such as *"What did we just do?"* and *"How do you understand . . . ?"* explore knowledge and understanding by using open-ended questions. The role of the group facilitator is to encourage participants to provide concrete, detailed answers, perhaps by having different participants describe different portions of the day.
- Analysis. This level of thought calls for participants to analyze their actions. Ask, *"Why do you think that you . . . ?"* *"Now that you have . . . how would you go about solving that particular problem in the future?"*
- Synthesis and evaluation. Synthesis leads to evaluation. Questions might be, *"What was the design of the course?"* *"In your opinion was the course well designed?"* *"What would you do differently if you were designing a climbing experience for beginners?"*
- Transference. This level follows synthesis and evaluation. One important goal of adventure education is to transfer adventure learning into constructive changes in everyday personal behavior. *"What have you learned about yourself?"*

An example of transference from an adventure to everyday behavior might involve communication. If you observed miscommunication during a climbing session, you can employ a sequence of questions to explore effective communication between participants.[14] For example, ask, *"Before you began to climb did you ask your belayer to keep a tight rope?"* *"How do you know that your belayer understood you?"* To explore whether the communication was effective when put into practice, you might follow with, *"While on the climb did your belayer's attention wander (away from the purpose of the communication)?"* *"If the belayer's attention wandered, what went wrong in the initial communication?"* *"What can you do differently next time to give a clearer message?"*

In his book, *Lasting Lessons*, Clifford E. Knapp makes many excellent suggestions for debriefing. Areas that are explored with sample questions include:

- communicating effectively
- expressing appropriate feelings
- deferring your judgment of others
- listening
- leading others
- following others
- making group decisions
- cooperating
- respecting human differences
- respecting human commonalties
- trusting the group
- closure

In conducting a verbal debriefing, ask clearly phrased and concise questions planned ahead of time. Give participants time to reflect and frame thoughtful answers, and listen carefully to them. Use follow-up questions to seek clarification and expand learning for other members of a group. Encourage students to ask questions so that group members, including yourself, can learn from them. Leading students into long-term learning through verbal debriefing is a skill acquired through practice. It can take only a few minutes or extended periods of time to reach course objectives.

Writing about the Climbing Experience

Asking participants to react to specific readings by writing is also a useful way for them to learn about themselves. Provide a reading list that touches on the experiences of others related to climbing. If you provide more than one selection, have the participants treat the material as a coherent whole to promote analysis and integration. Through reading and writing, participants can reflect, metaphorically, upon their own recent experiences. Each individual will arrive at a unique analysis that reflects personal beliefs and prior experiences. Read what students write, and share your own insights and experiences with them through notes in the margins or by brief discussions. These notes and discussions will validate the thoughts of participants and help them consider new ideas. Many students come to see climbing as a potential positive force in their lives. This type of analysis works well in concert with prior verbal debriefing.

Examples of readings that, at a surface level, touch on rules that climbers impose to keep climbs interesting, spiritual values, and technique include the selections by Lito Tejada-Flores, Benard Amy, and Michael Loughman, listed below under "References for Future Reading."

Reaction papers written by students show that they not only understand the surface significance of such material but also take away deeper personal meanings. Tejada-Flores's article shows how different types of climbing, such as bouldering or cliff climbing, can be viewed as different games with different rules designed to keep the outcome in doubt. This view of climbing provides an opportunity for many novices to see that their own desired outcomes and self-imposed rules can lead to personal definitions of success. Amy's metaphoric story allows the reader to examine personal spiritual values within the context of a physical activity and draws gentle parallels with how one conducts one's own life. The Loughman book uses extensive photography and practical problems of body movement to teach technique. The strongest message in the book for many readers, however, is that women can climb well. Almost all of the photographs are of Amy Loughman, who serves as a strong, confident role model.

REFERENCES FOR FUTURE READING

Amy, Benard. 1972. The greatest climber in the world. In *The games climbers play*. Ken Wilson, ed. San Francisco: Sierra Club Books.

Bacon, Stephen. 1983. *The conscious use of metaphor in Outward Bound*. Denver, Colorado: Colorado Outward Bound School.

Cockrell, David. 1991. Environmental ethics and backcountry practices. Chapter 4 in *The wilderness educator: The wilderness education association curriculum guide*. Merrillville, Indiana: ICS Books.

Direnfeld-Michael, Bonnie. 1989. A risk management primer for recreators. *Journal of Parks and Recreation*. March, 40–45.

Gass, Michael. 1990. Transfer of learning in adventure education. In *Adventure education*. John C. Miles and Simon Priest. State College, Pennsylvania: Venture Pub. Inc.

Hale, Alan. 1984. *Safety management for outdoor program leaders*. Bellefontaine, Ohio: National Safety Network.

Klokis, Holly. 1981. Outing centers—rowing, roller-skating & more. *College Union*. February, 13–16.

Knapp, Clifford E. 1984. Idea notebook: Designing processing questions to meet specific objectives. *Journal of Experiential Education*. 7(2):47–49.

———. 1990. Processing the adventure experience. In *Adventure Education*. John C. Miles and Simon Priest. State College, Pennsylvania: Venture Pub. Inc.

———. 1992. *Lasting lessons: A teacher's guide to reflecting on experience*. Charleston, West Virginia: Clearinghouse on Rural Education and Small Schools, Appalachian Educational Laboratory.

Kuller, Alison Murray, ed. 1986. *Readings*. Rockland, Maine: Hurricane Island Outward Bound School.

Loughman, Michael. 1981. Movement. Chapter 3 in *Learning to rock climb*. San Francisco: Sierra Club Books.

Meier, J. 1980. Is the risk worth taking? In *High adventure outdoor pursuits*. J. Meier et al., eds. Salt Lake: Brighton Pub. Co.

Miles, J. 1987. The value of high adventure activities. In *High adventure outdoor pursuits*. J. Meier et al., eds. Salt Lake: Brighton Pub. Co.

Piana, Paul. 1988. Salathé wall. *Climbing*. 110:50–60.

Plummer, Charles C, and David McGeary. 1991. *Physical geology*. Fifth edition. Dubuque, Iowa: Wm. C. Brown Co.

Priest, Simon, and Tim Dixon. 1990. *Safety practices in adventure programming*. Boulder: University of Colorado, The Association for Experiential Education, Safety Committee.

Rivera, Margo, and Stacy Stefan. 1992. The metaphor of rock climbing in a psychiatric setting. In *Proceedings manual of the 20th international conference of the association for experiential education*.

Schoel, Jim, and Mike Stratton, eds. 1990. *Golden nuggets: Readings for experiential educators*. Hamilton, Massachusetts: Project Adventure, Inc.

Tejada-Flores, Lito. 1978. Games climbers play. In *The games climbers play*. Ken Wilson, ed. San Francisco: Sierra Club Books.

Van der Smissen, Betty. 1980. Legal liability-adventure activities. Las Cruces, New Mexico: New Mexico State University. Educational Resources Information Center (ERIC), Clearinghouse on Rural Education and Small Schools (CRESS).

———. 1985. Releases, waivers, and agreements to participate. In *National safety network newsletter*. 1 (4).

Wade, I. R., and M. Fischesser. 1988. *The safety review manual: A guide to conducting safety reviews for assessing and upgrading safety in outdoor adventure programs*. Greenwich, Connecticut: Outward Bound USA.

ENDNOTES

1. Klokis, 1981.
2. Van der Smissen, 1980.
3. *Ibid.*
4. Van der Smissen, 1985.
5. Van der Smissen, 1980; Hale, 1984; Direnfield-Michael, 1989.
6. Priest and Dixon, 1990. This document is the standard reference of the outdoor recreation profession and has evolved in frequent revisions.
7. This section is adapted from the staff qualifications chapter in Priest and Dixon, 1990.
8. Knapp, 1992.
9. Bacon, 1983, explores the learning process of Outward Bound students.
10. Rivera and Stefan, 1992, discuss the extensive use of metaphors in the rock climbing sequence of a Challenge program in a dual-diagnosis psychiatric setting.
11. This is one of the favorite readings of Dr. Marty O'Keefe, from whom I took it. The original source is unknown.
12. From Kuller, 1986.
13. See Cockrell, 1991, 74–80, for a discussion of teaching strategies.
14. Clifford Knapp has a lifelong interest in learning about and teaching others about the educational value of debriefing. See "References for Future Reading" for three of his works.

18

Managing Risk

INTRODUCTION

From the very beginning, climbers have been concerned with accidents. Several fatalities occurred during the first ascent of the Matterhorn, on July 14, 1865. The party contained four gentlemen (Edward Whymper, Lord Francis Douglas, Mr. Hadrow, and Vicar Charles Hudson) and four guides (Michel Croz, Peter Taugwalder, and his two sons). On the descent, the entire party tied together, but without attachment to the rock, to pass the difficult bit below the summit. Mr. Hadrow slipped off his feet onto his back; his feet struck Croz and knocked him over. The connecting rope jerked Hudson and then Lord Douglas from their steps, and they fell down the slope. Old Peter Taugwalder and Edward Whymper, upon hearing Croz's exclamation, held on as tightly as possible, but the oldest of their manila ropes broke. The men continued falling until they reached the glacier 4,000 feet below. From this time, mountain climbing, and by inference all kinds of climbing, was considered dangerous.[1]

Today we better understand why, when, how, and to whom accidents occur. The wilderness recreation community has kept statistics for many years as it strives to improve our understanding of how to manage associated risks.[2] Recently, a number of agencies and organizations have redoubled and systematized these efforts. We have learned that climbing and wilderness recreation as a whole hold dangers, but that these are significantly fewer than the dangers associated with many other normal activities. Driving to a climbing site and back home is more dangerous than rock climbing.[3]

Only a small percentage of climbers are involved in accidents. There are an average of 2.5 deaths and a few serious injuries in Yosemite each year, in comparison to a range of 20 to 40 deaths and 140-plus serious injuries among all climbers in the United States. In addition, there are approximately 50 fractures and 15 to 25 rescues annually in Yosemite Valley, out of perhaps 25,000 to 50,000 climber-days on the rock.

Indeed, rock climbing is less dangerous than operating a power lawn mower or playing high-school football. A recent survey of injuries occurring to participants in the National Outdoor Leadership School found that mountaineering and rock climbing were lower-risk activities than backpacking, which is generally considered a low-risk activity.[4,5] It is important to note that instructors sustained a higher rate of injury than students, which may be associated with greater dangers in leading multipitch climbs.

The generally low rates of climbing injury should not lull us into taking a casual attitude toward safety. The fractures, head injuries, and internal traumas that occur in climbing accidents are potentially more serious than the sprains, strains, and soft-tissue injuries that result from backpacking.

The general public incorrectly perceives climbing as significantly more dangerous than high-school football and gymnastics, which have very high injury rates. Good statistical records will play a role in changing those perceptions, as well as in educating climbers to the dangers that they do face.

In part, climbers have a good safety record because we know that climbing is dangerous if we do not manage the risk by taking precautions and safeguarding ourselves. We know that falls from rock, out-of-control slides on snow slopes, collisions, encounters with avalanches, and lightning are the sources of injury. To deal with these dangers, we have developed leadership techniques, as well as engineering systems, and we are learning how the interactions of people and the environment contribute to accidents.

ROCK-CLIMBING ACCIDENTS

An examination of accident records in Yosemite National Park from 1970 to 1986 by John Dill found that "[s]hort climbs and Big Walls, easy routes and desperate ones—all get their share of accidents," that "[m]ost victims are experienced climbers: 60 percent have been climbing for three years or more, lead 5.10, and are in good condition, and climb frequently," and that "at least 80 percent of the climbing fatalities, and many injuries were easily preventable. In case after case, ignorance, a casual attitude, and/or some form of distraction proved to be the most dangerous aspects of the sport."[6] The cause of many of the accidents in both Yosemite and the United States and Canada was human error. In Yosemite and the United States, these errors include those listed in the categories given below.[7]

Learning to Lead

- Challenging oneself by learning to climb and protect at the same time. These are separate skills. Exceeding one's ability causes 12 accidents per year, and is a contributing cause for twice that number.
- Getting off route onto dangerous and/or difficult rock. Routefinding for longer climbs is a skill in itself (discussed on page 277 under "Classic 'Rules' for Speed on Big Climbs"). Approximately 4 accidents per year are due to this cause.
- Becoming overconfident before (or after) one's skills are solidified.

Leading

- Setting up a poor belay chain that turns an acceptable fall into an accident.
- Placing protection that failed when needed or was not placed frequently enough on easy run outs or to prevent groundfall. Approximately 38 accidents per year are due to no or inadequate protection or having a nut or chock pull.
- Trusting weathered fixed pins or bad bolts that pull.
- Falling after unroping to switch rappel anchors or to scramble on "easy terrain" to exit a climb.
- Being slow on long day climbs that turned into bivouacs followed by exposure and hypothermia.

Descending

- Not learning ahead of time the easy way off a climb. Approximately 12 accidents per year are due to rappel failure or error.
- Using single-point anchors for belays or rappels that fail.
- Rappelling off the end of ropes and/or using Prusik safety knots that melt.

Equipment Choice

- Discovering that rain and bivouac gear is inadequate in a storm followed by a retreat in cold weather. Proper preparation requires getting a weather report before you climb, learning about local weather conditions in order to anticipate and recognize changing weather patterns, and taking appropriate gear.
- Not wearing a helmet (8 percent of injuries are to the head). A helmet increases survival chances, and lessens or eliminates injuries for some victims in some accidents.

State of Mind

- Being unpracticed, unprepared, or uninformed about what to do when faced with a new task or situation.
- Being casual or inattentive; not taking climbing seriously.
- Being distracted, afraid, in a hurry, or argumentative with a partner.

Loose Rock

- Climbing beneath another party.
- Allowing ropes to knock off loose rock.
- Anchoring in rotten rock.

A broader report of accidents has been published by the American Alpine Club since 1951 (jointly with the Alpine Club of Canada since 1977) as *Accidents in North American Mountaineering*. From 1951 through 1998, 4,952 accidents involving 8,982 persons with 1,178 killed are reported for the United States. Approximately 61 percent of these accidents involved climbing on rock, 35 percent on snow, 3 percent on ice, 0.2 percent in rivers, and 0.4 percent for unknown reasons. Of accidents in Canada (1959 to 1998: 726 accidents, 1,534 persons, 249 killed) about 51 percent involved climbing on rock, 36 percent on snow, 12 percent on ice, 0.3 percent in rivers, and 0.8 percent for unknown reasons. Falls or slips on rock, snow, and ice account for 58 percent of all accidents. Environmental hazards, such as falling rock, avalanche, exposure, and lightning, are listed as the direct cause of approximately 18 percent of accidents.[8]

Human error contributed significantly to these accidents. Among the factors were climbing unroped or alone (accounting for about a quarter of all accidents); exceeding abilities; and using inadequate equipment, using equipment incorrectly, or trusting it mistakenly (pitons pulled). Climbers also set up rappels that failed and failed to follow established routes.

Many accidents happen to experienced climbers who make avoidable mistakes. In the United States as a whole, about 30 percent of accidents involve experienced people, and, in Yosemite, *most* victims are experienced (they have three years of climbing, lead 5.10 or more, and are in good condition) and climb frequently.

We must ask, then, why people make mistakes that result in accidents. Whatever we can learn will help us to protect ourselves. While this chapter explores risk management largely within the context of climbing, the question touches on human reactions to the many situations in which people find themselves while exploring the wild outdoors.

LEARNING TO MANAGE RISK

To learn to avoid making errors when we confront environmental hazards, we can draw on personal experience, education, and the experiences of others. Learning from one's own mistakes is a time-honored but self-limiting form of education. Participating in a structured program or working with a professional guide can teach us much, but here too the experience we can gain has practical limitations. An excellent way to learn without personal danger is by examining case studies that cover a multitude of situations. Sources that provide a starting point are listed below; detailed references appear at the end of the chapter.

Learning should result in a set of guidelines that you can store away until needed. These guidelines will never be the sole basis of decision-making, but they help you make decisions for the particular situation at hand. The process of internalizing a personal set of guidelines is a valuable one for future safety and ultimately can be as valuable as the written set below:

Chouinard, Yvon. 1978. Speed and Safety, in *Climbing Ice.*

Dill, John. 1987. Staying Alive, in *Yosemite Valley Climbs.*

Priest, Simon, and Tim Dixon. 1990. *Safety Practices in Adventure Programming.*

Snyder, J. 1985. A Collection of Accidents and Incidents to Learn from, Gleaned from the Records of the North Carolina Outward Bound School.

Walbridge, Charles C., ed. *River Safety Reports.*

Williams, Knox. 1975. *The Snowy Torrents: Avalanche Accidents in the United States 1967–71.*

Williamson, John E., A. Harvard, P. Lev, C. Bangs, and B. Shaw. 1986. Basecamp Program and Mount Hood Accident. Reports of the Base Camp Inquiry Committee to the Board of Trustees of Oregon Episcopal Church.

Williamson, John E., and O. Miskiw, eds. 1993. *Accidents in North American Mountaineering.*

Classic "Rules" for Speed on Big Climbs

Climbers have developed safety "rules" for moving on glaciers, big cliffs, and in the mountains where hazards of terrain and weather, such as storms, rockfall, and avalanches, are vitally important.

Many climbers believe that the first "rule" of safety is *speed*, that the faster that you get up a climb and back down, the safer you will be. What does the maxim *speed is safety* mean in practice?

It applies to competent, experienced parties consisting of fit and acclimatized individuals. These individuals make correct routefinding decisions, use efficient rope-management procedures, carry light packs, and resolve technical difficulties efficiently.

Yvon Chouinard, in his book *Climbing Ice*,[9] gives 27 suggestions to increase speed that come down to being fit, experienced, and having a desire to push one's limits. To paraphrase and elaborate on a few of these suggestions:

- Train for aerobic endurance as well as strength; acclimatize on lower-elevation climbs, and push yourself when you are on high climbs.
- Learn routefinding on shorter routes before you do longer routes. Memorize descent routes as well as ascent routes.
- Learn weather principles and local conditions, and study the forecast before you start; know when to turn back.
- Start early to have a full day and to avoid having any party ahead of you or encountering an afternoon thunderstorm or avalanche.
- Carry gear appropriate to what you need to climb, survive, and get down safely, but not enough to force a bivouac. Keep gear and food for the climb in an outside pocket. Eat and drink frequently at belays rather than plan a big lunch stop.
- Use efficient gear—long ropes to cut down belays, buckle-type rather than tied harnesses.
- Move efficiently over snow. Use long axes instead of shorter ones; cut a few steps instead of putting on crampons; belay from bollards instead of deadmen; follow low-angle alpine ice on tension with no or one hand tool; keep your tools sharp.

These suggestions do not cover every possibility. Each new situation demands that the climber analyze the situation, adapt the "rules" according to personal experience, and take appropriate action. It is helpful to have a model for looking at how environmental conditions and people interact to produce accidents, and to form general guidelines to avoid undesirable interactions.

Interactions of People and the Environment

The interplay of environmental and human factors creates accidents.[10] The guidelines discussed above help to prevent accidents by establishing a barrier between unwise human actions and environmental hazards. On the one side is the environment, with its steep slopes, avalanches, loose rock, gravity, storms, lightning, and other recurring natural hazards in an ongoing dynamic interaction. On the other side is what we take into the wilderness: knowledge and skill, personal goals, reaction to peer pressure and group dynamics, physical conditioning or fatigue, and a limited human perception of the time scale and processes involved in natural events.

A recurring accident at the Grand Teton National Park exemplifies how people make the same mistakes when they confront nature. The Symmetry Spire couloir is 2,500 feet long, with a rock cliff planted squarely in the middle a few hundred feet below the top (fig. 18-1). On the trip uphill, climbers usually scamper around this cliff using snow slopes on the cliff's left side. Above the cliff, climbers often cross a pronounced narrow groove in the broad upper fan and complete the ascent using the low-angle snow slope beneath Symmetry Spire.

From above, the view of the couloir appears somewhat different. A broad scoop leads down from the upper fan. Downhill, there is a long, gentle slope that seems to be made for sliding, but the center of the scoop is very icy and the slope becomes steeper as the scoop narrows to a trough just above the cliff. It is difficult to self-arrest in the icy center of the scoop, so the scoop funnels climbers over the cliff.

Below the cliff, the snow melts away from the rock during the spring to leave a moat, which

Figure 18-1. The Terrain Trap of Symmetry Spire Couloir. A—Sketch of the trap. B—The couloir.

might be dry or filled with water. If there is water, the out-of-control glissader will instantly submerge and suffer immersion hypothermia or drown. If the moat is dry, the glissader's fall could result in head injuries. Several fatalities have occurred in this particular place.[11] At least one glissader has escaped serious injury by jumping from the top of the cliff across the moat onto the snow slope below.

Being caught up in a terrain trap is one of many undesirable interactions with the environment that can lead to an accident. Individuals can develop guidelines to avoid these interactions and to manage risk.

Risk-management guidelines are presented below along with a few simplified case studies meant to illustrate these guidelines. A proper analysis of these case studies requires reading the original sources, which are often complex and bring to the analysis knowledge tempered by experience. The original sources are listed as references. Many of the case studies involve near-misses that did not result in injury; because we know that accidents are often preceded by a number of near-misses, these reports should lead to better judgment.

These guidelines are those of this author, tempered by the wisdom of others. Readers should ask their own questions, based on their own education and experience, in response to these and other examples. The guidelines that you form will serve you in any difficult situation. Remember, the purpose is to prevent accidents—not to criticize the mistakes of others.

Some Guidelines for Risk Management

Leaders' Reserve of Experience: Leaders should have more experience, knowledge, and skill than required for the activity at hand. This additional experience gives the leader a cushion of knowledge and skill to anticipate what might go wrong, take steps to prevent an accident, and handle the accident if it occurs.

This reserve of experience and skill is one component of what we call good judgment. We base good judgment on experience and the analysis of each specific situation, rather than

---

Anticipating Potential Danger

A group of outdoor leaders examined a rappel accident in which a member of an organized class fell to his death during his second rappel when the rope "popped" off the anchor rock.[12] They noted that anchor systems composed of two or more anchors that back up each other prevent failure of the entire system in case one anchor fails, and that it is common practice to belay beginning rappellers with a top rope throughout the beginning session and on the second rappel. They agreed that leaders need experience and knowledge of systems and people operating in groups to deal with situations that arise in the course of the outing. Leaders can be knowledgeable in one area but not in another; one of the hallmarks of good leaders is to know their own limitations and operate within them.

---

written rules to be followed to the letter. Another component of good judgment is self-knowledge. Leaders can be skilled in one area and not in another; they should know their own limitations and act as leaders only within their area of competency.

Approaching the Limits of our Abilities: While the dangers of exceeding our abilities are clear, we need also to understand the dangers of approaching our limits, especially when we are entrusted with the lives of others. Maintaining a large margin of safety and being extraordinarily well prepared can prevent a small setback from becoming life-threatening.

The line between life and death is narrow. We can perhaps learn more from near-misses than from fatal accidents (in the latter case, we can never know what people were thinking at the time). The accompanying case study (see box on page 280) represents a near-miss that might have a similar origin to that of a fatal accident on New Hampshire's Mt. Washington.[13] In the fatal accident, two experienced climbers completed a difficult climb in subzero conditions but were forced to bivouac at the top as jet-stream winds prevented their escape to the normal de-

---

Pushing the Limit

On New Hampshire's Mt. Washington, my partner and I had spent the evening in the Harvard cabin at tree line and awoke to a chilly 10 degrees inside the cabin. We fixed breakfast and noted that with an outside temperature of –20 degrees Fahrenheit our climbing would be limited. Still, since we had the day, we walked the mile or so to the base of Huntington Ravine, where we emerged from the trees. There was no wind, and the sky was clear. We hiked up the lower fan to the base of Damnation Gully, which is 1,500 feet long, mostly low-angle snow and a few ice bulges.

Before entering the gully, we checked for wind and reasoned that we could easily reverse the next few hundred feet of climbing. After reaching a short vertical ice bulge midway, we again checked for wind. We did the crux and decided that we could retreat easily if necessary. We found no frostbite, which would occur if any wind were present. Although we were in a sheltered gully, we could see no snow trails blowing off the Alpine Garden or summit that would indicate wind overhead. The air was wonderfully still.

The climb of the upper gully was long and uneventful. The gully ended in a short, steep wall that changed abruptly to the flat surface of the Alpine Garden. As we exited, we discovered that we had been climbing totally sheltered from the unheard and unseen jet-stream winds blowing from the west across the summit and Alpine Garden. A blast of this wind flattened Scott, who emerged before me, and then I was knocked down in turn. I stood up and was knocked over again. Scott's cheek was frostbitten as he helped me pull up my jacket over my climbing helmet. The new position of the jacket exposed my Adam's apple and it was instantly frostbitten by the –75-degree windchill. Covering ourselves, we raced the quarter mile to a simple downclimb and dropped out of the wind into the now calm –20-degree air. Because we were skilled at ice climbing, experienced on this mountain in winter, and constantly alert, we were willing to operate where all factors combined pushed us against a critical safety barrier. We crossed that barrier in an instant and were lucky to get down with as little injury as we had.

letter from a friend

---

scent route. After a night of extreme cold, they fell to their deaths as they attempted to descend another climb.

Novices and Mentors: A mentor can make a significant difference to a novice's well-being. A mentor, whether leader, instructor, or experienced partner, needs to have technical skills, people skills, knowledge of the environment, and knowledge of the rules of safety. In a group, the mentor's leadership style can have a direct impact upon safety.

In one situation (see box at right), two climbers shared a common adventure without a designated leader, as is usual with many climbing teams. In this case, each climber is responsible for his or her own safety as well as the safety of the team, but, in practice, the more experienced climber probably has a better understanding of the needs of the team and an ethical, if not a legal, responsibility for its safety. Most climbers accept this responsibility and pass their knowledge and skills on to their partners. Here, communication is the key to a safe outing.

In this near-miss, the experienced climber made an unrealistic assumption about the ability of his partner to undertake a technical glissade, and both climbers communicated poorly. They should have explored their differences in ability and experience more thoroughly by talking at greater length. If they had climbed a less committing route as a warm-up, they might have gotten a better sense of each other's abilities and experience and had a chance to discuss techniques and options.

Guidelines for Groups

Objectives: Frame objectives to fit the physical fitness and abilities of the group, whether it is an organized group or an informal group joined for a common adventure. One group might be goal-oriented, wanting for example to hike a particular trail; another might place primary emphasis on education.

A Novice and His Partner

I was in the Tetons seeking a partner. This was to be my first mountain route, although I had moderate experience rock climbing. I found a partner who had just climbed the North Ridge of the Grand and a number of other notable climbs, and I considered him experienced. We bivouacked at the base of the East Ridge, started out at first light, and did some interesting climbing throughout the long day. The highlight was the final 800-foot-high snow field adjacent to the 3,000-foot North Face. But in mountaineering, getting to the top is only half of the story. We had to return to the base of the ridge, which we did by crossing over the mountain and going down the regular Owen-Spalding route, then traversing the base of the mountain along the Black Dike Traverse.

At the end of the traverse, we reached the Tepe glacier after the light had left it. The soft surface of the sunlit glacier had quickly frozen into hard ice demanding crampons, an excellent glissading technique, or at least a few ice screws for belays. My partner started down, skiing on his feet. I followed but had not mastered the technique and repeatedly fell. I was wearing a smooth nylon cagoule that, combined with my lack of skill, acted as a runaway sledge. I self-arrested properly, but the steep glacier was fluted with alternating ridges and grooves extending up and down the glacier. With my axe in a ridge, I slowed but then my travel path would take me across a groove and my axe would be in the air. I needed to self-arrest again. Sometimes I was airborne, sometimes I did somersaults to self-arrest, but always after a few seconds of slowing, my axe

was in the air above the groove. This situation continued for a thousand very rapidly descended feet until the glacier became gentle enough for the self-arrest to work. I stood up and was miraculously unhurt, although my forearm was "pumped up" from hanging onto the axe. My partner, far above at the end of the slide, caught up and then passed me on the way, asking, "Who told you that you should wear nylon when glissading?" I later found out that this glacier was named for the climber who first died in a similar slide. I have also heard of a number of wiser parties who spent sleepless but safe nights at the top of the col looking down at their sleeping bags below. In the morning, after the sun softened the snow, they safely descended what had been a dangerous slope only hours before.

letter from a friend

Groups are normally goal-oriented, which can be positive or negative. Because goal orientation seems such a prominent part of group behavior in the outdoors, it might be successfully dealt with openly. Goal orientation is negative if a group is locked into a goal and continues to attempt to accomplish it without realistically considering alternatives in the face of environmental hazards.[14]

The goal need not be a summit; it might be pushing on through fatigue to camp at a particular site. Many of us have done this even though we could easily have camped earlier and proceeded the next morning when the group was fresh. Consider establishing acceptable alternatives or contingency plans before starting out to avoid locking into an inappropriate goal.

In small groups, members will benefit by discussing decision-making procedures before heading out. This discussion will help establish

consultation as an important procedure in decision-making.

Group Size: The number of people in a group influences its dynamics. Gregarious by nature, we often think there is safety in numbers, but more important is how well we, as individuals and team members, respond to situations that we encounter. Traveling in a group in a wilderness environment can test us all.

The advantages and disadvantages of large and small groups remain debatable. Undoubtedly, decision-making and organizational details are harder and more time consuming in large groups of inexperienced climbers who do not operate by a linear command structure, so size can give a false sense of security. On the other hand, having at least four in the party can be critical in an emergency: if a person is injured, two individuals can summon help while one remains with the victim. To evacuate a person, even with a minor injury such as a sprained ankle, requires several people to assist the injured person.

On the other hand, a small group might be able to evacuate itself more easily than a large group in a storm. When there are severe injuries requiring extensive medical care and mechanical evacuation, initial group size seems to be of more limited importance than obtaining outside help. Although there are no sure answers, wilderness travelers need to consider how group size in combination with experience might strengthen or hinder them for any given trip.

Peer Pressure: Peer pressure is ever present in our outings with others. It can be negative when one climber talks another into undertaking a climb that is too hazardous, and an accident occurs. Negative peer pressure usually involves the lack of resolved communication between climbers—a partner squelches or ignores a climber's concerns without the give and take of thoughtful debate. The incident described in the accompanying box is an example of how peer pressure can bring pleasure.

Peer pressure is a normal function of individuals in a group. Look for and openly discuss the concerns of party members before undertaking the activity whenever a single person opens the discussion. Members of a party might quickly reject voiced concerns as invalid, and the rejected person continues against his or her own best interest in order to remain a member of the group. In a structured group, leaders need to act in the group's best interest in order to avoid this tendency. Individuals with doubts concerning a peer group's course of action need to analyze the consequences to themselves and the group as a whole if they were to choose another course of action.

Time: Groups on a time schedule might consider picking at least two worthwhile potential goals, one of which all members of the group can achieve in almost any weather conditions. If the group does split up, each group should be under

---

A Great Climb

Two friends and I bivouacked at 11,500 feet in the Teton range. After a sleepless night, we awoke before first light and ate a cold breakfast of greasy sausage. About 5:30 A.M. we began working our way uphill into increasingly technical terrain. I was stiff with cold and sick to my stomach. The term nausea doesn't do it justice. I felt like quitting, but continued. After a half hour, I felt better and we had a good climb. Two years later, in a relaxed social atmosphere, I told this story to my friends, who revealed that they had felt the same way at that time. If anyone had brought up the idea of stopping at just the right (or wrong) moment, we all might have turned around and missed a great climb.

letter from a friend

---

competent leadership and contain enough internal strength to reach its goal safely.

The desire to achieve a goal within the limited time span of a vacation contributes to many accidents. Individuals and groups often are not willing to wait the two days needed for new snow to consolidate before skiing, or until unsettled weather clears before going high. Often, they expose themselves to avalanches, storms, and lightning in order to achieve goals conceived months earlier in their living rooms. To avoid this mind-set, it is useful to pick more than one original goal: for example, a summit on a fair day or a difficult but dry rock climb underneath an overhang in a drizzle. Or, take a cross-country ski trip through wooded terrain instead of venturing above tree line if avalanche conditions prevail. What is important here is that the participants believe both alternatives are worthy. They need to be ready to back away from one goal if it is no longer appropriate. We always need to remind ourselves that we are visitors in an environment that we cannot control.

In a program, participants should climb because they want to, not because they will fulfill some requirement. Programs also need to tailor the activities to the participants' abilities and give participants desirable options. Participants should always choose whether to take part in high-adventure activities that are potentially dangerous.

Staying Together: A basic rule of safety in backcountry travel is that members of the party not lose sight of one another, but it takes effort and organization to do so. To organize this effort, some groups assign functions to members as "guides," who find the way, and "sweeps," who bring up the rear without letting anyone out of sight at any time. To learn more about this technique, consult Paul Petzoldt's *New Wilderness Handbook* and "Adventure Skills and Travel Modes," chapter 8 in *Wilderness Educator.*

Many accidents stem from uncoordinated movement when one member of a group suffers injury. Individuals can become separated from the group and subsequently injure themselves in a fall or suffer hypothermia. In an unusual case described in *Snowy Torrents,*[15] a member of a group was buried by a very small avalanche while he was close to other group members. The avalanche ran about 50 feet and the uninvolved members of the group skied past the buried victim shortly after the slide. The victim might well have survived if group members had seen that he was caught in the slide.

Established Practices: Established practices can be a cause of accidents (see box at right). If you have initial doubts about an activity but the first trip succeeds without incident, you might dismiss your doubts. This produces a cyclic reasoning process that allows the activity to continue on the basis of its prior usage even though you suspect it may be unsafe. Breaking the cycle is difficult once it becomes established.

Other incidents have led to fatalities. One accident involved a routine long-established practice of guided parties eating lunch under a cornice because that was the only flat spot in the area. After many years, the cornice fell off and a number of deaths resulted.

Periodic safety review seems to be the only way to change established practices. In-house review panels can and probably should be estab-

---

Crossing the Train Trestle

A serious near-miss occurred to an Outward Bound group following an established procedure, when two instructors were accompanying students on a final expedition.

As Alan and Anne were partway across the Catawba River Railroad trestle (150 feet long and 30 feet above the river) a train suddenly appeared. At the far end of the trestle, Alan ran to get off the bridge and either leaped for the bank or was hit by the train. He sustained mild abrasions and a concussion and was consequently hospitalized overnight. He was X-rayed for possible head, neck, and spinal injuries. Anne was trapped in the middle of the trestle as the train appeared, jumped the railing and hung on to a parallel beam with her pack on until the train passed. She was shaken but did not require hospitalization. . . .

"A Collection of Accidents and Incidents to Learn From" by Jane Snyder[16]

---

lished for ongoing review. Outside reviewers can have a more objective view of practices as they see these without prejudice due to historical development.

SUMMARY

All climbers must be concerned about accidents because, sooner or later, most of us will be involved in one, either directly or indirectly. Accidents happen to experienced and highly skilled individuals as well as to the unwary novice. You should understand your own vulnerability and be committed to learning to climb safely.

Classic "rules" and guidelines tell us the best way to move safely and swiftly through the mountains, but these rules are ultimately not enough. As individuals and members of a group, we need to recognize what human behaviors we bring into the wilderness. We need to understand how these behaviors interact with environmental hazards and plan our climbs accordingly.

Climbing safely means gaining personal skills

and experiences in technical matters, learning about the natural environment, accepting our limits as human beings, and interacting in positive ways with climbing partners and others that we encounter while climbing. We need to be constantly on guard because everything can change quickly. This very alertness and the concentration that it demands makes climbing interesting and challenging enough to last a lifetime. By concentrating on safety, we do not necessarily become obsessed with it but simply see potential danger where others might not see it.

REFERENCES FOR FUTURE READING

Chouinard, Yvon. 1978. *Climbing ice*. San Francisco: Sierra Club Books in Association with the American Alpine Club.

Cinnamon, C. G. 1989. Risk management in high adventure outdoor pursuits. In *Proceedings of the 1988 national conference on outdoor recreation*. J. Gilbert and E. Brunner, eds. University: University of Mississippi, Department of Health, Physical Education and Recreation.

Cinnamon, J., and Ed Raiola. 1991. Adventure skills and travel modes. Chapter 8 in *The wilderness educator: The Wilderness Education Association's curriculum guide*. David Cockrell, ed. Maryville, Indiana: I.C.S. Books.

Cockrell, David. 1991. *The wilderness educator: The Wilderness Education Association's curriculum guide*. Maryville, Indiana: I.C.S. Books.

Couche, S. 1977. Avalanche awareness survey. *Mazama Journal*.

Dill, John. 1987. Staying alive. In *Yosemite climbs*. George Myers and Don Reid. Denver , Colorado: Chockstone Press.

Gentile, Douglas A., John A. Morris, Tod Schimelpfenig, Sue M. Bass, and Paul S. Auerbach. 1992. Wilderness injuries and illnesses. *Annals of Emergency Medicine*. 21(7):854–861.

Hale, Alan. 1984. *Safety management for outdoor program leaders*. Bellefontaine, Ohio: National Safety Network.

Hunt, Tom. 1988. Yosemite Valley: Study challenges common assumptions. *Climbing*. 108:116–117.

Meyer, D. 1979. The management of risk. *The Journal of Experiential Education* 2(2):9–14.

Petzoldt, Paul. 1984. *The wilderness handbook*, rev. ed. New York: W. W. Norton & Company.

Priest, Simon, and Tim Dixon. 1990. *Safety practices in adventure programming*. Boulder, Colorado: University of Colorado, The Association for Experiential Education, Safety Committee.

Roberts, David. 1986. Reflections on Mount Hood. *Outside*. September, 39–41.

Roskelly, John. 1986. Tragedy on Mt. Hood. *Backpacker*. September, 51–53.

Smutek, Ray, ed. 1972. Symmetry Spire—A very bad year. *Off-Belay*. January–February, 44.

Snyder, Howard. 1973. *The hall of the mountain king*. New York: Scribners.

Synder, Jane. 1985. A collection of accidents and incidents to learn from, gleaned from the records of the North Carolina Outward Bound School. Mankato, Minnesota: Mankato State University. Partial fulfillment of M.S. degree in Experiential Education.

Wade, Ian R. 1991. In *Safety management in adventure education*. John C. Miles and Simon Priest, eds. State College, Pennsylvania: Venture Publishing Co.

Walbridge, Charles C., ed. 1986. Fatal accident on the North Fork, American River. In *River safety report, 1982–1985*. Newington, Virginia: American Canoe Association, Inc.

Whymper, Edward. 1880. *The ascent of the Matterhorn*. London: John Murray.

Wilcox, Joe. 1981. *White winds: America's most tragic climb*. Los Alamitos, California: Hwong Publishing Co.

Williams, Knox. 1975a. Mt. Cleveland. In *The snowy torrents: Avalanche accidents in the United States 1967–71*. U.S. Department of Agriculture, Forest Service, General Technical Report RM-8. Washington, D.C.: Government Printing Office.

———. 1975b. Slide Mtn. Nevada. In *The snowy torrents: Avalanche accidents in the United States 1967–71*. U.S. Department of Agriculture, Forest Service, General Technical Report RM-8. Washington, D.C.: Government Printing Office.

Williamson, John E. 1983. Fall on snow, fall into moat, inadequate equipment, inexperience, Wyoming, Tetons. In *Accidents in North American Mountaineering*. John E. Williamson and O. Miskiw, eds. New York: The American Alpine Club, and Banff: The Alpine Club of Canada. 4(6):36, 67.

———. 1983. Rappel failure, inadequate protection, Utah, Diamond Fork. In *Accidents in North American Mountaineering*. John E. Williamson and O. Miskiw, eds. New York: The American Alpine Club, and Banf: The Alpine Club of Canada. 4(6):36, 58.

Williamson, John E., A. Harvard, P. Lev, C. Bangs, and B. Shaw. 1986. The base camp program and the Mount Hood accident, reports of the Base Camp Inquiry Committee to the Board of Trustees of Oregon Episcopal School. The Oregonian Publishing Co. 136: 44, 821, Friday, July 25, 1986, sunrise edition.

Williamson, John E., and E. Whalley, eds. 1980. Fall on snow, and ice, exposure, darkness, New Hampshire, Mt. Washington. In *Accidents in North American Mountaineering*. New York: The American Alpine Club, and Banff: The Alpine Club of Canada. 4(3):33, 36.

Williamson, John E., and J. Whitteker, eds. 1987. Preface. In *Accidents in North American Mountaineering*. New York: The American Alpine Club, and Banff: The Alpine Club of Canada.

———. 1988. Statistical tables. In *Accidents in North American Mountaineering*. New York: The American Alpine Club, and Banff: The Alpine Club of Canada.

Williamson, John E., and R. Plasman, eds. 1999. Statistical tables. In *Accidents in North American Mountaineering*. New York: The American Alpine Club, and Banff: The Alpine Club of Canada.

ENDNOTES

1. *The ascent of the Matterhorn* (Whymper, 1880) describes the race between two parties attempting to reach the summit of the Matterhorn on the same day. When Whymper and his party reached the summit, they saw the competing party far below on a different route and rolled rocks from the summit to catch their attention. The accident during the descent is described in the book.

2. See, especially, Meyer, 1979; Hale, 1984; Dill, 1987; Wade, 1991; and Williamson and Whitteker, 1988.

3. Meyer, 1979.

4. Williamson and Whitteker, 1987.

5. Results and conclusions are taken from a study of injuries and illnesses occurring in the National Outdoor Leadership School over a five-year period, September 1984 through September 1989. See Gentile et al., 1992.

6. Dill, 1987, and Hunt, 1988.

7. U.S. and Canadian data are from statistical tables in the 1999 issue of *Accidents in North American Mountaineering*, published jointly by the American Alpine Club and the Alpine Club of Canada. This data is available in graph form at <http://www.klab.caltech.edu/~peter/climbing>.

8. From statistical tables in Williamson and Plasman, 1999.

9. Chouinard, 1978, 153.

10. Hale, 1984.

11. Smutek, 1972; Williamson, ed., 1983, 67.

12. Williamson, 1983, 58. Outward Bound, with over 19,000 participants and 1,000 instructors, has been able to reduce its accidental death rate sevenfold in the last decade to achieve safety results comparable to the risk of everyday life. See Wade, 1991.

13. Williamson, John E., and E. Whalley, 1980, 36.

14. Williams, 1975, 102. As an example of an accident that might be related to goal orientation, see the case study on Mt. Cleveland.

15. Williams, 1975, 56.

16. Snyder , 1985.

First-Aid Programs

WILDERNESS FIRST AID

Wilderness travelers can gain skills and the critical personal confidence required to administer first aid by completing a Wilderness First Responder (WFR) or Wilderness Emergency Medical Technician (WEMT) course. There is a growing list of nationally recognized schools now offering basic and advanced wilderness first aid for backcountry travelers. These courses teach basic life-support techniques, how to stabilize a spine, and how to recognize and treat head injuries, shock, and hypothermia. Most important, they teach you to think about potential changes in a victim's condition over the few hours after an accident and what you can do to stabilize the victim's condition.

FIRST-AID SCHOOLS

Stonehearth Open Learning (SOLO)
P.O. Box 3150
Conway NH 03818
603-447-6711
Fax 603-447-2310
E-mail: solo@stonehearth.com
http://www.stonehearth.com

Wilderness Medical Associates (WMA)
189 Dudley Rd., #2
Bryant Pond ME 04219
207-665-2707
Fax 207-665-2747
E-mail: office@wildmed.com
http://www.wildmed.com

Wilderness Medicine Institute (WMI)
P.O. Box 9
413 Main St.
Pitkin CO 81241
970-641-3572
Fax 970-641-0882
E-mail: wmi@nols.edu
http://wmi.nols.edu

APPENDIX B

Fitness

PHYSICAL FITNESS AND CLIMBING

Being physically fit enables you to climb at your best and to avoid soreness, fatigue, and injury. These pages do not outline a complete fitness program, which could fill a whole book, or offer personalized advice such as you can get from a sports trainer, but rather aim to get you started in the proper direction.

To achieve fitness you can train for cardio-vascular (aerobic) endurance; muscular endurance, flexibility, strength, and power; balance, agility, and coordination; and body composition. You can also pay attention to proper nutrition in order to reach peak performance. Before undertaking more than a generalized training program, have fun climbing and develop good technique and concentration while gaining experience. When you do start a generalized training program, do so to improve your entire body rather than concentrating on only a few specific muscle groups.

If you have any doubts about whether to start a fitness program, given your age and health, consult your physician. To help you get started and to understand the principles underlying many forms of fitness, refer to Hoeger's *Lifetime Physical Fitness and Wellness*, and Hoeger and Hoeger's *Fitness and Wellness*. (All publications mentioned in this appendix are listed under "References for Future Reading.")

Once you are motivated and are well into a fitness program, do not overdo your training, because this can result in injury. Once injured, you must avoid training until you heal, and you will be susceptible to further injury.

Aerobic Endurance

Endurance is important on each pitch and allows you to function well pitch after pitch. Aerobic, meaning *with oxygen*, fitness is necessary for the muscular endurance required during longer climbs. Aerobic endurance will help avoid soreness that comes from prematurely calling upon your less efficient *anaerobic* energy system. The objective of aerobic training is to strengthen your heart, lungs, blood vessels, etc., so that your body can collect, transport, and use oxygen efficiently at the cell level, where it helps produce energy. Aerobic training involves groups of large muscles, mainly your legs or upper body and legs combined, in a sustained effort. The aerobic system is the body's most efficient system for delivering energy to muscle cells and provides the main source of energy involved in any sustained effort.

Mountain biking on rough trails, for example, gives good general aerobic training and uses the upper body as well as the lower body. This form of exercise is easy on the knee joints, while it strengthens the muscles of the legs, back, and arms. Other aerobic activities include taking long walks, hiking, running, road bicycling, and cross-country skiing. Enjoying the training activity is important, since good results require that you train systematically for 8 to 12 weeks at about 75 to 80 percent of maximum effort before the climbing season starts.

Stretching

The object of stretching is to extend the operating range of a muscle group so that you can use and strengthen the muscles throughout their entire range of motion. Before stretching, warm up by engaging in an aerobic activity for five minutes to increase the temperature of your muscles. This activity will also increase the blood supply to these muscles and remove waste products produced in exercise more efficiently. If you are stretching as part of an aerobic workout, stretch lightly before exercising and spend more time stretching during a cool-down phase of your exercise. Stretching should occur statically—hold a muscle in a slightly extended position, where there is some muscular discomfort but no pain. Stretching by bouncing can tear muscles, ligaments, and tendons.

The standard work on stretching is *Stretching*, by Bob Anderson, which includes a pretraining routine for weight training and running.

Muscular Endurance Training

Generalized training should work on the muscles of your upper, middle, and lower body. The easiest and most enjoyable generalized training to prepare for climbing is to boulder on large holds two or more times a week in hour-long sessions. Vary the aerobic-workout intensity by the size of footholds that you use, and the workout duration by the length of time spent without touching down. You are unlikely to injure your tendons if you stay away from repeated laps on small holds. Injury often results because muscles of your shoulders, arms, and forearms strengthen more quickly than tendons connecting these joints. You will quickly be strong enough to pull harder with these muscles than the connecting ligaments and tendons can sustain[1], so they will tear instead. A slow buildup in an 8- to 12-week training program will allow your tendons and ligaments to get stronger slowly, keep up with increases in muscular strength, and thus help prevent injury.

When you get into the gym, incorporate into your program exercises where you push or pull against a solid object. Push-ups, sit-ups, curls, squats, dips, pull-ups, and chin-ups fall into this group. Lifting light weights 15 to 20 or more times is another type of muscular endurance training. Muscular endurance depends upon both muscular strength and aerobic conditioning. Muscular strength programs, discussed later, depend on prior muscular endurance programs to succeed. *Weight Training for Life* by James Hesson, *Climbing Fit* by Martyn Hurn and Pat Ingle, and *The Outdoor Athlete* by Steve Ilg are good guides for muscular endurance and strength training; *Climbing Fit* was written specifically for climbers. A video on training for rock climbing is also available from the Vertical Club.[2]

Muscular Strength

At some point when you climb a steep wall, your aerobic energy production system may begin to overload and your anaerobic energy system kicks in. Operating without oxygen, you can put out sustained energy for only a few minutes. The anaerobic system also produces lactic acid as a by-product, which remains after exercise and promotes soreness. When you train to improve muscular endurance, you are trying to elevate the critical effort level at which your anaerobic system comes into play, and improve the ability of your body to remove lactic acid once it has been created.

Muscular strength is gained by anaerobic training, which relies on the overload. If you overload specific muscle cells beyond their normal use, they will increase in size, strength, and/or endurance. Women who weight-train show increases in muscular strength, but do not experience large increases in muscular size.[3] To increase strength systematically, progressively, and without injury, increase the demands placed upon your muscles over a planned period of time involving a training program. Your body needs rest periods of 48 hours or longer between workouts, so that its aerobic systems can repair damaged tissue and build new cells. Insufficient rest between workouts prevents improvement and may lead to injury. Normally you should work out a set of muscles only every second or third day, depending on your personal rate of recovery.

To stimulate strength development in weight training, you should use a weight that you can lift 6 to 12 times before momentary failure. This might be between 70 and 80 percent of your body weight, with the higher resistance levels more likely to lead to injury. Refer to listed references for specific training exercises, techniques, and lifting patterns.

Training Programs

Programs of training involve both aerobic and anaerobic training and accompanying stretching exercises. A training program might be the equivalent of running three miles, three times a week,[4] and spending two days a week strength training. Advanced climbers may benefit from strength training on three days each week. Each session might begin with stretching to warm up, then training, followed by cool-down stretching. Be sure that you allow 48 hours of rest or longer between strength-training sessions. When you plan to climb, be sure to rest or only train lightly the day before.

Year-long muscular training programs begin during the winter when you spend most of the time building endurance and strength in the gym.[5] As rock season comes around, you gradually spend more time climbing, with weekly trips to the gym to maintain your strength. When you begin to spend all your time on the rock and reduce strength training, you will find that your performance level picks up and peaks. After you peak, you probably will be mentally and physically stale for a while, so train and climb less intensely until you are ready to begin the cycle again.

Injuries

The most common climbing injuries are to tendons and ligaments of the elbow, shoulder, or fingers. Treatment begins with rest; do not climb. You can help reduce swelling and promote healing in a sore joint by applying ice frequently throughout the day. Move the ice around and take care not to cause cold-induced nerve damage. When the pain from the injury goes away, your joint may not be inflamed or swollen, but it has not healed. You need to wait a few more weeks before beginning to train at a level appropriate to the injury and stage of healing.

A complete program of recovery that avoids reinjury may require eight weeks or longer to work back to a high level of fitness. Adopt a slow, systematic increase in activity while avoiding the movement or error that caused the original injury. Start with a full range of motion stretching followed by high-repetition, low-weight isolation exercises, such as using dumbbells, after you experience no pain during stretching. Continue to ice after each session.

Dr. Mark Robinson, a physician and a climber, recommends that you add "eccentric" exercises once you regain 80 percent of your lost strength. For example, he recommends that you lower from a bar, stretching your muscles slowly and controlling your descent. Take care, as these exercises are stressful, and limit them to once every three to five days. Your first climbs should be on low-angle, big-hold slabs. As you continue to recover, emphasize improving balance, flexibility, and smooth static moves on steeper climbs with large holds. Rehabilitation is not training, and you can easily reinjure yourself by following routines suitable to an uninjured climber or by attempting dynamic moves to small holds. Seek help in dealing with the complex steps of recovery by consulting a physician or trainer who specializes in sports injuries.

REFERENCES FOR FUTURE READING

Anderson, Bob. 1980. *Stretching*. Bolinas, California: Shelter Publications.

Cooper, Kenneth H. 1968. *Aerobics*. New York: Bantam Books.

———. 1982. *The aerobics program for total well-being: Exercise, diet, emotional balance*. New York: Bantam Books.

Hesson, James L. 1991. *Weight training for life*. Englewood, Colorado: Morton Publishing Co.

Hoeger, Werner W. K. 1989. *Lifetime physical fitness & wellness: A personalized program*. Second edition. Englewood, Colorado: Morton Publishing Co.

Hoeger, Werner W. K., and Sharon A. Hoeger. 1990. *Fitness and wellness*. Englewood, Colorado: Morton Publishing Co.

Horst, J. Eric. 1989. Happiness is a pair of big guns. *Climbing*. 116:118.

Hurn, Martyn, and Pat Ingle. 1988. *Climbing fit*. Seattle: Cloudcap.

Ilg, Steve. 1985. Weight training for rock climbers. *Climbing*. 91:58–62.

Robinson, Mark. 1988a. Fingers: Get a grip on injury prevention and treatment. *Climbing*. 109:108–113.

———. 1988b. The shoulder: A powerful joint with a delicate construction. *Climbing*. 111:111–116.

———. 1989. The elbow: Understanding a common "sore" subject. *Climbing*. 113:130–137.

———. 1992. Climbing injuries to fingers and forearm. *Climbing*. 138:141–150.

Smith, Nathan J., and Bonnie Worthington-Roberts. 1989. *Food for sport*. Palo Alto, California: Bull Publishing Co.

ENDNOTES

1. See Robinson, 1988a and b and 1989.
2. This video is hosted by Christen Griffen and includes stretching, bouldering, proper use of hang boards, and weight exercises to prevent shoulder injuries. Available from the Vertical Club, Inc., Seattle, Washington; (206) 283-8056.
3. Hesson, 1991, indicates that this may be related to low levels of the hormone testosterone and high levels of the hormone estrogen.
4. See Horst, 1989, for a general rundown on training.
5. See Robinson, 1988a and b and 1989.

APPENDIX C

Lightning

INTRODUCTION

Lightning is the leading direct meteorological cause of casualties in the United States. Snowstorms cause more indirect deaths and tornadoes cause more property damage, but lightning kills about 100 and injures about 300 Americans each year. For this reason, lightning is of concern to all who use the outdoors for recreation.

Rock climbers and mountaineers, of course, play a part in the statistics. Thirty-seven mountaineering accidents involving lightning were reported in the United States from 1951 to 1991.[1] Lightning encounters by mountaineers in Canada appear to occur at a lower rate, with only six incidents reported between 1959 and 1991.

Lightning occurs when warm moisture-laden air is lifted into the atmosphere and water vapor condenses to form thunderstorms. Towering *cumulonimbus thunderclouds* contain the up and down air currents associated with heavy rain, hail, wind gusts, and lightning. Orographic or mountain lifting (fig. C-1) is of particular interest to climbers and hill hikers alike. In summer, by afternoon, the solar heating of moist air during the morning coupled with air rising over a mountain range produces thunderstorms and lightning. After an hour or two, its energy dissipated, the storm blows over and the sky clears.

The weather in many major alpine areas follows this pattern in summer, affecting rock-climbing areas located in the mountains or at their base. Climbers who do not wish to get caught climbing in the midst of a storm ascend their route and descend by early afternoon, before the storm begins.

Other kinds of thunderstorms are those associated with cold fronts, air-mass heating, and severe thunderstorms (that can spawn tornadoes). Frontal thunderstorms originate as a cold air mass burrows under a warm air mass along a

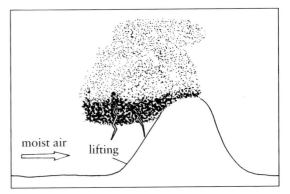

Figure C-1. Orographic Lifting of Warm Moist Air: Mountain lifting often produces summer afternoon thunderstorms with hail, a torrential downpour, and lightning.

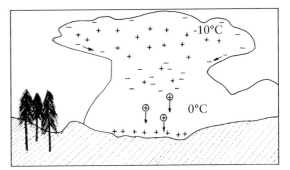

Figure C-2. Thunderstorm Charge Distribution: Charge separation occurs in the middle of the cloud, the upper part becoming positively charged (+) and the lower part negatively charged (–). The ground takes on a positive charge and the air acts as an insulator to the flow of electricity. After Uman and Krider, 1989.

291

Lightning on the Chouinard-Becky

On August 3 . . . two climbers left the Bugaboo Hut and climbed in good weather to the base of Great White Headwall on the Chouinard-Becky route on the west face of the South Howser Tower (3,300 meters). The following day the pair reached the start of the lower-angle summit ridge immediately following the tension traverse pitch. The weather had deteriorated over the preceding half hour with scattered squalls moving through the area, but none affecting the Howsers. Continuing over the summit and down the standard route seemed preferable to rappelling the ascent route. They were not far below the summit when a nearby small pinnacle on the ridge began to hum. The climbers got rid of their hardware and sat on their packs and ropes in a notch beneath the pinnacle. Then the humming stopped, and they did not feel the prickling skin or hair sensation that would indicate a gathering charge. But within one or two minutes, there was a sharp crack, and both climbers were hit by ground current.

Afterward, one climber had lost feeling in both legs, and his right leg was paralyzed. Later, entrance and exit wounds were found on his right hip and on both sides of his ankle. The other climber had generalized numbness and muscle weakness. His right forearm was painful, and he could see holes burned through several layers of clothing. Entrance and exit wounds were later found on both sides of his forearm and on his right ankle. In addition to the small full-thickness burns at the entrance and exit wounds, there were patches of superficial burns where his polypropylene underwear had ignited.

The climbers gradually regained motor control over the next half hour, and they rappelled their ascent route. They then hiked back to the Kain Hut where their burns were cleaned and dressed.

(From Williamson and Whitteker, 1988; original source: J. Bird and C. Atkinson, Bugaboo Glacier National Park.)

Analysis: The climbers did all the classic, right things. They were not on the summit or under overhangs. They insulated themselves by sitting on their packs.

---

boundary that may extend over many states. These storms can occur at any time of the day or night throughout the year and often last for half a day or longer. Air-mass thunderstorms occur in the afternoon of a hot summer day, when warm moist air is heated and lifted within an air mass that may cover an area that is the size of many states. This air-mass lifting may assist mountain lifting, but it may also produce thunderstorms over flat areas. Severe thunderstorms are associated with fairly unique conditions of colliding air masses, shear between air layers and spin, and strong air flow aloft. These storms are of interest to climbers because they may lead to serious weather changes in specific locations at specific times, but climbers must cope with the thunderstorms produced by mountain lifting on a daily basis. Lightning usually occurs during the mature stage of the thunderstorm. As a cumulonimbus cloud develops, charge separations occur in it very quickly (fig. C-2), making the middle of the cloud negative and the top positive.

Lightning, a transient high-current discharge with a path length kilometers long, can occur within clouds, from cloud to cloud, from cloud to air, and from cloud to ground. Discharges connecting clouds and the earth are of primary interest because of the possibility of injury and death associated with them. There are four identified types of lightning connecting cloud to earth, categorized by whether the initial discharge (leader) moves downward or upward and whether the initial leader is positive or negative. The most common discharge initiates in a cloud and connects the negative charges in the middle of the cloud to positive charges induced at ground level, like a shadow, by the negative charges in the lower part of the cloud. A small percentage of the cloud-to-ground leaders are positive. Upward-initiated leaders usually occur from mountain peaks and tall structures, with the most common having a positive leader.[2]

Charge Separation and Updrafts

The origin of the charge separation that leads to lightning is not fully understood. It must relate to the rapid vertical movements, updrafts, and formation of frozen precipitation within the building cumulonimbus cloud. The processes of freezing and melting produce charged particles. Collisions between falling pea-size white ice pellets (called *graupel*), ice crystals, and supercooled water drops appear to be important in producing the distribution of charges.[3] In laboratory experiments, when the temperature is below a critical value called the charge-reversal temperature, T_R, the falling graupel particles acquire a negative charge in collisions with the ice crystals. At temperatures above T_R, they acquire a positive charge. T_R is thought to be about 5 degrees Fahrenheit (–15 degrees Celsius). This reading coincides with the temperature of the region in thunderclouds where the main negative charge is found. When graupel falls below this altitude, to a region of higher temperature, it picks up a positive charge. There is evidence that these positively charged graupel particles form a small lower positive region of the thundercloud that lies beneath the main negative region.

The Lightning Stroke

The lightning flash, which is the total discharge from the cloud, is actually a sequence of strokes. Each stroke lasts about a millisecond, and the separation between strokes is typically several tens of milliseconds. The sequence of cloud-to-ground flash is illustrated in figure C-3. The primary breakdown in the cloud may occur when a flow of electrons (negatively charged particles) from the middle of the cloud rushes toward the base. The initial stroke is the first of a series of stepped leaders. *Stepped leaders* are tens of meters long and last about a millionth of a second; there is a pause of 20 to 50 millionths of a second between steps. The average downward speed of propagation is about 200,000 meters/second; our eyes cannot distinguish the individual steps at this speed.

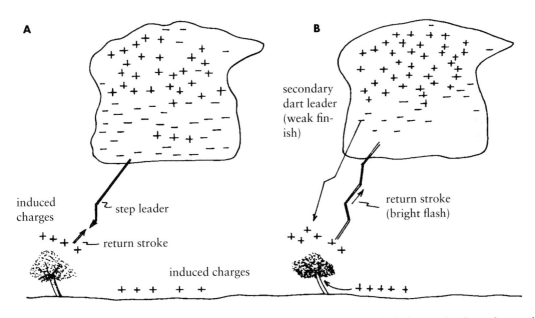

Figure C-3. Steps in the Lightning Stroke: A—A step leader (discharge) initiates the stroke from the base of the cloud, ionizing the air. When the step leader has almost reached the ground, a return leader leaps up to meet it.

B—The return stroke lights up the sky and neutralizes the lower part of the cloud. Higher in the cloud a secondary dart leader begins its path toward earth, taking electrons with it, repeating the earlier sequence.

As the tip of the leader nears the ground, the electrical field increases until it exceeds the resistance of air at sharp objects or at irregularities on the ground. The earth and cloud join by an ionized path. Up this path rushes a return stroke that imparts energy to the atoms and molecules of the air, which in turn give off light to the branches of the descending step leader. The *return stroke* somewhat neutralizes the cloud, since the initial stroke only discharges the lowest portions of the cloud. The drama of discharge continues as a secondary return occurs through the ionized channel, prepared by the initial strike, to discharge higher and higher regions of the negatively charged portion of the cloud. This secondary return is the dart leader, of which there are usually three or four. The elapsed time from step leader to final dart leader occurs in about a second—too fast for our eyes to see individual steps, although high-speed photography has captured them on film.

Upward Lightning

Lightning is sometimes initiated by upward-moving leaders that arise from TV towers and from tall mountain peaks. Upward-moving leaders can be distinguished from downward-moving strokes because the flash branches upward (fig. C-4). These leaders are usually positive and produce a more or less continuous flow of current at the ground. In about half of the upward-initiated events, however, the continuous current is followed by a sequence of dart leaders and return strokes that are similar to those following the first strokes in natural cloud-to-ground discharges.[4]

Thunder

Thunder is a direct effect of lightning. Lightning heats the air in a narrow channel to around 54,000 degrees Fahrenheit (30,000 degrees Celsius) as it propagates earthward. This heating causes explosive expansion of the air, producing the sound that we call thunder. Thunder rumbles because different parts of the lightning stroke are different distances away from the observer.

We can use the different rates of travel for light and sound for the practical purpose of calculating how far away we are from a lightning storm. Light travels so fast that a flash from a lightning stroke appears to an observer almost as it happens. However, sound travels at a much slower rate—about 4.8 seconds per mile, or approximately one-fifth mile per second. In figure

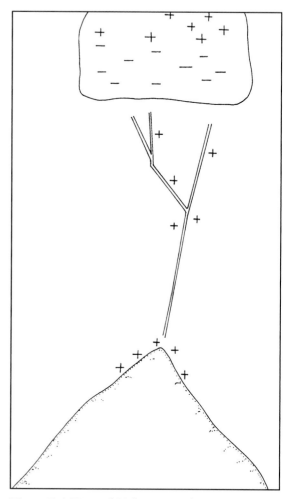

Figure C-4. Upward Lightning: Lightning may sometimes be initiated by upward-moving discharge leaders. These discharge leaders are usually positive and can produce a continuous flow of current, or a sequence of dart leaders and return strokes. This phenomenon is well documented in association with TV towers and appears to occur on tall mountains. Modified from a figure by Uman and Krider, 1989.

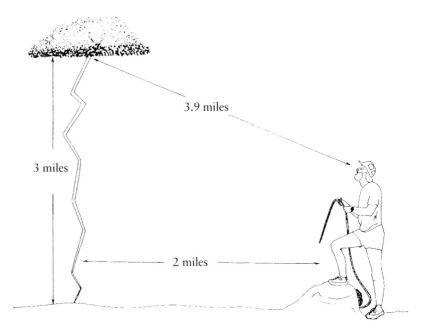

Figure C-5. Thunder, or Maybe We Shouldn't Do This Climb: Because sound waves from the lower part of the lightning stroke reach the observer before those from the upper part of the stroke, the thunder appears to rumble.

C-5, the sound of the bottom portion of the stroke reaches the observer in about 10 seconds, whereas sound from the top part of the stroke takes about 19 seconds to arrive. The rumbling "sound on sound" effect results from the sound traveling different distances. The lag time between lightning and thunder is approximately 5 seconds for each mile that the storm is distant from the observer's position. A lag of 10 seconds between lightning and thunder thus indicates that a storm is 2 miles away. This 10-second lag is a strong warning to seek safety.

LIGHTNING DANGERS

During a lightning storm, climbers are in direct danger from the storm's electricity in three ways: (1) a direct lightning strike, (2) induced currents in the vicinity of a strike, and (3) ground currents.

The Direct Strike

If you cannot descend from a mountain or leave the area before a storm, you should avoid locations that might be hit by a direct strike. Seek a place where nearby projections, such as a pinnacle, are above your own head. Such projections

provide a 45-degree cone of protection (fig. C-6). On an exposed ridge with trees, the safest shelter is amid the shorter trees in the middle of the ridge. Avoid trees at the edges or shoulders of the ridge. On a bare mountain top it might be

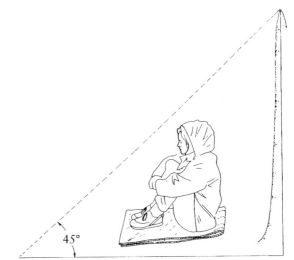

Figure C-6. The 45-Degree Cone of Protection from Lightning Strike: The climber sits halfway between the top of the rock pinnacle and the edge of the cone. The projection should be 5 to 10 times the climber's height.

possible to use the peak itself as a lightning rod to take the direct strike, but it is always preferable to get lower, out of the strike zone, before the storm begins.

Induced Currents

In a cloud-to-ground lightning strike, a climber may be the projection that takes on the induced positive charge (fig. C-7). (A climber can also be the chief discharge point for a lightning flash in ground-to-cloud lightning.) In either case, the

Figure C-7. Induced Charges on a Climber: The climber is in immediate danger of experiencing a lightning strike. The climber may hear the "buzzing of bees" and smell ozone. The climber should immediately get below the summit and seek a cone of protection, leaving the axe where it can be found after the storm has passed.

air around the climber will become ionized and lose its insulating ability. It can give off a crackling noise, known in the Alps as the "buzzing of bees," and the distinctive odor of ozone may be present. If the climber's hair stands on end and crackles, and ice axes, carabiners, and other metal tools discharge, giving off a bluish glow or corona called St. Elmo's Fire, lightning is about to strike.

The literature on mountaineering suggests that climbers usually toss aside ice axes, carabiners, and other gear when they hear and see these phenomena in an attempt to avoid the lightning stroke,[5] returning to pick up their gear when the storm is over. While it is realistic to be afraid of a lightning storm, climbers should also fear doing dangerous things to get out of the path of a storm. You can get hurt as seriously by falling when your rappel anchor fails or while running down a mountain as when you get hit by lightning.

Ground Currents and Body Position

Your major concerns in a lightning storm are to avoid a direct strike and prevent the passage of ground current through your body. Two factors determine the extent of human injury caused by ground currents: the quantity of current and the part of the body affected. A current passing from one hand to the other, through the heart or lungs, or from head to foot through the brain and other organs, is most dangerous, since vital functions can be impaired. As the boxed excerpt on page 292 indicates, you can also suffer burns at entry and exit points, as well as medical shock.

To avoid the worst effects of ground currents, assume one of the body positions illustrated in figure C-8. You may crouch low in a balanced position on a doubled insulated pad. Both feet should be together and touch the pad so that lightning cannot enter one foot, travel through the body and exit via the second foot. Because the crouching position is difficult to hold for very long, you may need to sit if the storm continues. In the sitting position, the feet are together, and feet and buttocks touch the pad.

Figure C-8. Body Positions to Minimize Damage from Lightning Storm: All positions keep the climber low to avoid direct strikes. The feet are held together to make one entry point for ground currents, and to prevent the body from providing a conducting path.

Hold arms out to the side or wrap them around the knees for stability. (It is difficult to hold the arms out to the side for any period of time, but theoretically ground currents are less likely to pass through the heart and lungs in this position.) Both sitting positions are intended to keep you low to avoid a direct strike, and require less balance and muscular control than to maintain a crouching position.

Ground Currents and Positions on a Peak

When an electrical discharge strikes a point, electricity flows outward. On rock, the major path of flow is along the wet surface, because water is a better conductor than rock. Electricity travels down wet cracks, through depressions with saturated soils, or along water-rich vegetation. Electrical currents can jump short gaps, such as from the roof to the floor of a shallow cave, so you should not seek shelter from storms in the shallow caves and overhangs normally found on peaks. Figure C-9A, B, and C illustrate three dangerous choices: leaning against a wall (ground currents may pass through heart and lungs), sitting underneath a shallow overhang (the climber provides a path for ground currents from roof to the floor), and sitting in a depression (the climbers provide a shortened path for ground currents and a pool of conducting water may accumulate). Figure C-9D shows the only position that is potentially safe: the climber sits on an insulating pad (a pack would also serve) on a shelf, above the path of ground currents, which should pass safely underneath.

FIRST AID

Any climbers who are struck directly by lightning or have ground current pass through their body will need first aid and subsequent examination by a physician. Common effects of severe electrical disturbances to the body are burns, stoppage of respiratory and cardiac functions, severe muscular contractions, and even functional failure of the brain. In addition, the victim may experience serious secondary injuries from a fall.

The fact that lightning is a high-voltage event of very short duration leads to characteristic patterns of injury. Second-degree burns from lightning usually cover skin surfaces and do not normally lead to entrance or exit wounds, which do occur from contact with alternating-current power lines. The short encounter also protects victims from the excessive internal burning associated with alternating currents.

It is important for rescuers to realize that victims of lightning do not retain any electrical charge. You can safely touch victims to give first aid immediately after they are struck.

Look first for signs that lightning has interfered with heart and lung function. If respiratory and cardiac arrest occur together, you can revive the victim by prompt action. In some victims who experience both heart and lung arrest, the heart may spontaneously start up, leaving them only in respiratory arrest. In other victims, only respiratory arrest occurs initially, but cardiac arrest follows if they are not promptly re-

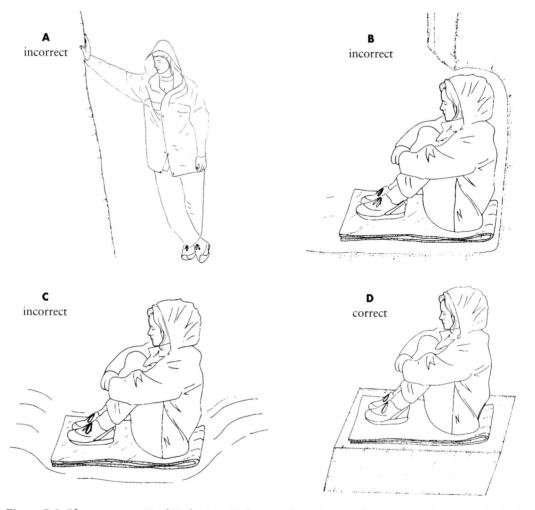

Figure C-9. Placement on a Rock Ridge in a Lightning Storm (A, B, and C are dangerous): A—Leaning against wet rock (currents go in one arm and through the body). B—Sitting under a shallow overhang or cave (currents jump the gap and go through the body). C—Sitting in a depression (currents pass through wet soil or water and through the body). Better Placement: D—Sitting on a rock—with added insulation—above the surface of a shelf and well below the direct strike zone (ground currents may pass beneath the climber).

vived. Individuals who are only in respiratory arrest can be saved with prompt ventilation at a rate that makes their chest rise and fall normally after establishing an open airway.

Climbers and others who spend time adventuring outdoors need to know rescue breathing and heart massage as taught in American Red Cross or American Heart Association cardiopulmonary resuscitation (CPR) courses. Since lightning can strike a CPR-trained member of a climbing team, all climbers should learn CPR to safeguard each other.

Other injuries and symptoms that can occur in lightning encounters include strong muscular contractions, related to the electrical impulse of lightning, that can lead to fractured bones and muscular injuries. Approximately half the victims of direct lightning strikes also have at least one eardrum ruptured. Amnesia, postconcussion swelling of the brain, and even paralysis may occur. Victims of direct strikes can literally have their clothes blown off as the lightning current explosively vaporizes skin moisture. Because of possible hidden complications that may not present for hours after injury, all victims of lightning encounters should undergo observation by a physician in a hospital after first aid has been administered.

REFERENCES FOR FUTURE READING

Peters, Ed, ed. 1982. *Mountaineering: The freedom of the hills.* Fourth edition. Seattle: The Mountaineers.

Uman, Martin A., and E. Philip Krider. 1989. Natural and artificially initiated lightning. *Science.* 246: 457–464.

Williams, Earle R. 1988. The electrification of thunderstorms. *Scientific American.* November: 88–99.

Williamson, J. and J. Whitteker, eds. 1988. *Accidents in North American Mountaineering.* New York: The American Alpine Club and Banff: The Alpine Club of Canada.

Williamson, John E., and O. Miskiw, eds. 1992. *Accidents in North American Mountaineering.* New York: The American Alpine Club and Banff: The Alpine Club of Canada.

ENDNOTES

1. Williamson and Miskiw, 1992.
2. Uman and Krider, 1989.
3. Williams, 1988.
4. Uman and Krider, 1989.
5. This is my observation as well.

Pulley System Basics

INTRODUCTION

Pulleys connected by rope form a system, often called a *tackle*, that provides leverage for lifting or lowering heavy objects. There are a number of reasons why climbers might want to know about pulley systems. A pulley system is commonly used to rescue climbers from a crevasse and for the construction of hauling systems for big-wall rescues.[1] Knowing how to set up pulley systems will allow you to lift heavy panels single-handedly if you build a climbing wall—or to pull your car out of the mud at the base of the climbing site.

Pulley systems create *mechanical advantage* by using a tensioned rope that changes direction at the pulleys, making it possible to lift people or gear. The stresses pulleys produce can break ropes and anchors because tensioned ropes are susceptible to cutting or breaking. Hence, belays and backup systems are important when using pulleys for rescues. And be sure that you do not climb again on a rope after you destroy its shock-absorbing character by using it in a pulley system.

Mechanical advantage is defined as the ratio of the weight to be lifted divided by the applied force, or:

$$\text{Mechanical advantage} = \frac{\text{Weight to be lifted}}{\text{Applied force}}$$

The mechanical advantage is normally written as a ratio—3:1, 2:1, 1:1. No units are involved. In the ideal mechanical-advantage systems examined in this appendix, friction does not exist, though of course it does in real systems, where the friction of pulleys reduces work efficiency to 70 to 93 percent of the theoretical value. If you use carabiners in place of pulleys, efficiency drops to less than two-thirds of the theoretical value.[2] For example, a 3:1 mechanical advantage is reduced to less than a 2:1 advantage when carabiners take the place of pulleys in the system.

SINGLE-PULLEY SYSTEMS

1:1 Systems

In a one-to-one system a single rope supports the load. When you directly lift a weight, as the climber does in figure D-1A by using her arm and shoulder muscles, the lifting force equals the load, and the lifting force is in the direction of the applied force. The same 1:1 advantage occurs when you lift a weight by means of a pulley and a rope (fig. D-1B). The rope on the right side of the pulley does not give any additional lifting force, but it does offer the advantage of a change of direction of the applied force.

The climber using the pulley system finds lifting the weight easier than the first climber because pulling down on the rope after it changes direction at the pulley allows her to employ her muscles more efficiently; she uses her legs, both arms, and her shoulder, chest, back, and stomach muscles to lift the weight. When the climber using the pulley system suspends the load in the air without moving, the load is in a state of *equilibrium*: a balanced state between the force of gravity trying to pull the load downward and the force of the climber trying to lift the weight. To upset equilibrium and lift the weight, the climber has only to supply a small additional force.

2:1 Systems

If two people lift the same weight, a new situation occurs (fig. D-2A). To share equally in lift-

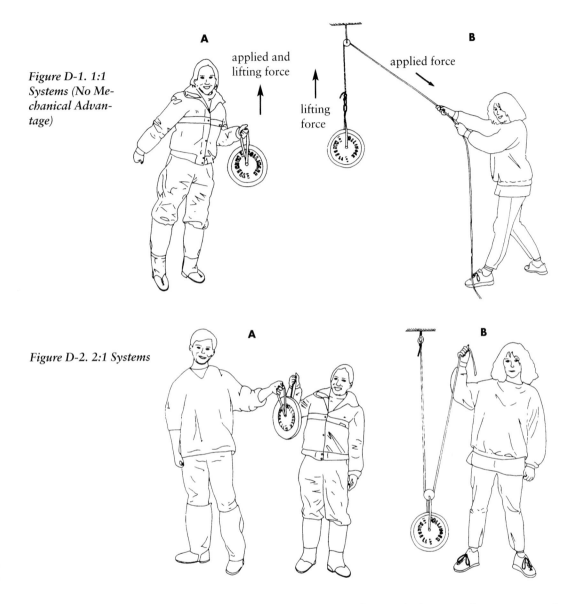

Figure D-1. 1:1 Systems (No Mechanical Advantage)

A applied and lifting force

B applied force lifting force

Figure D-2. 2:1 Systems

A

B

ing the weight, they each must lift one-half the total. They do this by compensating for differences in height and strength by conscious *coordination*. If we substitute a rope for the climbers' arms (fig. D-2B), there are still two "arms" supporting the weight. The climber in figure D-2B can now lift the weight from its position of equilibrium by lifting one of the rope "arms." The rope automatically coordinates

sharing the weight between the two supporting rope arms. In general, if two "arms" support a weight (in this case, the two arms of rope in the pulley system), they create a 2:1 advantage. If the climber runs the rope she holds through a second pulley at the ceiling, she can change the direction of the applied force again, so that she can use her leg, shoulder, arm, and back muscles to help lift the weight, as in figure D-1B.

4:1 Systems

Now imagine that four people get together to lift the weight, as shown in figure D-3A. We could call this a 4:1 people-advantage system. Of course, four people have to coordinate their efforts to raise the weight. The coordination problem is simplified by using a rope and pulleys as illustrated in figure D-3B. In this 4:1 mechanical-advantage system, the rope provides continuity. When the weight and system are at rest, one person supports just one-fourth of the total weight, while three-quarters of the weight is supported by the other "arms" of the system. When she pulls with slightly more force, she unbalances the system and starts the weight moving upward.

PULLEY SYSTEM NOTATION

Pulley systems employ two different types of pulleys, those that are fixed in position and those that are free to move. A *fixed pulley,* such as that of figure D-1B, attached to a structural support simply provides a change of direction.

A *floating pulley* (fig. D-2B) moves as the load moves while providing a change of direction. Pulley systems that give higher ratios of mechanical advantage use both types of pulleys, as illustrated by the 4:1 systems of figure D-3B. Here, one fixed pulley and two floating pulleys alter rope direction to provide four rope "arms" to support the weight; these floating pulleys replace the two sticks in figure D-3A.

As more pulleys, changes of direction, and "arms" are added to pulley systems, it is useful to employ a system of notation to describe the system and to calculate mechanical advantage provided by the system. We use a system that denotes properties of pull, or *tensional force* (T). A subscript to the right of the T (for example, T_a) indicates the *location* of a specific tensional force; a number to the left of the T (for example, 2T) gives the *size* or *magnitude* of the tensional force. Hence, $2T_b$ is a tensional force of size 2 at the location b.

In figure D-3B, the rope producing forces of $1T_a$, $1T_b$, $1T_c$, and $1T_d$ replaces the pulls or tension provided by the four arms of the young people.

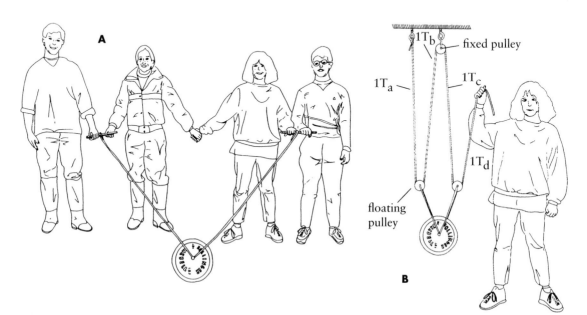

Figure D-3. 4:1 Systems

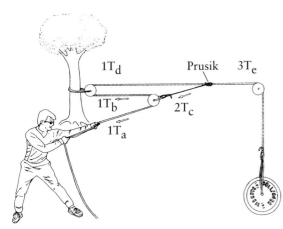

Figure D-4A. 3:1 System Using a Prusik Knot to Increase Efficiency

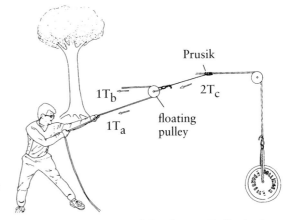

Figure D-4B. Function of the Floating Pulley in the System

PULLEY SYSTEMS WITH PRUSIKS

A Prusik knot can be used to enhance the mechanical advantage of a pulley system. Systems with Prusiks have mechanical advantages with ratios of 3:1, 6:1, or 9:1, and so on. The Prusik knot is purposely made of a smaller and weaker rope so that if you overload the system, the Prusik—not the main rope—will break. Because there is a backup, the lifted load will not drop if the Prusik breaks.

This section explains the theory of how pulley systems with Prusiks work. In the field, of course, there are many practical considerations when you use these systems for safeguarding yourself or for rescues. Because rescue can be (and is) the topic of entire books, coverage here has been limited to the theoretical aspects.

3:1 Systems

The climber in figure D-4A provides the initial pulling or tensional force that passes to the rope at T_a. The tensional forces on the rope labeled T_a, T_b, etc., act much like the human arms in the previous examples in supporting and lifting the weight. The initial pull force at location a is assigned a value of 1, giving $1T_a$. $1T_a$ passes around the floating pulley unaltered in magnitude so that T_b has the same value as T_a, namely 1. These two pulling forces act through

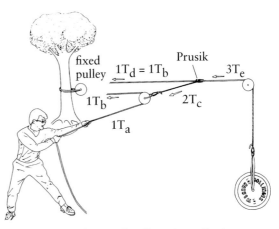

Figure D-4C. The Fixed Pulley's Contribution

the floating pulley and its associated Prusik sling to exert a force of $1T_a + 1T_b = 2T_c$ on the weight in the direction indicated by the arrows. If we isolate subparts of the system (by not showing part of the rope), the result would be as shown in figure D-4B: $1T_a$ and $1T_b$ each share equally in holding the total load.

The rope passes from location b around a fixed pulley on the tree (fig. D-4A) to change the rope's direction. Now consider positions b and d in figure D-4C. Here there is another pull on the load, $1T_d$, that owes its existence to force $1T_b$, in that $1T_b$ transfers around the fixed pulley on the tree to create T_d. This means that the

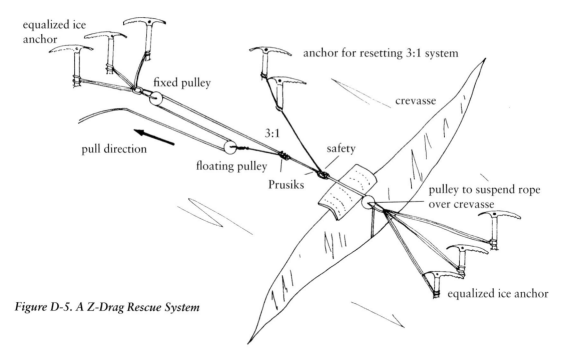

Figure D-5. A Z-Drag Rescue System

total lifting force on the weight is the combination of $[(1T_a + 1T_b) = 2T_c] + 1T_d = 3T_e$. Thus, the system is a 3:1 mechanical-advantage system, and the climber needs to apply a force slightly greater than one-third of the load's weight to start it moving upward.

In examining the system note that the direction of pull arrows may actually be in a different direction than the rope moves as it maintains coordination between various parts of the system. These opposed directions are illustrated at position b (fig. D-4A), where the tensional forces act to pull the floating pulley to the left, while the rope runs to the right as the climber pulls on it.

In any pulley system you need to pull an amount of rope through to raise a weight a given distance: the weight rises a distance that is inversely proportional to the mechanical advantage of the system. In a 3:1 system, the weight rises only 33 feet for every 100 feet of rope pulled through. The climber in figure D-4 does not have to exert a lot of effort to lift the weight, but he has to pull in lots of rope.

When you pull a rope to raise a weight using a pulley system, Prusik knots and floating pulleys move toward fixed pulleys until they touch, or until mechanical advantage is lost by removing changes of direction at the pulleys. As a result, you must periodically restore the system or reset it to its original state.

Z-Drag Systems: A Z-drag system is a 3:1 pulley system combined with Prusik knots that maintain the load in a lifted position while you release tension on the system to reset it. A Z-drag system should also provide anchors for rescuers who work around a crevasse lip or are endangered while operating the system. When you use the Z-drag for crevasse rescue, friction is caused by the rope cutting into the lip of the crevasse. To prevent this you pad the edge, cut away any protruding lip, and possibly use ice axes laid horizontally to keep the rope from cutting into the edge. In addition, you need to safeguard pads, ice axes, and people working at the edge. Another way to avoid the problem of edge friction is to suspend a pulley in the air directly above the middle of the crevasse. Attach this pulley to anchors on the opposite side of the crevasse to the 3:1 pulley, as shown in figure D-5.

In order to gain the full mechanical advantage of this system, you must pull the rope parallel to the system's arms, and not at an angle, which would destroy mechanical advantage.

HIGHER RATIOS OF MECHANICAL ADVANTAGE

Higher ratios of mechanical advantage make it easier to lift heavy loads with fewer people. These systems are rescue systems that tax the strength of Prusiks and ropes and require safety backups for the system as well as for people working with it. They commonly use specially made rollers to reduce friction where the rope passes over an edge.

Higher systems are formed by combining either a simple system with one that uses Prusiks, or two-Prusik systems. For example, a 2:1 system pulling a 3:1 system gives rise to a 6:1 system of mechanical advantage, a 3:1 system pulling a 3:1 system gives rise to a 9:1 system of mechanical advantage, and so on. To help you learn to analyze these systems, their description is set up in the form of problems to solve. After working on both problems, turn the page to compare your analyses to those presented here.

Problem One

Our climber has set up a higher ratio of mechanical advantage in figure D-6A. He wants to determine what mechanical advantage exists for the total system: Is this a 6:1 system, a 12:1 system, or a system with some other ratio of me-

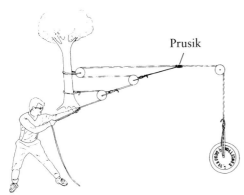

Figure D-6A. A System of Higher Mechanical Advantage

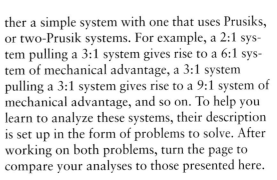

Figure D-6B. The System Related to the First Floating Pulley

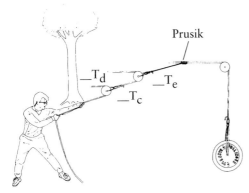

Figure D-6C. The Second Floating Pulley and Prusik

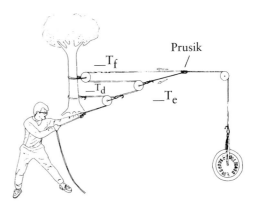

Figure D-6D. The Fixed Pulley and Total Mechanical Advantage

chanical advantage? We will analyze each sub-part in turn to understand the total system.

First look at figure D-6A; then, on figure D-6B, fill in the pull forces encountered for each side of the pulley on the blank lines labeled $\_T_x$. The initial pull force has a value of 1T at location a in the direction indicated by the arrow. Next, use the pull forces or T values, derived in figure D-6B, to determine those in figure D-6C and D-6D in turn. Use arrows to show pull directions for each rope segment. Finally, fill in the final value of mechanical advantage at T_g, located to the right of the Prusik knot in figure D-6D.

Therefore, to lift a weight of 60 pounds you need to exert a starting force of ____ pounds to offset equilibrium and to cause lifting to start.

This system is an example of a ____ : ____ mechanical-advantage system.

Problem Two

Draw the hook-up, showing rope travel, pulleys, Prusiks, trees, and weights required to set up a 9:1 mechanical advantage system. Label the forces exerted on the subparts of the system.

This problem tests your understanding of the main points discussed thus far. If necessary, review the material presented above. When you do begin, try a number of combinations of fixed and floating pulleys and figure out the mechanical advantage on scrap paper. Put the result of this trial-and-error figuring below before turning the page.

Answer to Problem One

(A) Figure D-7 shows the completely sketched setup of problem one of figure D-6. This is basically a 2:1 system pulling a 3:1 system to give rise to a 6:1 system of mechanical advantage.

(B) Starting with a pull of force 1T at a, the pull is transferred by a change in direction at the first free-floating pulley to an equal pull of 1T at b. This means that there is a pull on the rope attached to the first free-floating pulley at c of 1T + 1T = 2T. Note that the arrows at the lettered positions show the direction in which the pull is exerted, not the direction in which the rope is moving. Indeed, the rope is moving in the direction of the pull at a, but in the opposite direction at d.

(C) The pull of strength 2T calculated above for c transfers around the second free-floating pulley by the continuous rope to the opposite side at d. This means that there is a pull of 2T + 2T = 4T at e on the second Prusik sling.

(D) At the Prusik sling at e is a pull of 4T. In addition, the pull of 2T at d changes direction at the fixed pulley on the tree and exerts a force of 2T directly on the weight at f. When you add up these tensional forces, the weight is being pulled with 4T (e) + 2T (f) = 6T at g.

(E) This is a system of 6:1 mechanical advantage. If you use it, you can lift a weight of 60 pounds with a starting force of slightly more than 10 pounds, neglecting friction. With a fair amount of friction the mechanical advantage is lower, possibly about 4:1.

Answer to Problem Two

This is a 9:1 mechanical-advantage system (fig. D-8) that is basically one 3:1 system pulling another 3:1 system. Begin the analysis at a, where 1T is the amount of pull. This also occurs on the left side of the lowest free-floating pulley at b. The combined effect of these two pulls, of 1T each, on the Prusik sling at c produces a pull of 2T on that sling.

Each of the pulleys fixed to the tree is a 1:1 system that alters the direction but not the amount of pull. Therefore, the force on the far side of these pulleys is the same as on the near side. The 1T pull of b transfers around the lower fixed pulley to become 1T at d. This combines with the 2T pull on the Prusik in c to exert a combined pull of 3T on the second free-floating pulley at e.

This 3T pull occurs on both sides of the higher of the free-floating pulleys, at both e and f, producing a combined pull of 6T on the higher Prusik at g. The 3T pull at f transfers around the upper fixed pulley as a 3T pull at h.

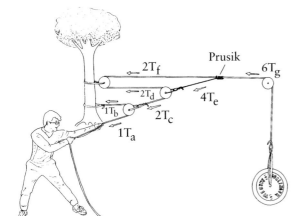

Figure D-7. 6:1 System

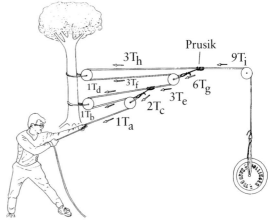

Figure D-8. 9:1 System of Mechanical Advantage

This 3T pull of h combines with the 6T pull of the Prusik at g to give a total of 9T at i. The components of this system up to e comprise a 3:1 system that pulls on a second 3:1 system from e to i.

In a frictionless system, you might be able to initiate a pull of 50 pounds or more, allowing you to lift 450 pounds, using this imaginary system. In a real system, friction would reduce this advantage considerably—perhaps by one-third—limiting the weight being lifted to a maximum of about 300 pounds.

REFERENCES FOR FUTURE READING

May, W. G. 1973. Hauling systems. Chapter 26 in *Mountain search and rescue techniques*. Boulder, Colorado: Rocky Mountain Rescue Group, Inc.

Setnicka, Tim. 1980. Raising systems. Chapter 19 in *Wilderness search and rescue*. Boston: Appalachian Mountain Club.

Selters, Andy. 1990. *Glacier travel and crevasse rescue*. Seattle: The Mountaineers.

Smutek, Ray, ed. 1977. Notes on equipment & technique: Efficiencies, advantages, and factors. *Off-Belay*. 36:8–19.

ENDNOTES

1. May, 1973; Setnicka, 1980.
2. Smutek, 1977, lists the two-thirds value. This article includes a letter by John Lawton commenting on test data by Don Wenzel. A value of approximately 60 percent is listed in appendix D of the Ontario Rock Climbing Association Safety Manual.

Index